NEGIMA! 14

Ken Akamatsu

TRANSLATED BY
Toshifumi Yoshida

ADAPTED BY
Ikoi Hiroe

LETTERING AND RETOUCH BY
Steve Palmer

DEL
REY

BALLANTINE BOOKS · NEW YORK

Negima! volume 14 is a work of fiction. Names, characters, places, and incidents are the products of the author's imagination or are used fictitiously. Any resemblance to actual events, locales, or persons, living or dead, is entirely coincidental.

A Del Rey Trade Paperback Original

Published in the United States by Del Rey Books, an imprint of The Random House Publishing Group, a division of Random House, Inc., New York.

Publication rights arranged through Kodansha Ltd.

First published in Japan in 2006 by Kodansha Ltd., Tokyo

ISBN 978-0-345-49614-0

Printed in the United States of America

www.delreymanga.com

9 8 7 6 5 4 3 2 1

Translator—Toshifumi Yoshida
Adaptor—Ikoi Hiroe
Lettering and retouch—Steve Palmer

Honorifics Explained

Throughout the Del Rey Manga books, you will find Japanese honorifics left intact in the translations. For those not familiar with how the Japanese use honorifics and, more important, how they differ from American honorifics, we present this brief overview.

Politeness has always been a critical facet of Japanese culture. Ever since the feudal era, when Japan was a highly stratified society, use of honorifics—which can be defined as polite speech that indicates relationship or status—has played an essential role in the Japanese language. When addressing someone in Japanese, an honorific usually takes the form of a suffix attached to one's name (example: "Asuna-san"), is used as a title at the end of one's name, or appears in place of the name itself (example: "Negi-sensei," or simply "Sensei!").

Honorifics can be expressions of respect or endearment. In the context of manga and anime, honorifics give insight into the nature of the relationship between characters. Many translations into English leave out these important honorifics and therefore distort the feel of the original Japanese. Because Japanese honorifics contain nuances that English honorifics lack, it is our policy at Del Rey not to translate them. Here, instead, is a guide to some of the honorifics you may encounter in Del Rey Manga.

-*san:* This is the most common honorific and is equivalent to Mr., Miss, Ms., or Mrs. It is the all-purpose honorific and can be used in any situation where politeness is required.

-*sama:* This is one level higher than "-san" and is used to confer great respect.

-*dono:* This comes from the word "tono," which means "lord." It is an even higher level than "-sama" and confers utmost respect.

-kun: This suffix is used at the end of boys' names to express familiarity or endearment. It is also sometimes used by men among friends, or when addressing someone younger or of a lower station.

-chan: This is used to express endearment, mostly toward girls. It is also used for little boys, pets, and even among lovers. It gives a sense of childish cuteness.

Bozu: This is an informal way to refer to a boy, similar to the English terms "kid" and "squirt."

Sempai/senpai: This title suggests that the addressee is one's senior in a group or organization. It is most often used in a school setting, where underclassmen refer to their upperclassmen as "sempai." It can also be used in the workplace, such as when a newer employee addresses an employee who has seniority in the company.

Kohai: This is the opposite of "sempai" and is used toward underclassmen in school or newcomers in the workplace. It connotes that the addressee is of a lower station.

Sensei: Literally meaning "one who has come before," this title is used for teachers, doctors, or masters of any profession or art.

Anesan (or *nesan*): A generic term for a girl, usually older, that means sister.

Ojôsama: A way of referring to the daughter or sister of someone with high political or social status.

-[blank]: This is usually forgotten in these lists, but it is perhaps the most significant difference between Japanese and English. The lack of honorific means that the speaker has permission to address the person in a very intimate way. Usually, only family, spouses, or very close friends have this kind of permission. Known as *yobisute,* it can be gratifying when someone who has earned the intimacy starts to call one by one's name without an honorific. But when that intimacy hasn't been earned, it can be very insulting.

A Word from the Author

Negima! will be an animated series! Please check the website below for more information.

There may be more news in the future!

The Mahora Budōkai is finally over, so we're going back to stories of various classmates.

The spotlight will shine on different girls and different groups not featured before...

I wonder if your favorite classmate will be introduced soon?

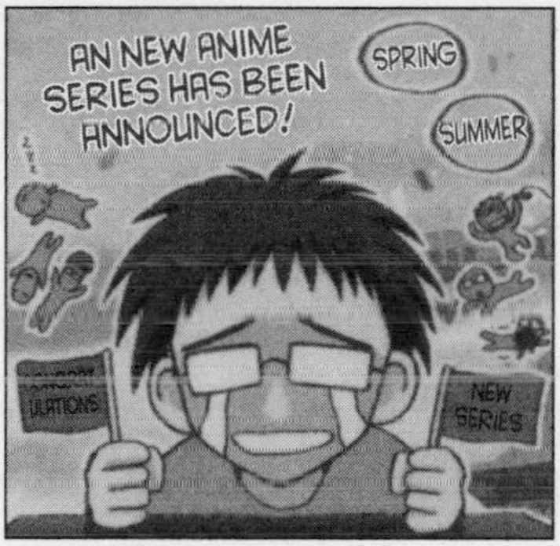
AN NEW ANIME SERIES HAS BEEN ANNOUNCED!
SPRING
SUMMER
ULATIONS
NEW SERIES

The background stories for all of the students have been laid out since the beginning of the series. If you don't recall details, reread the series from the beginning to refresh your memory.

Ken Akamatsu
www.ailove.net

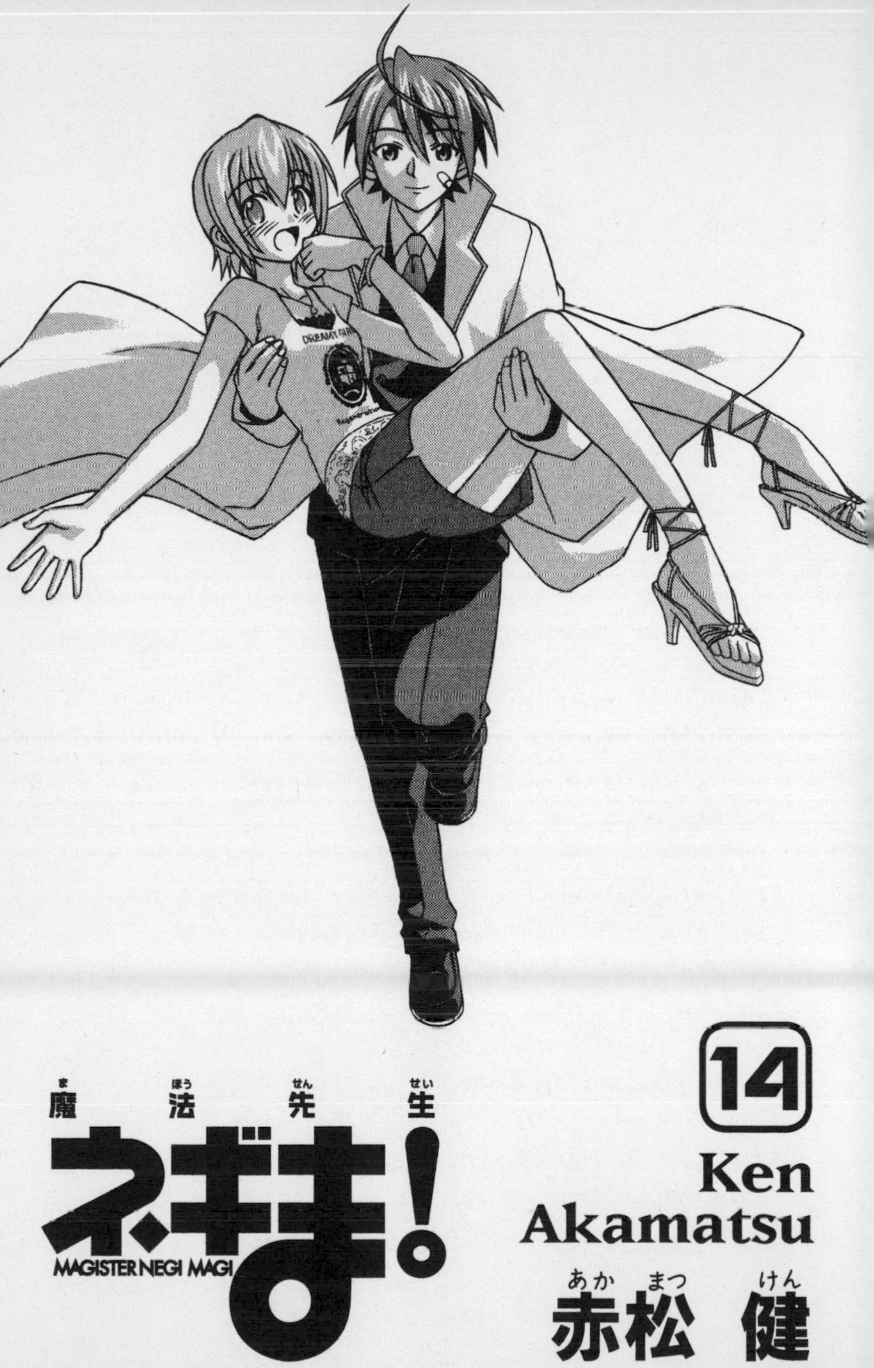

魔法先生ネギま!

MAGISTER NEGI MAGI

14

Ken Akamatsu

赤松 健

Contents

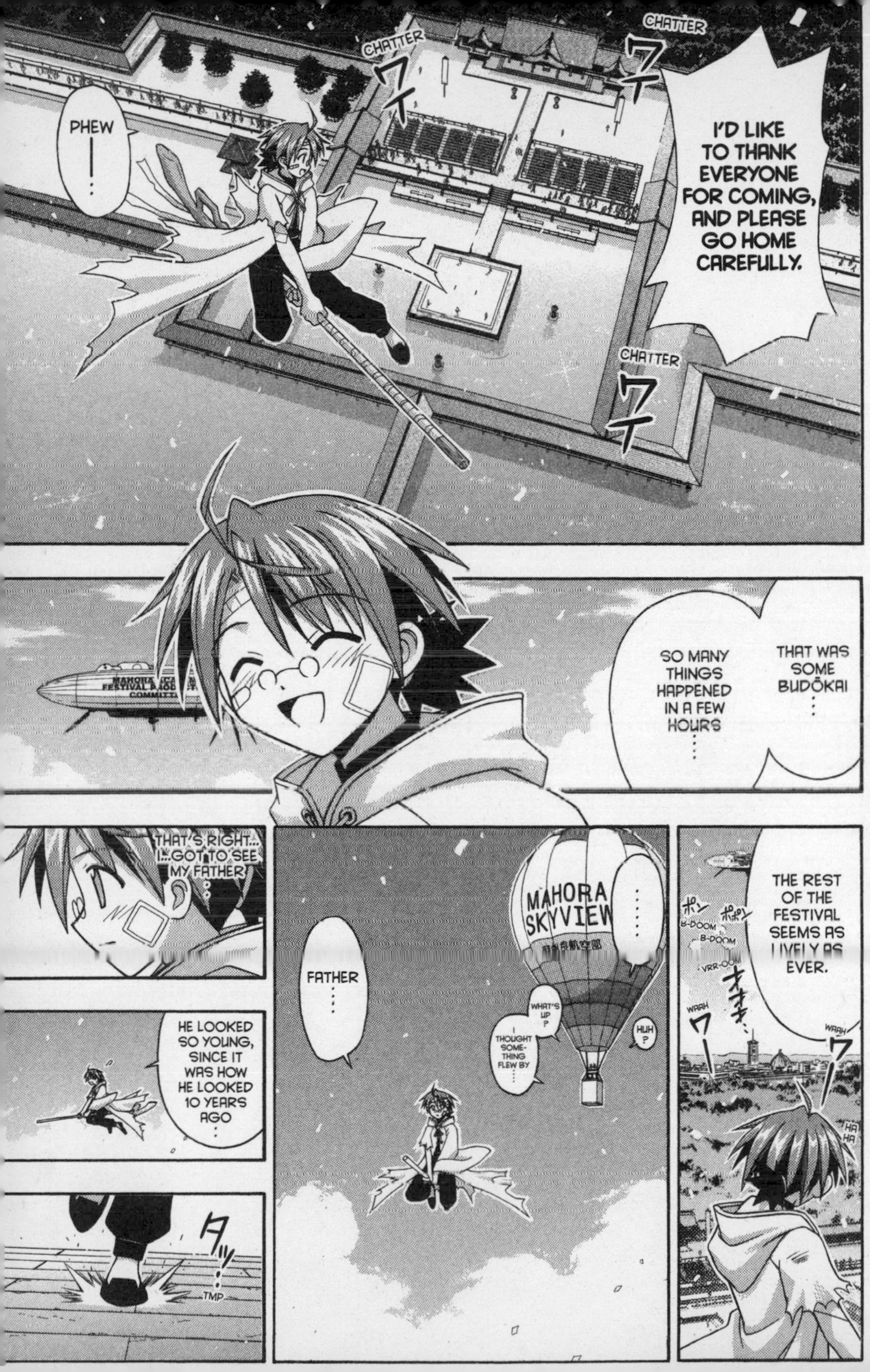
CHATTER
ワイ
I'D LIKE TO THANK EVERYONE FOR COMING, AND PLEASE GO HOME CAREFULLY.
CHATTER
ワイ
PHEW ...
CHATTER
ワイ
THAT WAS SOME BUDŌKAI ...
SO MANY THINGS HAPPENED IN A FEW HOURS ...
THE REST OF THE FESTIVAL SEEMS AS LIVELY AS EVER.
ポン B-DOOM
ポポン B-DOOM
VRR-OOM オォォ
WAAH ワー
WAAH ワー
HA HA
......
MAHORA SKYVIEW
FATHER ...
WHAT'S UP?
I THOUGHT SOMETHING FLEW BY ...
HUH?
THAT'S RIGHT... I...GOT TO SEE MY FATHER ...
HE LOOKED SO YOUNG, SINCE IT WAS HOW HE LOOKED 10 YEARS AGO ...
タッ TMP

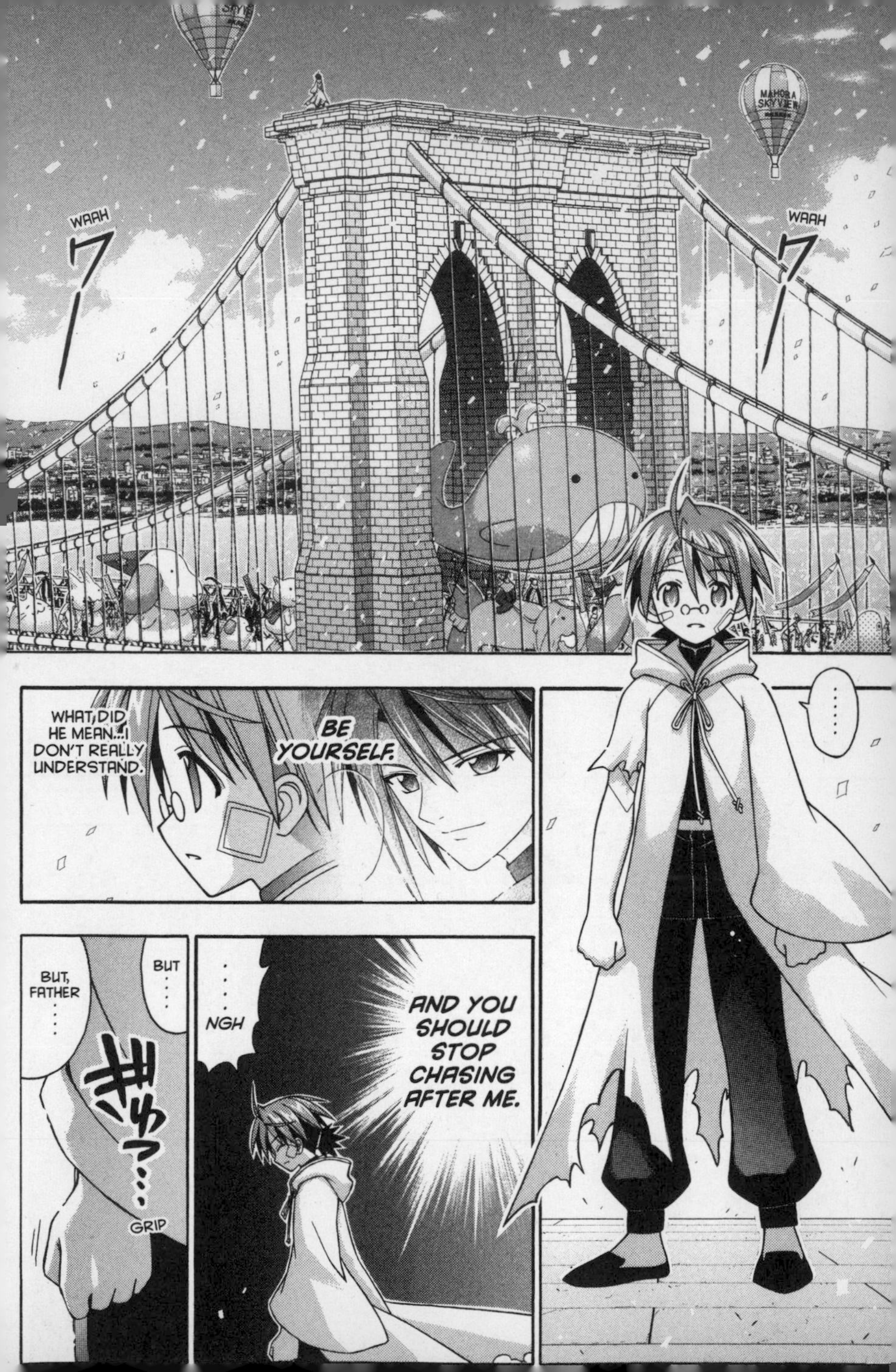

MAHORA SKYVIEW
WAAH
WAAH
......
BE YOURSELF.
WHAT DID HE MEAN...I DON'T REALLY UNDERSTAND.
AND YOU SHOULD STOP CHASING AFTER ME.
......NGH
BUT......
BUT, FATHER......
GRIP

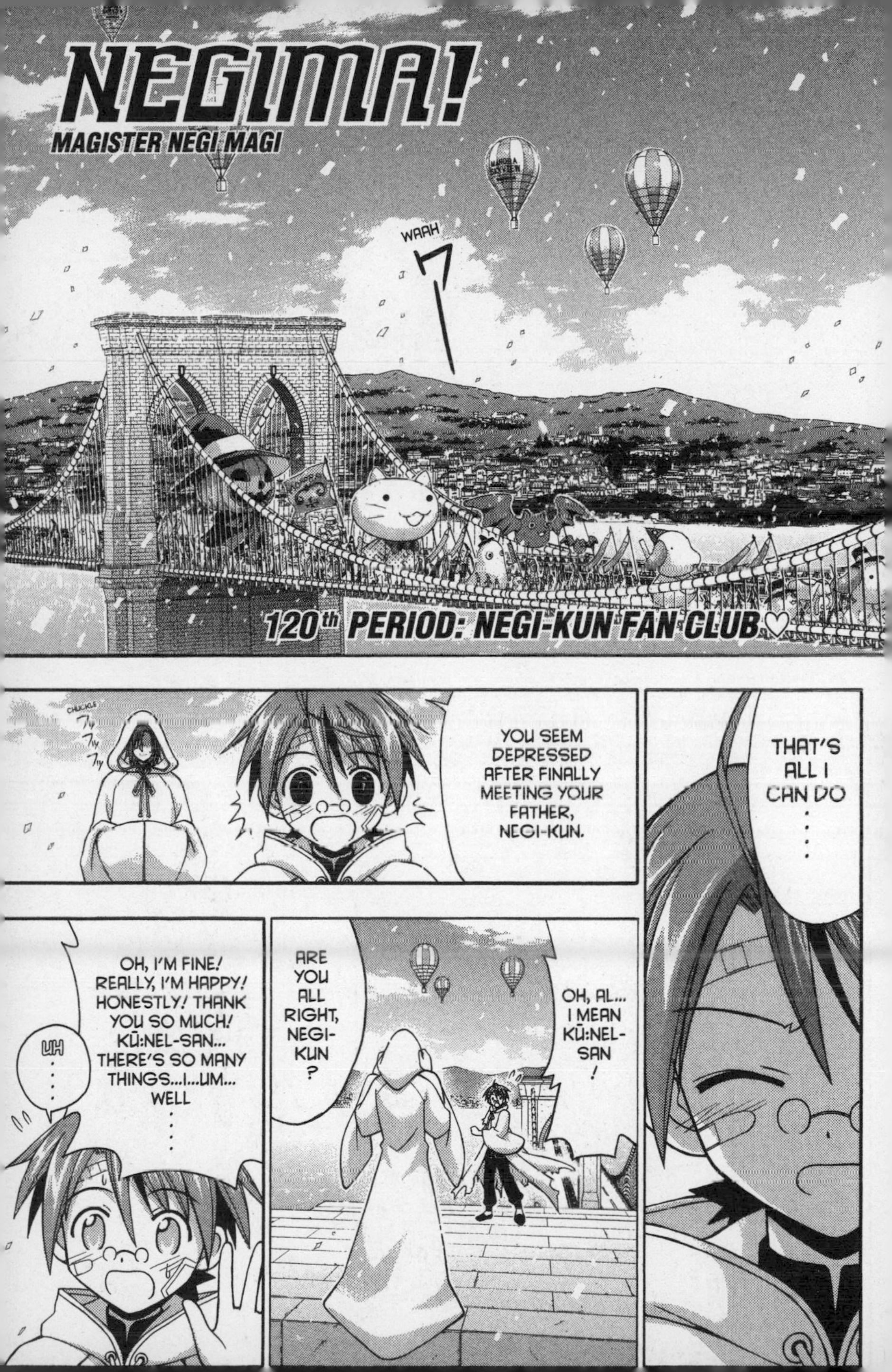
NEGIMA!
MAGISTER NEGI MAGI
WAAH
120th PERIOD: NEGI-KUN FAN CLUB♡
THAT'S ALL I CAN DO ....
CHUCKLE
YOU SEEM DEPRESSED AFTER FINALLY MEETING YOUR FATHER, NEGI-KUN.
OH, AL... I MEAN KŪ:NEL-SAN!
ARE YOU ALL RIGHT, NEGI-KUN?
OH, I'M FINE! REALLY, I'M HAPPY! HONESTLY! THANK YOU SO MUCH! KŪ:NEL-SAN... THERE'S SO MANY THINGS...I...UM... WELL ....
UH ....

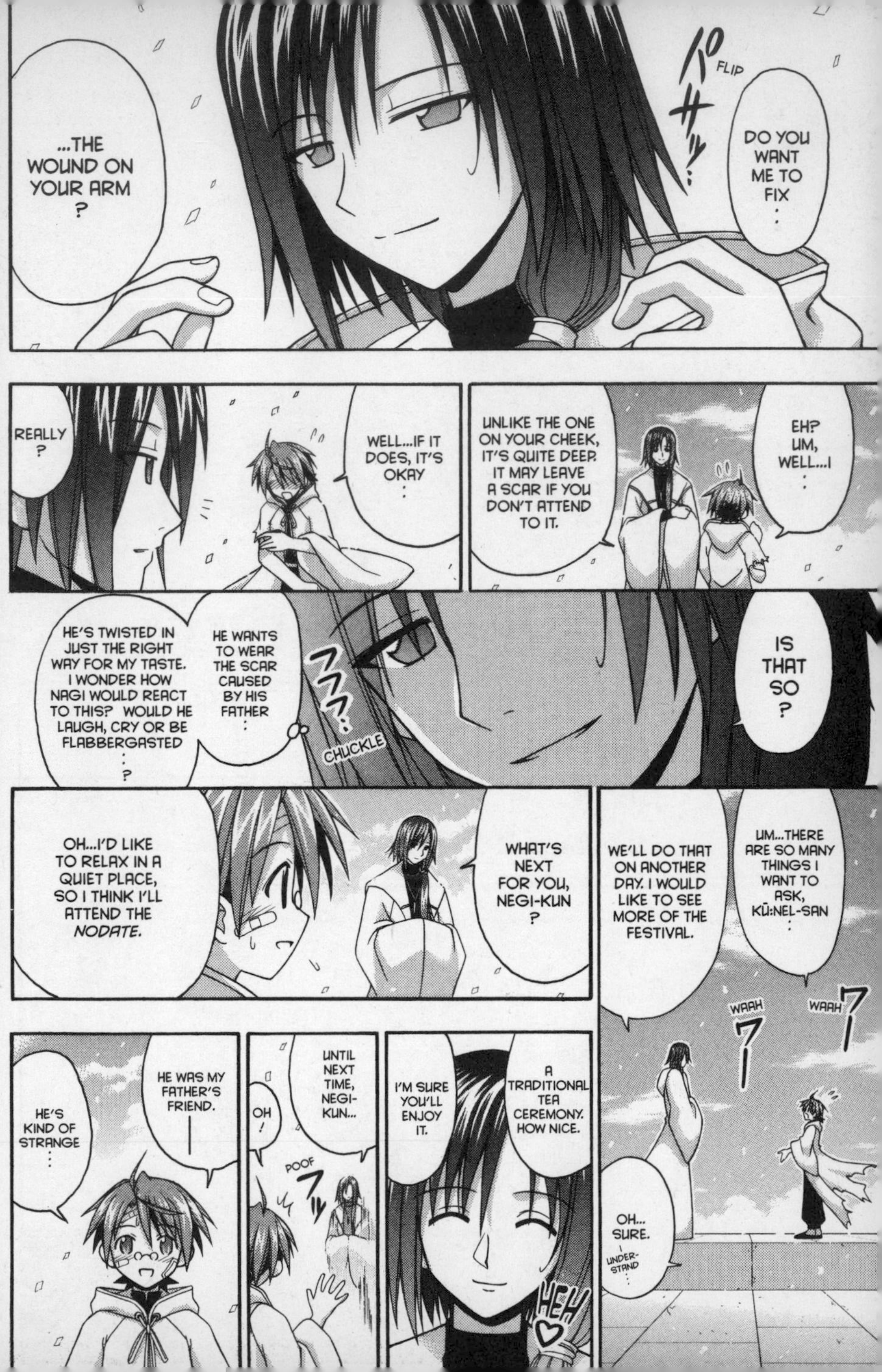
DO YOU WANT ME TO FIX ...
FLIP
...THE WOUND ON YOUR ARM ?
EH? UM, WELL...I ...
UNLIKE THE ONE ON YOUR CHEEK, IT'S QUITE DEEP. IT MAY LEAVE A SCAR IF YOU DON'T ATTEND TO IT.
WELL...IF IT DOES, IT'S OKAY ...
REALLY ?
IS THAT SO ?
CHUCKLE
HE WANTS TO WEAR THE SCAR CAUSED BY HIS FATHER ...
HE'S TWISTED IN JUST THE RIGHT WAY FOR MY TASTE. I WONDER HOW NAGI WOULD REACT TO THIS? WOULD HE LAUGH, CRY OR BE FLABBERGASTED ...?
UM...THERE ARE SO MANY THINGS I WANT TO ASK, KŪ:NEL-SAN ...
WE'LL DO THAT ON ANOTHER DAY. I WOULD LIKE TO SEE MORE OF THE FESTIVAL.
WAAH
WAAH
OH... SURE. I UNDERSTAND ...
WHAT'S NEXT FOR YOU, NEGI-KUN ?
OH...I'D LIKE TO RELAX IN A QUIET PLACE, SO I THINK I'LL ATTEND THE *NODATE*.
A TRADITIONAL TEA CEREMONY. HOW NICE.
I'M SURE YOU'LL ENJOY IT.
HEH
UNTIL NEXT TIME, NEGI-KUN...
OH !
POOF
HE WAS MY FATHER'S FRIEND.
HE'S KIND OF STRANGE ...

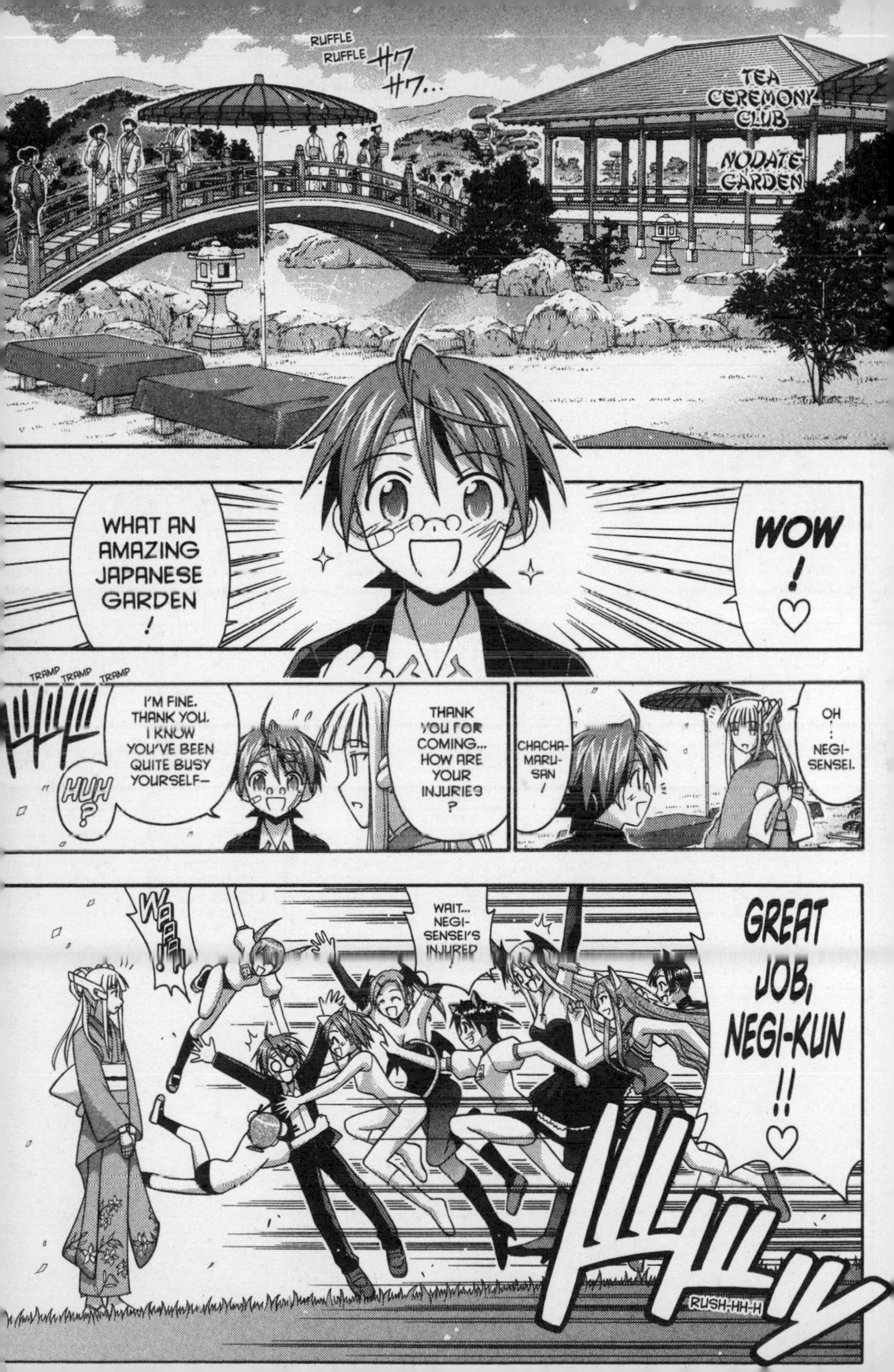
TEA CEREMONY CLUB
NODATE GARDEN
RUFFLE RUFFLE
サワ サワ…
WOW! ♡
WHAT AN AMAZING JAPANESE GARDEN!
OH… NEGI-SENSEI.
CHACHAMARU-SAN!
THANK YOU FOR COMING… HOW ARE YOUR INJURIES?
I'M FINE. THANK YOU. I KNOW YOU'VE BEEN QUITE BUSY YOURSELF—
HUH?
TRAMP TRAMP TRAMP
GREAT JOB, NEGI-KUN!! ♡
WAIT… NEGI-SENSEI'S INJURED
RUSH-HH-H

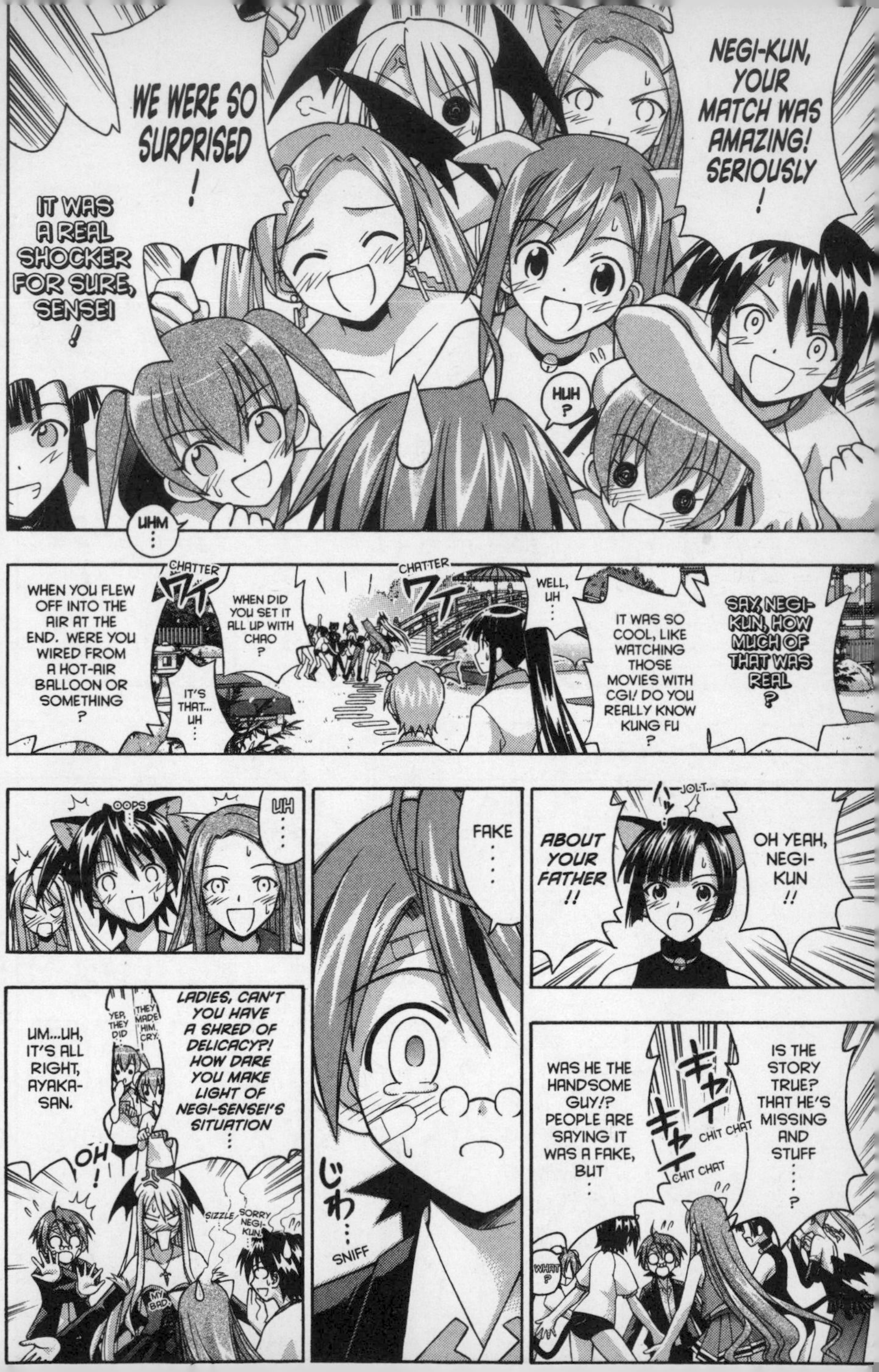
NEGI-KUN, YOUR MATCH WAS AMAZING! SERIOUSLY!
WE WERE SO SURPRISED!
IT WAS A REAL SHOCKER FOR SURE, SENSEI!
HUH?
UHM...
SAY, NEGI-KUN, HOW MUCH OF THAT WAS REAL?
IT WAS SO COOL, LIKE WATCHING THOSE MOVIES WITH CGI! DO YOU REALLY KNOW KUNG FU?
WELL, UH...
CHATTER
WHEN DID YOU SET IT ALL UP WITH CHAO?
IT'S THAT... UH...
CHATTER
WHEN YOU FLEW OFF INTO THE AIR AT THE END. WERE YOU WIRED FROM A HOT-AIR BALLOON OR SOMETHING?
JOLT...
OH YEAH, NEGI-KUN!!
ABOUT YOUR FATHER!!
IS THE STORY TRUE? THAT HE'S MISSING AND STUFF...?
WAS HE THE HANDSOME GUY!? PEOPLE ARE SAYING IT WAS A FAKE, BUT...
CHIT CHAT
CHIT CHAT
WHAT?
FAKE...
SNIFF
UH...
OOPS
LADIES, CAN'T YOU HAVE A SHRED OF DELICACY?! HOW DARE YOU MAKE LIGHT OF NEGI-SENSEI'S SITUATION...
THEY MADE HIM CRY.
YEP, THEY DID
UM...UH, IT'S ALL RIGHT, AYAKA-SAN.
OH!
SORRY NEGI-KUN.
SIZZLE
MY BAD.

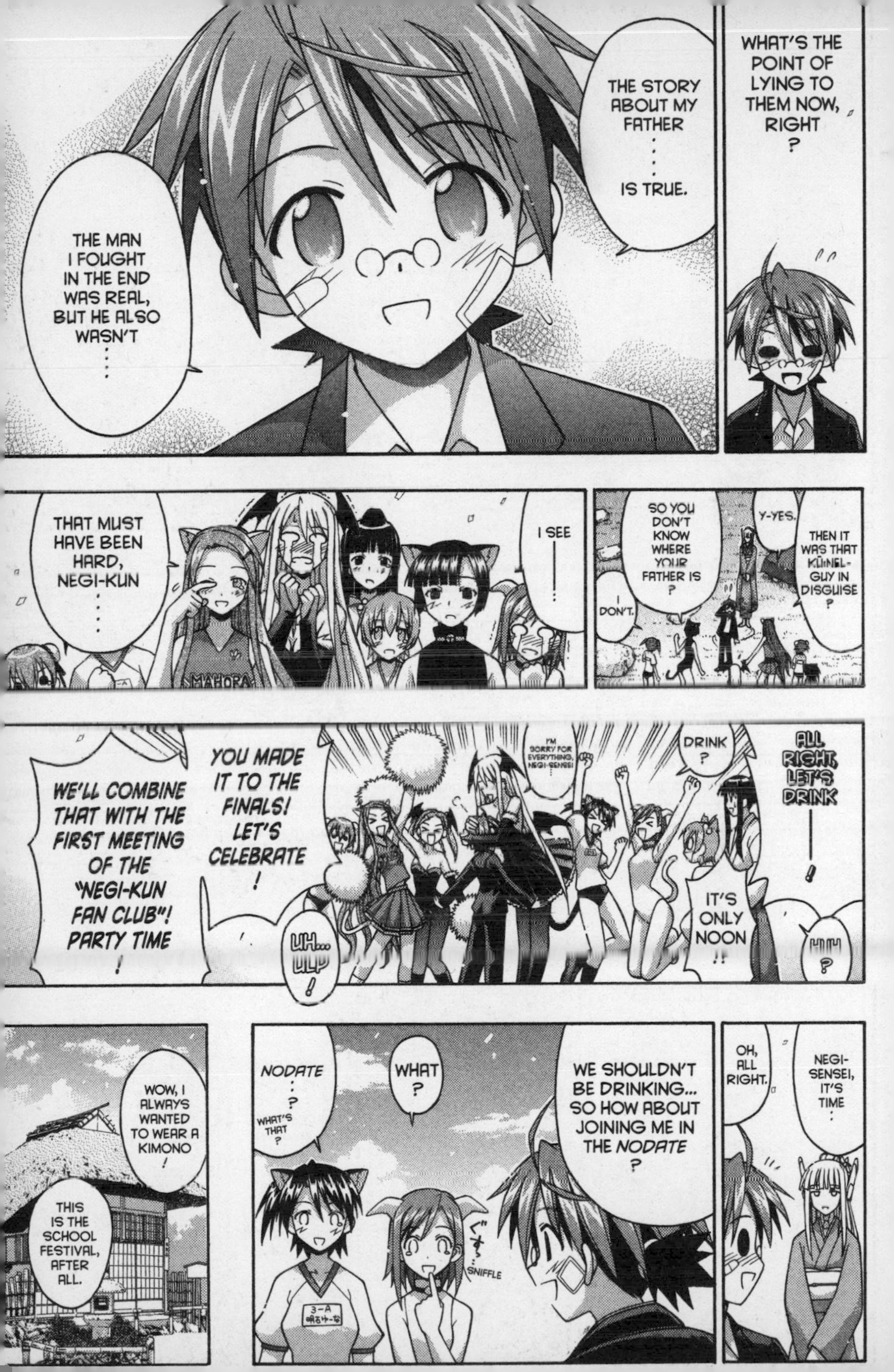

WHAT'S THE POINT OF LYING TO THEM NOW, RIGHT?
THE STORY ABOUT MY FATHER.... IS TRUE.
THE MAN I FOUGHT IN THE END WAS REAL, BUT HE ALSO WASN'T...
THEN IT WAS THAT KÜNEL-GUY IN DISGUISE?
Y-YES.
SO YOU DON'T KNOW WHERE YOUR FATHER IS?
I DON'T.
I SEE———!
THAT MUST HAVE BEEN HARD, NEGI-KUN....
MAHORA
ALL RIGHT, LET'S DRINK———!
HM?
DRINK?
IT'S ONLY NOON!!
I'M SORRY FOR EVERYTHING, NEGI-SENSEI...
UH... ULP!
YOU MADE IT TO THE FINALS! LET'S CELEBRATE!
WE'LL COMBINE THAT WITH THE FIRST MEETING OF THE "NEGI-KUN FAN CLUB"! PARTY TIME!
NEGI-SENSEI, IT'S TIME...
OH, ALL RIGHT.
WE SHOULDN'T BE DRINKING... SO HOW ABOUT JOINING ME IN THE NODATE?
WHAT?
NODATE..?
WHAT'S THAT?
SNIFFLE
WOW, I ALWAYS WANTED TO WEAR A KIMONO!
THIS IS THE SCHOOL FESTIVAL, AFTER ALL.

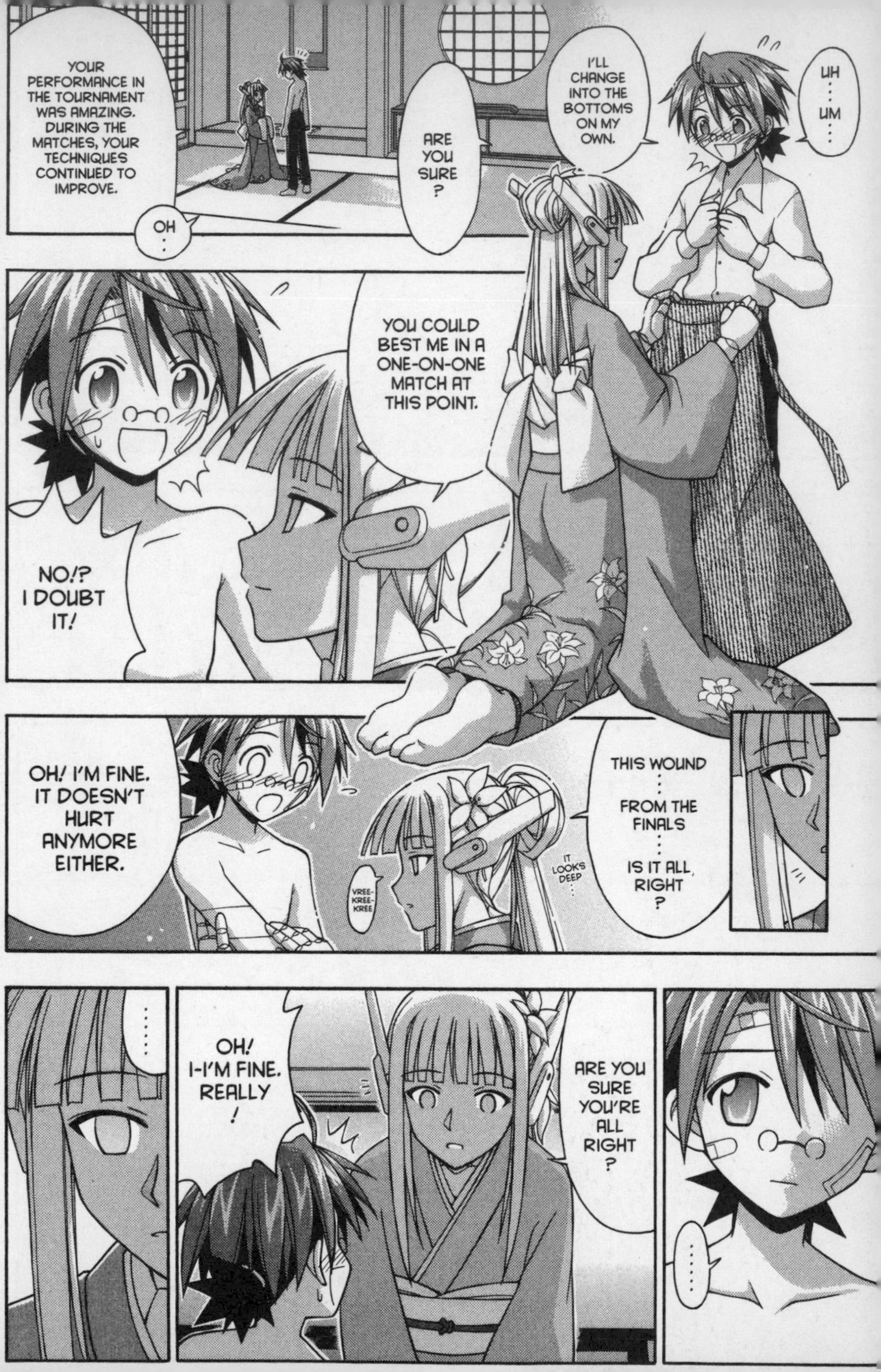
UH... UM...
I'LL CHANGE INTO THE BOTTOMS ON MY OWN.
ARE YOU SURE?
YOUR PERFORMANCE IN THE TOURNAMENT WAS AMAZING. DURING THE MATCHES, YOUR TECHNIQUES CONTINUED TO IMPROVE.
OH...
YOU COULD BEST ME IN A ONE-ON-ONE MATCH AT THIS POINT.
NO!? I DOUBT IT!
THIS WOUND... FROM THE FINALS... IS IT ALL RIGHT?
IT LOOKS DEEP...
VREE-KREE-KREE
OH! I'M FINE. IT DOESN'T HURT ANYMORE EITHER.
ARE YOU SURE YOU'RE ALL RIGHT?
......
OH! I-I'M FINE. REALLY!
......

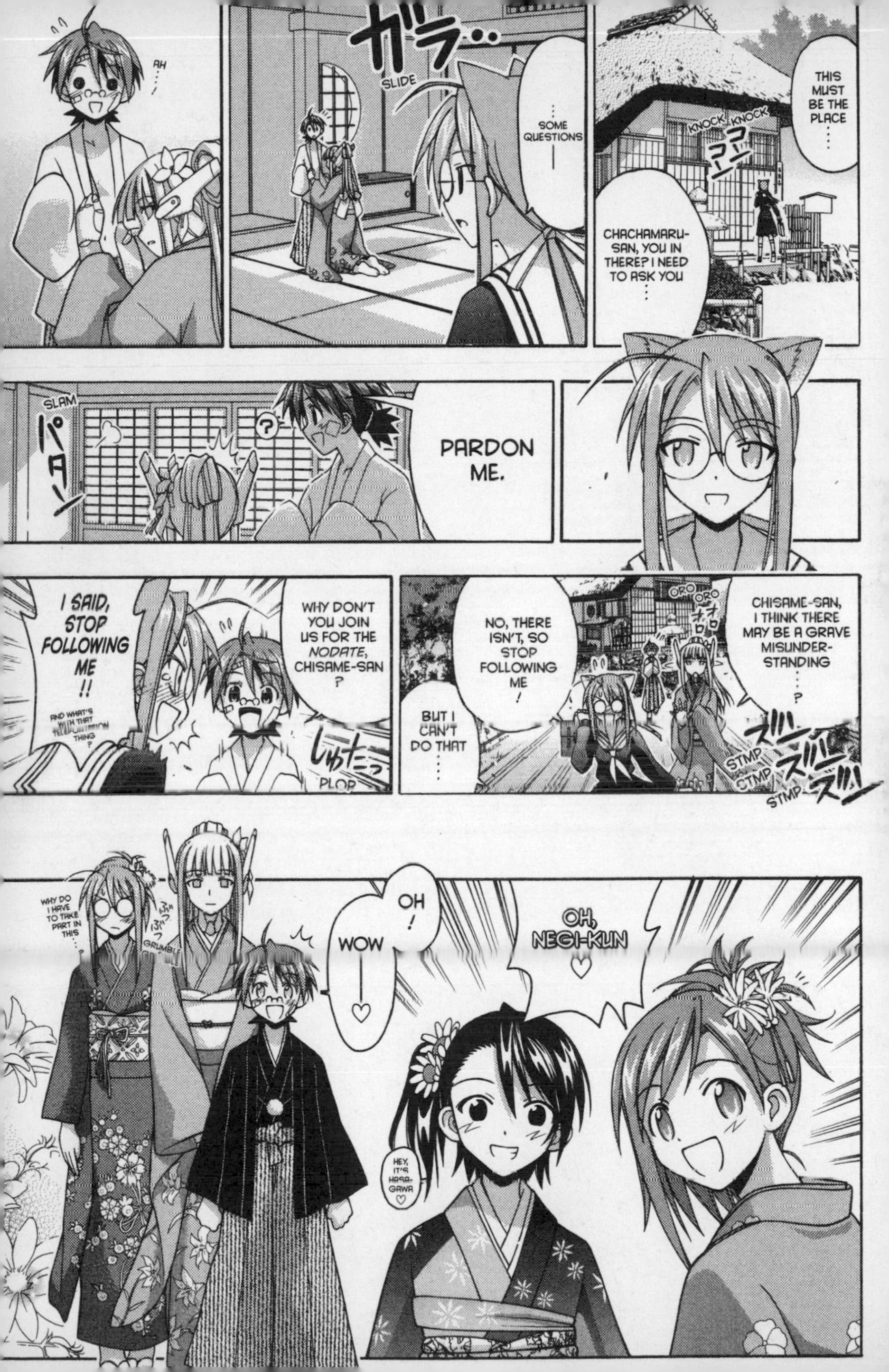
THIS MUST BE THE PLACE . . . .
KNOCK KNOCK
CHACHAMARU-SAN, YOU IN THERE? I NEED TO ASK YOU . . .
SLIDE
. . . SOME QUESTIONS —
AH . . . !
PARDON ME.
SLAM
?
CHISAME-SAN, I THINK THERE MAY BE A GRAVE MISUNDER-STANDING . . . ?
ORO ORO
NO, THERE ISN'T, SO STOP FOLLOWING ME!
BUT I CAN'T DO THAT . . . .
STMP STMP STMP
WHY DON'T YOU JOIN US FOR THE *NODATE*, CHISAME-SAN?
I SAID, STOP FOLLOWING ME!!
AND WHAT'S WITH THAT THING?
PLOP
OH, NEGI-KUN ♡
OH!
WOW — ♡
HEY, IT'S HASA-GAWA ♡
WHY DO I HAVE TO TAKE PART IN THIS . . . ?
GRUMBLE

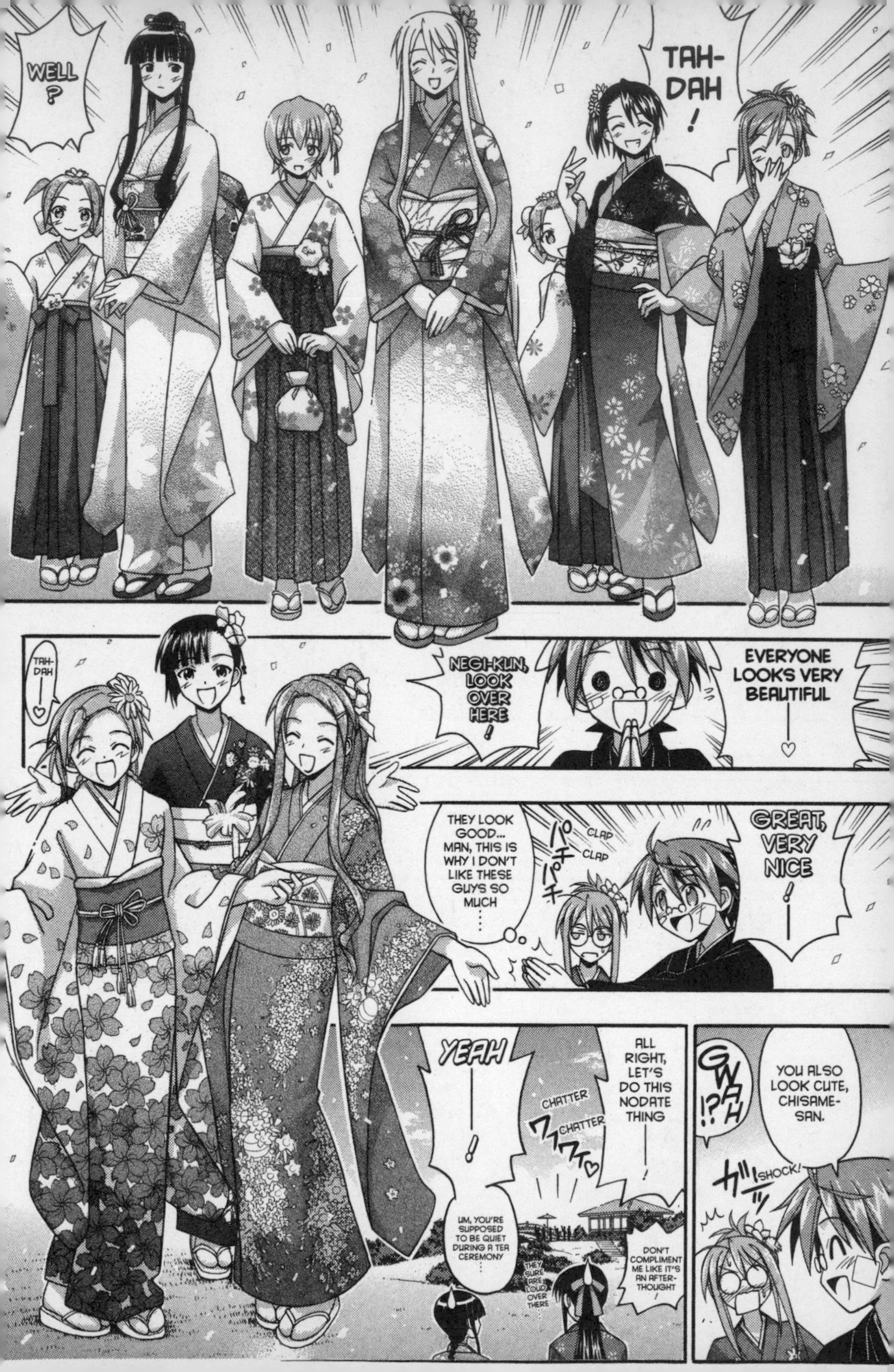
TAH-DAH!
WELL?
EVERYONE LOOKS VERY BEAUTIFUL ♡
NEGI-KUN, LOOK OVER HERE!
GREAT, VERY NICE!
CLAP CLAP
THEY LOOK GOOD... MAN, THIS IS WHY I DON'T LIKE THESE GUYS SO MUCH ......
YOU ALSO LOOK CUTE, CHISAME-SAN.
GWAH!?
SHOCK!
DON'T COMPLIMENT ME LIKE IT'S AN AFTER-THOUGHT!
ALL RIGHT, LET'S DO THIS NODATE THING!
YEAH!
CHATTER CHATTER
UM, YOU'RE SUPPOSED TO BE QUIET DURING A TEA CEREMONY ......
THEY SURE ARE LOUD OVER THERE
TAH-DAH ♡

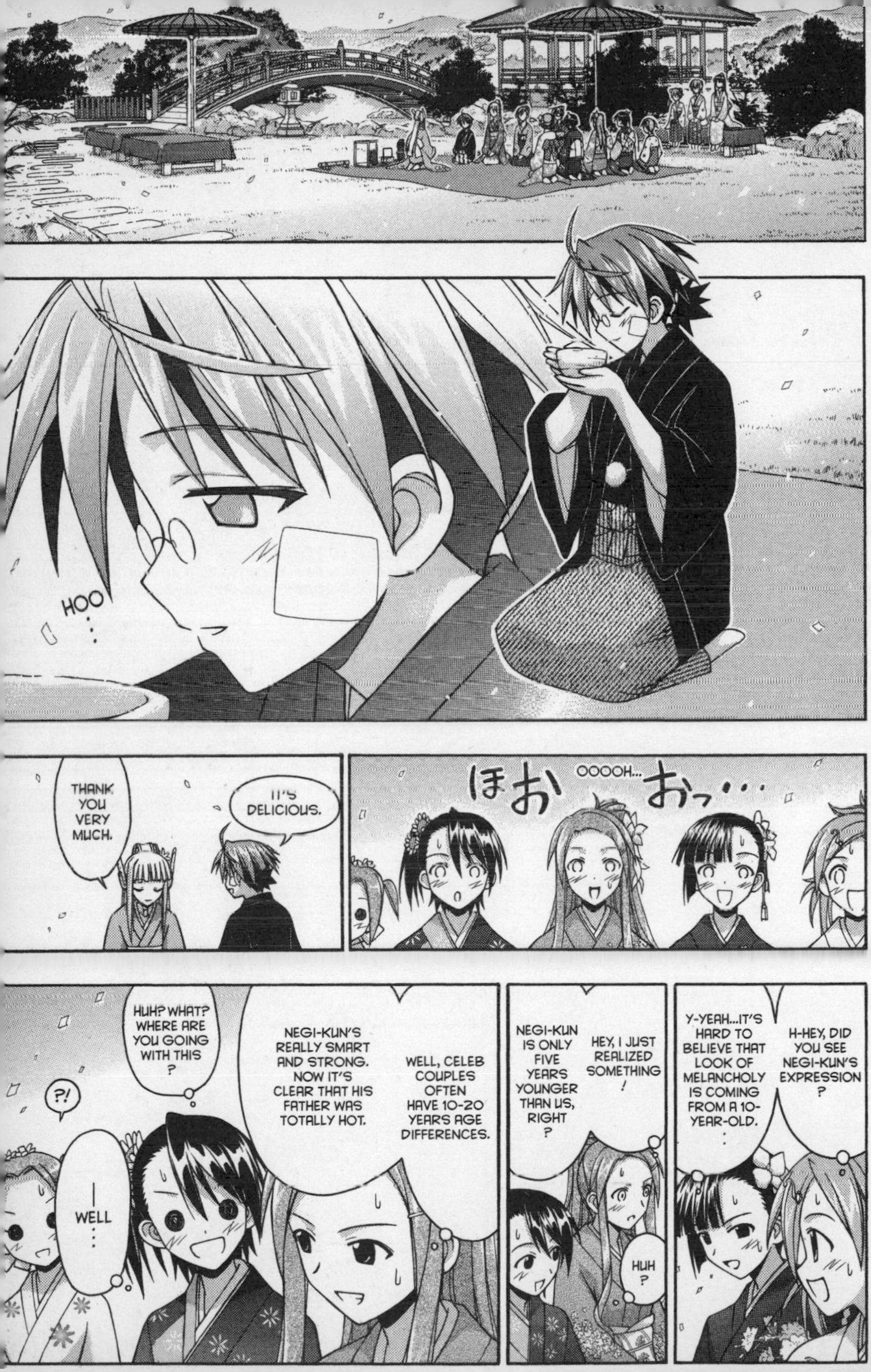
HOO…
ほお
OOOOH…
おっ…
IT'S DELICIOUS.
THANK YOU VERY MUCH.
H-HEY, DID YOU SEE NEGI-KUN'S EXPRESSION?
Y-YEAH…IT'S HARD TO BELIEVE THAT LOOK OF MELANCHOLY IS COMING FROM A 10-YEAR-OLD.
HEY, I JUST REALIZED SOMETHING!
NEGI-KUN IS ONLY FIVE YEARS YOUNGER THAN US, RIGHT?
HUH?
WELL, CELEB COUPLES OFTEN HAVE 10-20 YEARS AGE DIFFERENCES.
NEGI-KUN'S REALLY SMART AND STRONG. NOW IT'S CLEAR THAT HIS FATHER WAS TOTALLY HOT.
HUH? WHAT? WHERE ARE YOU GOING WITH THIS?
?!
—WELL…

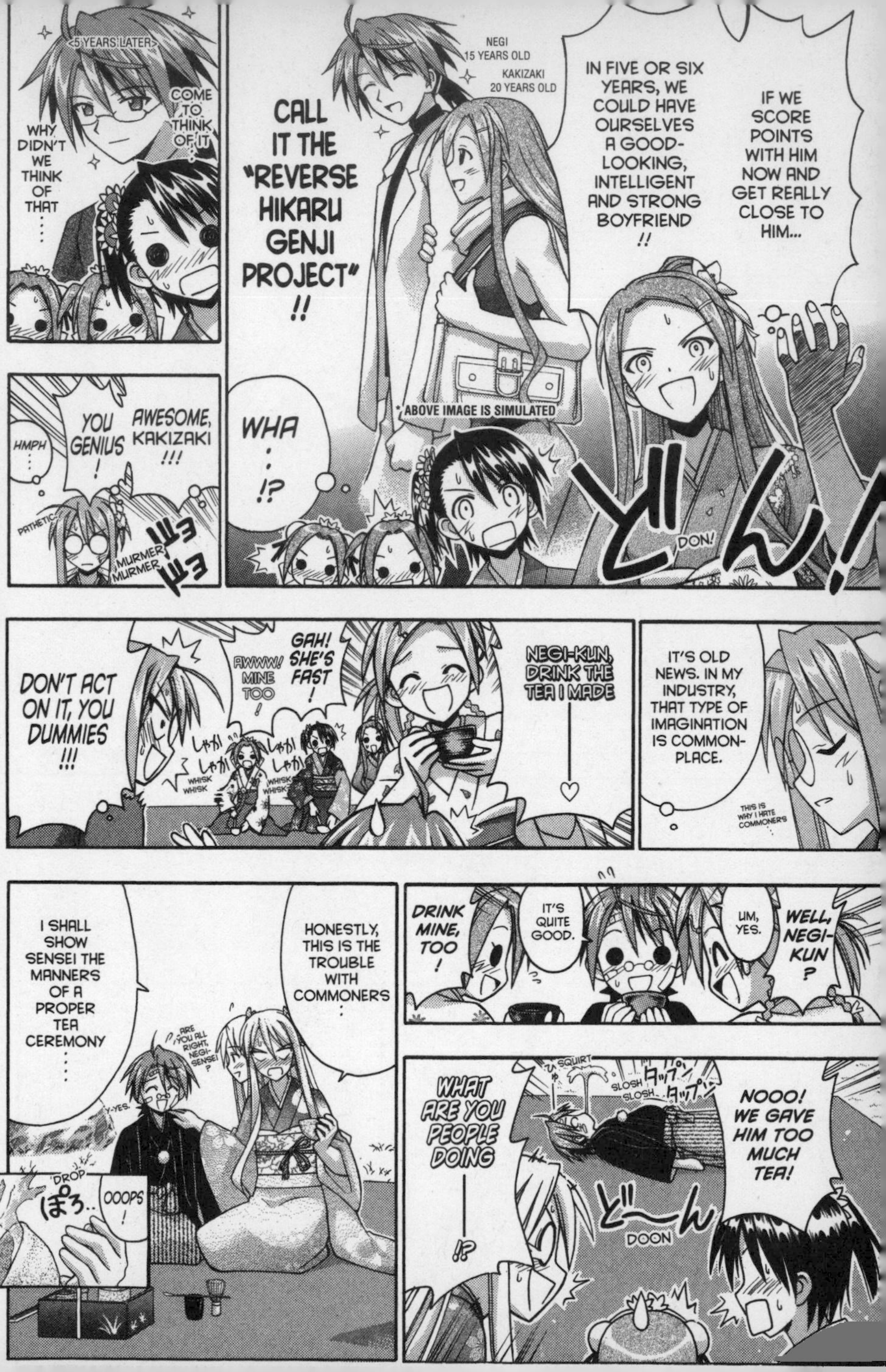
IF WE SCORE POINTS WITH HIM NOW AND GET REALLY CLOSE TO HIM...
IN FIVE OR SIX YEARS, WE COULD HAVE OURSELVES A GOOD-LOOKING, INTELLIGENT AND STRONG BOYFRIEND !!
NEGI 15 YEARS OLD
KAKIZAKI 20 YEARS OLD
CALL IT THE "REVERSE HIKARU GENJI PROJECT" !!
* ABOVE IMAGE IS SIMULATED
WHA...!?
どん!
DON!
<5 YEARS LATER>
COME TO THINK OF IT...
WHY DIDN'T WE THINK OF THAT...
AWESOME, KAKIZAKI !!!
YOU GENIUS !
HMPH...
PATHETIC
MURMER MURMER
IT'S OLD NEWS. IN MY INDUSTRY, THAT TYPE OF IMAGINATION IS COMMONPLACE.
THIS IS WHY I HATE COMMONERS...
NEGI-KUN, DRINK THE TEA I MADE ♡
GAH! SHE'S FAST!
AWWW! MINE TOO!
しゃかしゃか
WHISK WHISK
しゃかしゃか
WHISK WHISK
DON'T ACT ON IT, YOU DUMMIES !!!
WELL, NEGI-KUN?
UM, YES.
IT'S QUITE GOOD.
DRINK MINE, TOO!
NOOO! WE GAVE HIM TOO MUCH TEA!
タップン タップン
SLOSH SLOSH
SQUIRT
WHAT ARE YOU PEOPLE DOING—!?
ど〜ん
DOON
HONESTLY, THIS IS THE TROUBLE WITH COMMONERS...
I SHALL SHOW SENSEI THE MANNERS OF A PROPER TEA CEREMONY...
ARE YOU ALL RIGHT, NEGI-SENSEI?
Y-YES.
OOOPS!
ぽろ..
DROP

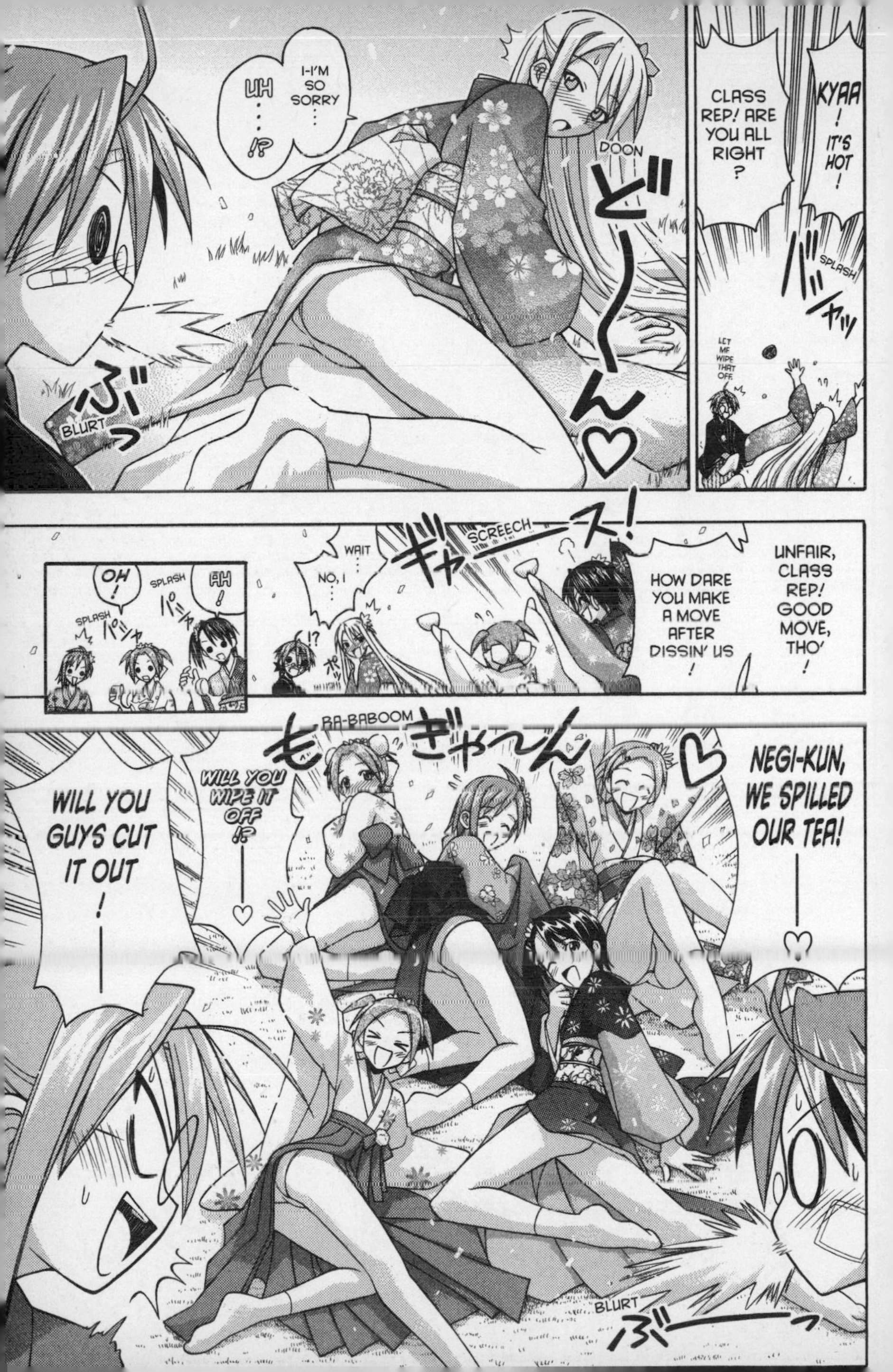
KYAA! IT'S HOT!
CLASS REP! ARE YOU ALL RIGHT?
バシャッ
SPLASH
LET ME WIPE THAT OFF.
DOON
どーん♡
I-I'M SO SORRY...
UH...!?
ぶ
BLURT
UNFAIR, CLASS REP! GOOD MOVE, THO'!
HOW DARE YOU MAKE A MOVE AFTER DISSIN' US!
ギャース!
SCREECH
WAIT... NO, I...
!?
AH!
パシャ
SPLASH
OH!
パシャ
SPLASH
NEGI-KUN, WE SPILLED OUR TEA!—♡
ぎゃーん♡
RA-BABOOM
WILL YOU WIPE IT OFF!?—♡
WILL YOU GUYS CUT IT OUT!—
ぶー
BLURT

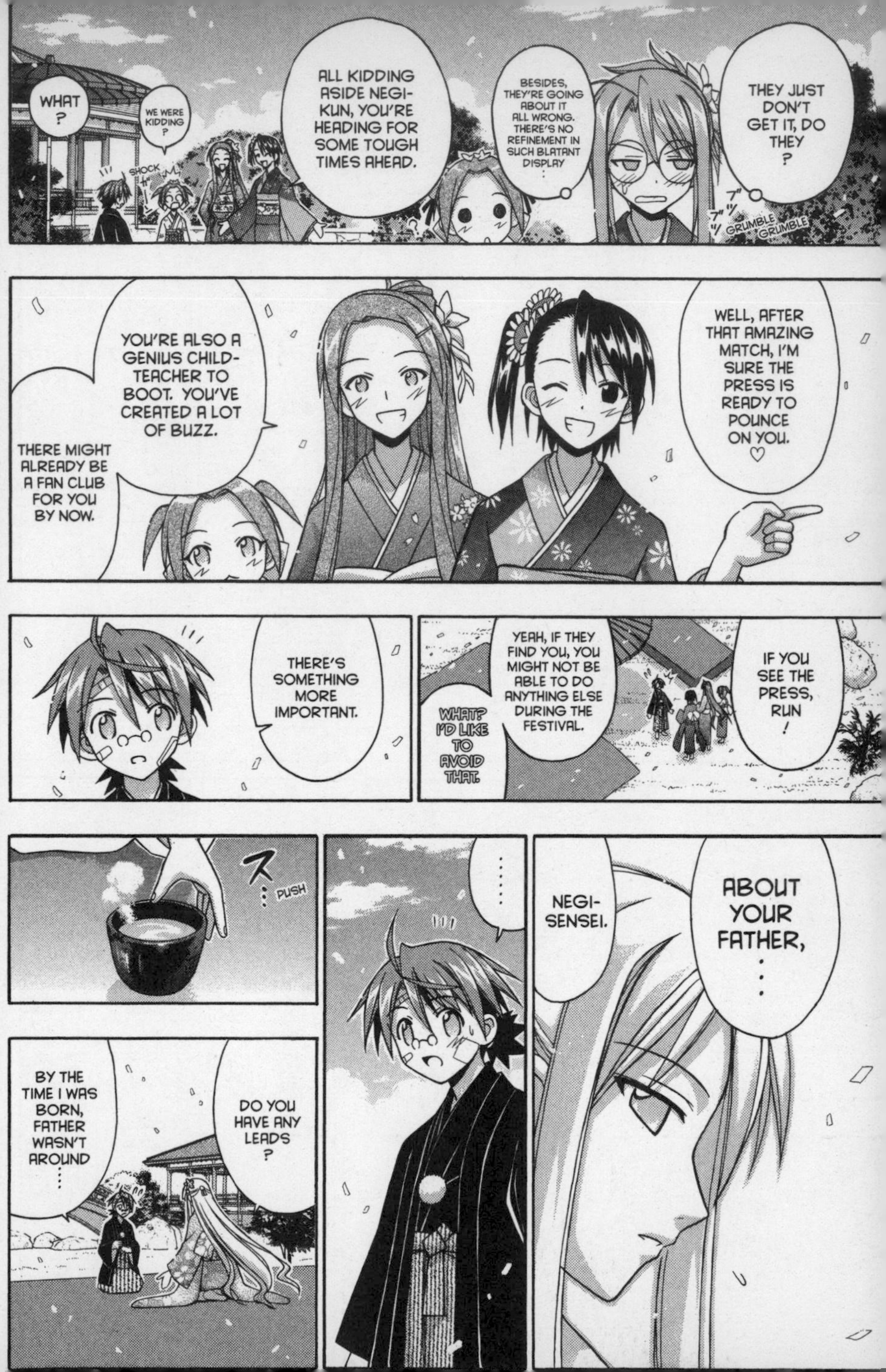
THEY JUST DON'T GET IT, DO THEY?
GRUMBLE GRUMBLE
BESIDES, THEY'RE GOING ABOUT IT ALL WRONG. THERE'S NO REFINEMENT IN SUCH BLATANT DISPLAY...
ALL KIDDING ASIDE NEGI-KUN, YOU'RE HEADING FOR SOME TOUGH TIMES AHEAD.
WE WERE KIDDING?
SHOCK
WHAT?
WELL, AFTER THAT AMAZING MATCH, I'M SURE THE PRESS IS READY TO POUNCE ON YOU. ♡
YOU'RE ALSO A GENIUS CHILD-TEACHER TO BOOT. YOU'VE CREATED A LOT OF BUZZ.
THERE MIGHT ALREADY BE A FAN CLUB FOR YOU BY NOW.
IF YOU SEE THE PRESS, RUN!
YEAH, IF THEY FIND YOU, YOU MIGHT NOT BE ABLE TO DO ANYTHING ELSE DURING THE FESTIVAL.
WHAT? I'D LIKE TO AVOID THAT.
THERE'S SOMETHING MORE IMPORTANT.
ABOUT YOUR FATHER, ...
NEGI-SENSEI.
......
PUSH
DO YOU HAVE ANY LEADS?
BY THE TIME I WAS BORN, FATHER WASN'T AROUND...

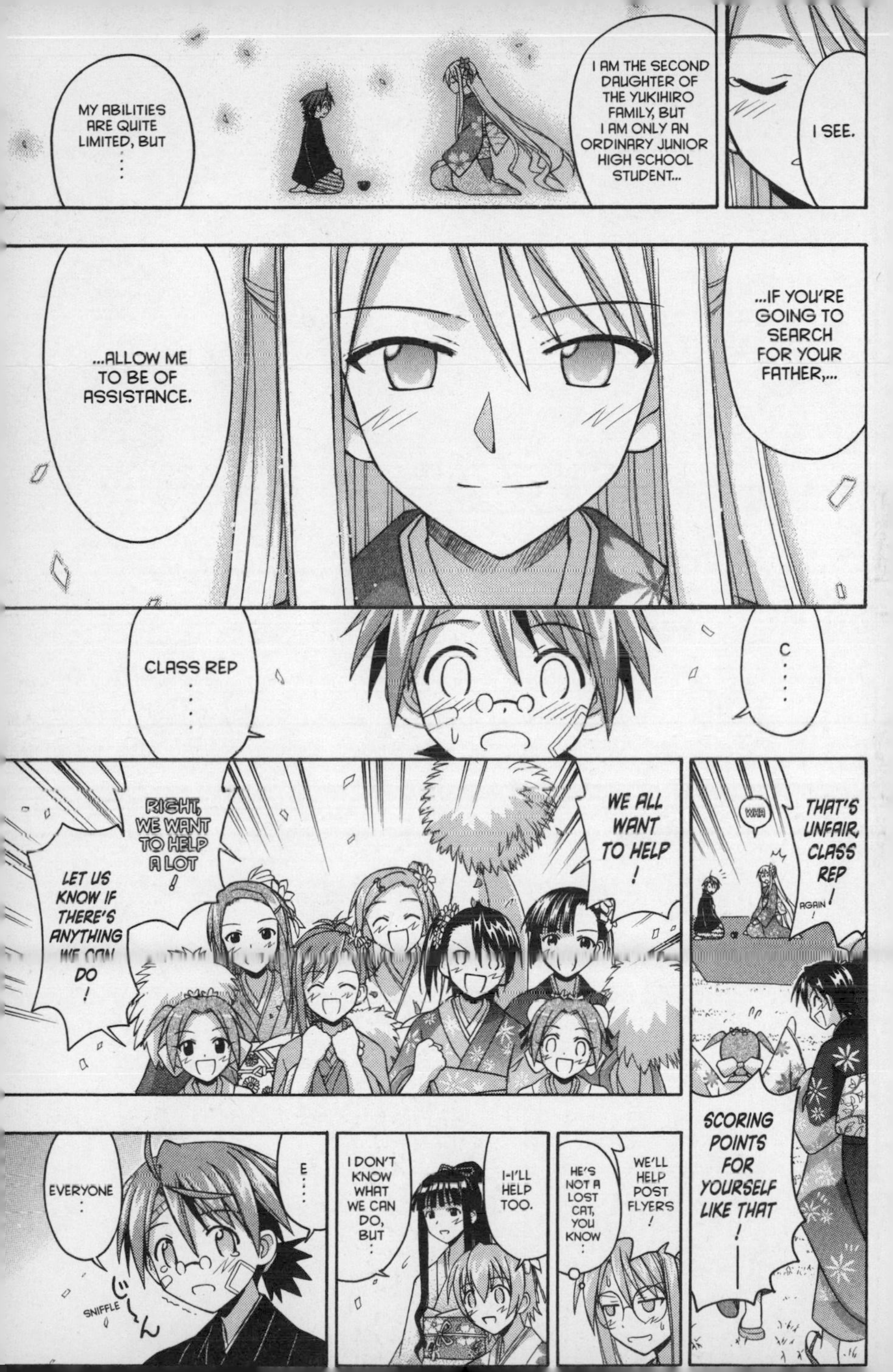
I SEE.
I AM THE SECOND DAUGHTER OF THE YUKIHIRO FAMILY, BUT I AM ONLY AN ORDINARY JUNIOR HIGH SCHOOL STUDENT...
MY ABILITIES ARE QUITE LIMITED, BUT ...
...IF YOU'RE GOING TO SEARCH FOR YOUR FATHER,...
...ALLOW ME TO BE OF ASSISTANCE.
C...
CLASS REP...
WHA
THAT'S UNFAIR, CLASS REP!
AGAIN!
SCORING POINTS FOR YOURSELF LIKE THAT!
WE ALL WANT TO HELP!
RIGHT, WE WANT TO HELP A LOT!
LET US KNOW IF THERE'S ANYTHING WE CAN DO!
WE'LL HELP POST FLYERS!
HE'S NOT A LOST CAT, YOU KNOW...
I-I'LL HELP TOO.
I DON'T KNOW WHAT WE CAN DO, BUT...
E...
EVERYONE...
じ～ん
SNIFFLE

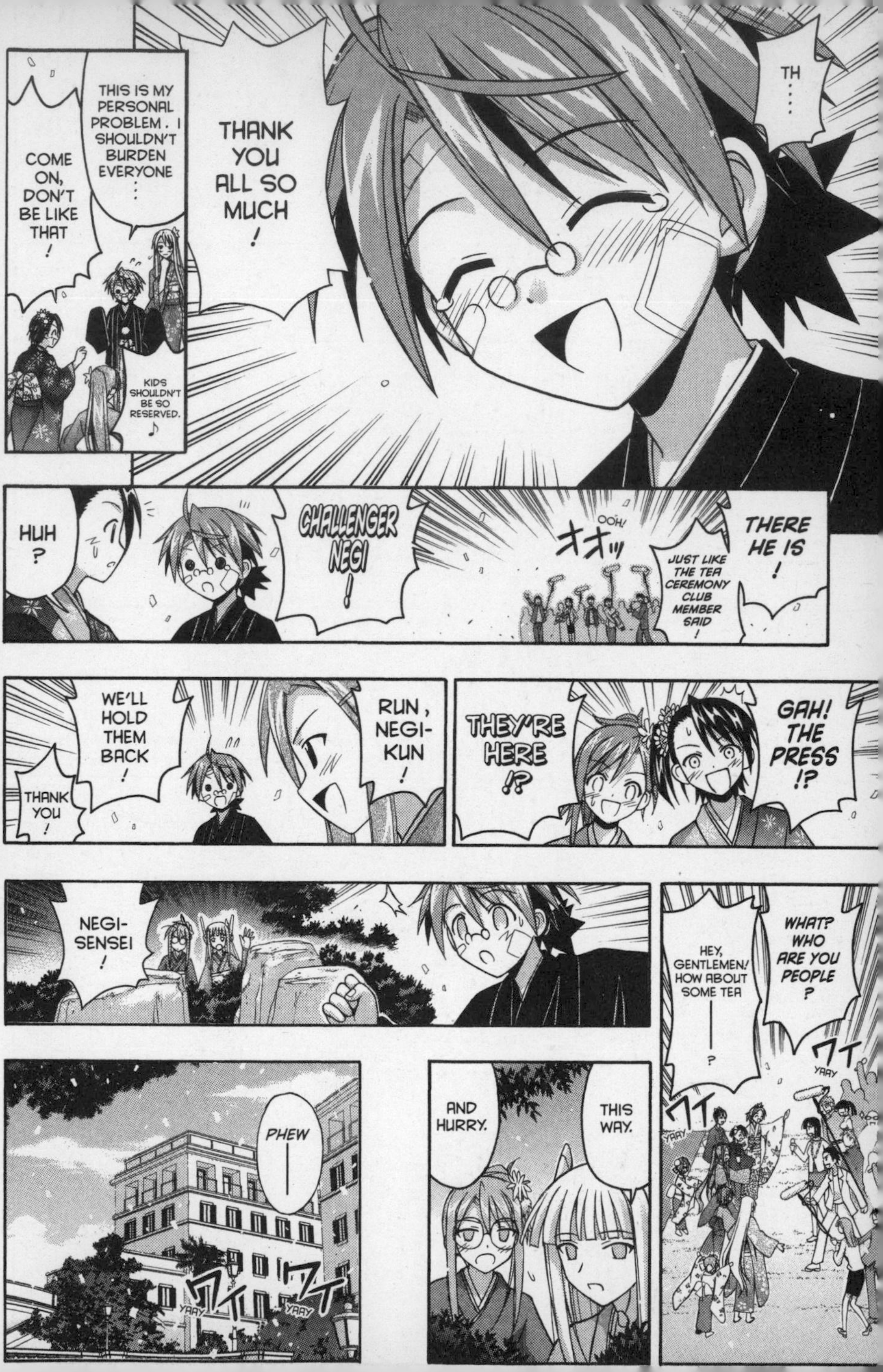
TH....
THANK YOU ALL SO MUCH!
THIS IS MY PERSONAL PROBLEM. I SHOULDN'T BURDEN EVERYONE...
COME ON, DON'T BE LIKE THAT!
KIDS SHOULDN'T BE SO RESERVED. ♪
THERE HE IS!
JUST LIKE THE TEA CEREMONY CLUB MEMBER SAID!
OOH!
CHALLENGER NEGI!
HUH?
GAH! THE PRESS!?
THEY'RE HERE!?
RUN, NEGI-KUN!
WE'LL HOLD THEM BACK!
THANK YOU!
WHAT? WHO ARE YOU PEOPLE?
HEY, GENTLEMEN! HOW ABOUT SOME TEA—?
YAAY
YAAY
NEGI-SENSEI!
THIS WAY.
AND HURRY.
PHEW—
YAAY
YAAY

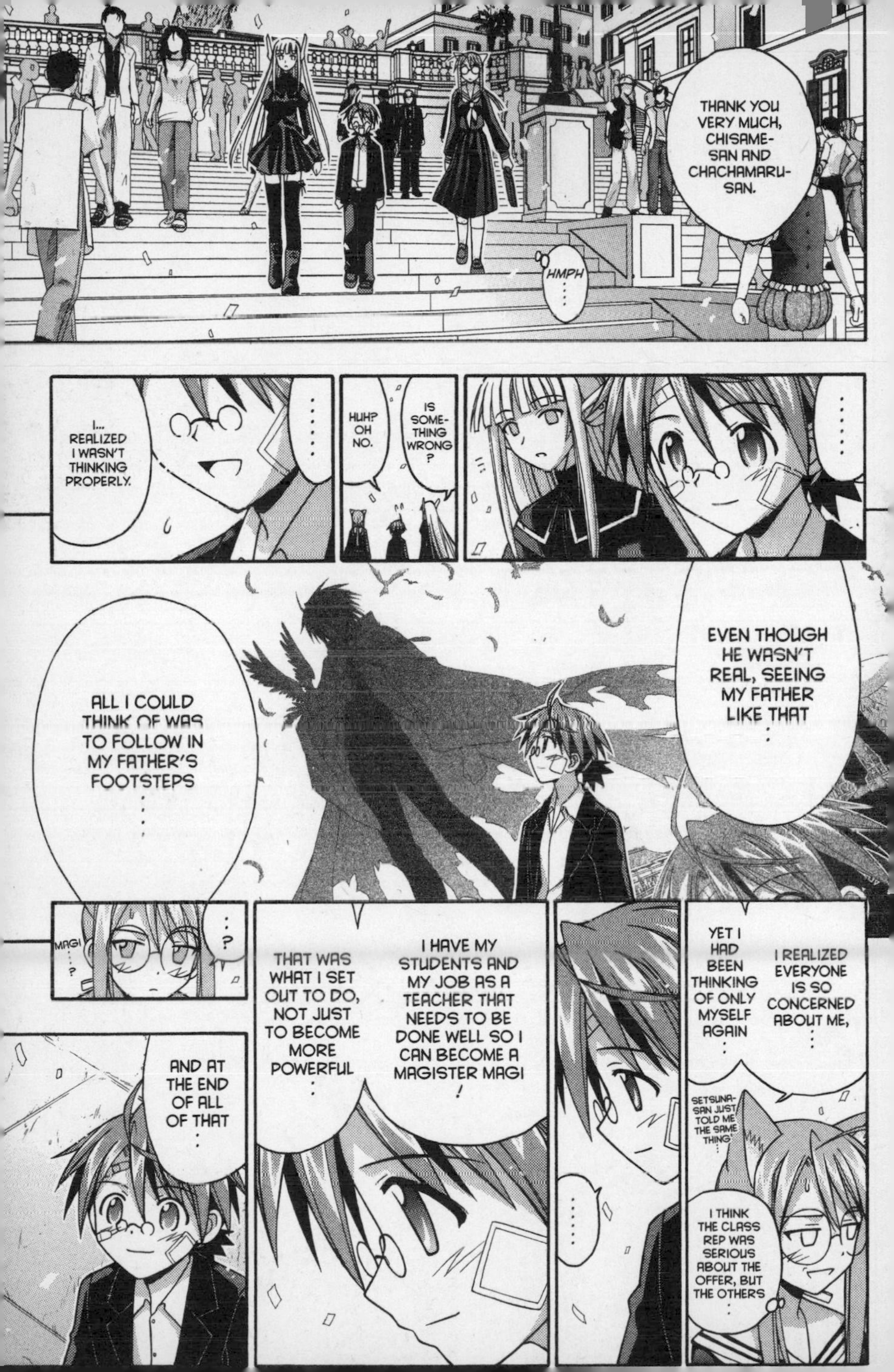
THANK YOU VERY MUCH, CHISAME-SAN AND CHACHAMARU-SAN.
HMPH....
......
IS SOMETHING WRONG?
HUH? OH NO.
......
I... REALIZED I WASN'T THINKING PROPERLY.
EVEN THOUGH HE WASN'T REAL, SEEING MY FATHER LIKE THAT..
ALL I COULD THINK OF WAS TO FOLLOW IN MY FATHER'S FOOTSTEPS......
I REALIZED EVERYONE IS SO CONCERNED ABOUT ME,...
YET I HAD BEEN THINKING OF ONLY MYSELF AGAIN..
SETSUNA-SAN JUST TOLD ME THE SAME THING...
I THINK THE CLASS REP WAS SERIOUS ABOUT THE OFFER, BUT THE OTHERS..
......
I HAVE MY STUDENTS AND MY JOB AS A TEACHER THAT NEEDS TO BE DONE WELL SO I CAN BECOME A MAGISTER MAGI!
THAT WAS WHAT I SET OUT TO DO, NOT JUST TO BECOME MORE POWERFUL...
..?
MAGI...?
AND AT THE END OF ALL OF THAT..

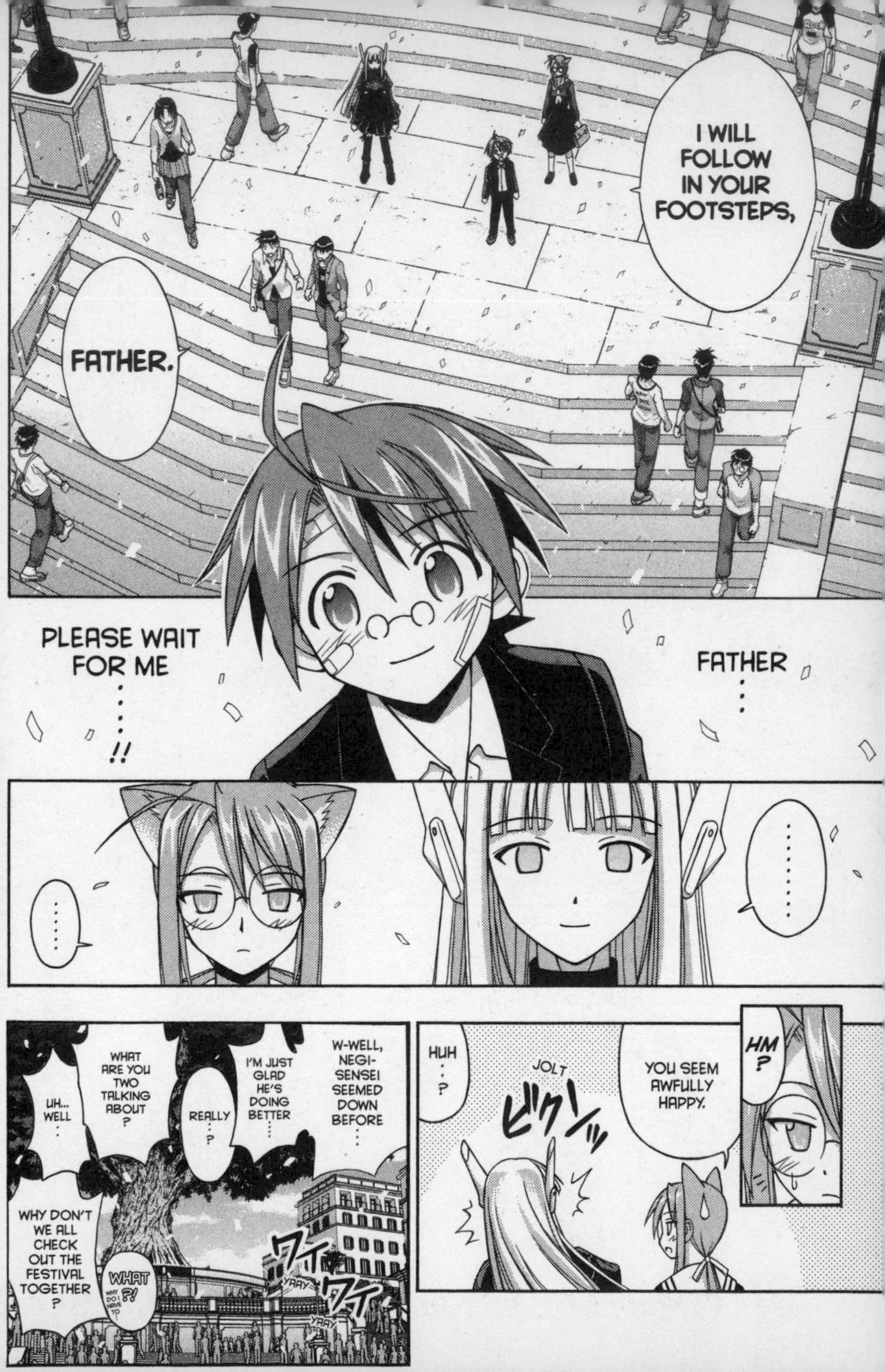
I WILL FOLLOW IN YOUR FOOTSTEPS,
FATHER.
FATHER . . .
PLEASE WAIT FOR ME . . . !!
. . . .
. . . . . .
HM ?
YOU SEEM AWFULLY HAPPY.
JOLT
ビクッ
HUH . . ?
W-WELL, NEGI-SENSEI SEEMED DOWN BEFORE . . .
I'M JUST GLAD HE'S DOING BETTER . . .
REALLY . . . ?
WHAT ARE YOU TWO TALKING ABOUT ?
UH... WELL . . .
WHY DON'T WE ALL CHECK OUT THE FESTIVAL TOGETHER ?
WHAT ?!
WHY DO I HAVE TO?
ワイワイ
YAAY
YAAY

NEGIMA!

MAGISTER NEGI MAGI

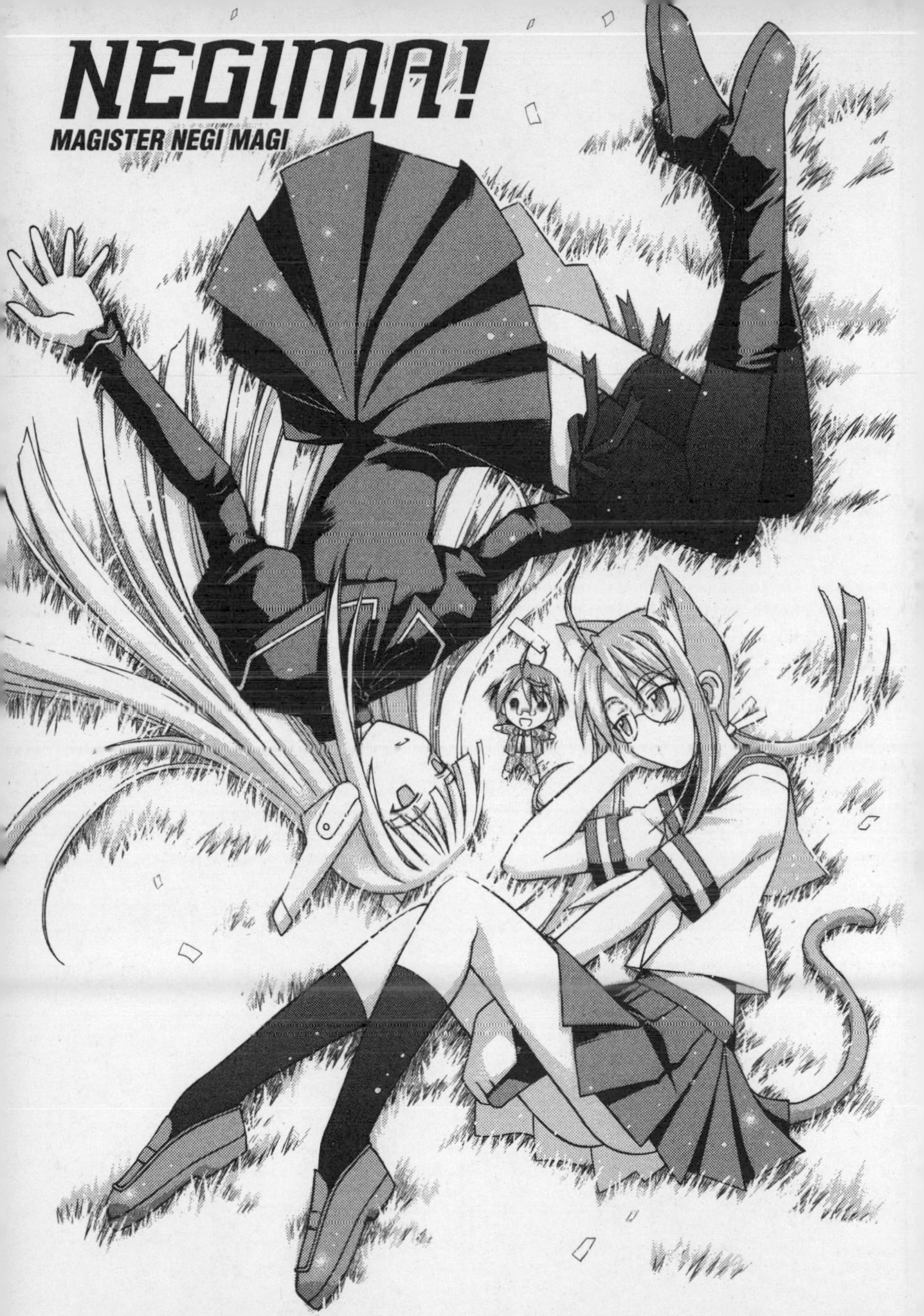

121ST PERIOD: NEGI MAJORLY BUSTED MAGISTER MAGI

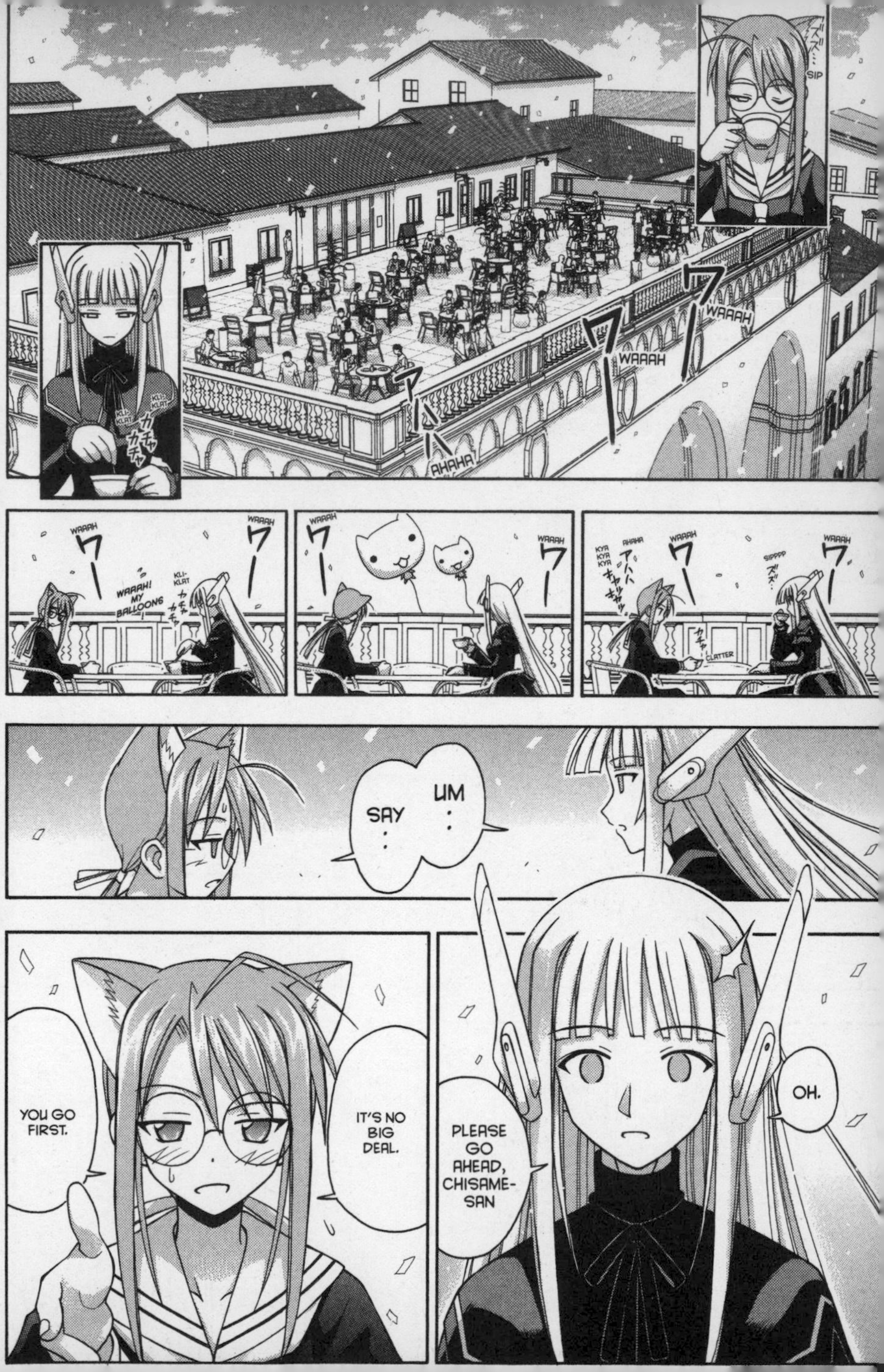

ズズー…
SIP
ワー
WAAAH
ワー
WAAAH
アハハ
AHAHA
KLI-KLAT
KLI-KLAT
カチャ カチャ
ワー
WAAAH
ズズ
SIPPPP
ワー
WAAAH
アハハ
AHAHA
キャッキャッ
KYA KYA KYA
カチャ
CLATTER
ワー
WAAAH
ワー
WAAAH
ワー
WAAAH
カチャ カチャ
KLI-KLAT
WAAAH! MY BALLOONS!
UM :
SAY :
OH.
PLEASE GO AHEAD, CHISAME-SAN
IT'S NO BIG DEAL.
YOU GO FIRST.

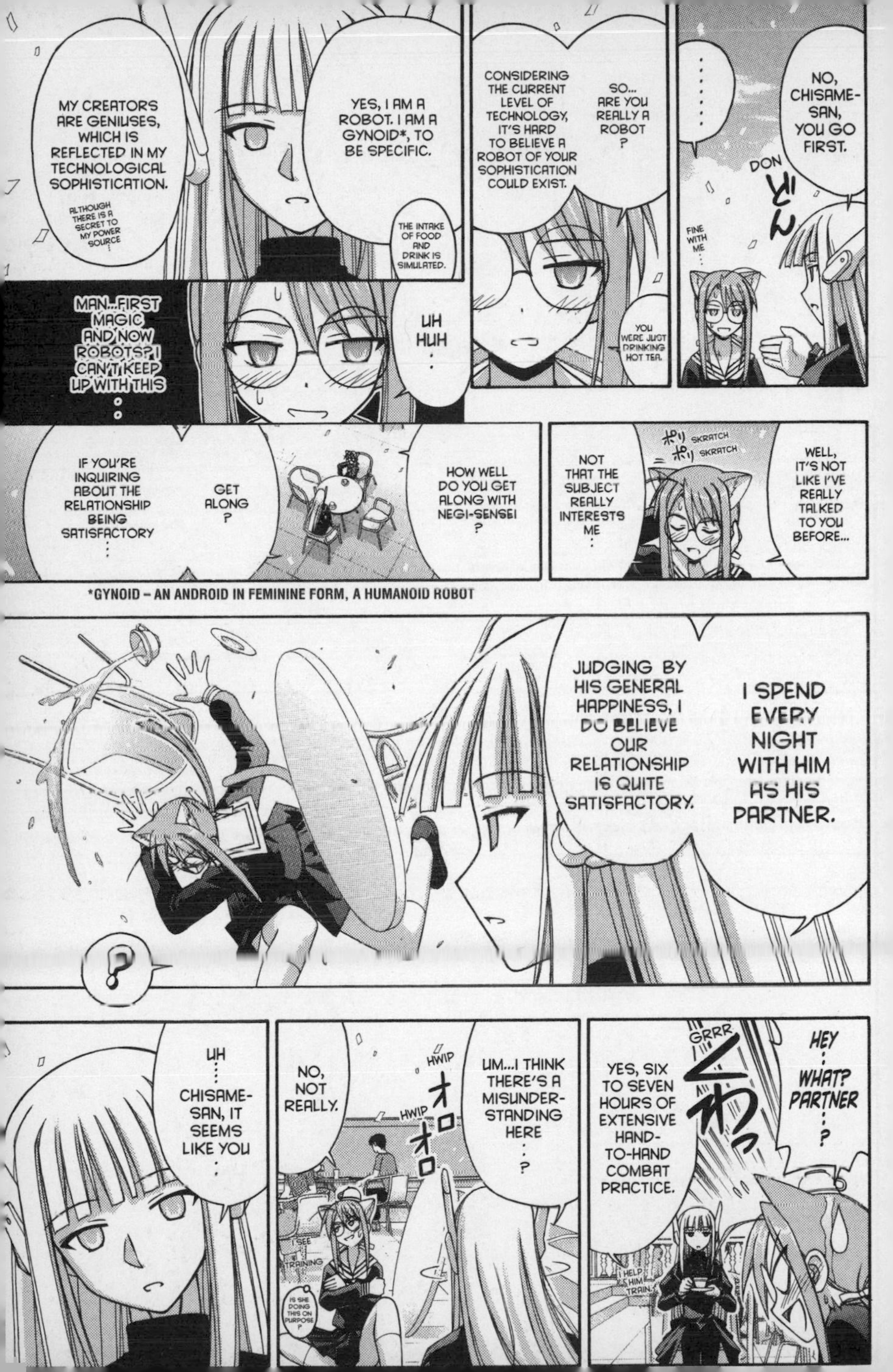

NO, CHISAME-SAN, YOU GO FIRST.
DON どん
FINE WITH ME...
......
SO... ARE YOU REALLY A ROBOT?
CONSIDERING THE CURRENT LEVEL OF TECHNOLOGY, IT'S HARD TO BELIEVE A ROBOT OF YOUR SOPHISTICATION COULD EXIST.
YOU WERE JUST DRINKING HOT TEA.
YES, I AM A ROBOT. I AM A GYNOID*, TO BE SPECIFIC.
THE INTAKE OF FOOD AND DRINK IS SIMULATED.
MY CREATORS ARE GENIUSES, WHICH IS REFLECTED IN MY TECHNOLOGICAL SOPHISTICATION.
ALTHOUGH THERE IS A SECRET TO MY POWER SOURCE...
UH HUH...
MAN...FIRST MAGIC AND NOW ROBOTS? I CAN'T KEEP UP WITH THIS...
WELL, IT'S NOT LIKE I'VE REALLY TALKED TO YOU BEFORE...
ポリ SKRATCH ポリ SKRATCH
NOT THAT THE SUBJECT REALLY INTERESTS ME...
HOW WELL DO YOU GET ALONG WITH NEGI-SENSEI?
GET ALONG?
IF YOU'RE INQUIRING ABOUT THE RELATIONSHIP BEING SATISFACTORY...
I SPEND EVERY NIGHT WITH HIM AS HIS PARTNER.
JUDGING BY HIS GENERAL HAPPINESS, I DO BELIEVE OUR RELATIONSHIP IS QUITE SATISFACTORY.
?
HEY... WHAT? PARTNER...?
GRRR わっ
YES, SIX TO SEVEN HOURS OF EXTENSIVE HAND-TO-HAND COMBAT PRACTICE.
I HELP HIM TRAIN.
UM...I THINK THERE'S A MISUNDER-STANDING HERE...?
HWIP オロ HWIP オロ
NO, NOT REALLY.
I SEE TRAINING
IS SHE DOING THIS ON PURPOSE?
UH... CHISAME-SAN, IT SEEMS LIKE YOU...

*GYNOID – AN ANDROID IN FEMININE FORM, A HUMANOID ROBOT

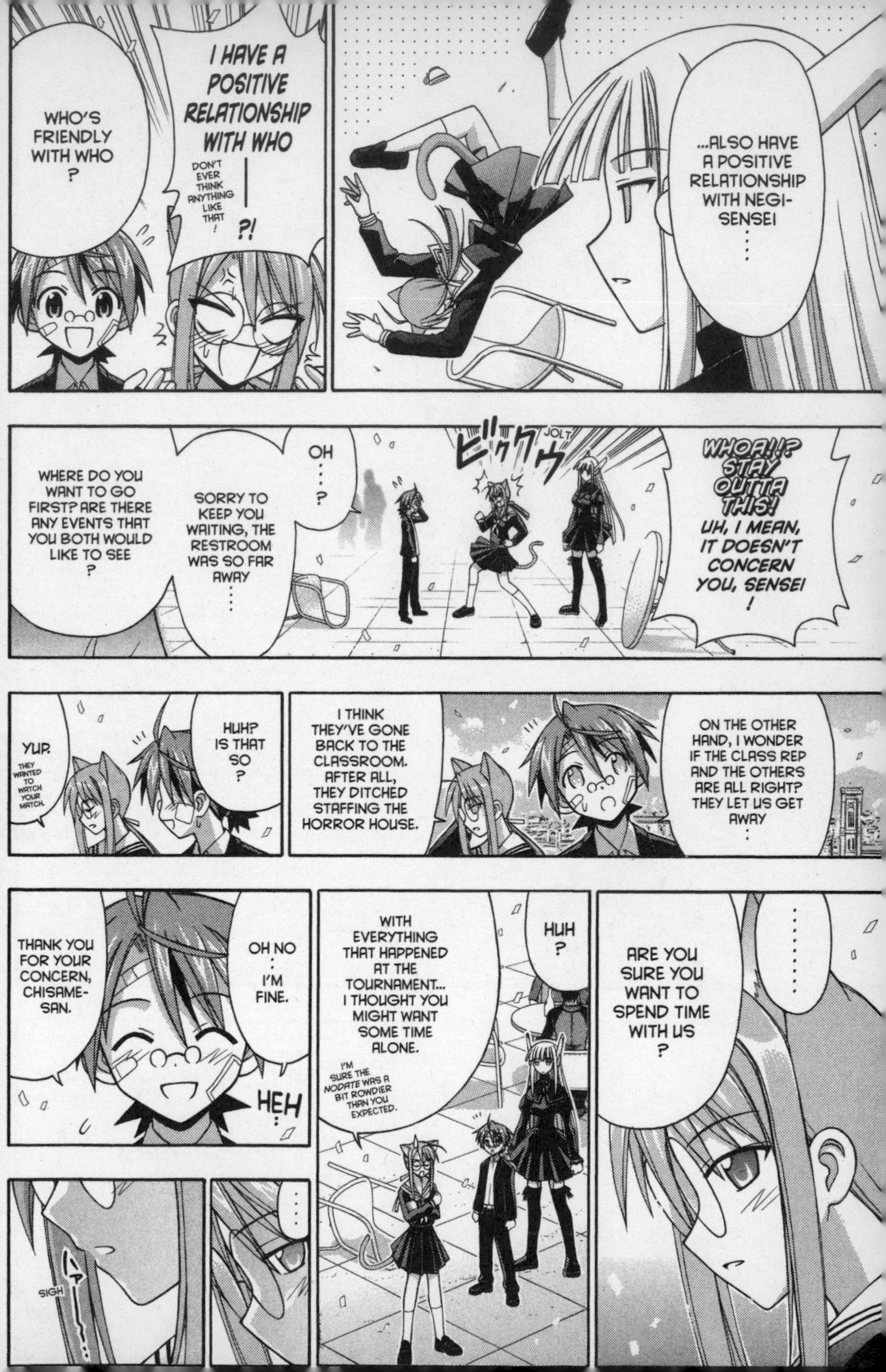

...ALSO HAVE A POSITIVE RELATIONSHIP WITH NEGI-SENSEI ....
I HAVE A POSITIVE RELATIONSHIP WITH WHO —
DON'T EVER THINK ANYTHING LIKE THAT!
?!
WHO'S FRIENDLY WITH WHO ?
WHOA!!? STAY OUTTA THIS! UH, I MEAN, IT DOESN'T CONCERN YOU, SENSEI!
JOLT
OH ...?
SORRY TO KEEP YOU WAITING, THE RESTROOM WAS SO FAR AWAY ....
WHERE DO YOU WANT TO GO FIRST? ARE THERE ANY EVENTS THAT YOU BOTH WOULD LIKE TO SEE ?
ON THE OTHER HAND, I WONDER IF THE CLASS REP AND THE OTHERS ARE ALL RIGHT? THEY LET US GET AWAY ...
I THINK THEY'VE GONE BACK TO THE CLASSROOM. AFTER ALL, THEY DITCHED STAFFING THE HORROR HOUSE.
HUH? IS THAT SO ?
YUP.
THEY WANTED TO WATCH YOUR MATCH.
....
ARE YOU SURE YOU WANT TO SPEND TIME WITH US ?
HUH ?
WITH EVERYTHING THAT HAPPENED AT THE TOURNAMENT... I THOUGHT YOU MIGHT WANT SOME TIME ALONE.
I'M SURE THE *NODATE* WAS A BIT ROWDIER THAN YOU EXPECTED.
OH NO ... I'M FINE.
THANK YOU FOR YOUR CONCERN, CHISAME-SAN.
HEH ...
....
SIGH

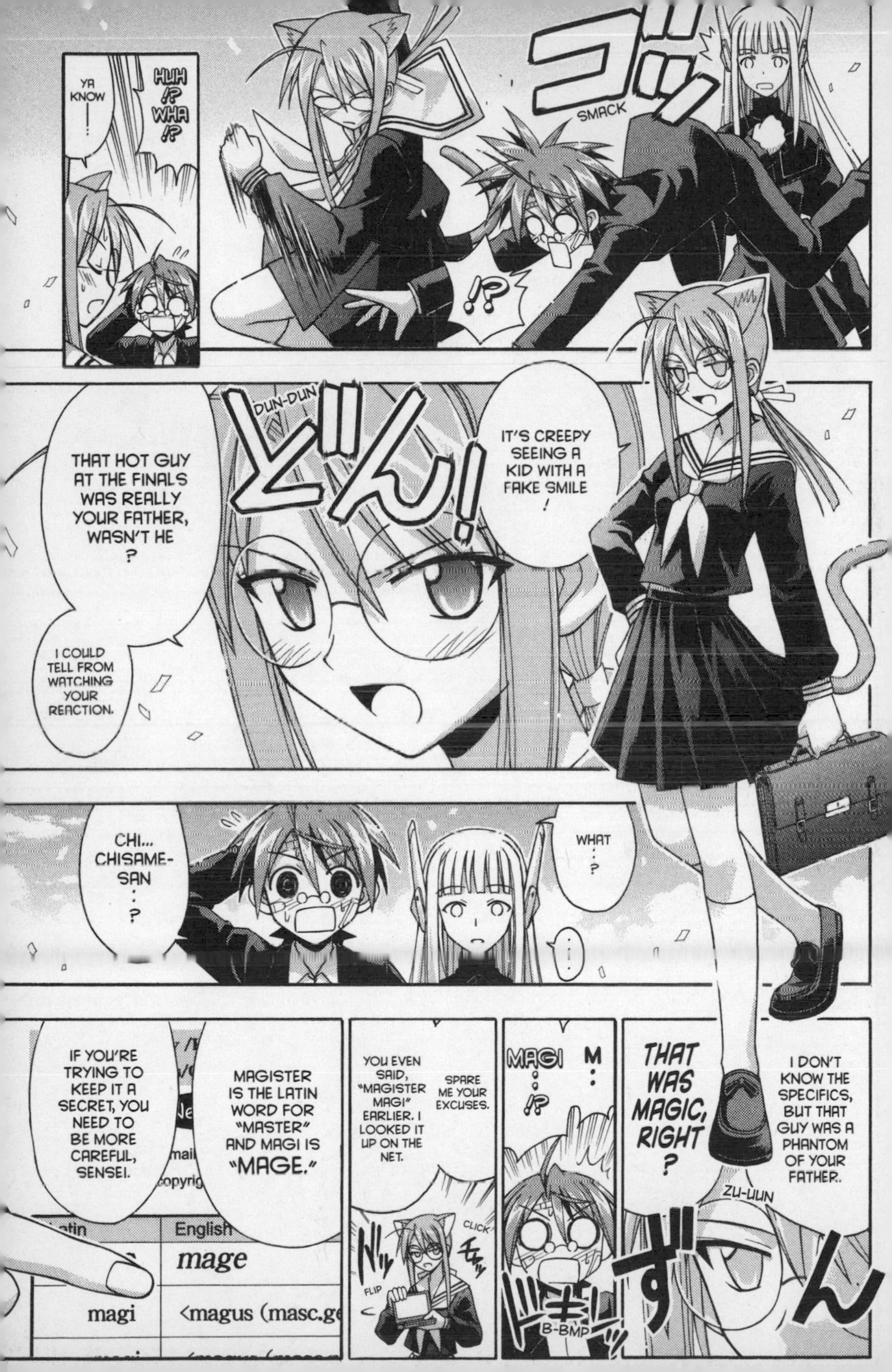
SMACK
!?
HUH !? WHA !?
YA KNOW......
IT'S CREEPY SEEING A KID WITH A FAKE SMILE!
DUN-DUN
THAT HOT GUY AT THE FINALS WAS REALLY YOUR FATHER, WASN'T HE?
I COULD TELL FROM WATCHING YOUR REACTION.
WHAT...?
...
CHI... CHISAME-SAN...?
I DON'T KNOW THE SPECIFICS, BUT THAT GUY WAS A PHANTOM OF YOUR FATHER.
THAT WAS MAGIC, RIGHT?
ZU-UUN
M...
MAGI...!?
B-BMP
SPARE ME YOUR EXCUSES.
YOU EVEN SAID, "MAGISTER MAGI" EARLIER. I LOOKED IT UP ON THE NET.
CLICK
FLIP
MAGISTER IS THE LATIN WORD FOR "MASTER" AND MAGI IS "MAGE."
IF YOU'RE TRYING TO KEEP IT A SECRET, YOU NEED TO BE MORE CAREFUL, SENSEI.
English
mage
magi

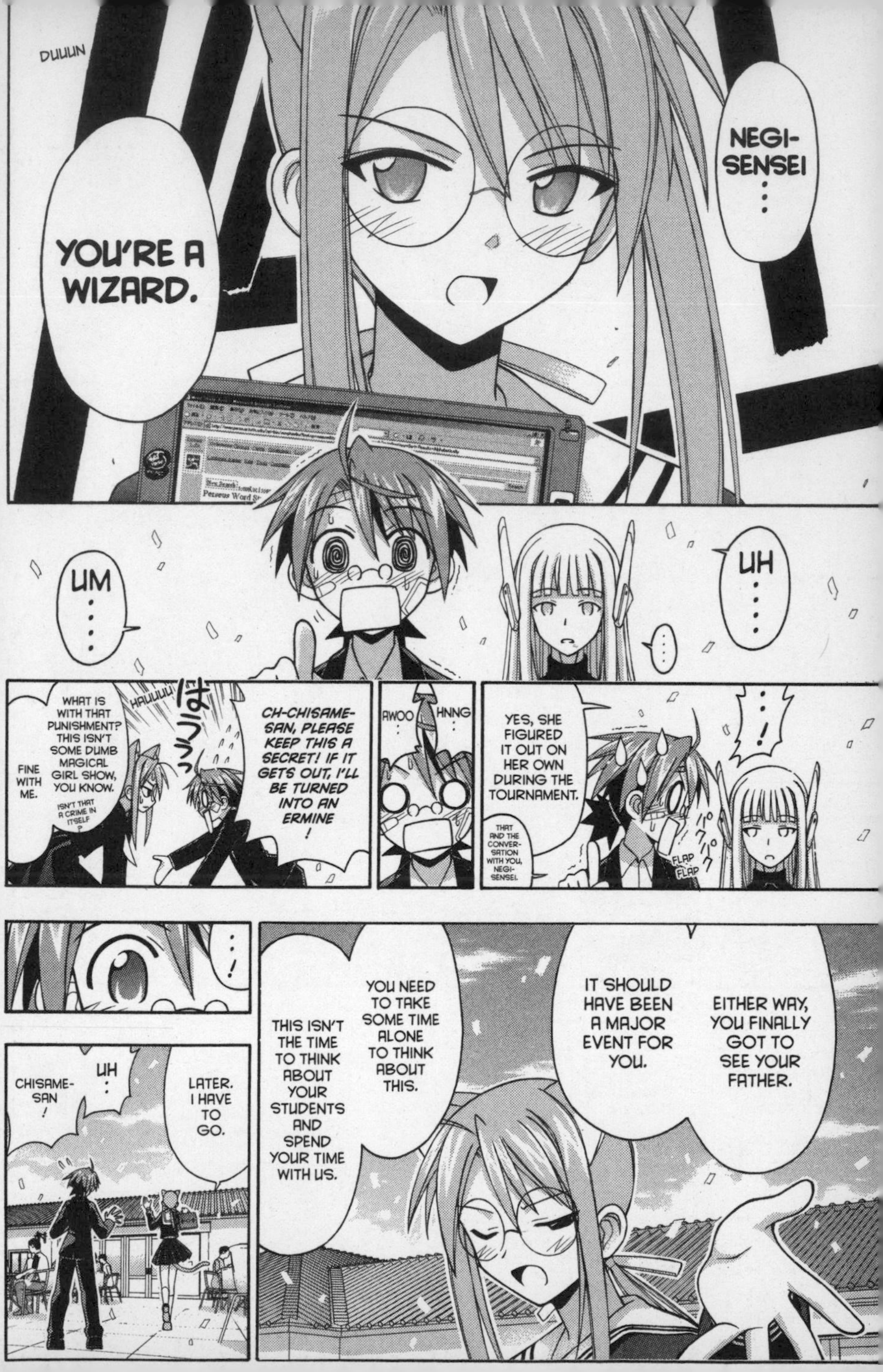

NEGI-SENSEI...
DUUUN
YOU'RE A WIZARD.
UH...
...
UM...
...!
YES, SHE FIGURED IT OUT ON HER OWN DURING THE TOURNAMENT.
THAT AND THE CONVERSATION WITH YOU, NEGI-SENSEI.
FLAP FLAP
HNNG
AWOO
CH-CHISAME-SAN, PLEASE KEEP THIS A SECRET! IF IT GETS OUT, I'LL BE TURNED INTO AN ERMINE!
HAUUUU
WHAT IS WITH THAT PUNISHMENT? THIS ISN'T SOME DUMB MAGICAL GIRL SHOW, YOU KNOW.
FINE WITH ME.
ISN'T THAT A CRIME IN ITSELF?
EITHER WAY, YOU FINALLY GOT TO SEE YOUR FATHER.
IT SHOULD HAVE BEEN A MAJOR EVENT FOR YOU.
YOU NEED TO TAKE SOME TIME ALONE TO THINK ABOUT THIS.
THIS ISN'T THE TIME TO THINK ABOUT YOUR STUDENTS AND SPEND YOUR TIME WITH US.
...!
LATER. I HAVE TO GO.
UH...
CHISAME-SAN!

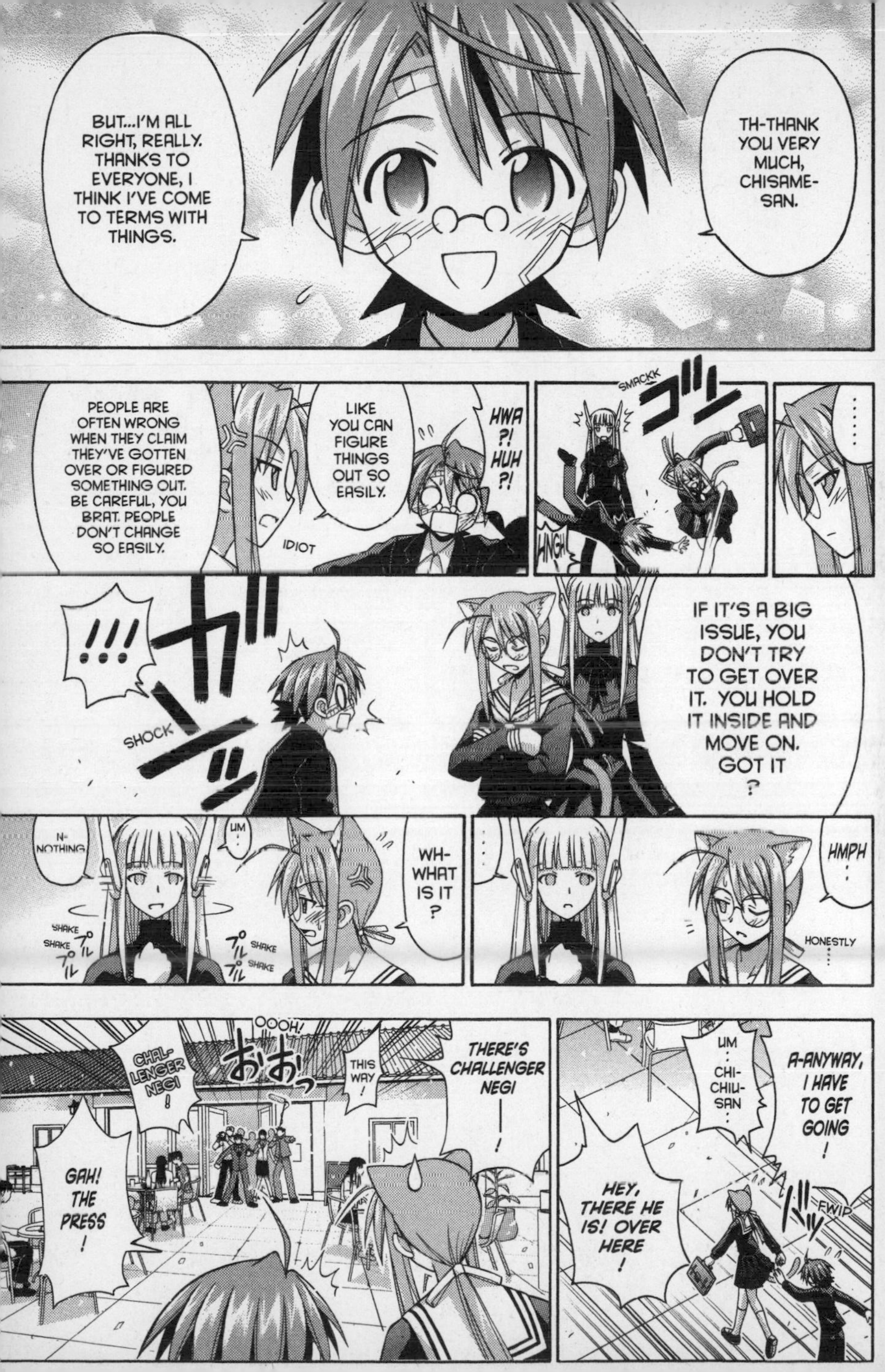
TH-THANK YOU VERY MUCH, CHISAME-SAN.
BUT...I'M ALL RIGHT, REALLY. THANKS TO EVERYONE, I THINK I'VE COME TO TERMS WITH THINGS.
......
SMACKK
HNGH
HWA?! HUH?!
LIKE YOU CAN FIGURE THINGS OUT SO EASILY.
PEOPLE ARE OFTEN WRONG WHEN THEY CLAIM THEY'VE GOTTEN OVER OR FIGURED SOMETHING OUT. BE CAREFUL, YOU BRAT. PEOPLE DON'T CHANGE SO EASILY.
IDIOT
IF IT'S A BIG ISSUE, YOU DON'T TRY TO GET OVER IT. YOU HOLD IT INSIDE AND MOVE ON. GOT IT?
SHOCK
!!!
HMPH...
HONESTLY......
....
WH-WHAT IS IT?
UM...
N-NOTHING
SHAKE SHAKE
SHAKE SHAKE
A-ANYWAY, I HAVE TO GET GOING!
UM... CHI-CHIU-SAN...
HEY, THERE HE IS! OVER HERE!
FWIP
THERE'S CHALLENGER NEGI—!
OOOH!
THIS WAY!
CHALLENGER NEGI!
GAH! THE PRESS!

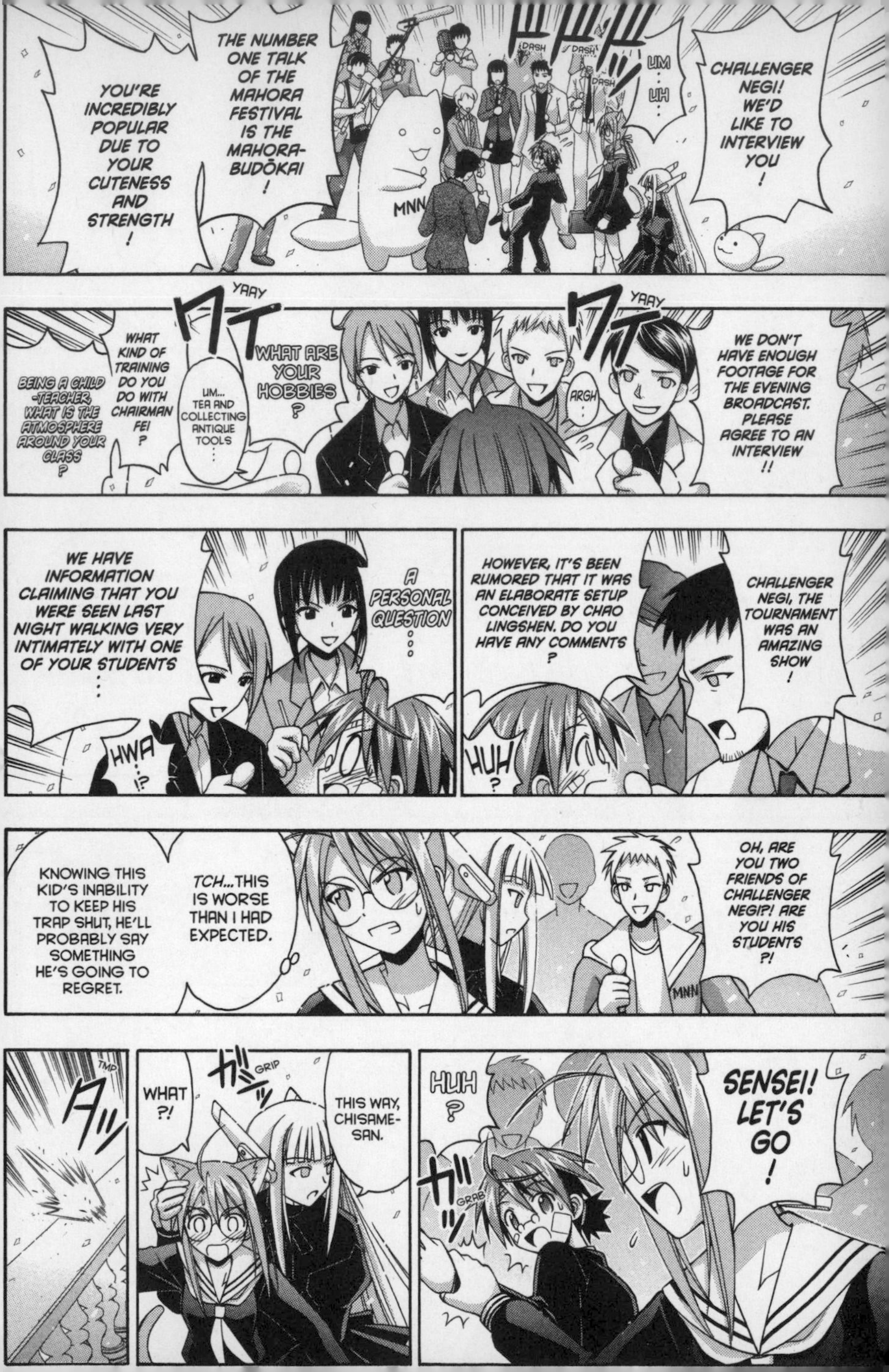
CHALLENGER NEGI! WE'D LIKE TO INTERVIEW YOU!
UM... UH...
DASH
DASH
DASH
THE NUMBER ONE TALK OF THE MAHORA FESTIVAL IS THE MAHORA-BUDŌKAI!
YOU'RE INCREDIBLY POPULAR DUE TO YOUR CUTENESS AND STRENGTH!
MNN
YAAY
WE DON'T HAVE ENOUGH FOOTAGE FOR THE EVENING BROADCAST. PLEASE AGREE TO AN INTERVIEW!!
ARGH...
YAAY
WHAT ARE YOUR HOBBIES?
UM... TEA AND COLLECTING ANTIQUE TOOLS...
WHAT KIND OF TRAINING DO YOU DO WITH CHAIRMAN FEI?
BEING A CHILD-TEACHER, WHAT IS THE ATMOSPHERE AROUND YOUR CLASS?
CHALLENGER NEGI, THE TOURNAMENT WAS AN AMAZING SHOW!
HOWEVER, IT'S BEEN RUMORED THAT IT WAS AN ELABORATE SETUP CONCEIVED BY CHAO LINGSHEN. DO YOU HAVE ANY COMMENTS?
HUH?
A PERSONAL QUESTION...
WE HAVE INFORMATION CLAIMING THAT YOU WERE SEEN LAST NIGHT WALKING VERY INTIMATELY WITH ONE OF YOUR STUDENTS...
HWA...!?
OH, ARE YOU TWO FRIENDS OF CHALLENGER NEGI?! ARE YOU HIS STUDENTS?!
MNN
TCH...THIS IS WORSE THAN I HAD EXPECTED.
KNOWING THIS KID'S INABILITY TO KEEP HIS TRAP SHUT, HE'LL PROBABLY SAY SOMETHING HE'S GOING TO REGRET.
SENSEI! LET'S GO!
HUH?
GRAB
THIS WAY, CHISAME-SAN.
GRIP
WHAT?!
TMP

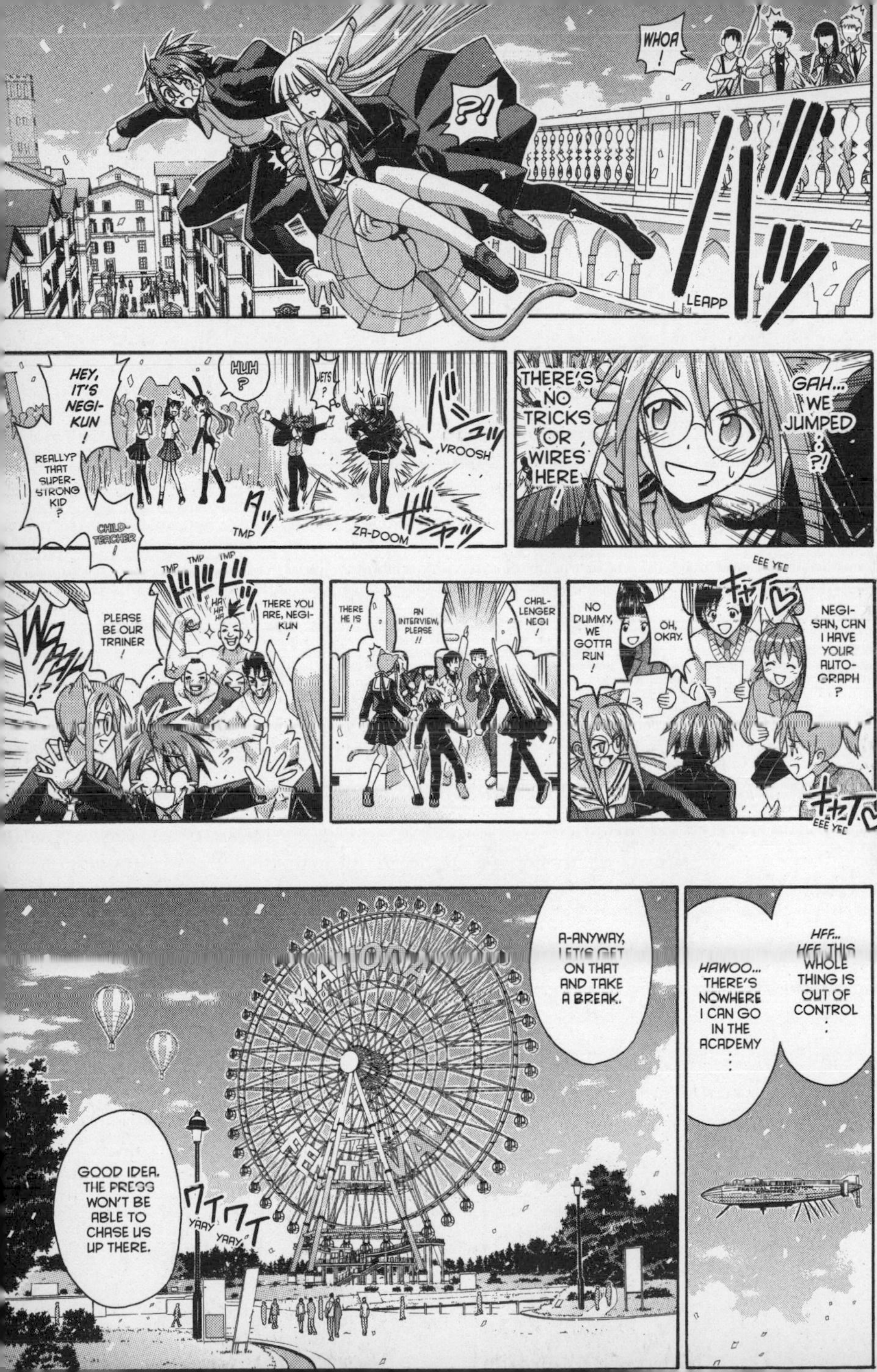
WHOA!
?!
LEAPP
GAH... WE JUMPED?!
THERE'S NO TRICKS OR WIRES HERE!
JETS?
HUH?
HEY, IT'S NEGI-KUN!
REALLY? THAT SUPER-STRONG KID?
CHILD-TEACHER!
VROOSH
ZA-DOOM
TMP
EEE YEE
NEGI-SAN, CAN I HAVE YOUR AUTOGRAPH?
OH, OKAY.
NO DUMMY, WE GOTTA RUN!
EEE YEE
CHALLENGER NEGI!
AN INTERVIEW, PLEASE!!
THERE HE IS!
TMP TMP TMP
THERE YOU ARE, NEGI-KUN!
HA HA HA
PLEASE BE OUR TRAINER!
HFF... HFF THIS WHOLE THING IS OUT OF CONTROL...
HAWOO... THERE'S NOWHERE I CAN GO IN THE ACADEMY...
A-ANYWAY, LET'S GET ON THAT AND TAKE A BREAK.
MAHORA
GOOD IDEA. THE PRESS WON'T BE ABLE TO CHASE US UP THERE.
YAAY YAAY

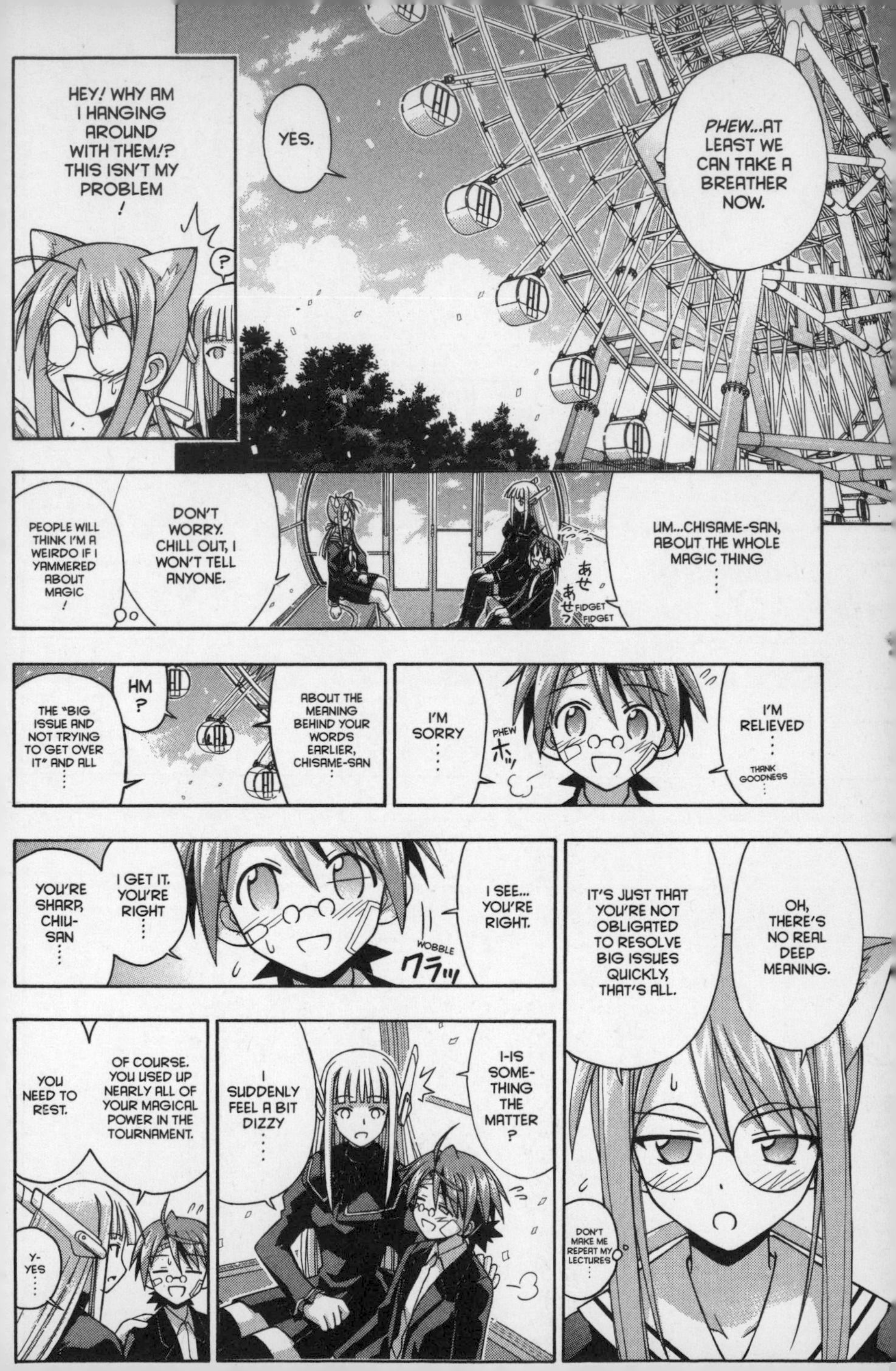

PHEW...AT LEAST WE CAN TAKE A BREATHER NOW.
YES.
HEY! WHY AM I HANGING AROUND WITH THEM!? THIS ISN'T MY PROBLEM!
?
UM...CHISAME-SAN, ABOUT THE WHOLE MAGIC THING...
あせあせっ
FIDGET FIDGET
DON'T WORRY. CHILL OUT, I WON'T TELL ANYONE.
PEOPLE WILL THINK I'M A WEIRDO IF I YAMMERED ABOUT MAGIC!
I'M RELIEVED...
THANK GOODNESS...
ホッ
PHEW
I'M SORRY...
ABOUT THE MEANING BEHIND YOUR WORDS EARLIER, CHISAME-SAN...
HM?
THE "BIG ISSUE AND NOT TRYING TO GET OVER IT" AND ALL...
OH, THERE'S NO REAL DEEP MEANING.
IT'S JUST THAT YOU'RE NOT OBLIGATED TO RESOLVE BIG ISSUES QUICKLY, THAT'S ALL.
DON'T MAKE ME REPEAT MY LECTURES...
I SEE... YOU'RE RIGHT.
WOBBLE
クラッ
I GET IT. YOU'RE RIGHT...
YOU'RE SHARP, CHIU-SAN...
I-IS SOMETHING THE MATTER?
I SUDDENLY FEEL A BIT DIZZY...
OF COURSE. YOU USED UP NEARLY ALL OF YOUR MAGICAL POWER IN THE TOURNAMENT.
YOU NEED TO REST.
Y-YES...

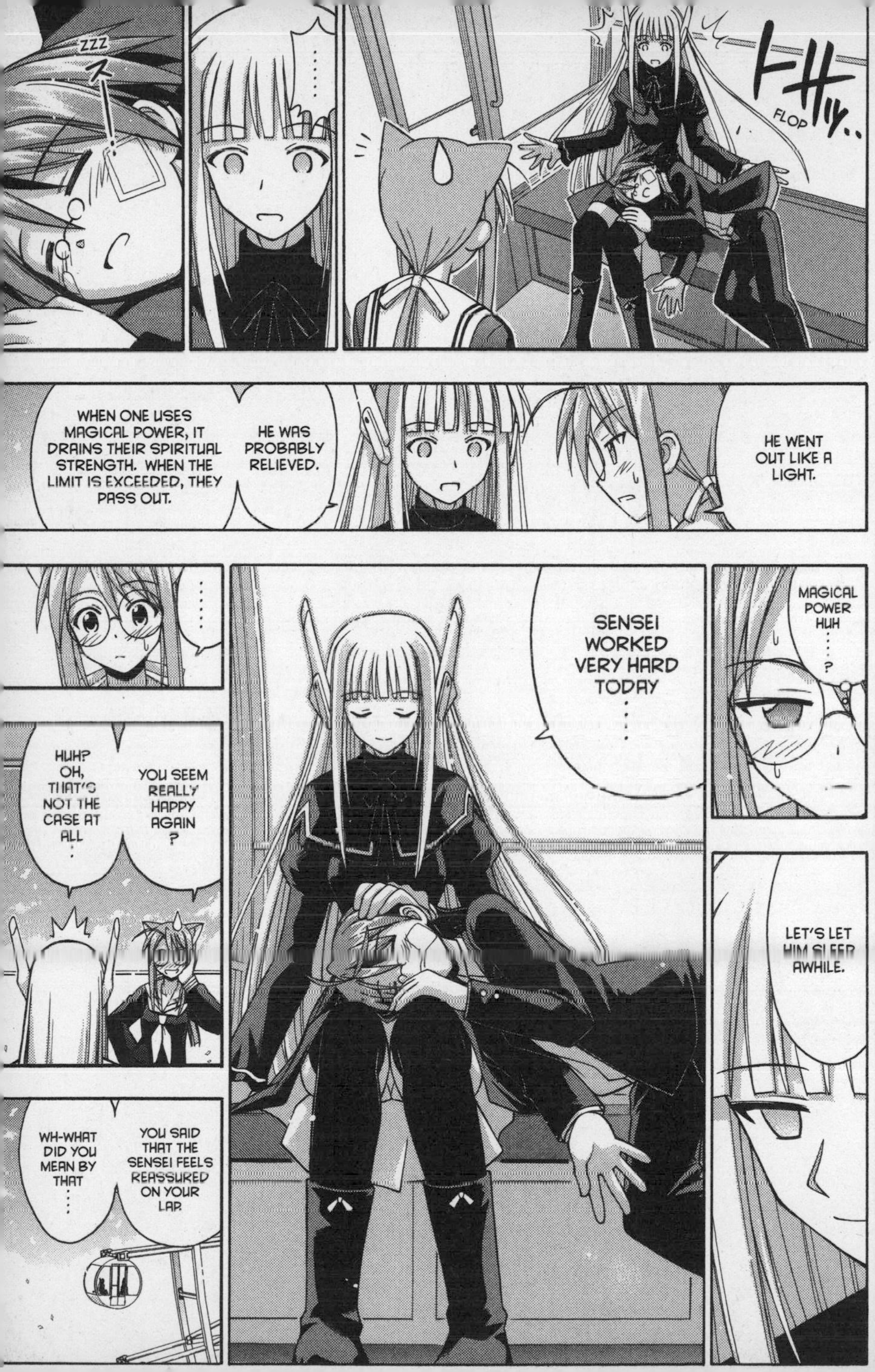
トサッ
FLOP
......
ZZZ
ス
HE WENT OUT LIKE A LIGHT.
HE WAS PROBABLY RELIEVED.
WHEN ONE USES MAGICAL POWER, IT DRAINS THEIR SPIRITUAL STRENGTH. WHEN THE LIMIT IS EXCEEDED, THEY PASS OUT.
MAGICAL POWER HUH ......?
LET'S LET HIM SLEEP AWHILE.
SENSEI WORKED VERY HARD TODAY ......
......
YOU SEEM REALLY HAPPY AGAIN?
HUH? OH, THAT'S NOT THE CASE AT ALL...
YOU SAID THAT THE SENSEI FEELS REASSURED ON YOUR LAP.
WH-WHAT DID YOU MEAN BY THAT ......

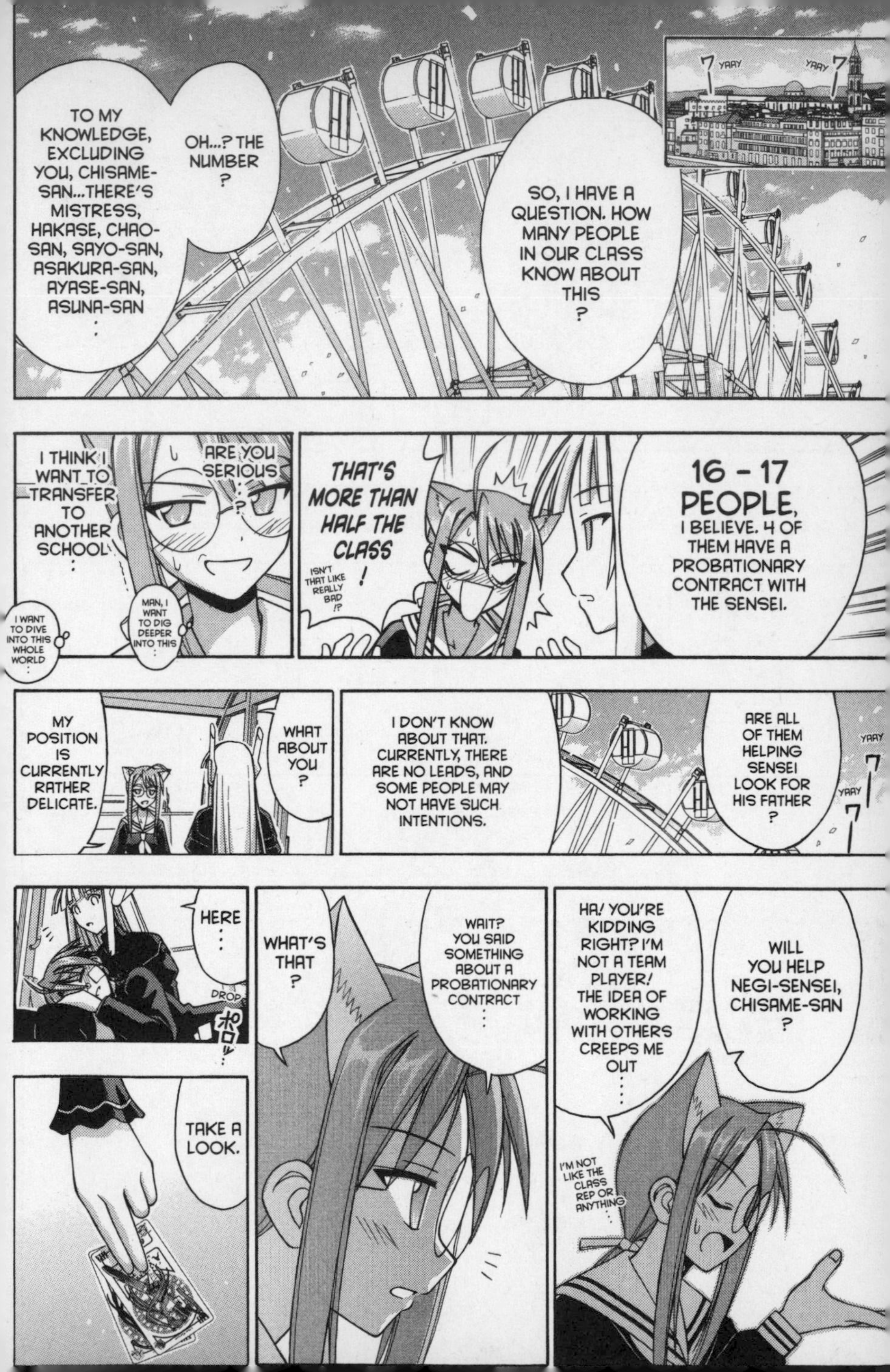
YAAY
YAAY
SO, I HAVE A QUESTION. HOW MANY PEOPLE IN OUR CLASS KNOW ABOUT THIS ?
OH...? THE NUMBER ?
TO MY KNOWLEDGE, EXCLUDING YOU, CHISAME-SAN...THERE'S MISTRESS, HAKASE, CHAO-SAN, SAYO-SAN, ASAKURA-SAN, AYASE-SAN, ASUNA-SAN ...
16 - 17 PEOPLE, I BELIEVE. 4 OF THEM HAVE A PROBATIONARY CONTRACT WITH THE SENSEI.
THAT'S MORE THAN HALF THE CLASS !
ISN'T THAT LIKE REALLY BAD !?
ARE YOU SERIOUS ...?
I THINK I WANT TO TRANSFER TO ANOTHER SCHOOL ...
MAN, I WANT TO DIG DEEPER INTO THIS ...
I WANT TO DIVE INTO THIS WHOLE WORLD ...
YAAY
YAAY
ARE ALL OF THEM HELPING SENSEI LOOK FOR HIS FATHER ?
I DON'T KNOW ABOUT THAT. CURRENTLY, THERE ARE NO LEADS, AND SOME PEOPLE MAY NOT HAVE SUCH INTENTIONS.
WHAT ABOUT YOU ?
MY POSITION IS CURRENTLY RATHER DELICATE.
WILL YOU HELP NEGI-SENSEI, CHISAME-SAN ?
HA! YOU'RE KIDDING RIGHT? I'M NOT A TEAM PLAYER! THE IDEA OF WORKING WITH OTHERS CREEPS ME OUT ...
I'M NOT LIKE THE CLASS REP OR ANYTHING ...
WAIT? YOU SAID SOMETHING ABOUT A PROBATIONARY CONTRACT ...
WHAT'S THAT ?
HERE ...
DROP
TAKE A LOOK.

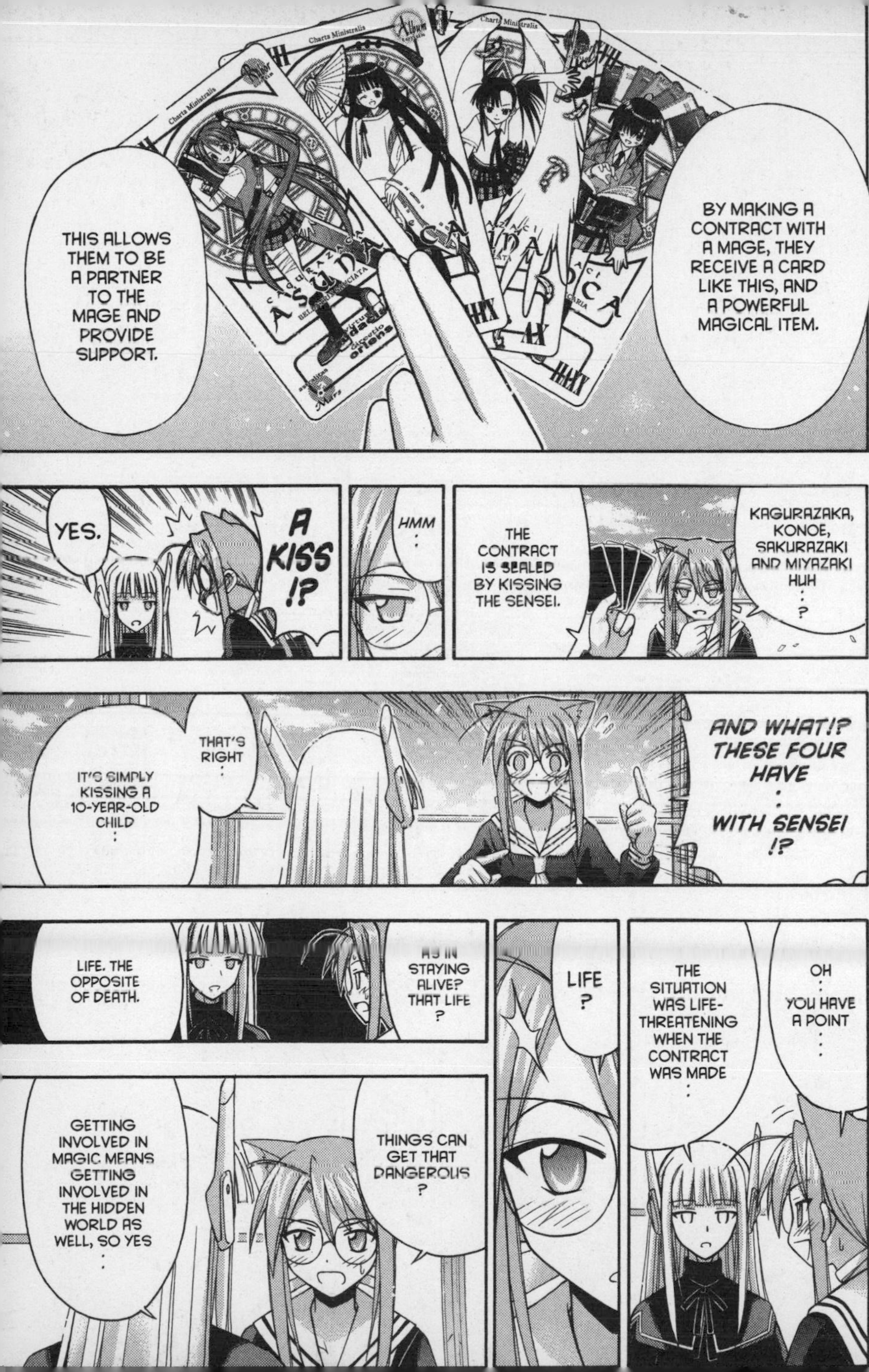

BY MAKING A CONTRACT WITH A MAGE, THEY RECEIVE A CARD LIKE THIS, AND A POWERFUL MAGICAL ITEM.
THIS ALLOWS THEM TO BE A PARTNER TO THE MAGE AND PROVIDE SUPPORT.
KAGURAZAKA, KONOE, SAKURAZAKI AND MIYAZAKI HUH..?
THE CONTRACT IS SEALED BY KISSING THE SENSEI.
HMM..
A KISS!?
YES.
AND WHAT!? THESE FOUR HAVE.. WITH SENSEI!?
THAT'S RIGHT..
IT'S SIMPLY KISSING A 10-YEAR-OLD CHILD..
OH.. YOU HAVE A POINT...
THE SITUATION WAS LIFE-THREATENING WHEN THE CONTRACT WAS MADE..
LIFE?
AS IN STAYING ALIVE? THAT LIFE?
LIFE. THE OPPOSITE OF DEATH.
THINGS CAN GET THAT DANGEROUS?
GETTING INVOLVED IN MAGIC MEANS GETTING INVOLVED IN THE HIDDEN WORLD AS WELL, SO YES..

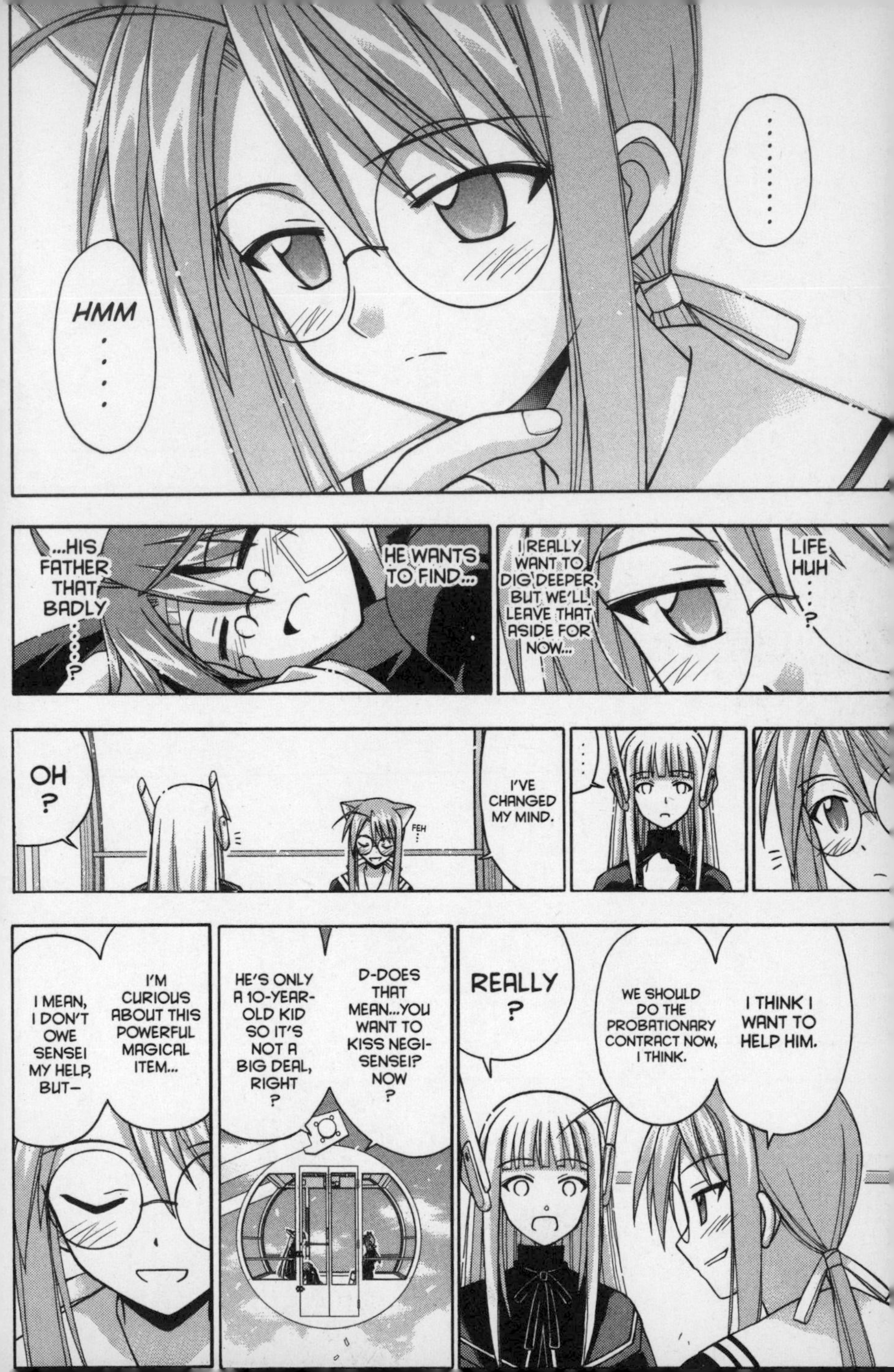
......
HMM.....
LIFE HUH...?
I REALLY WANT TO DIG DEEPER, BUT WE'LL LEAVE THAT ASIDE FOR NOW...
HE WANTS TO FIND...
...HIS FATHER THAT BADLY......?
...
I'VE CHANGED MY MIND.
FEH...
OH?
I THINK I WANT TO HELP HIM.
WE SHOULD DO THE PROBATIONARY CONTRACT NOW, I THINK.
REALLY?
D-DOES THAT MEAN...YOU WANT TO KISS NEGI-SENSEI? NOW?
HE'S ONLY A 10-YEAR-OLD KID SO IT'S NOT A BIG DEAL, RIGHT?
I'M CURIOUS ABOUT THIS POWERFUL MAGICAL ITEM...
I MEAN, I DON'T OWE SENSEI MY HELP, BUT–

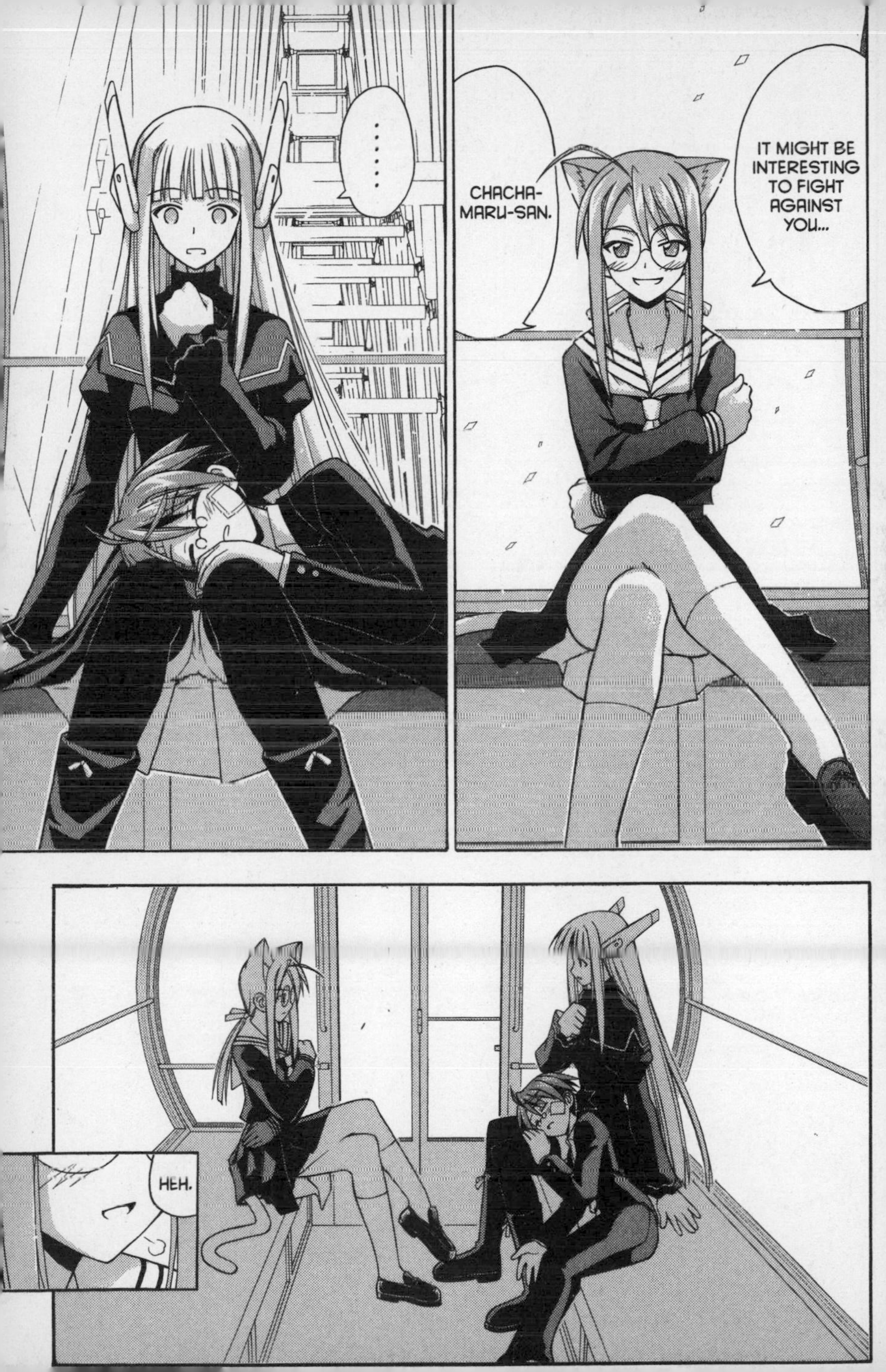
IT MIGHT BE INTERESTING TO FIGHT AGAINST YOU...
CHACHA-MARU-SAN.
......
HEH.

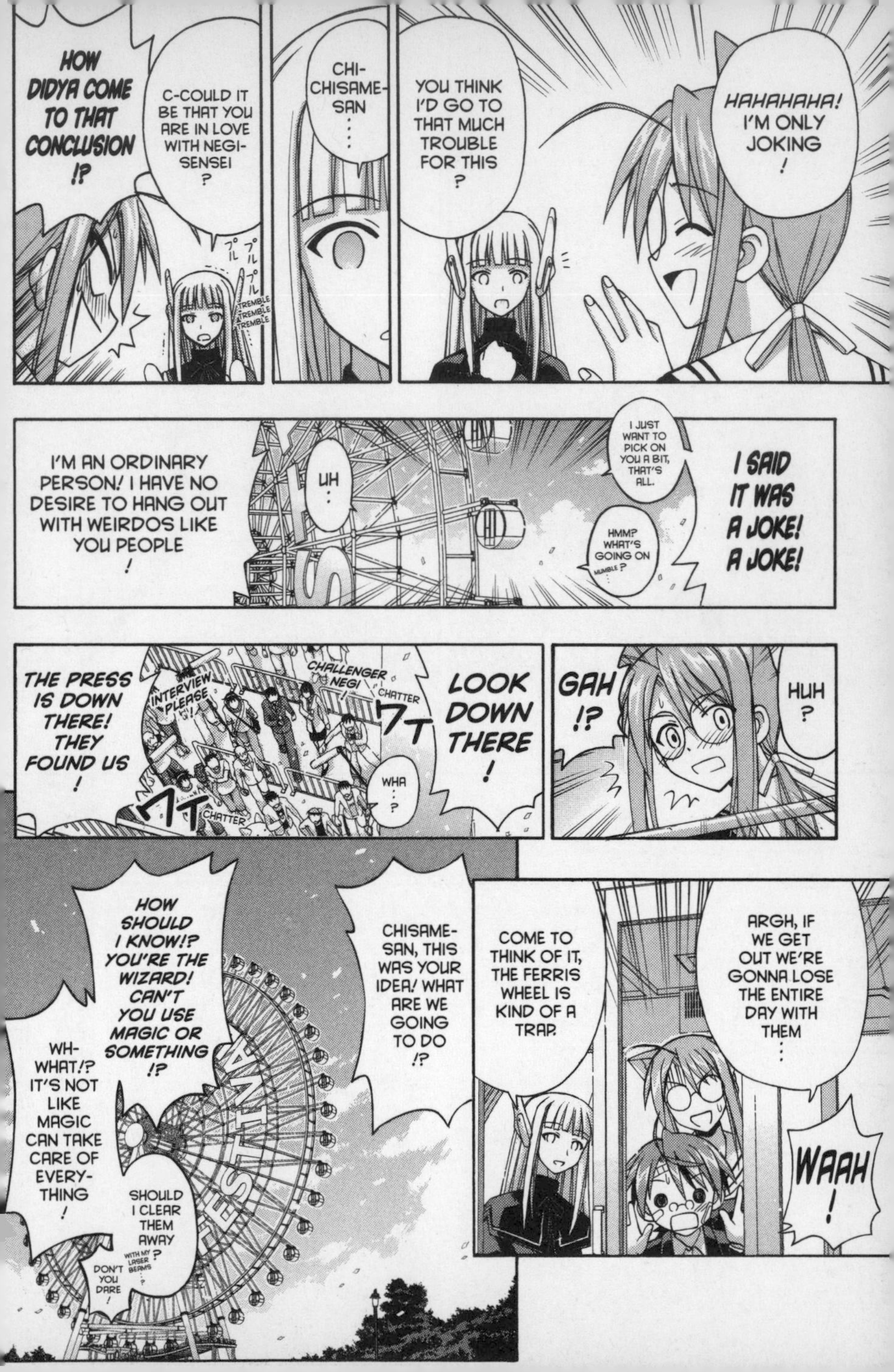
HAHAHAHA! I'M ONLY JOKING!
YOU THINK I'D GO TO THAT MUCH TROUBLE FOR THIS?
CHI-CHISAME-SAN...
C-COULD IT BE THAT YOU ARE IN LOVE WITH NEGI-SENSEI?
プルプル
TREMBLE TREMBLE TREMBLE
HOW DIDYA COME TO THAT CONCLUSION!?
I SAID IT WAS A JOKE! A JOKE!
I JUST WANT TO PICK ON YOU A BIT, THAT'S ALL.
HMM? WHAT'S GOING ON MUMBLE?...
UH...
I'M AN ORDINARY PERSON! I HAVE NO DESIRE TO HANG OUT WITH WEIRDOS LIKE YOU PEOPLE!
HUH?
GAH!?
LOOK DOWN THERE!
WHA...?
CHALLENGER NEGI!
CHATTER
INTERVIEW PLEASE
THE PRESS IS DOWN THERE! THEY FOUND US!
CHATTER
ARGH, IF WE GET OUT WE'RE GONNA LOSE THE ENTIRE DAY WITH THEM...
WAAH!
COME TO THINK OF IT, THE FERRIS WHEEL IS KIND OF A TRAP.
CHISAME-SAN, THIS WAS YOUR IDEA! WHAT ARE WE GOING TO DO!?
HOW SHOULD I KNOW!? YOU'RE THE WIZARD! CAN'T YOU USE MAGIC OR SOMETHING!?
WH-WHAT!? IT'S NOT LIKE MAGIC CAN TAKE CARE OF EVERYTHING!
SHOULD I CLEAR THEM AWAY? WITH MY LASER BEAMS...?
DON'T YOU DARE!

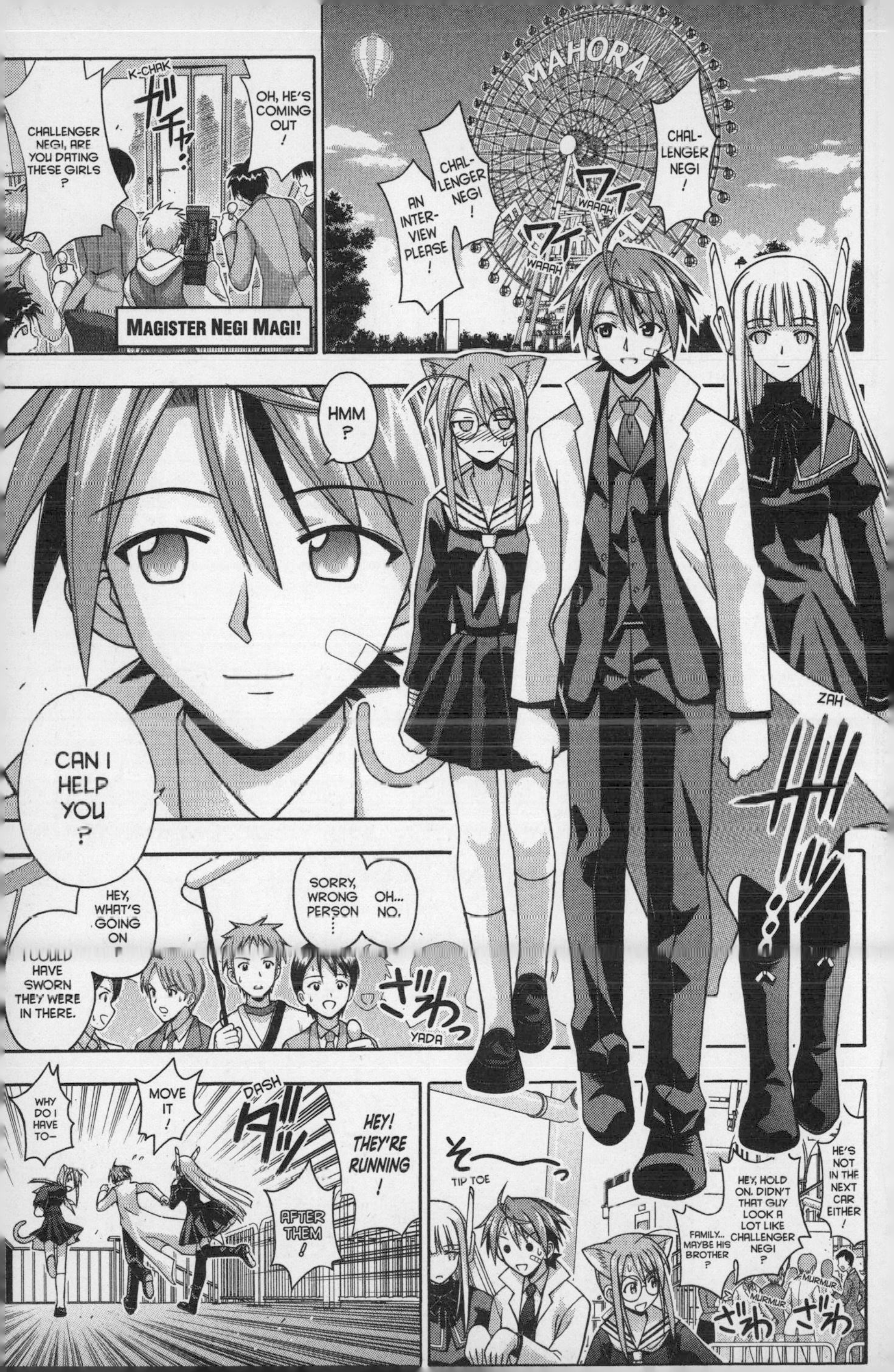
CHAL-LENGER NEGI!
WAAAH
WAAAH
CHAL-LENGER NEGI!
AN INTER-VIEW PLEASE!
OH, HE'S COMING OUT!
K-CHAK
CHALLENGER NEGI, ARE YOU DATING THESE GIRLS?
MAGISTER NEGI MAGI!
HMM?
ZAH
CAN I HELP YOU?
SORRY, WRONG PERSON......
OH... NO.
YADA
HEY, WHAT'S GOING ON
I COULD HAVE SWORN THEY WERE IN THERE.
HE'S NOT IN THE NEXT CAR EITHER!
HEY, HOLD ON. DIDN'T THAT GUY LOOK A LOT LIKE CHALLENGER NEGI?
FAMILY... MAYBE HIS BROTHER?
TIP TOE
MURMUR
MURMUR
HEY! THEY'RE RUNNING!
AFTER THEM!
DASH
MOVE IT!
WHY DO I HAVE TO—

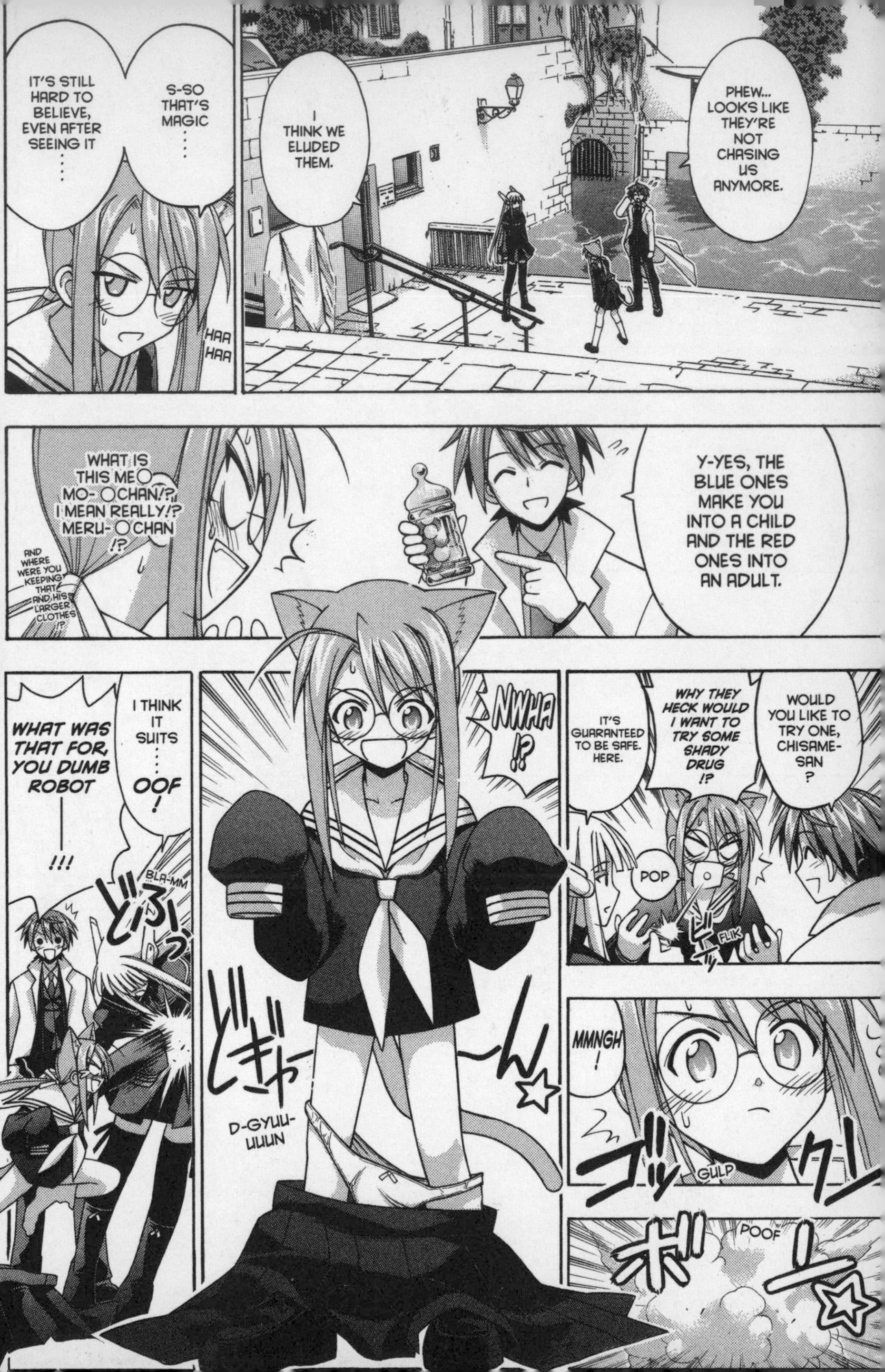
PHEW... LOOKS LIKE THEY'RE NOT CHASING US ANYMORE.
I THINK WE ELUDED THEM.
S-SO THAT'S MAGIC....
IT'S STILL HARD TO BELIEVE, EVEN AFTER SEEING IT....
HAA HAA
Y-YES, THE BLUE ONES MAKE YOU INTO A CHILD AND THE RED ONES INTO AN ADULT.
WHAT IS THIS ME○ MO-○CHAN!? I MEAN REALLY!? MERU-○CHAN!?
AND WHERE WERE YOU KEEPING THAT AND HIS LARGER CLOTHES!?
WOULD YOU LIKE TO TRY ONE, CHISAME-SAN?
WHY THEY HECK WOULD I WANT TO TRY SOME SHADY DRUG!?
IT'S GUARANTEED TO BE SAFE. HERE.
POP
FLIK
MMNGH!
GULP
POOF
NWHA!?
D-GYUU-UUUN
I THINK IT SUITS.... OOF!
WHAT WAS THAT FOR, YOU DUMB ROBOT——!!!
BLA-MM

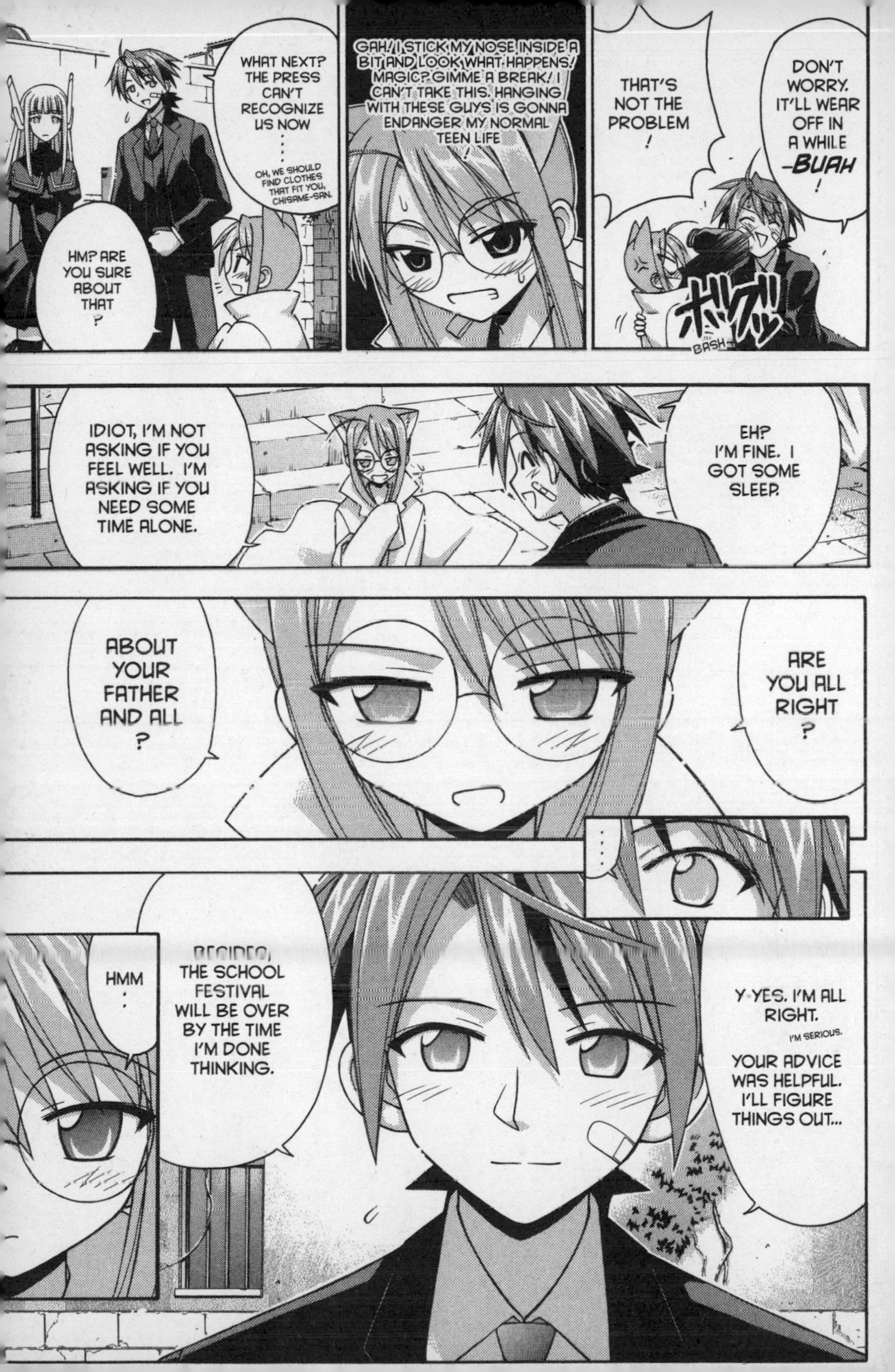
DON'T WORRY. IT'LL WEAR OFF IN A WHILE -BUAH!
THAT'S NOT THE PROBLEM!
BASH
GAH! I STICK MY NOSE INSIDE A BIT AND LOOK WHAT HAPPENS! MAGIC? GIMME A BREAK! I CAN'T TAKE THIS. HANGING WITH THESE GUYS IS GONNA ENDANGER MY NORMAL TEEN LIFE!
WHAT NEXT? THE PRESS CAN'T RECOGNIZE US NOW . . .
OH, WE SHOULD FIND CLOTHES THAT FIT YOU, CHISAME-SAN.
HM? ARE YOU SURE ABOUT THAT?
EH? I'M FINE. I GOT SOME SLEEP.
IDIOT, I'M NOT ASKING IF YOU FEEL WELL. I'M ASKING IF YOU NEED SOME TIME ALONE.
ARE YOU ALL RIGHT?
ABOUT YOUR FATHER AND ALL?
. . . .
Y-YES. I'M ALL RIGHT.
I'M SERIOUS.
YOUR ADVICE WAS HELPFUL. I'LL FIGURE THINGS OUT...
BESIDES, THE SCHOOL FESTIVAL WILL BE OVER BY THE TIME I'M DONE THINKING.
HMM . .

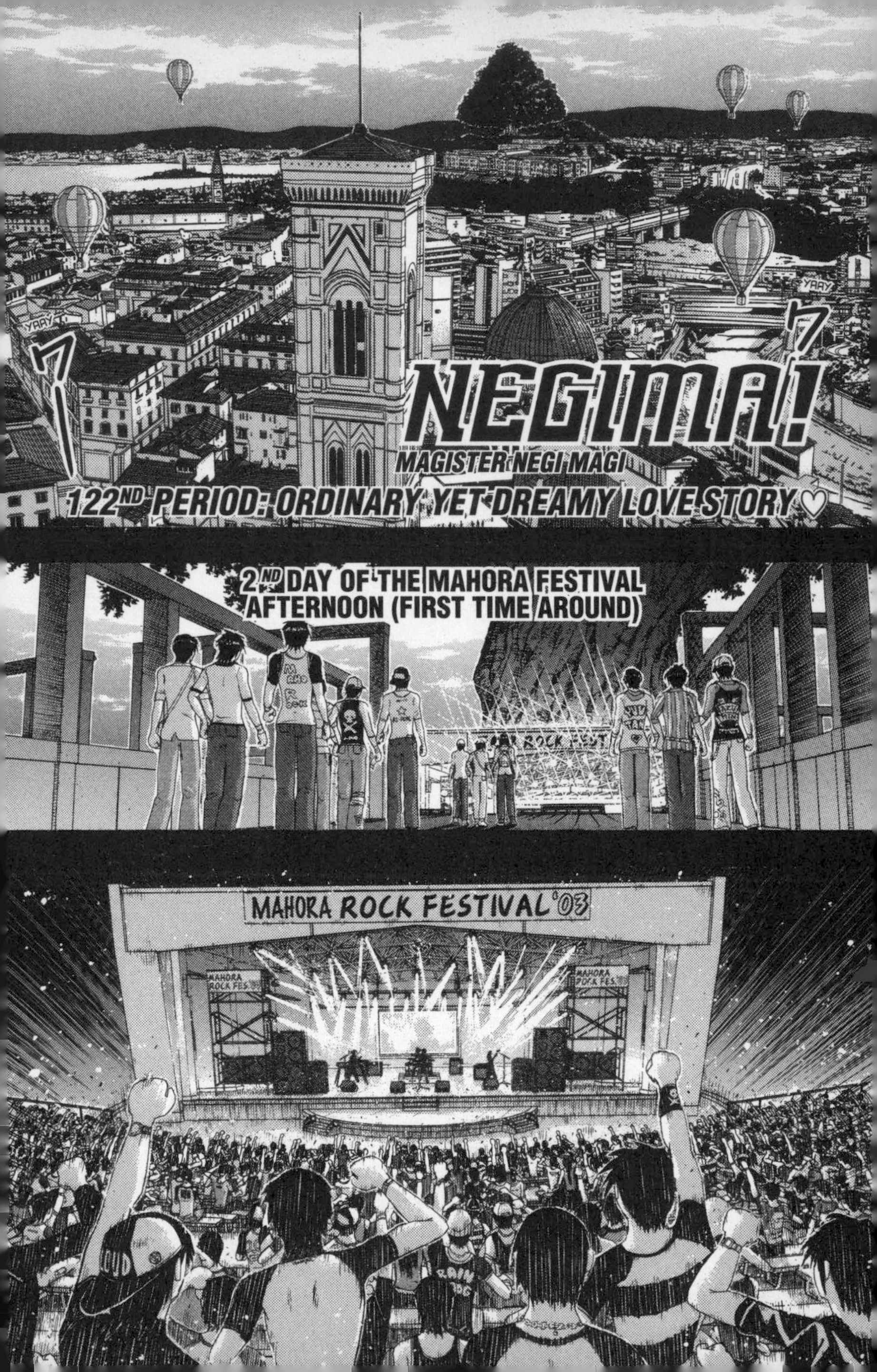
YAAY
YAAY
NEGIMA!
MAGISTER NEGI MAGI
122ND PERIOD: ORDINARY YET DREAMY LOVE STORY♡
2ND DAY OF THE MAHORA FESTIVAL
AFTERNOON (FIRST TIME AROUND)
MAHORA ROCK FESTIVAL '03
MAHORA ROCK FES.
MAHORA ROCK FES

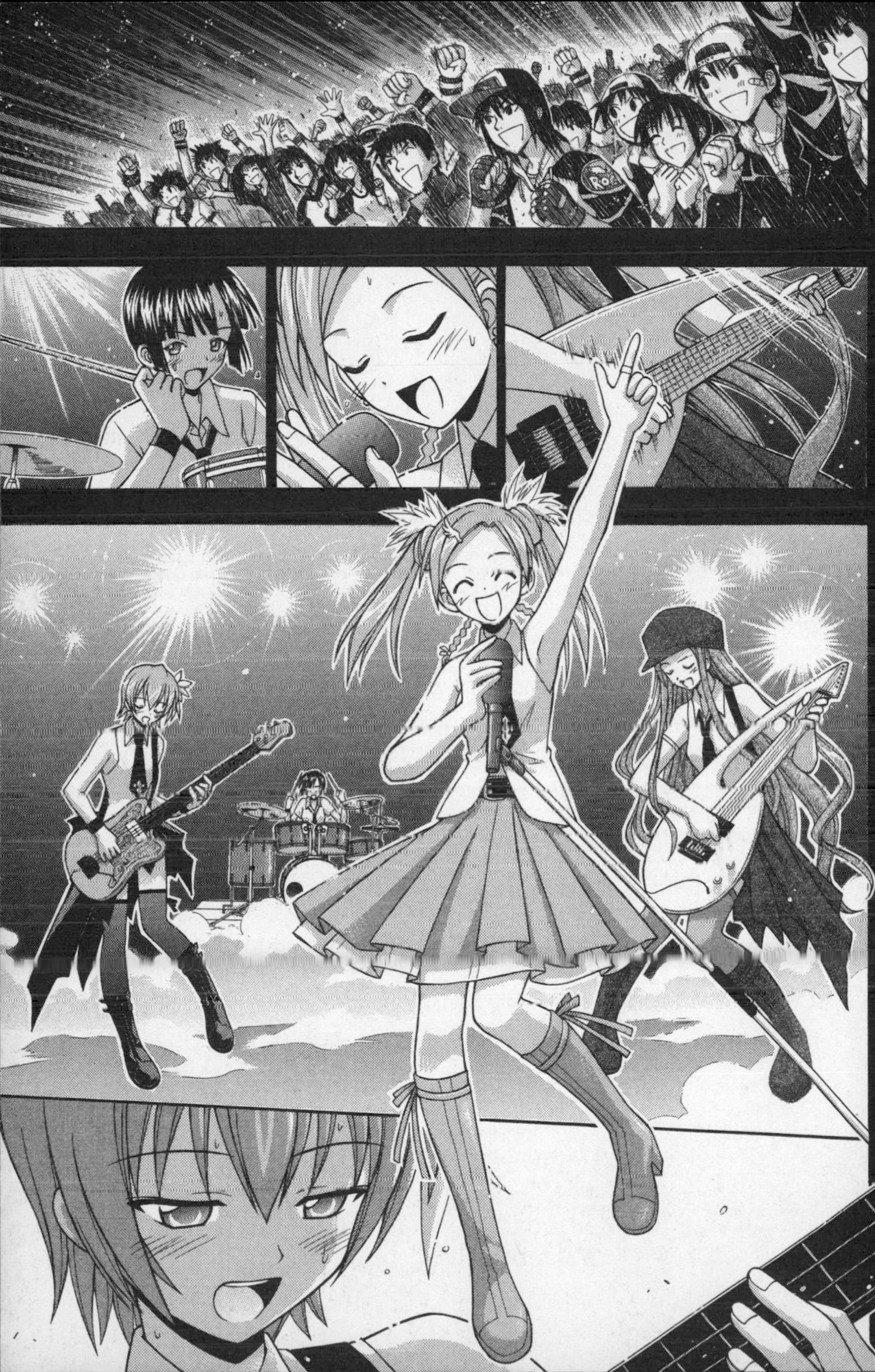

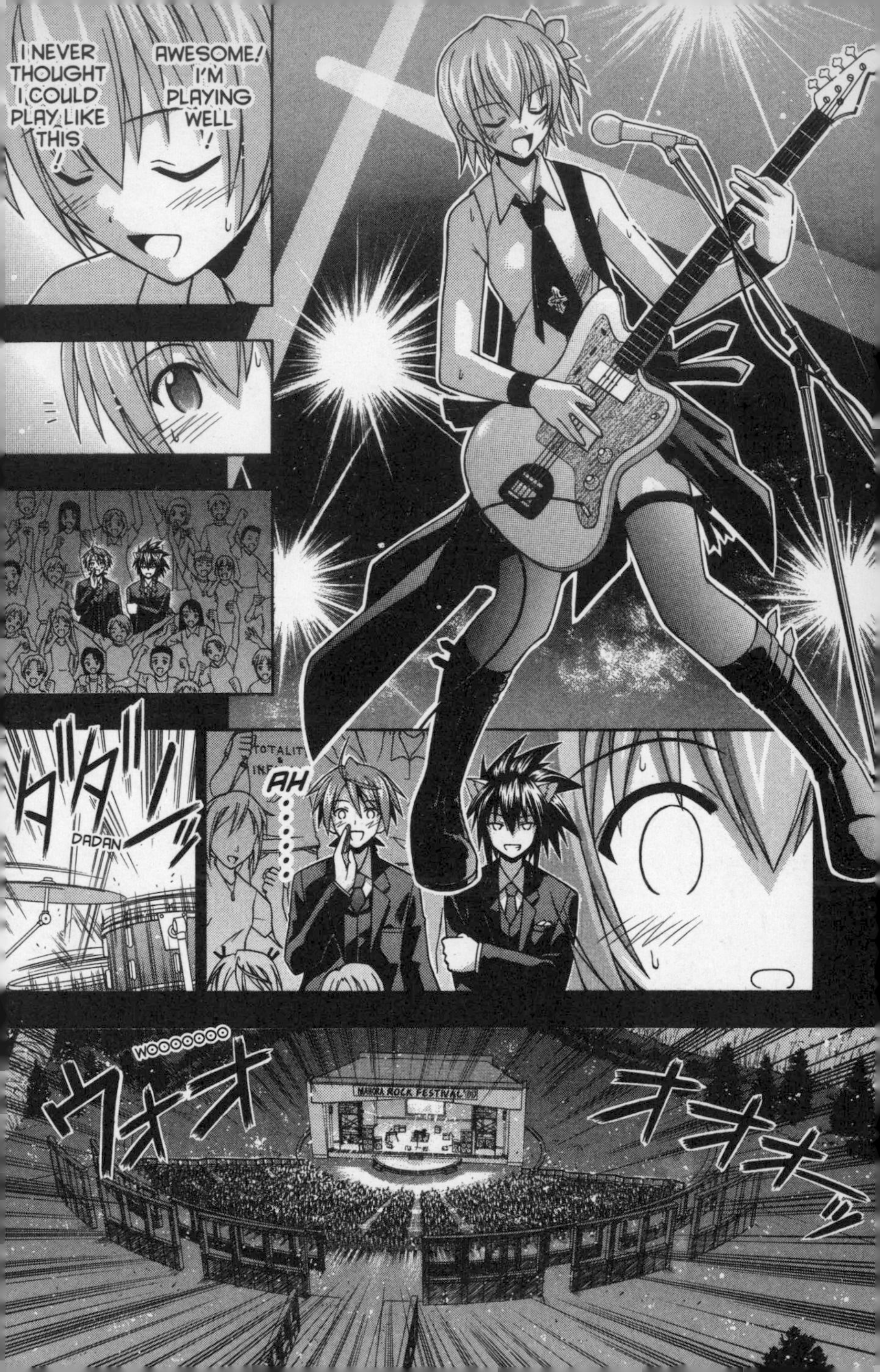
AWESOME! I'M PLAYING WELL!
I NEVER THOUGHT I COULD PLAY LIKE THIS!
AH......
DADAN
WOOOOOOO
MAHORA ROCK FESTIVAL

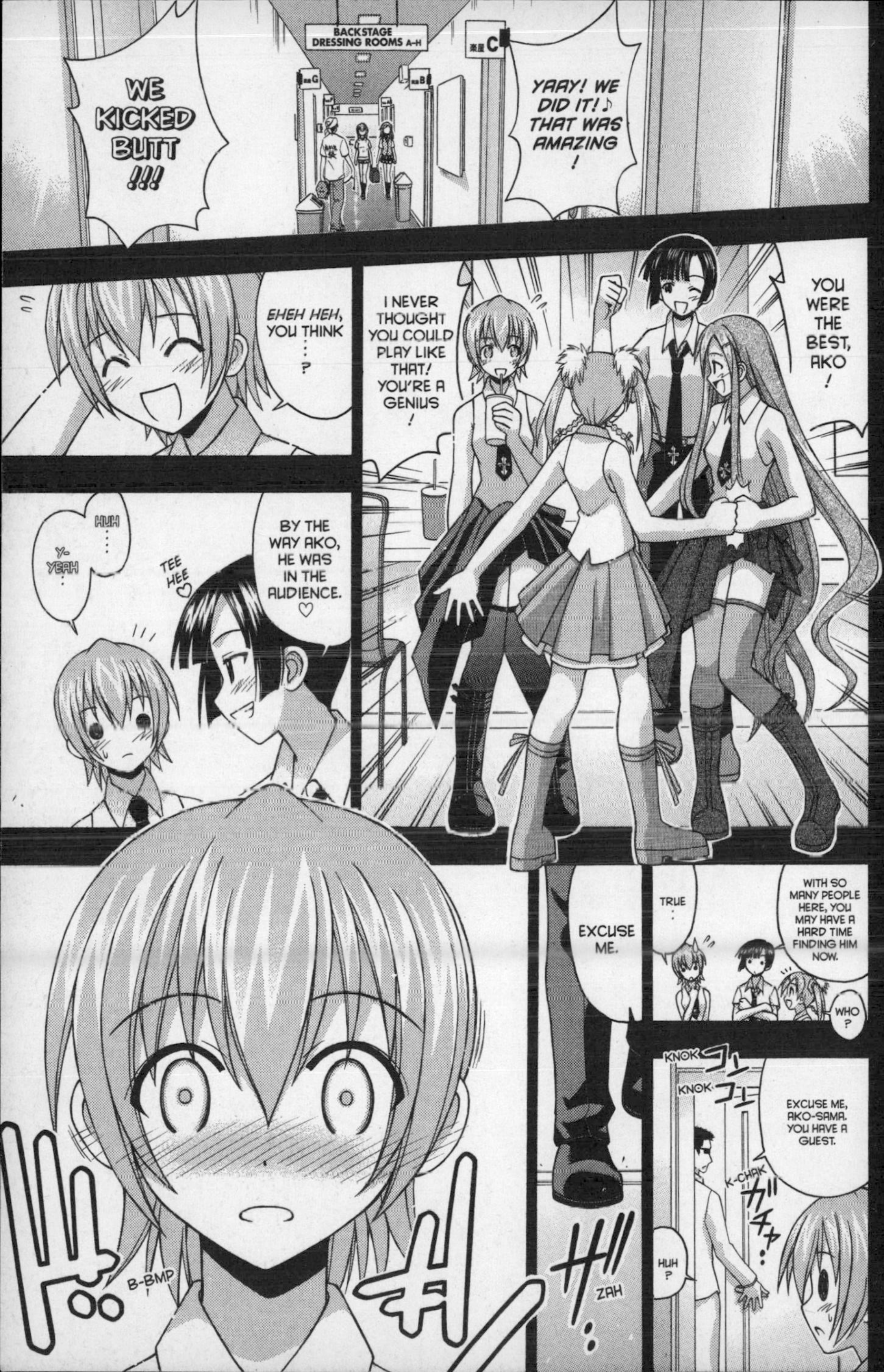
BACKSTAGE DRESSING ROOMS A–H
楽屋 C
YAAY! WE DID IT!♪ THAT WAS AMAZING!
WE KICKED BUTT!!!
YOU WERE THE BEST, AKO!
I NEVER THOUGHT YOU COULD PLAY LIKE THAT! YOU'RE A GENIUS!
EHEH HEH, YOU THINK...?
BY THE WAY AKO, HE WAS IN THE AUDIENCE. ♡
TEE HEE ♡
HUH...
Y-YEAH...
WITH SO MANY PEOPLE HERE, YOU MAY HAVE A HARD TIME FINDING HIM NOW.
TRUE...
WHO?
KNOK
KNOK
EXCUSE ME, AKO-SAMA. YOU HAVE A GUEST.
K-CHAK
HUH?
EXCUSE ME.
ZAH
B-BMP

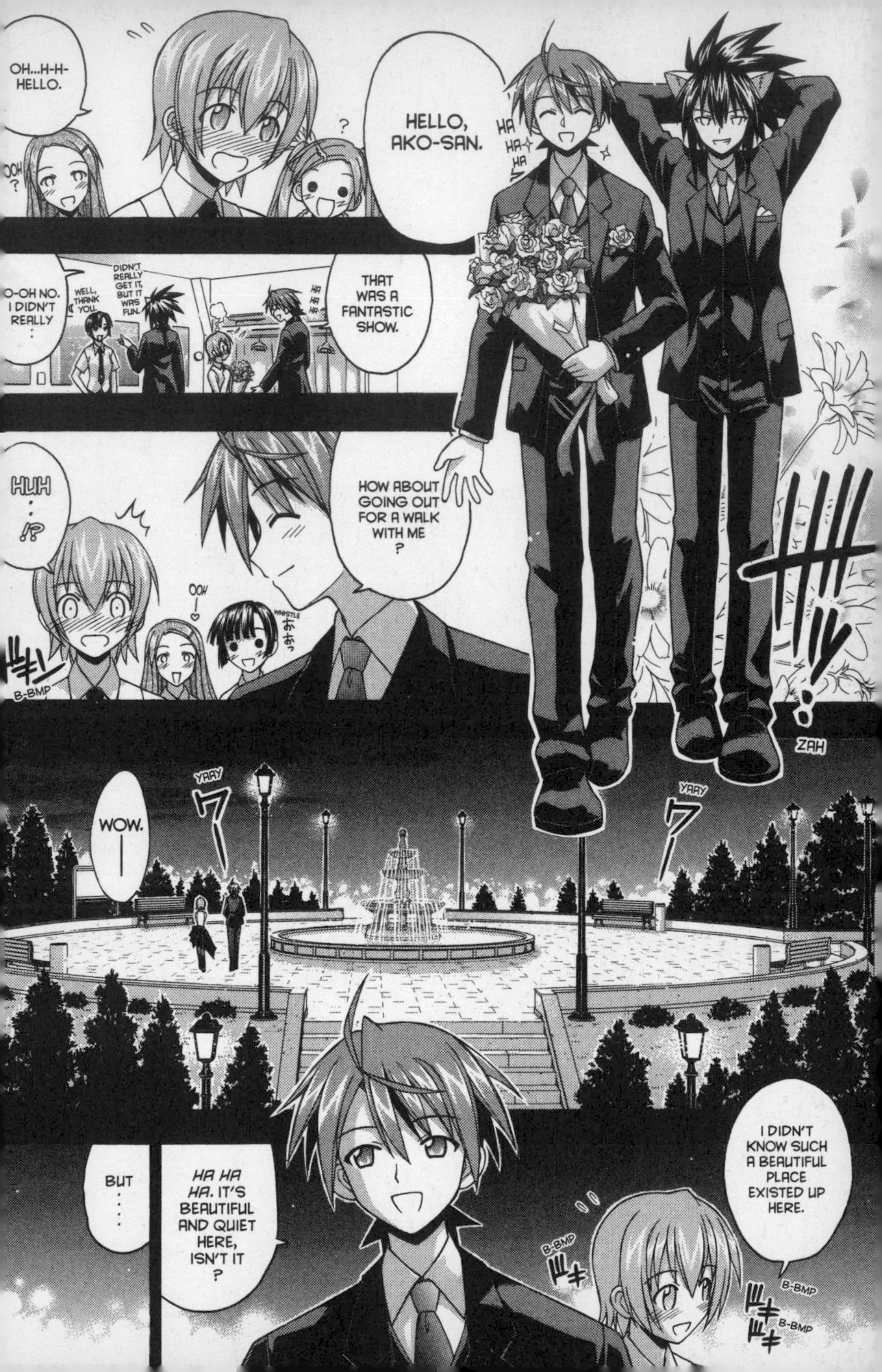
HELLO, AKO-SAN.
HA HA HA
ZAH
OH...H-H-HELLO.
OOH?
?
THAT WAS A FANTASTIC SHOW.
HA HA HA
DIDN'T REALLY GET IT, BUT IT WAS FUN.
WELL, THANK YOU.
O-OH NO. I DIDN'T REALLY...
HOW ABOUT GOING OUT FOR A WALK WITH ME?
HUH...!?
OOH
WHISTLE おおっ
B-BMP
YAAY
WOW.
YAAY
I DIDN'T KNOW SUCH A BEAUTIFUL PLACE EXISTED UP HERE.
B-BMP
B-BMP
B-BMP
HA HA HA. IT'S BEAUTIFUL AND QUIET HERE, ISN'T IT?
BUT....

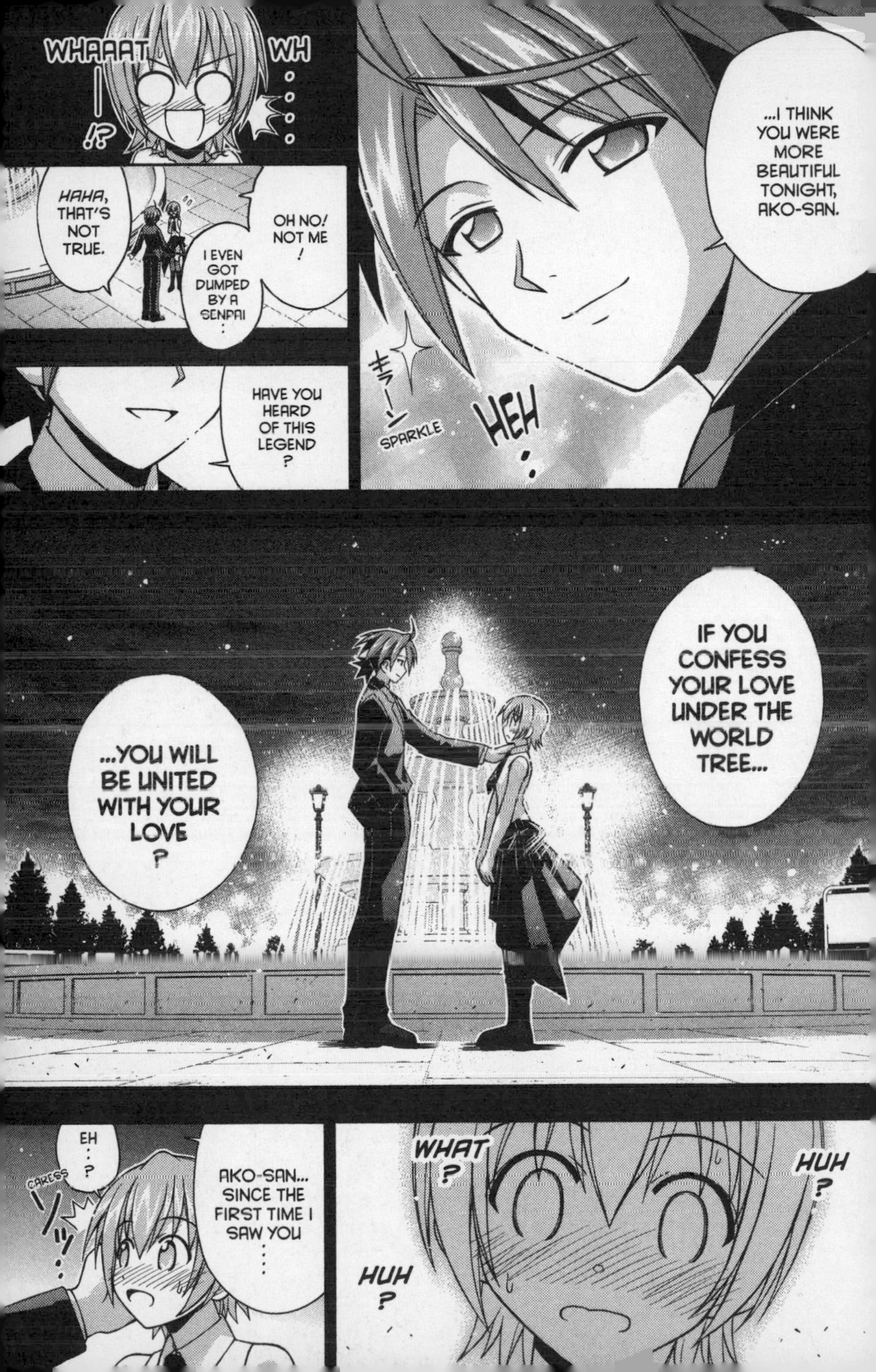
...I THINK YOU WERE MORE BEAUTIFUL TONIGHT, AKO-SAN.
キラーン
SPARKLE
HEH..
WHOOOO
WHAAAT—!?
OH NO! NOT ME!
I EVEN GOT DUMPED BY A SENPAI...
HAHA, THAT'S NOT TRUE.
HAVE YOU HEARD OF THIS LEGEND?
IF YOU CONFESS YOUR LOVE UNDER THE WORLD TREE...
...YOU WILL BE UNITED WITH YOUR LOVE?
HUH?
WHAT?
HUH?
AKO-SAN... SINCE THE FIRST TIME I SAW YOU...
EH...?
CARESS

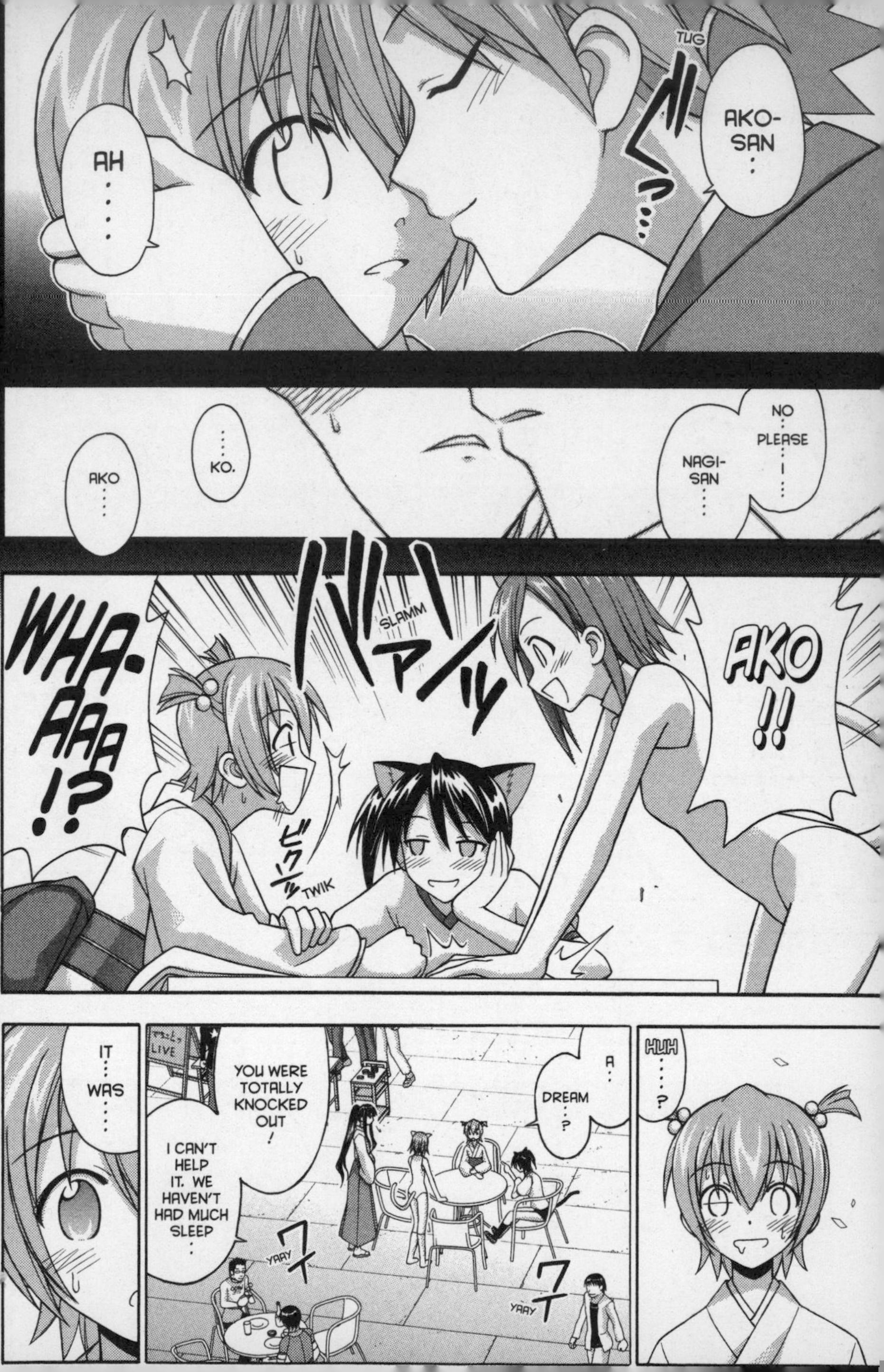
TUG
AKO-SAN...
AH......
NO... PLEASE... I...
NAGI-SAN...
...KO.
AKO...
AKO!!
SLAMM
TWIK
WHA-AAAA!?
HUH...?
A... DREAM...?
YOU WERE TOTALLY KNOCKED OUT!
I CAN'T HELP IT. WE HAVEN'T HAD MUCH SLEEP...
LIVE
YAAY
YAAY
IT... WAS......

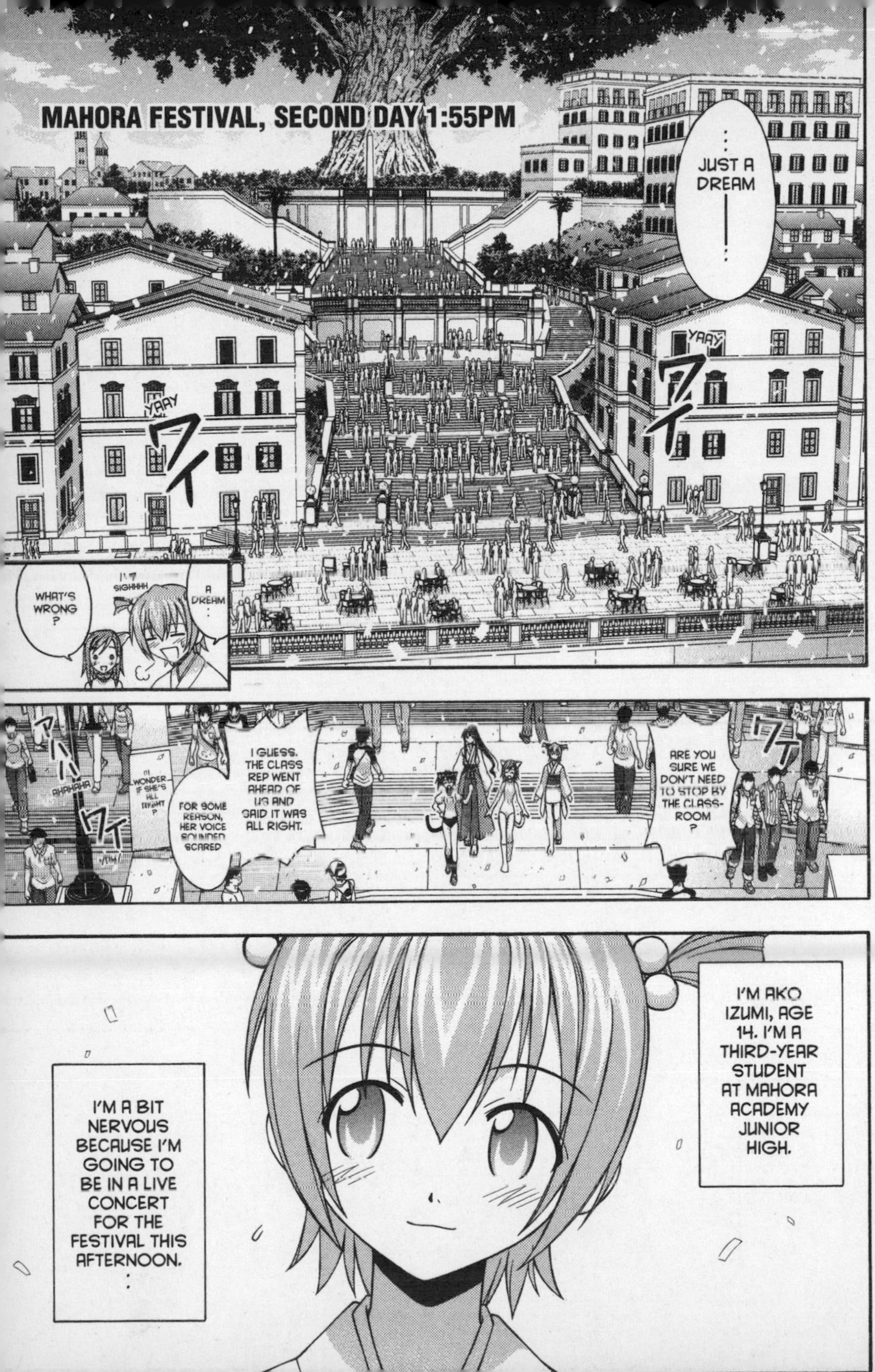
MAHORA FESTIVAL, SECOND DAY 1:55PM
...JUST A DREAM—
YAAY
YAAY
A DREAM...
SIGHHHH
WHAT'S WRONG?
ARE YOU SURE WE DON'T NEED TO STOP BY THE CLASSROOM?
I GUESS. THE CLASS REP WENT AHEAD OF US AND SAID IT WAS ALL RIGHT.
FOR SOME REASON, HER VOICE SOUNDED SCARED
I WONDER IF SHE'S ALL RIGHT?
AHAHAHA
I'M AKO IZUMI, AGE 14. I'M A THIRD-YEAR STUDENT AT MAHORA ACADEMY JUNIOR HIGH.
I'M A BIT NERVOUS BECAUSE I'M GOING TO BE IN A LIVE CONCERT FOR THE FESTIVAL THIS AFTERNOON...

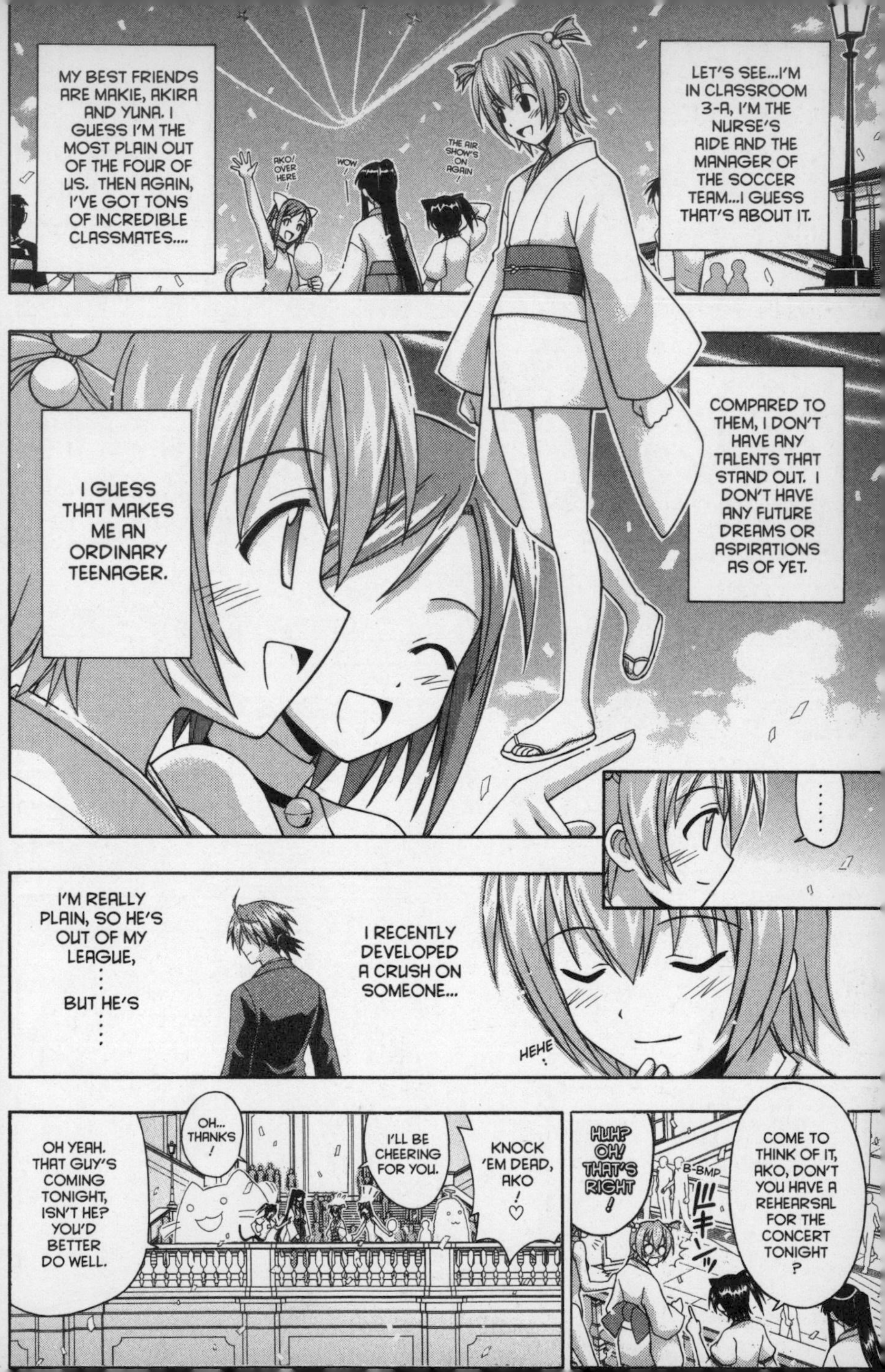
LET'S SEE...I'M IN CLASSROOM 3-A, I'M THE NURSE'S AIDE AND THE MANAGER OF THE SOCCER TEAM...I GUESS THAT'S ABOUT IT.
THE AIR SHOW'S ON AGAIN!
WOW!
AKO! OVER HERE!
MY BEST FRIENDS ARE MAKIE, AKIRA AND YUNA. I GUESS I'M THE MOST PLAIN OUT OF THE FOUR OF US. THEN AGAIN, I'VE GOT TONS OF INCREDIBLE CLASSMATES....
COMPARED TO THEM, I DON'T HAVE ANY TALENTS THAT STAND OUT. I DON'T HAVE ANY FUTURE DREAMS OR ASPIRATIONS AS OF YET.
I GUESS THAT MAKES ME AN ORDINARY TEENAGER.
......
HEHE
I RECENTLY DEVELOPED A CRUSH ON SOMEONE...
I'M REALLY PLAIN, SO HE'S OUT OF MY LEAGUE, ... BUT HE'S ...
COME TO THINK OF IT, AKO, DON'T YOU HAVE A REHEARSAL FOR THE CONCERT TONIGHT?
B-BMP
HUH? OH! THAT'S RIGHT!
KNOCK 'EM DEAD, AKO! ♡
I'LL BE CHEERING FOR YOU.
OH... THANKS!
OH YEAH. THAT GUY'S COMING TONIGHT, ISN'T HE? YOU'D BETTER DO WELL.

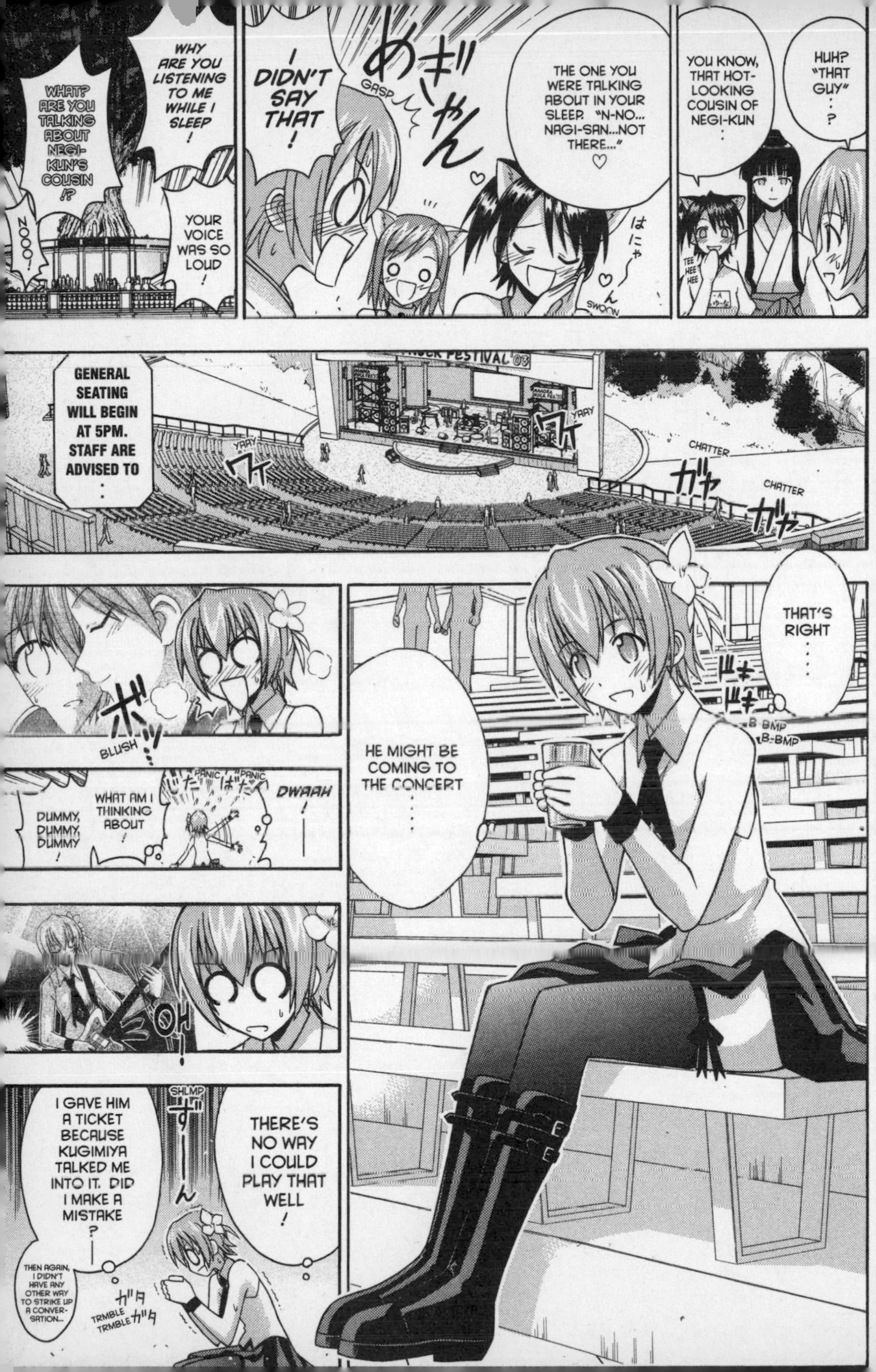
HUH? "THAT GUY"...?
YOU KNOW, THAT HOT-LOOKING COUSIN OF NEGI-KUN:
TEE HEE HEE
THE ONE YOU WERE TALKING ABOUT IN YOUR SLEEP. "N-NO... NAGI-SAN...NOT THERE..." ♡
はにゃ～ん
SWOON
あぎゃん
GASP
I DIDN'T SAY THAT!
WHY ARE YOU LISTENING TO ME WHILE I SLEEP!
YOUR VOICE WAS SO LOUD!
WHAT? ARE YOU TALKING ABOUT NEGI-KUN'S COUSIN!?
NOOO!
ガヤ
CHATTER
ガヤ
CHATTER
ワイ
YAAY
ワイ
YAAY
GENERAL SEATING WILL BEGIN AT 5PM. STAFF ARE ADVISED TO:
THAT'S RIGHT....
ドキドキ
B-BMP B-BMP
HE MIGHT BE COMING TO THE CONCERT....
ボッ
BLUSH
DWAAH!
じたばた
PANIC PANIC
WHAT AM I THINKING ABOUT!
DUMMY, DUMMY, DUMMY!
OH!
THERE'S NO WAY I COULD PLAY THAT WELL!
ずーん
SHLMP
I GAVE HIM A TICKET BECAUSE KUGIMIYA TALKED ME INTO IT. DID I MAKE A MISTAKE?
THEN AGAIN, I DIDN'T HAVE ANY OTHER WAY TO STRIKE UP A CONVERSATION...
ガタガタ
TRMBLE TRMBLE

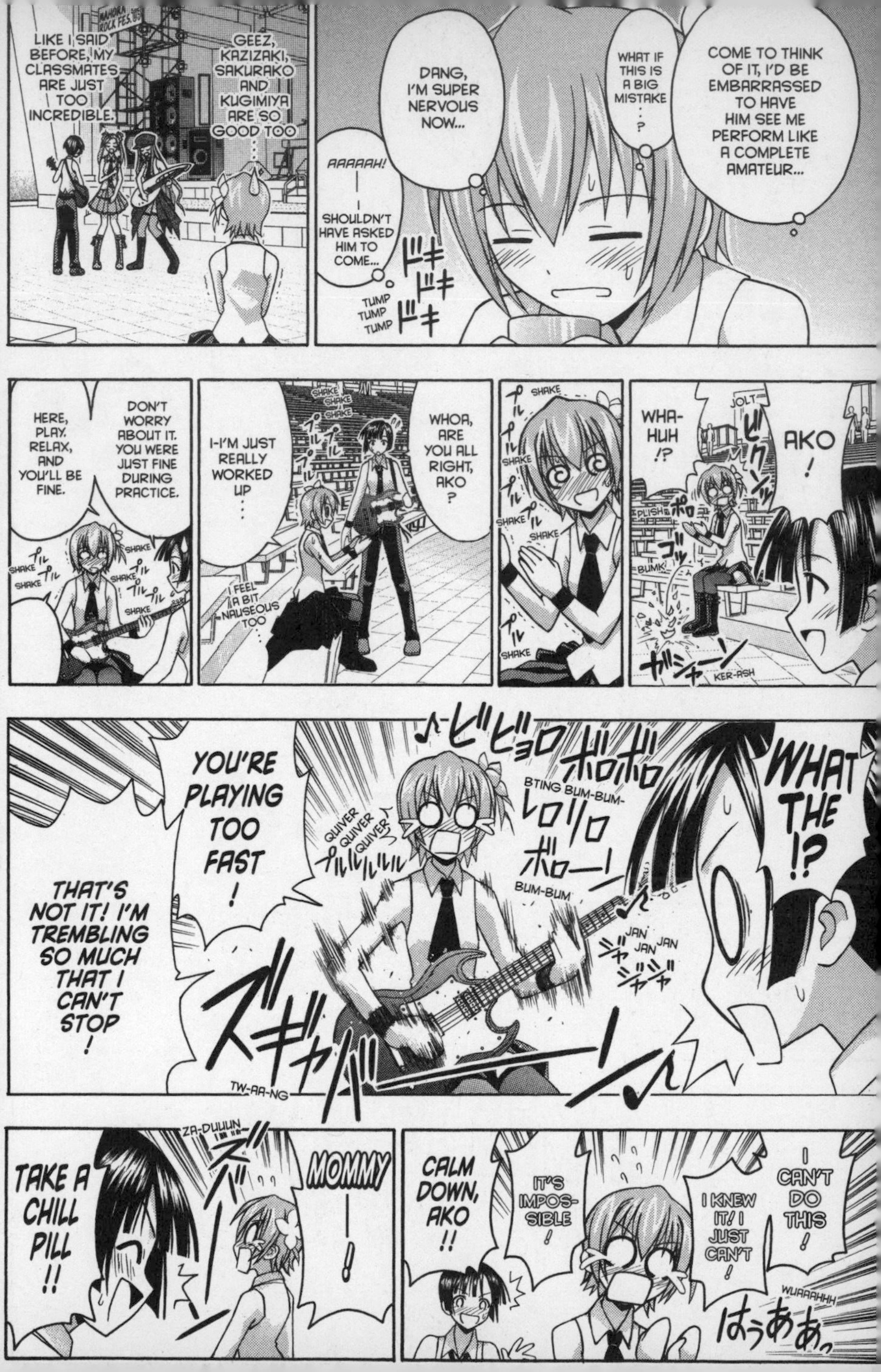
COME TO THINK OF IT, I'D BE EMBARRASSED TO HAVE HIM SEE ME PERFORM LIKE A COMPLETE AMATEUR...
WHAT IF THIS IS A BIG MISTAKE...?
DANG, I'M SUPER NERVOUS NOW...
AAAAAH! — I SHOULDN'T HAVE ASKED HIM TO COME...
ドキドキドキ
TUMP TUMP TUMP
GEEZ, KAZIZAKI, SAKURAKO AND KUGIMIYA ARE SO GOOD TOO
LIKE I SAID BEFORE, MY CLASSMATES ARE JUST TOO INCREDIBLE.
AKO!
JOLT
WHA-HUH!?
PLISH
BUMK
KER-ASH
SHAKE SHAKE SHAKE SHAKE
WHOA, ARE YOU ALL RIGHT, AKO?
SHAKE SHAKE SHAKE
I-I'M JUST REALLY WORKED UP...
I FEEL A BIT NAUSEOUS TOO...
DON'T WORRY ABOUT IT. YOU WERE JUST FINE DURING PRACTICE.
HERE, PLAY. RELAX, AND YOU'LL BE FINE.
SHAKE SHAKE SHAKE SHAKE SHAKE
WHAT THE!?
BTING BUM-BUM-
BUM-BUM
JAN JAN JAN
QUIVER QUIVER QUIVER
YOU'RE PLAYING TOO FAST!
THAT'S NOT IT! I'M TREMBLING SO MUCH THAT I CAN'T STOP!
TW-AA-NG
I CAN'T DO THIS!
I KNEW IT! I JUST CAN'T!
IT'S IMPOSSIBLE!
CALM DOWN, AKO!!
WUAAAHHH
MOMMY—!
ZA-DUUUN
TAKE A CHILL PILL!!

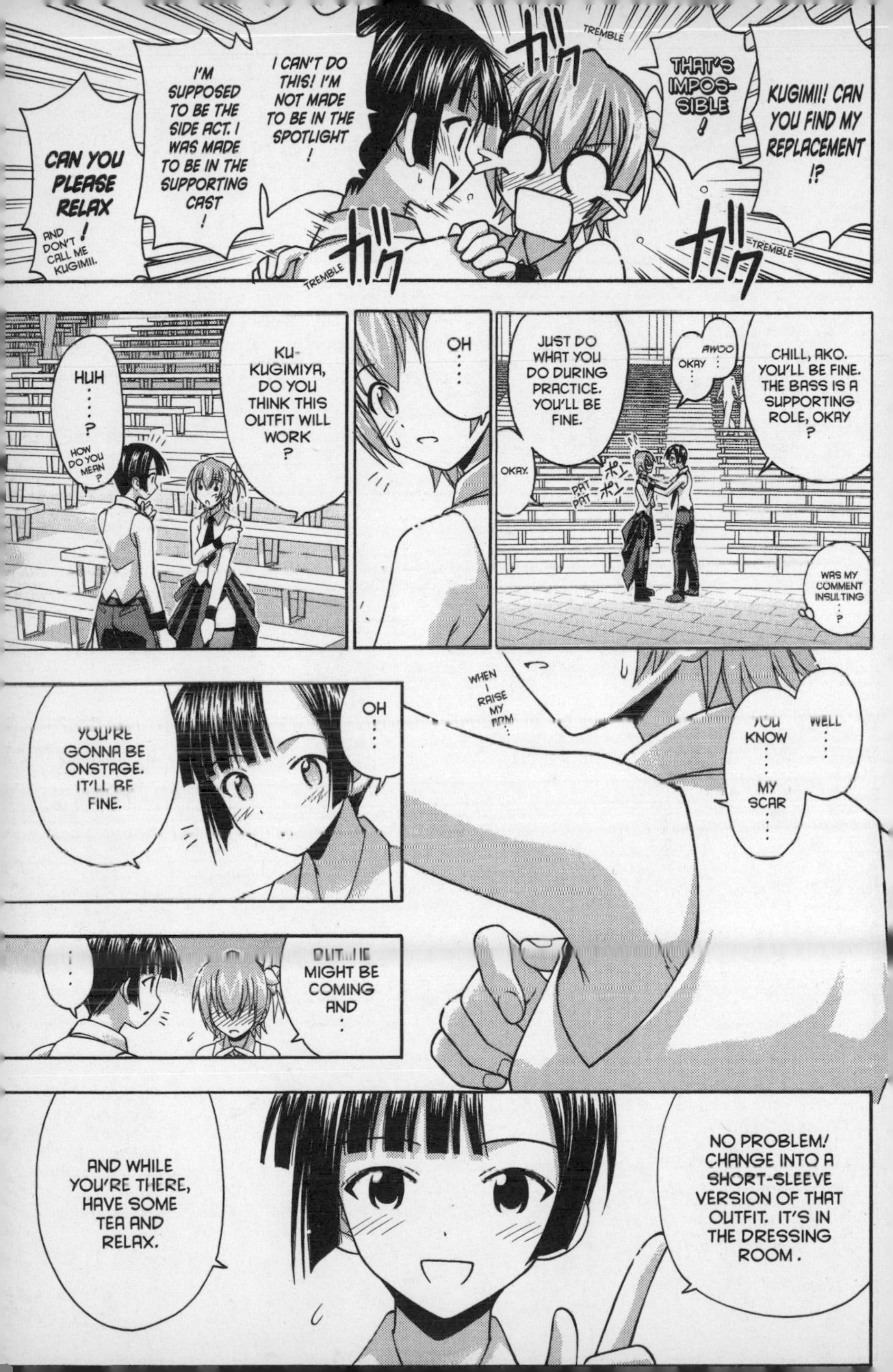
KUGIMII! CAN YOU FIND MY REPLACEMENT!?
THAT'S IMPOSSIBLE!
TREMBLE
TREMBLE
I CAN'T DO THIS! I'M NOT MADE TO BE IN THE SPOTLIGHT!
I'M SUPPOSED TO BE THE SIDE ACT. I WAS MADE TO BE IN THE SUPPORTING CAST!
TREMBLE
CAN YOU PLEASE RELAX!
AND DON'T CALL ME KUGIMII.
CHILL, AKO. YOU'LL BE FINE. THE BASS IS A SUPPORTING ROLE, OKAY?
AWOO... OKAY...
JUST DO WHAT YOU DO DURING PRACTICE. YOU'LL BE FINE.
PAT PAT
OKAY.
WAS MY COMMENT INSULTING...?
OH...
KU-KUGIMIYA, DO YOU THINK THIS OUTFIT WILL WORK?
HUH...?
HOW DO YOU MEAN?
WELL...
YOU KNOW... MY SCAR...
WHEN I RAISE MY ARM...
OH...
YOU'RE GONNA BE ONSTAGE. IT'LL BE FINE.
BUT HE MIGHT BE COMING AND...
...
NO PROBLEM! CHANGE INTO A SHORT-SLEEVE VERSION OF THAT OUTFIT. IT'S IN THE DRESSING ROOM.
AND WHILE YOU'RE THERE, HAVE SOME TEA AND RELAX.

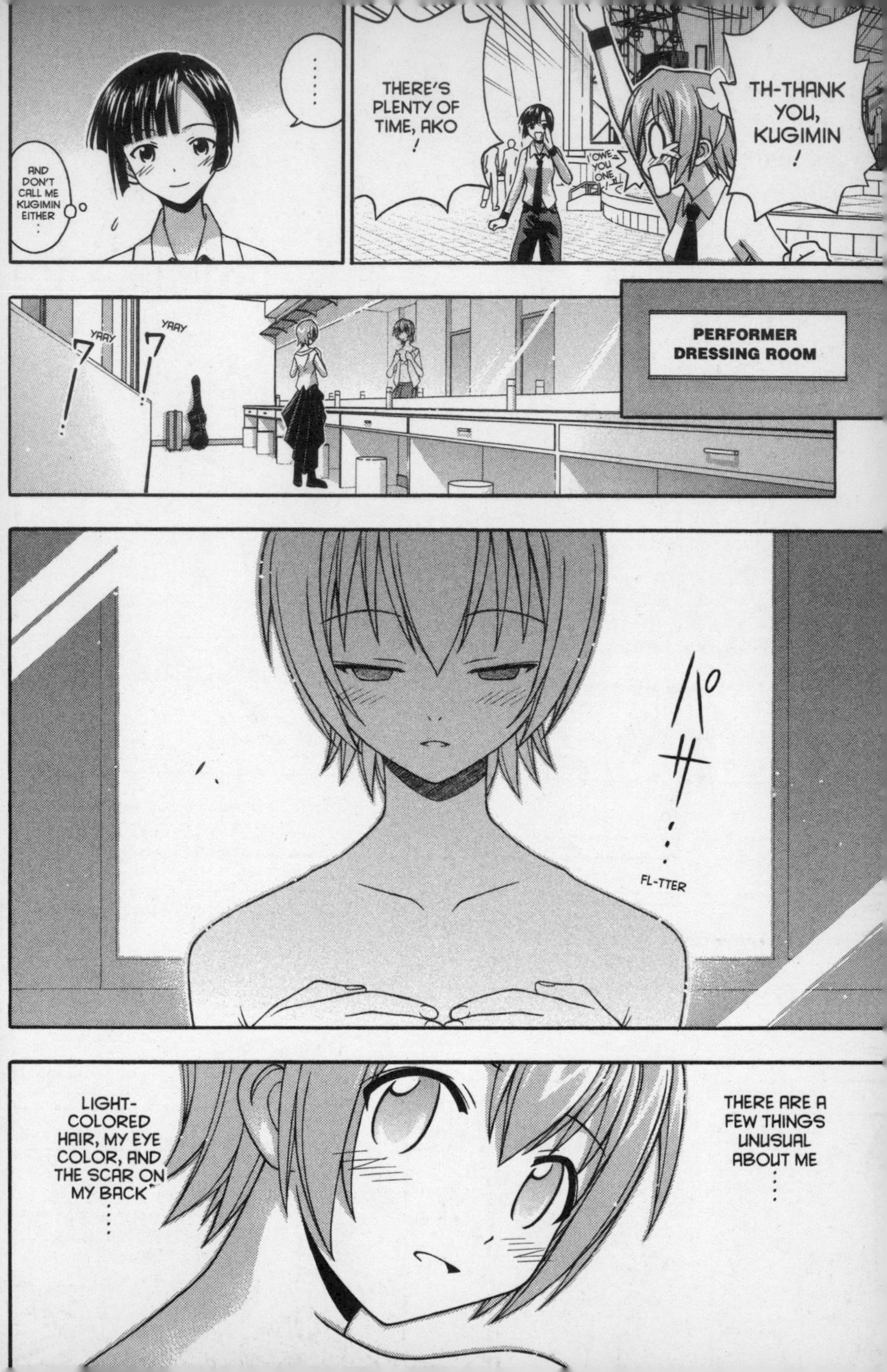
TH-THANK YOU, KUGIMIN!
I OWE YOU ONE!
THERE'S PLENTY OF TIME, AKO!
......
AND DON'T CALL ME KUGIMIN EITHER...
PERFORMER DRESSING ROOM
YAAY
YAAY
FL-TTER
THERE ARE A FEW THINGS UNUSUAL ABOUT ME...
LIGHT-COLORED HAIR, MY EYE COLOR, AND THE SCAR ON MY BACK...

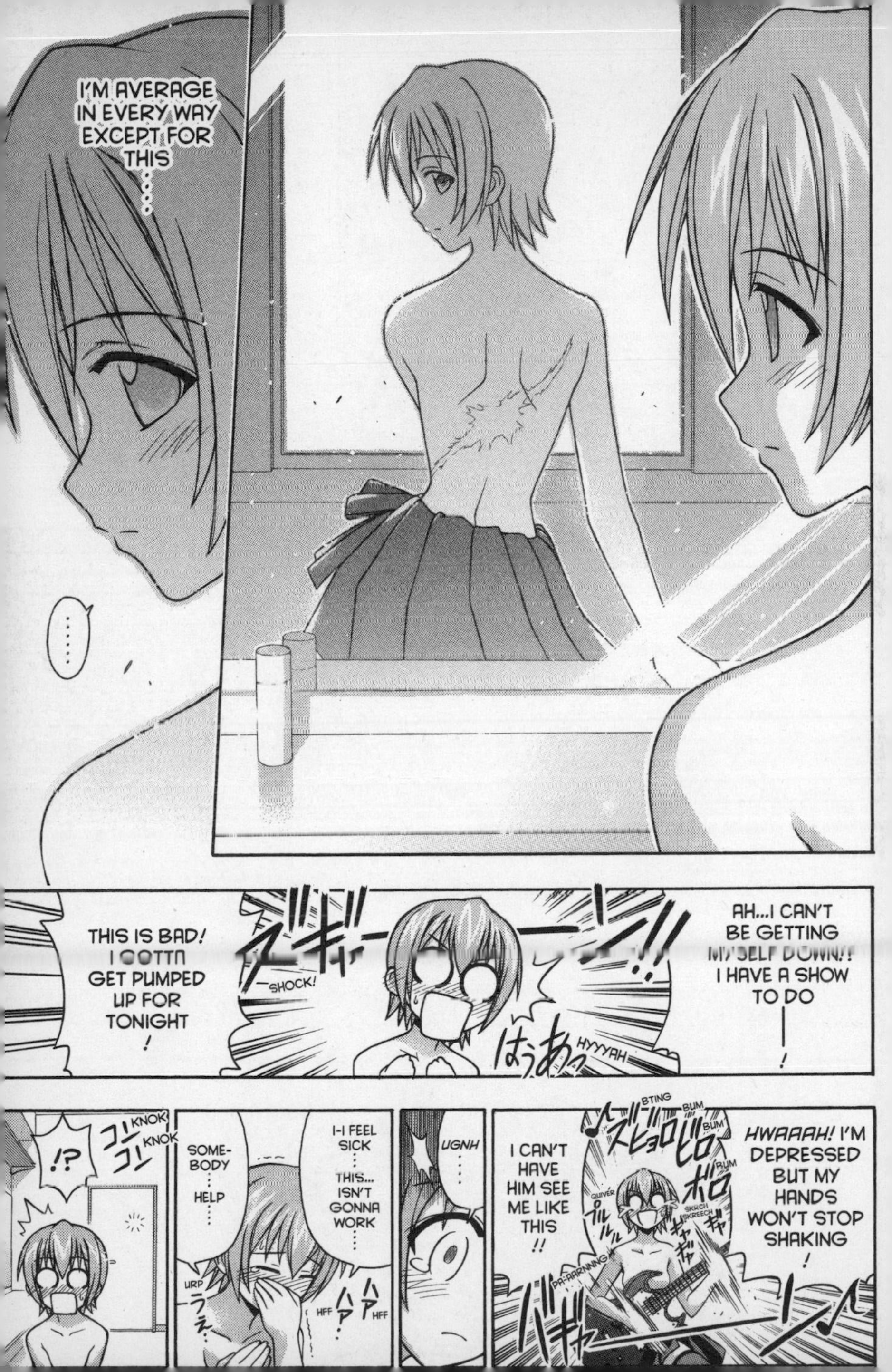
I'M AVERAGE IN EVERY WAY EXCEPT FOR THIS......
......
AH...I CAN'T BE GETTING MYSELF DOWN!! I HAVE A SHOW TO DO—!
HYYYAH
SHOCK!
THIS IS BAD! I GOTTA GET PUMPED UP FOR TONIGHT!
HWAAAH! I'M DEPRESSED BUT MY HANDS WON'T STOP SHAKING!
BTING
BUM
BUM
BUM
SKRCH SKREECH
QUIVER
PA-RARNNNG
I CAN'T HAVE HIM SEE ME LIKE THIS!!
UGNH...
I-I FEEL SICK... THIS... ISN'T GONNA WORK...
SOMEBODY... HELP...
URP
HFF
HFF
KNOK
KNOK
!?

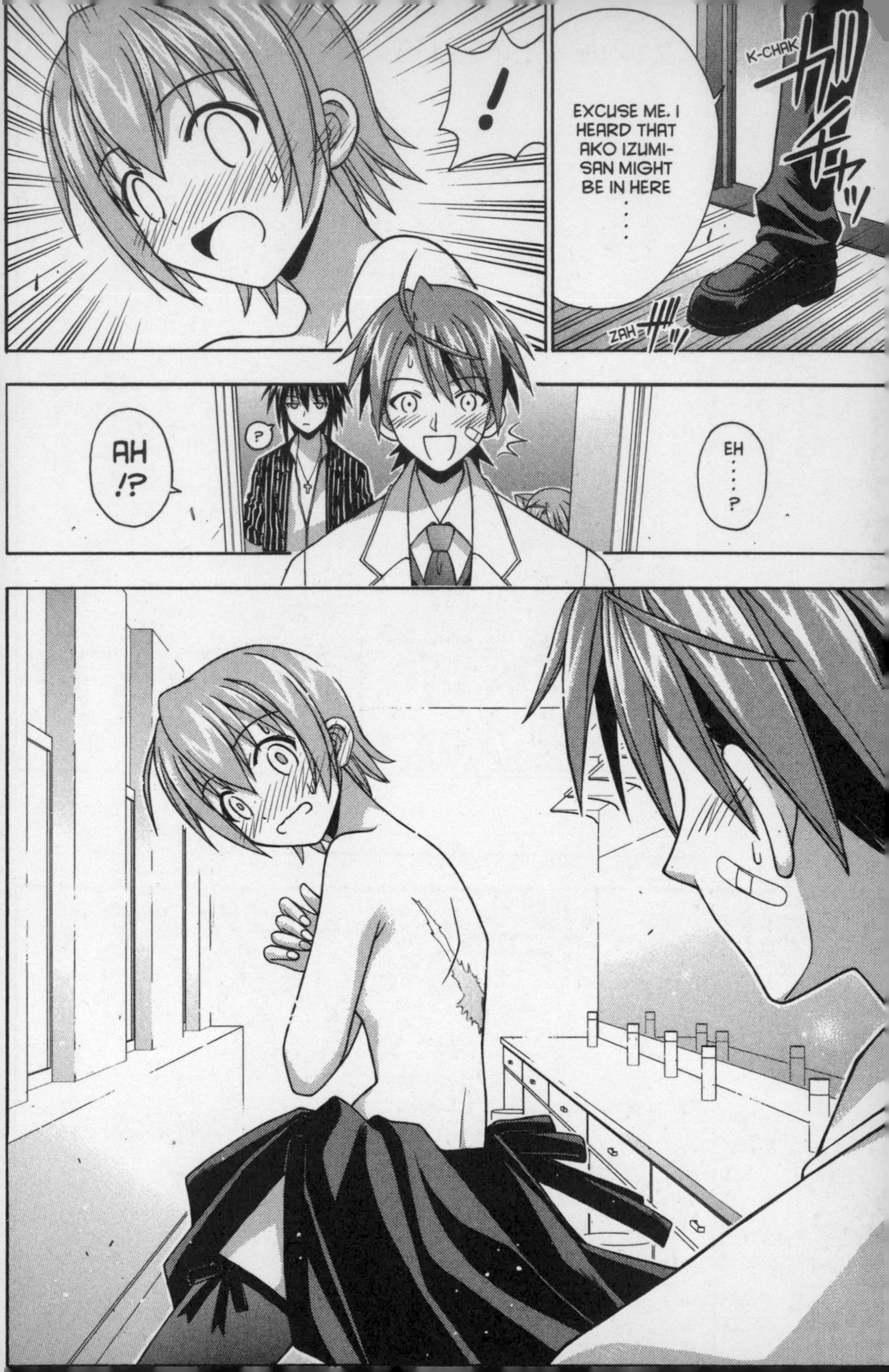
K-CHAK
ガチャッ
EXCUSE ME. I HEARD THAT AKO IZUMI-SAN MIGHT BE IN HERE . . . .
ZAH
ザッ
!
EH . . . . ?
AH !?

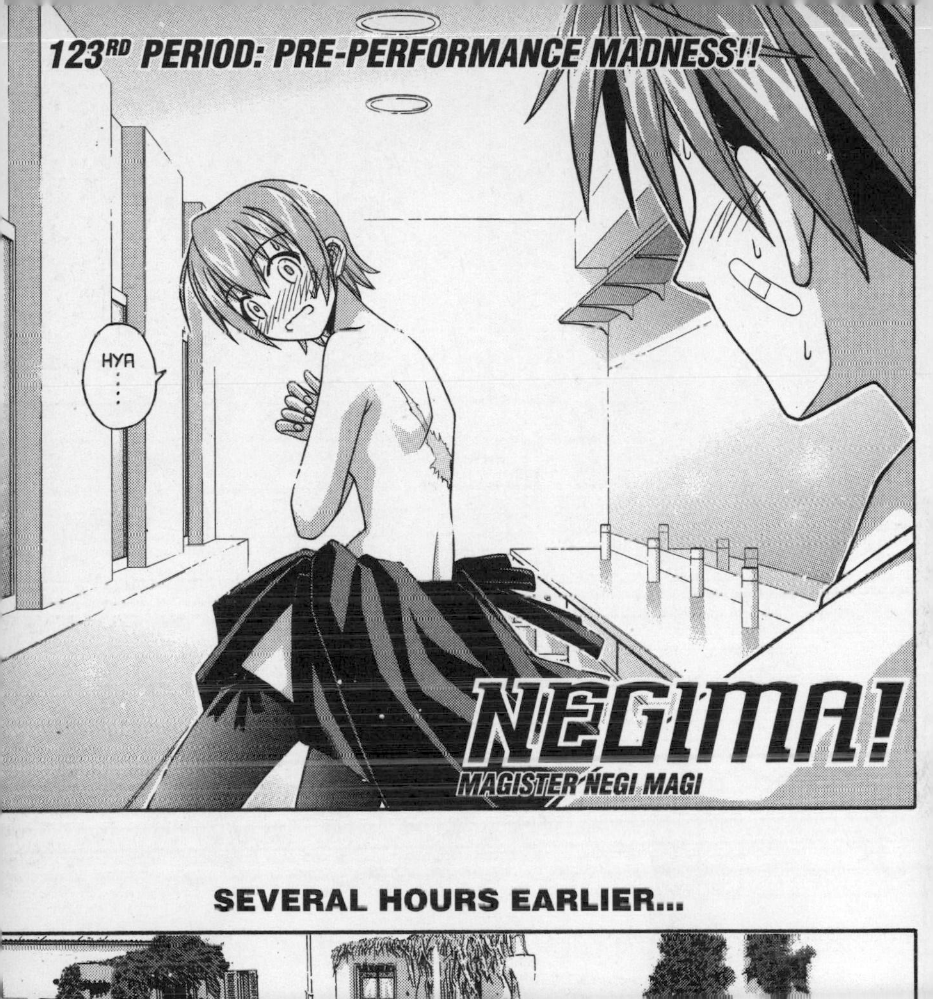
123RD PERIOD: PRE-PERFORMANCE MADNESS!!
HYA ....
NEGIMA!
MAGISTER NEGI MAGI

SEVERAL HOURS EARLIER...

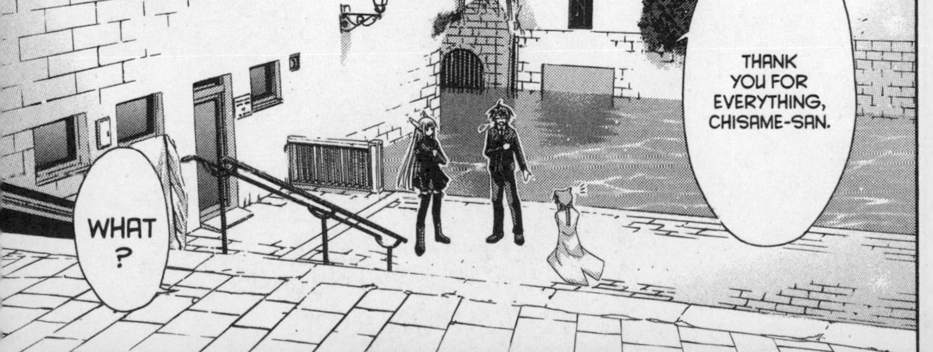
THANK YOU FOR EVERYTHING, CHISAME-SAN.
WHAT ?

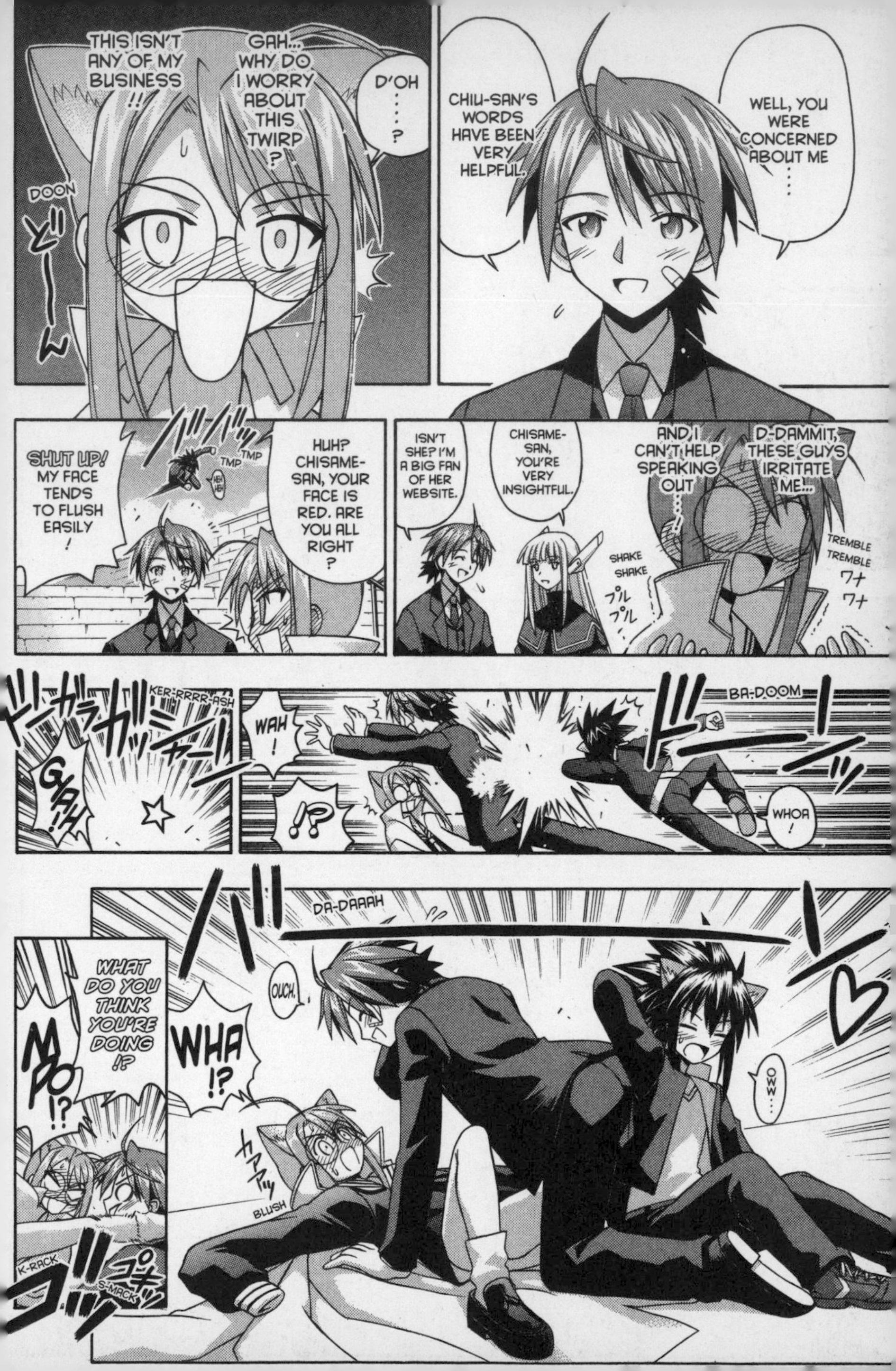

WELL, YOU WERE CONCERNED ABOUT ME ....
CHIU-SAN'S WORDS HAVE BEEN VERY HELPFUL.
D'OH ....?
GAH... WHY DO I WORRY ABOUT THIS TWIRP?
THIS ISN'T ANY OF MY BUSINESS!!
DOON
どーーん
D-DAMMIT, THESE GUYS IRRITATE ME...
AND I CAN'T HELP SPEAKING OUT ....
TREMBLE TREMBLE
ワナワナ
SHAKE SHAKE
プルプル
CHISAME-SAN, YOU'RE VERY INSIGHTFUL.
ISN'T SHE? I'M A BIG FAN OF HER WEBSITE.
HUH? CHISAME-SAN, YOUR FACE IS RED. ARE YOU ALL RIGHT?
TMP TMP
HEH HEH
SHUT UP! MY FACE TENDS TO FLUSH EASILY!
BA-DOOM
WHOA!
WAH!
!?
KER-RRRR-ASH
GYAH!!
DA-DAAAH
OUCH.
OWW...
WHA!?
BLUSH
WHAT DO YOU THINK YOU'RE DOING!?
MPO!?
K-RACK
S-MACK

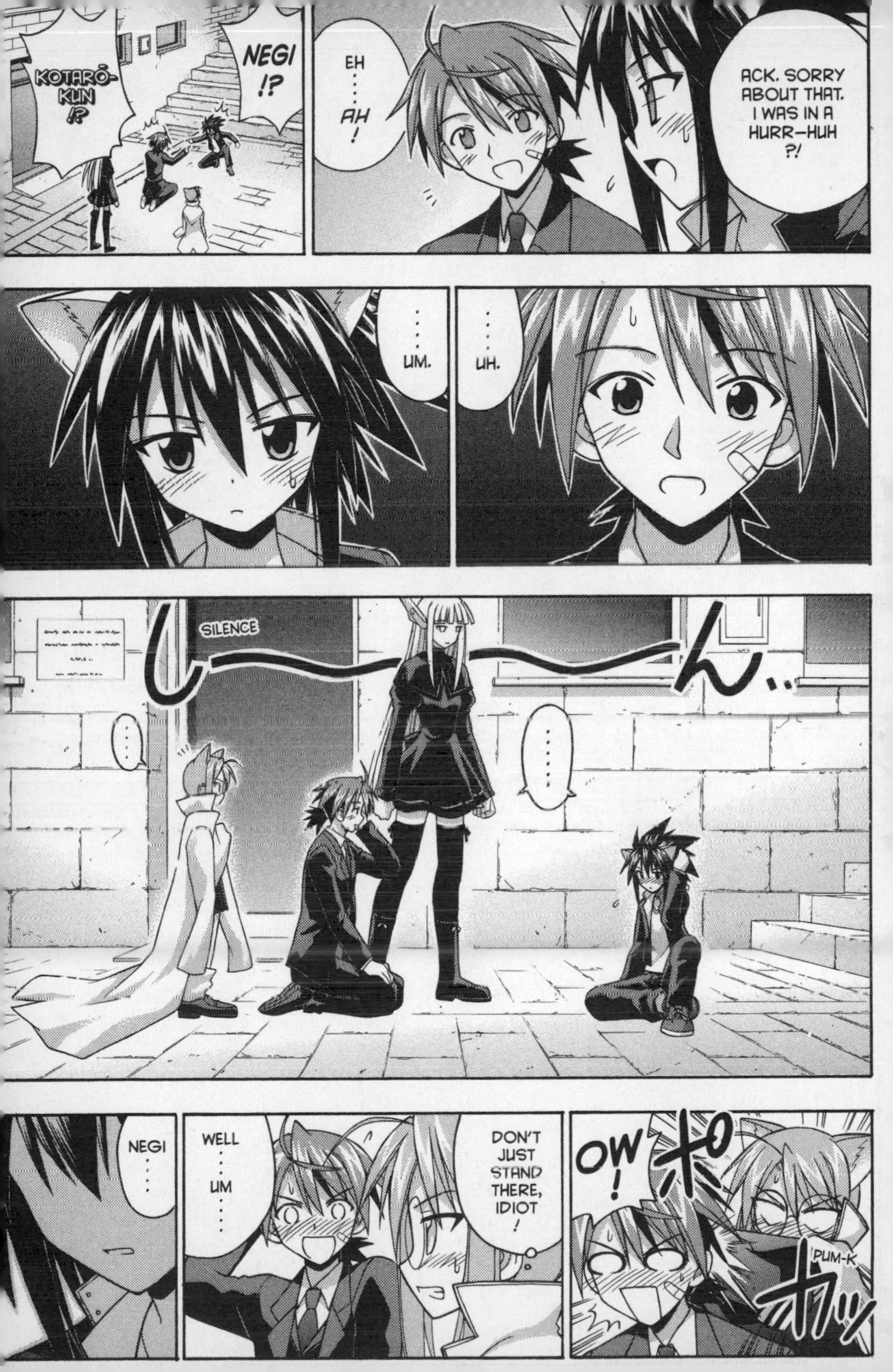
ACK. SORRY ABOUT THAT. I WAS IN A HURR—HUH ?!
EH ... AH !
NEGI !?
KOTARŌ-KUN !?
... UH.
... UM.
SILENCE
し——ん..
......
....
OW !
PUM-K
DON'T JUST STAND THERE, IDIOT !
WELL ... UM ....
NEGI ....

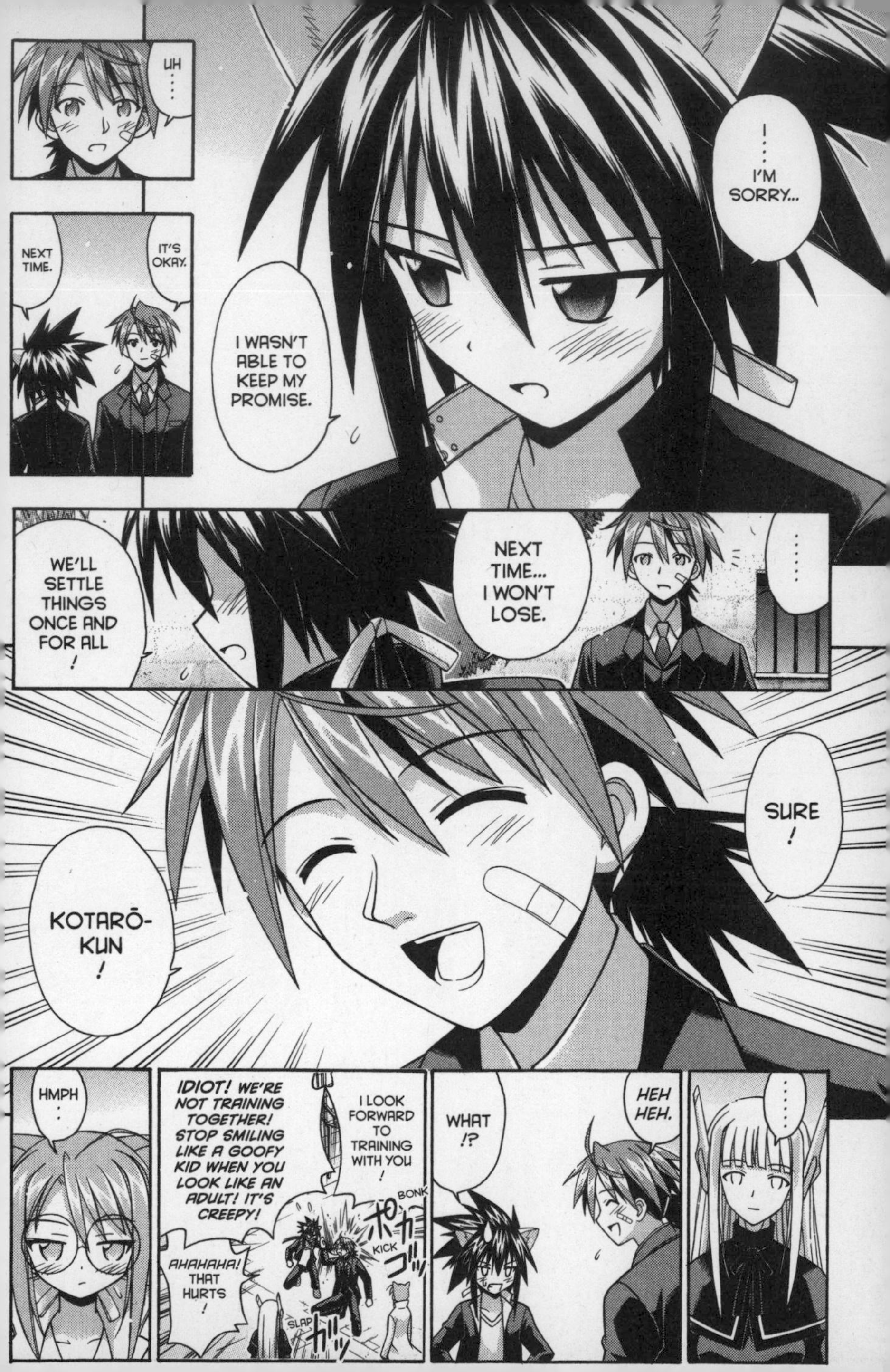
I... I'M SORRY...
I WASN'T ABLE TO KEEP MY PROMISE.
UH...
IT'S OKAY.
NEXT TIME.
......
NEXT TIME... I WON'T LOSE.
WE'LL SETTLE THINGS ONCE AND FOR ALL!
SURE!
KOTARŌ-KUN!
......
HEH HEH.
WHAT!?
I LOOK FORWARD TO TRAINING WITH YOU!
IDIOT! WE'RE NOT TRAINING TOGETHER! STOP SMILING LIKE A GOOFY KID WHEN YOU LOOK LIKE AN ADULT! IT'S CREEPY!
BONK
KICK
AHAHAHA! THAT HURTS!
SLAP
HMPH...

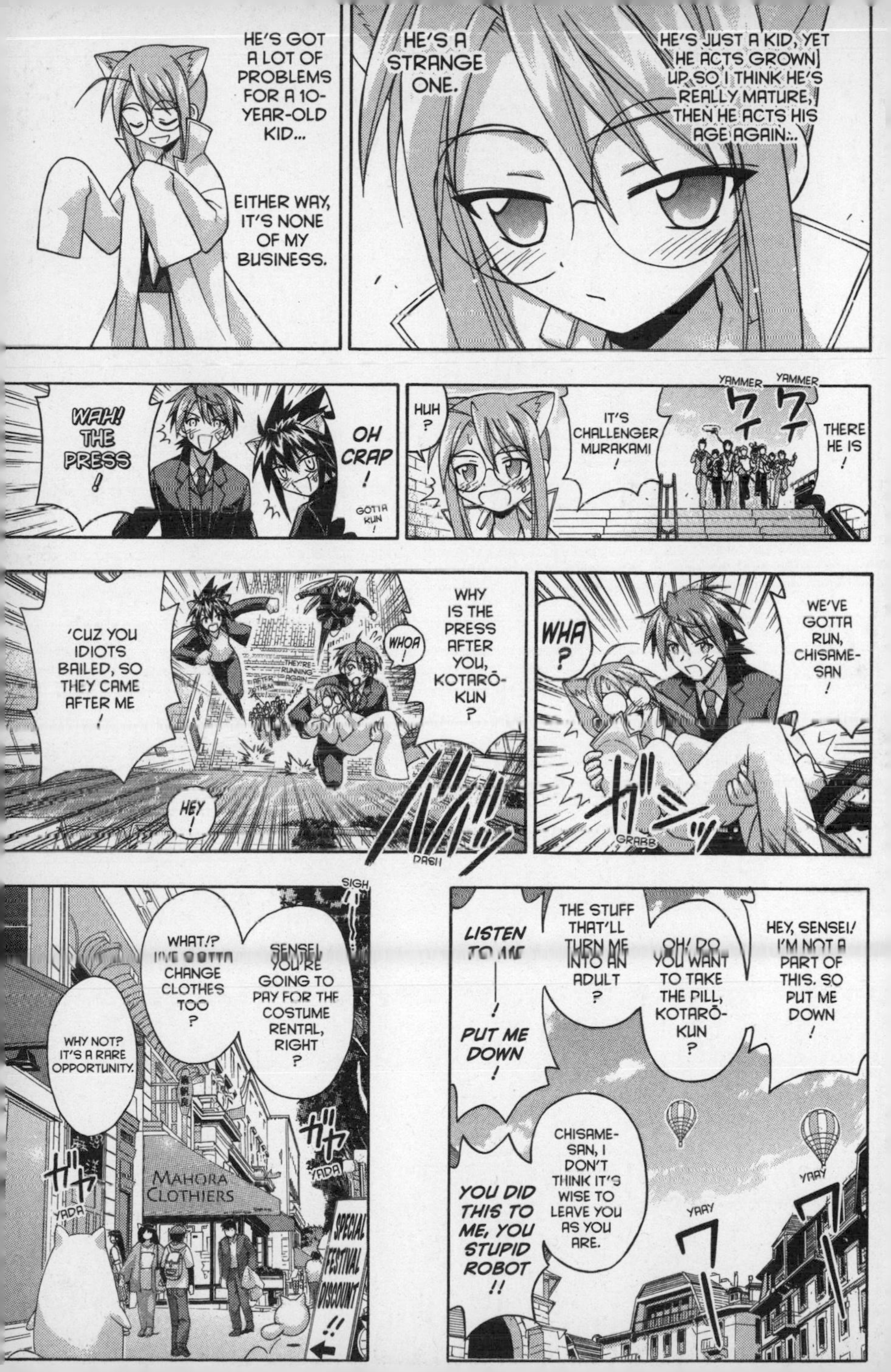
HE'S JUST A KID, YET HE ACTS GROWN UP SO I THINK HE'S REALLY MATURE, THEN HE ACTS HIS AGE AGAIN...
HE'S A STRANGE ONE.
HE'S GOT A LOT OF PROBLEMS FOR A 10-YEAR-OLD KID...
EITHER WAY, IT'S NONE OF MY BUSINESS.
YAMMER
YAMMER
THERE HE IS!
IT'S CHALLENGER MURAKAMI!
HUH?
OH CRAP!
WAH! THE PRESS!
WE'VE GOTTA RUN, CHISAME-SAN!
WHA?
GRABB
WHY IS THE PRESS AFTER YOU, KOTARŌ-KUN?
WHOA!
THEY'RE RUNNING AGAIN
AFTER THEM
'CUZ YOU IDIOTS BAILED, SO THEY CAME AFTER ME!
HEY!
DASH
HEY, SENSEI! I'M NOT A PART OF THIS. SO PUT ME DOWN!
OH! DO YOU WANT TO TAKE THE PILL, KOTARŌ-KUN?
THE STUFF THAT'LL TURN ME INTO AN ADULT?
LISTEN TO ME—! PUT ME DOWN!
CHISAME-SAN, I DON'T THINK IT'S WISE TO LEAVE YOU AS YOU ARE.
YOU DID THIS TO ME, YOU STUPID ROBOT!!
YAAY
YAAY
SIGH
SENSEI, YOU'RE GOING TO PAY FOR THE COSTUME RENTAL, RIGHT?
WHAT!? I'VE GOTTA CHANGE CLOTHES TOO?
WHY NOT? IT'S A RARE OPPORTUNITY.
YADA
YADA
MAHORA CLOTHIERS
SPECIAL FESTIVAL DISCOUNT!!

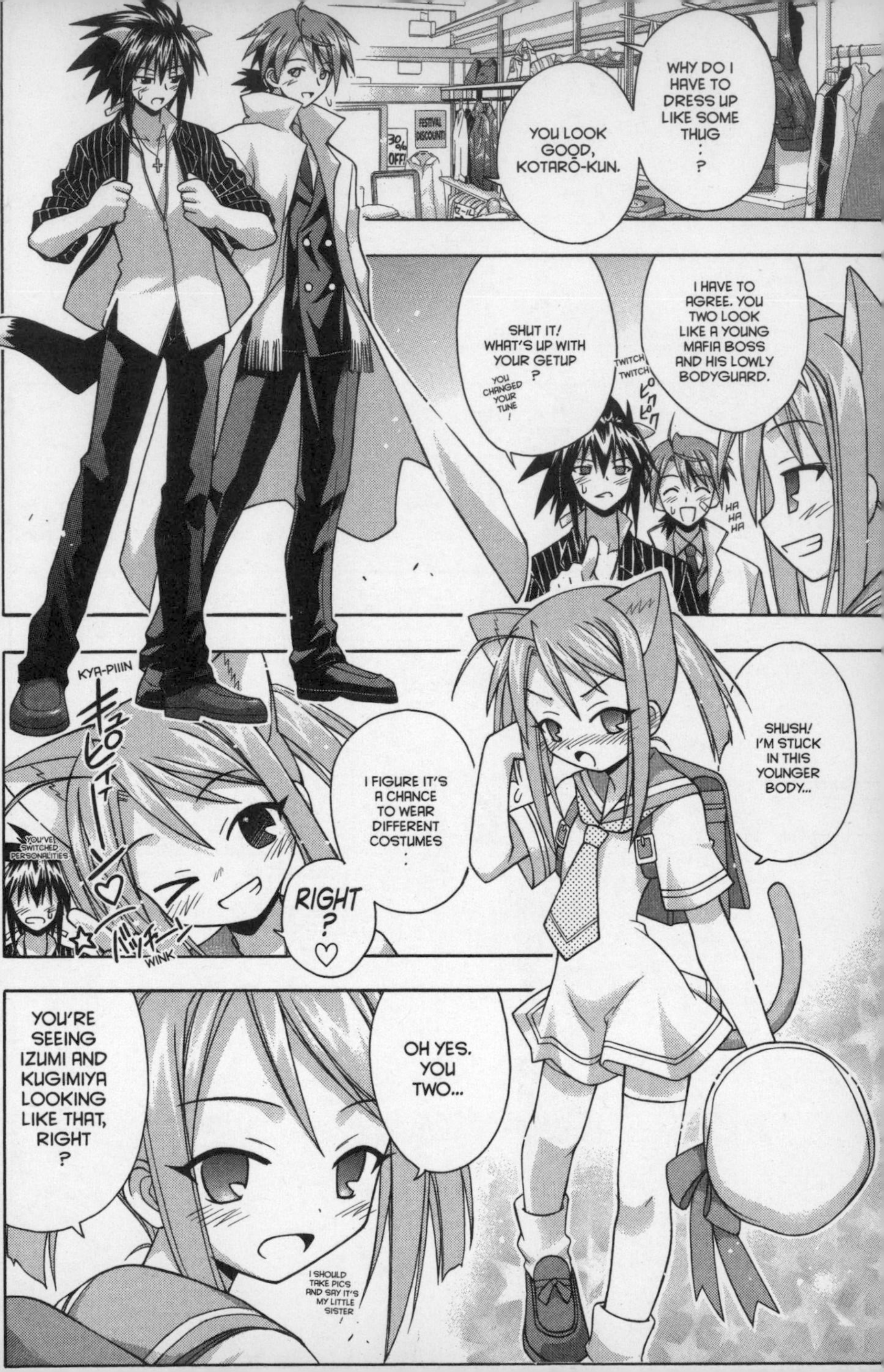
WHY DO I HAVE TO DRESS UP LIKE SOME THUG . . ?
YOU LOOK GOOD, KOTARŌ-KUN.
FESTIVAL DISCOUNT!
30% OFF!
I HAVE TO AGREE. YOU TWO LOOK LIKE A YOUNG MAFIA BOSS AND HIS LOWLY BODYGUARD.
TWITCH TWITCH
SHUT IT! WHAT'S UP WITH YOUR GETUP ?
YOU CHANGED YOUR TUNE !
HA HA HA
SHUSH! I'M STUCK IN THIS YOUNGER BODY...
I FIGURE IT'S A CHANCE TO WEAR DIFFERENT COSTUMES . .
RIGHT ? ♡
KYA-PIIN
WINK
YOU'VE SWITCHED PERSONALITIES
OH YES. YOU TWO...
YOU'RE SEEING IZUMI AND KUGIMIYA LOOKING LIKE THAT, RIGHT ?
I SHOULD TAKE PICS AND SAY IT'S MY LITTLE SISTER !

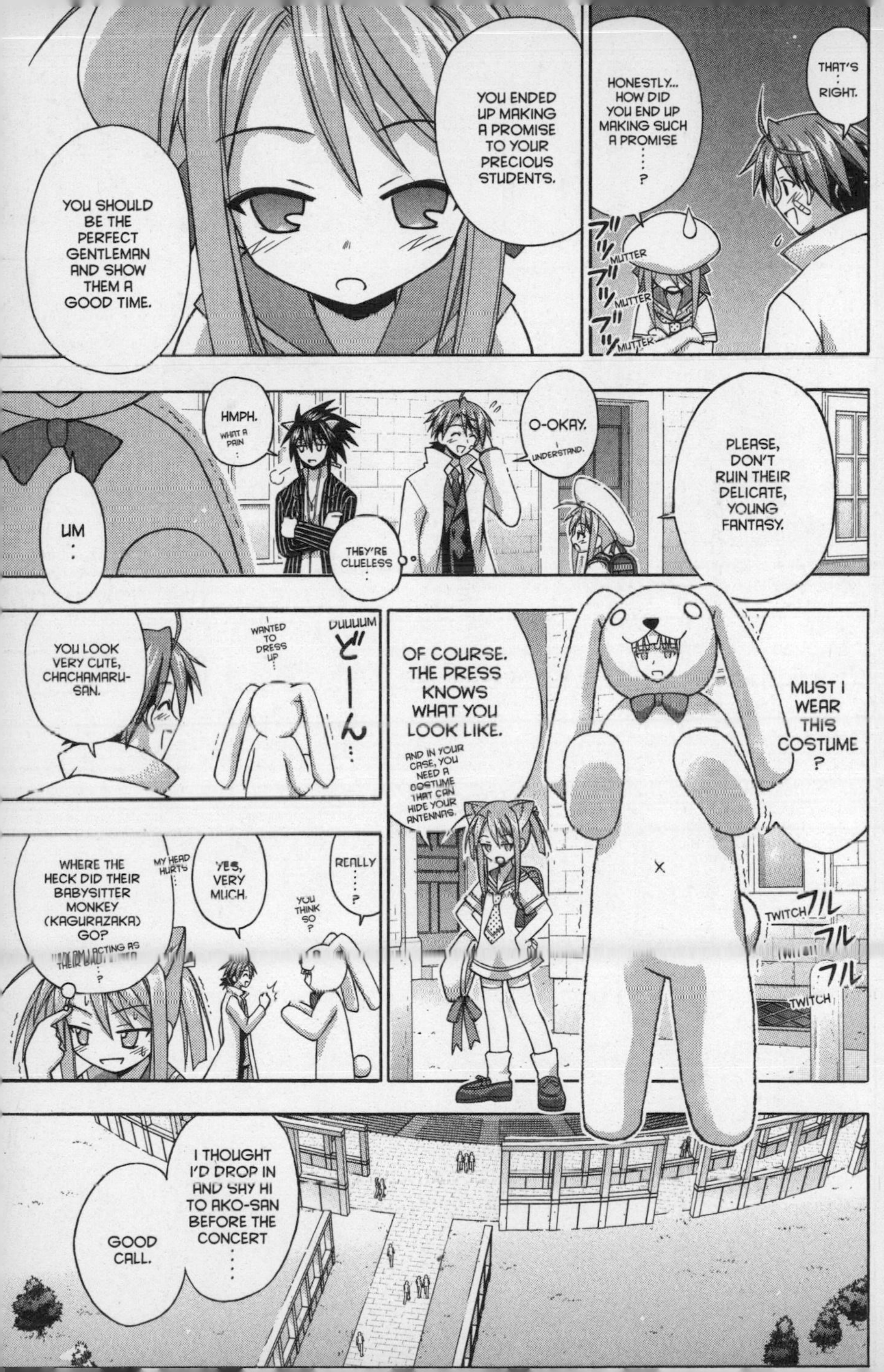
THAT'S... RIGHT.
HONESTLY... HOW DID YOU END UP MAKING SUCH A PROMISE...?
ブツ MUTTER
ブツ MUTTER
ブツ MUTTER
YOU ENDED UP MAKING A PROMISE TO YOUR PRECIOUS STUDENTS.
YOU SHOULD BE THE PERFECT GENTLEMAN AND SHOW THEM A GOOD TIME.
PLEASE, DON'T RUIN THEIR DELICATE, YOUNG FANTASY.
O-OKAY.
I UNDERSTAND.
HMPH.
WHAT A PAIN...
THEY'RE CLUELESS...
UM...
MUST I WEAR THIS COSTUME?
OF COURSE. THE PRESS KNOWS WHAT YOU LOOK LIKE.
AND IN YOUR CASE, YOU NEED A COSTUME THAT CAN HIDE YOUR ANTENNAS.
フル TWITCH
フル TWITCH
フル TWITCH
YOU LOOK VERY CUTE, CHACHAMARU-SAN.
I WANTED TO DRESS UP...
DUUUUM どーん...
REALLY...?
YOU THINK SO?
YES, VERY MUCH.
MY HEAD HURTS...
WHERE THE HECK DID THEIR BABYSITTER MONKEY (KAGURAZAKA) GO?
I THOUGHT I'D DROP IN AND SAY HI TO AKO-SAN BEFORE THE CONCERT...
GOOD CALL.

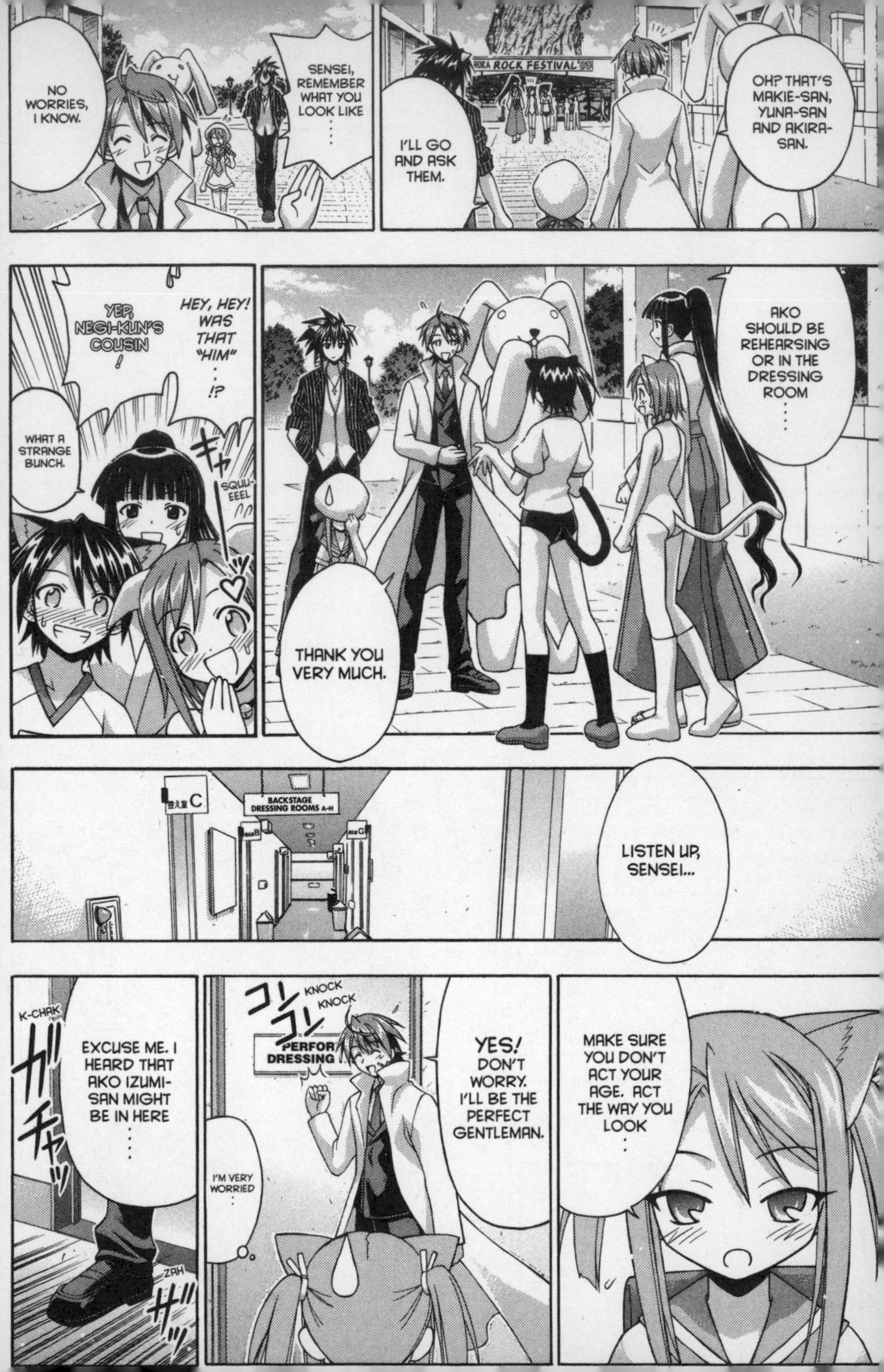
ROCK FESTIVAL
OH? THAT'S MAKIE-SAN, YUNA-SAN AND AKIRA-SAN.
I'LL GO AND ASK THEM.
SENSEI, REMEMBER WHAT YOU LOOK LIKE ...
NO WORRIES, I KNOW.
AKO SHOULD BE REHEARSING OR IN THE DRESSING ROOM ...
THANK YOU VERY MUCH.
HEY, HEY! WAS THAT "HIM" ...!?
YEP, NEGI-KUN'S COUSIN!
WHAT A STRANGE BUNCH.
SQUU-EEEL
LISTEN UP, SENSEI...
BACKSTAGE DRESSING ROOMS A-H
MAKE SURE YOU DON'T ACT YOUR AGE. ACT THE WAY YOU LOOK ...
YES! DON'T WORRY. I'LL BE THE PERFECT GENTLEMAN.
KNOCK KNOCK
I'M VERY WORRIED ...
K-CHAK
EXCUSE ME. I HEARD THAT AKO IZUMI-SAN MIGHT BE IN HERE ...
ZAH

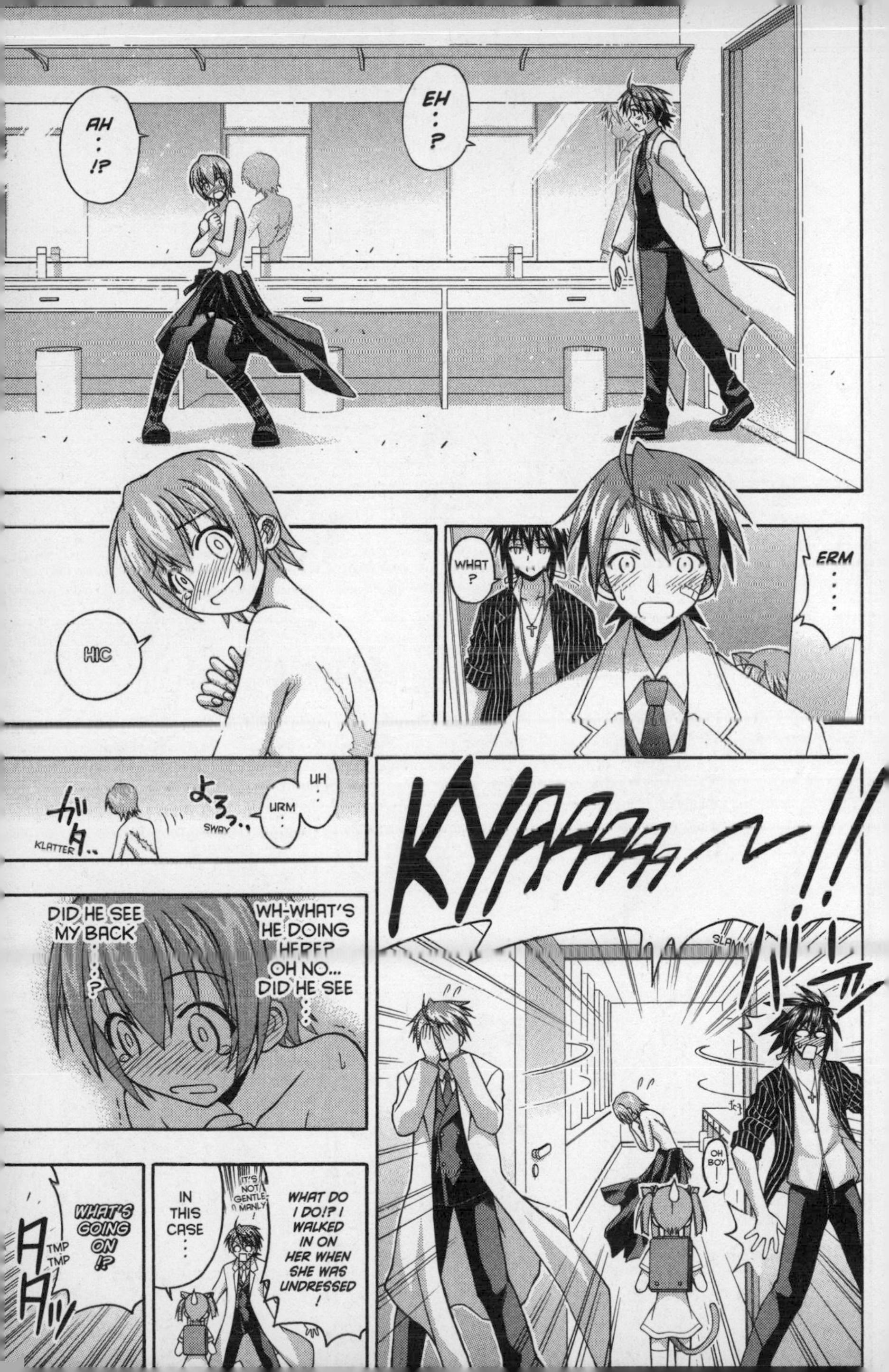
EH...?
AH...!?
ERM....
WHAT?
HIC
KYAAAAA~~!!
SLAM
OH BOY!
UH...
URM...
よろっ.. SWAY
ガタ.. KLATTER
WH-WHAT'S HE DOING HERE? OH NO... DID HE SEE...
DID HE SEE MY BACK...?
WHAT DO I DO!? I WALKED IN ON HER WHEN SHE WAS UNDRESSED!
IT'S NOT GENTLE-MANLY!
IN THIS CASE...
WHAT'S GOING ON!?
TMP TMP

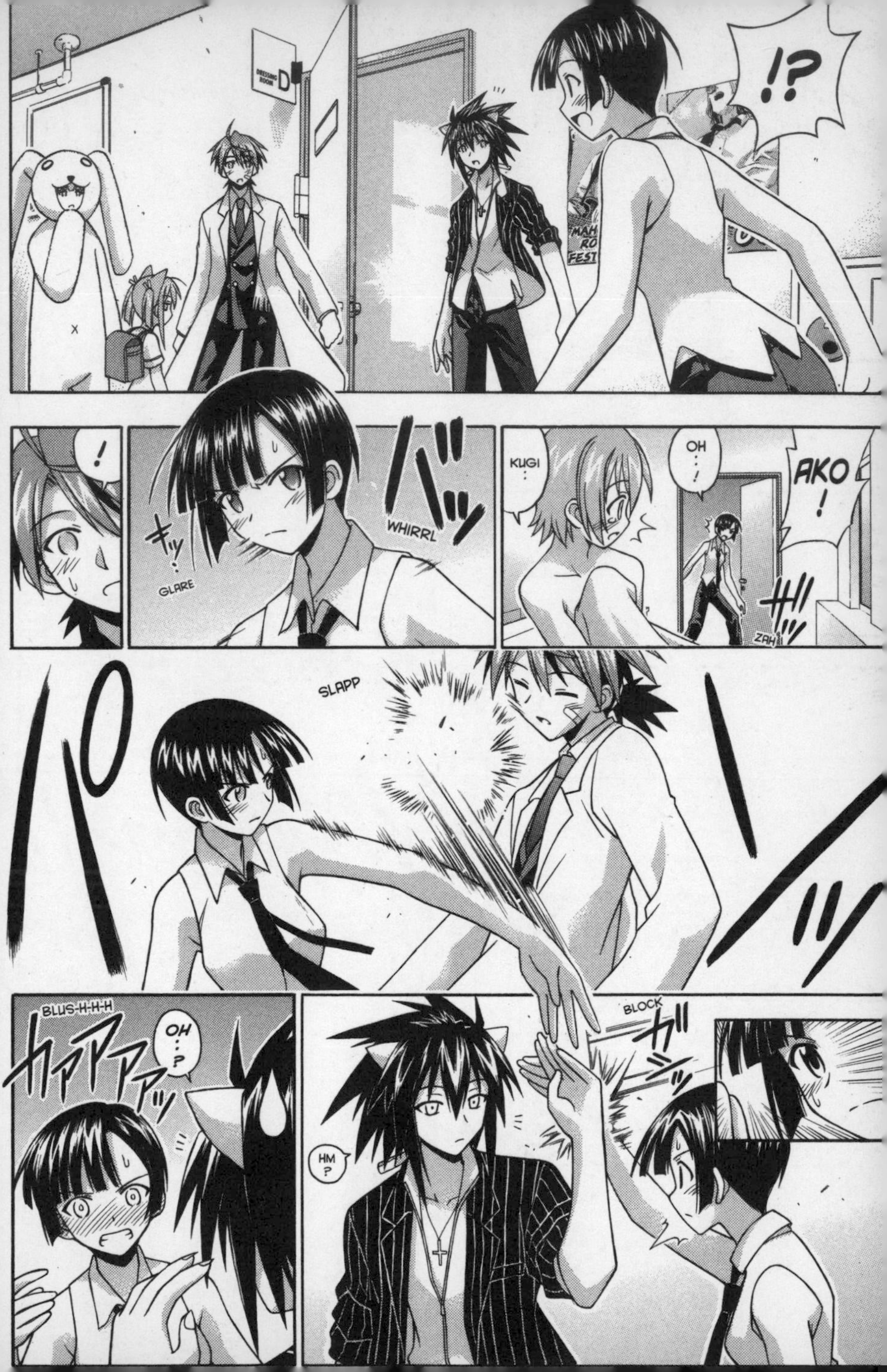
!?
DRESSING ROOM D
AKO !
ZAH
OH... !
KUGI...
バッ
WHIRRL
キッ
GLARE
!
SLAPP
パーンッ
BLOCK
ガッ
HM ?
BLUS-H-H-H
カァアアァッ
OH...?

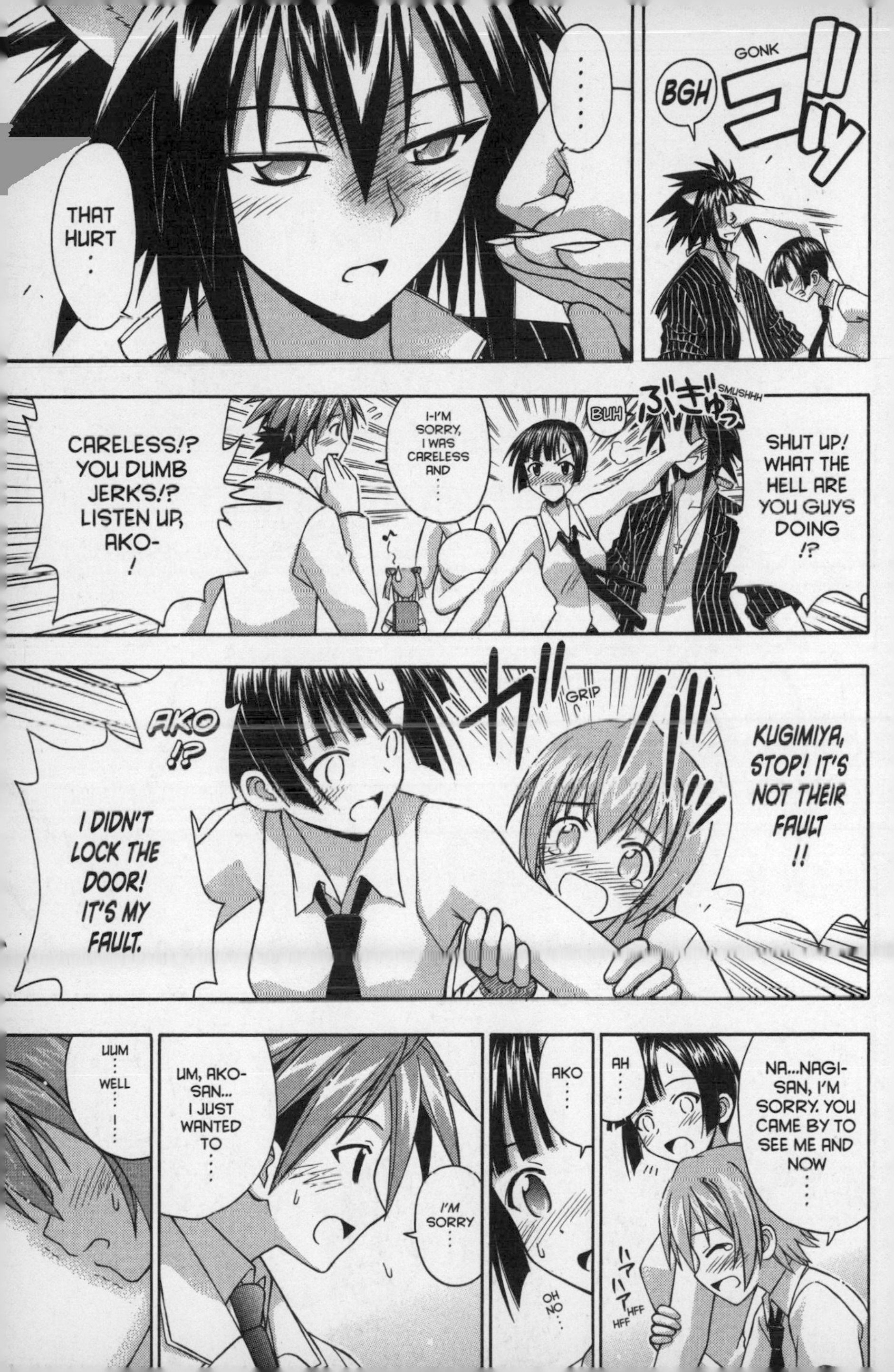
GONK
BGH
......
THAT HURT ...
SHUT UP! WHAT THE HELL ARE YOU GUYS DOING !?
SMUSHHH
BUH
I-I'M SORRY, I WAS CARELESS AND ...
CARELESS!? YOU DUMB JERKS!? LISTEN UP, AKO- !
KUGIMIYA, STOP! IT'S NOT THEIR FAULT !!
GRIP
AKO !?
I DIDN'T LOCK THE DOOR! IT'S MY FAULT.
NA...NAGI-SAN, I'M SORRY. YOU CAME BY TO SEE ME AND NOW ...
AH ...
HFF HFF
AKO ...
OH NO...
UM, AKO-SAN... I JUST WANTED TO ...
I'M SORRY ...
UUM ... WELL ... !...

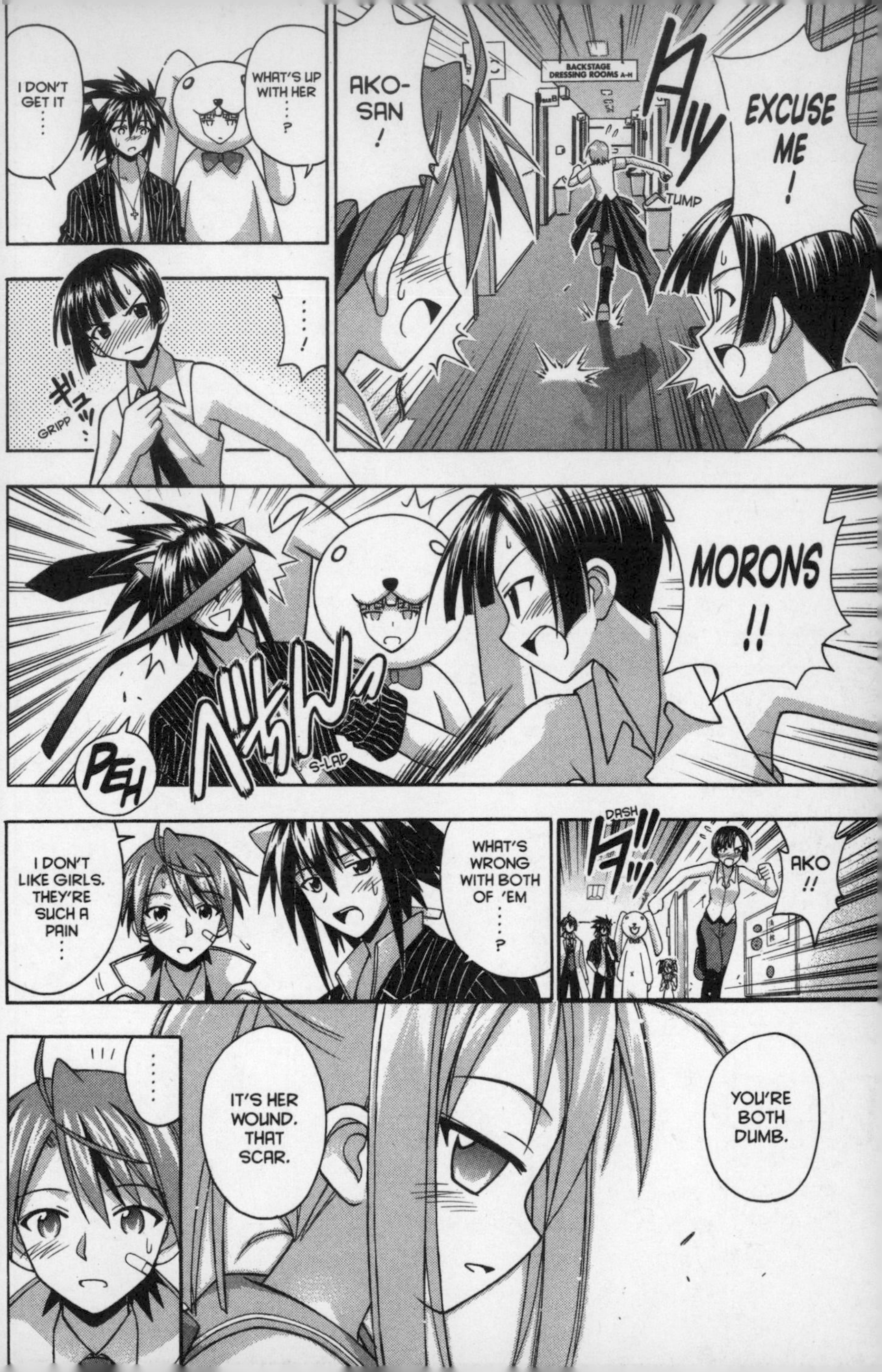

EXCUSE ME!
TUMP
BACKSTAGE DRESSING ROOMS A-H
AKO-SAN!
WHAT'S UP WITH HER ....?
I DON'T GET IT ....
....!
GRIPP
MORONS!!
S-LAP
PEH
AKO!!
DASH
WHAT'S WRONG WITH BOTH OF 'EM ....?
I DON'T LIKE GIRLS. THEY'RE SUCH A PAIN ....
YOU'RE BOTH DUMB.
IT'S HER WOUND. THAT SCAR.
......

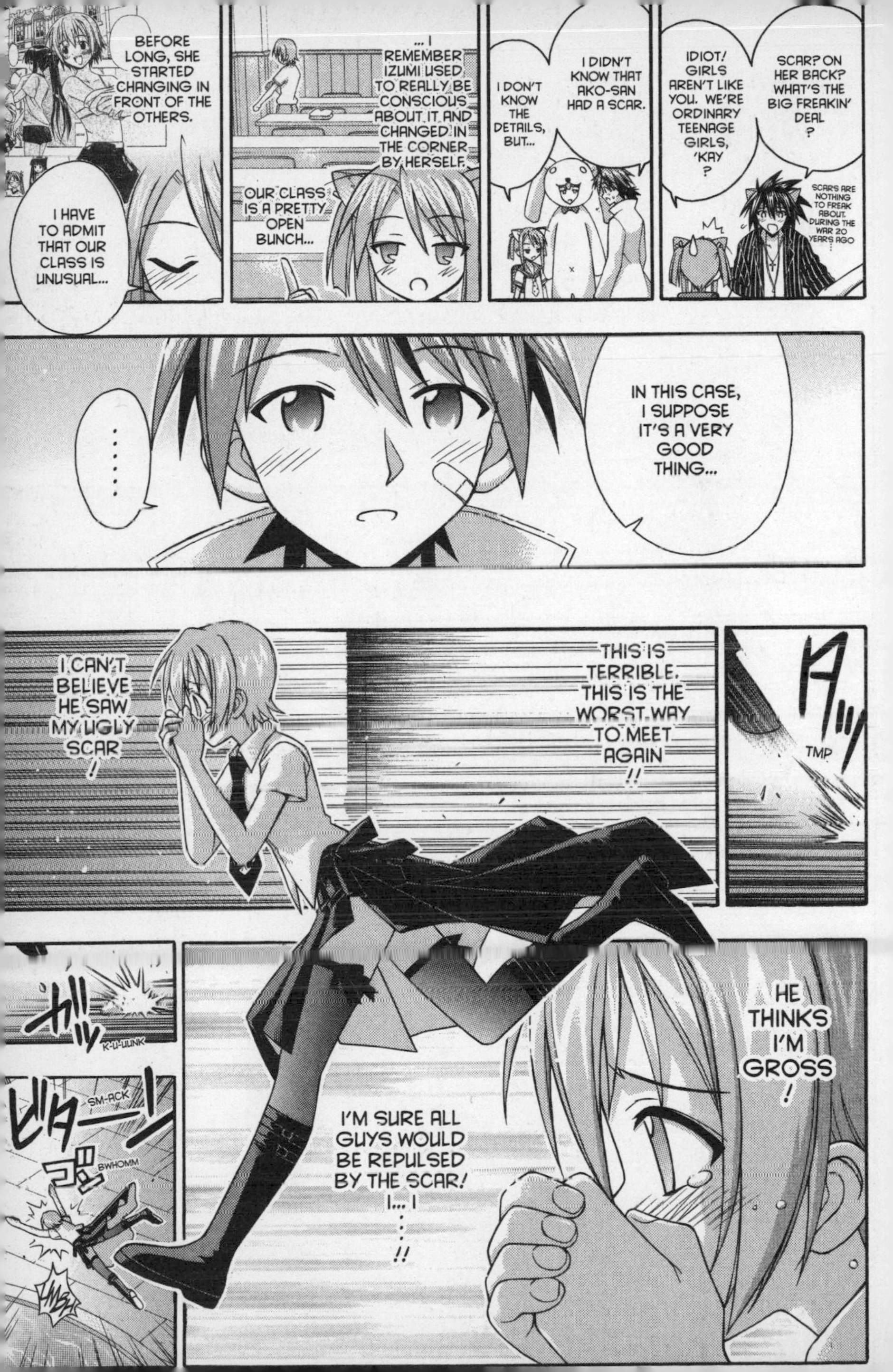

SCAR? ON HER BACK? WHAT'S THE BIG FREAKIN' DEAL?
IDIOT! GIRLS AREN'T LIKE YOU. WE'RE ORDINARY TEENAGE GIRLS, 'KAY?
SCARS ARE NOTHING TO FREAK ABOUT. DURING THE WAR 20 YEARS AGO...
I DIDN'T KNOW THAT AKO-SAN HAD A SCAR.
I DON'T KNOW THE DETAILS, BUT...
... I REMEMBER IZUMI USED TO REALLY BE CONSCIOUS ABOUT IT AND CHANGED IN THE CORNER BY HERSELF.
OUR CLASS IS A PRETTY OPEN BUNCH...
BEFORE LONG, SHE STARTED CHANGING IN FRONT OF THE OTHERS.
I HAVE TO ADMIT THAT OUR CLASS IS UNUSUAL...
IN THIS CASE, I SUPPOSE IT'S A VERY GOOD THING...
......
TMP
THIS IS TERRIBLE. THIS IS THE WORST WAY TO MEET AGAIN!!
I CAN'T BELIEVE HE SAW MY UGLY SCAR!
HE THINKS I'M GROSS!
I'M SURE ALL GUYS WOULD BE REPULSED BY THE SCAR! I... I...!!
K-U-UNK
SM-ACK
BWHOMM

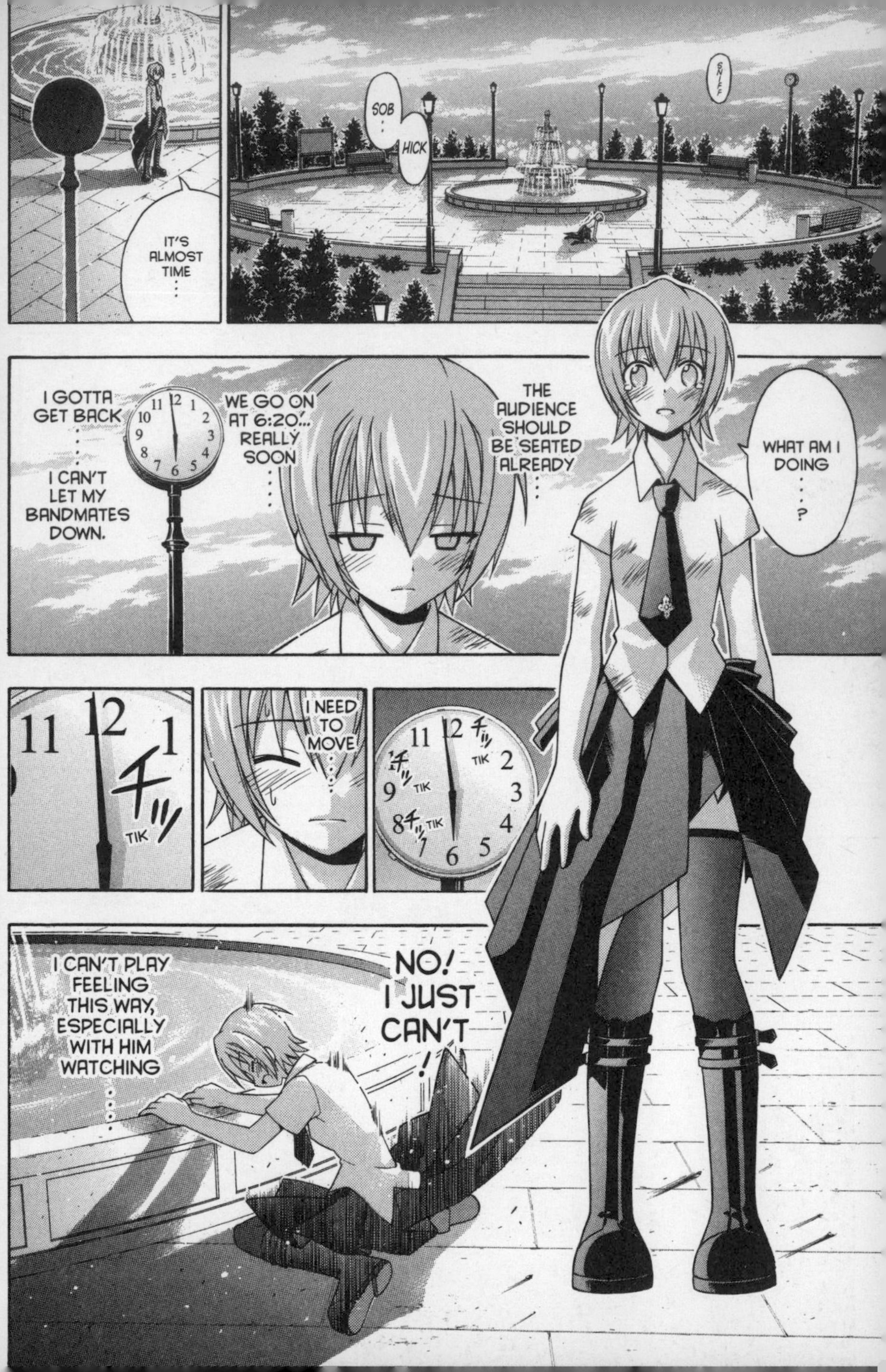

SNIFF
SOB...
HICK
IT'S ALMOST TIME...
WHAT AM I DOING...?
THE AUDIENCE SHOULD BE SEATED ALREADY...
WE GO ON AT 6:20... REALLY SOON...
I GOTTA GET BACK...
I CAN'T LET MY BANDMATES DOWN.
チッ TIK
チッ TIK
チッ TIK
I NEED TO MOVE...
チッ TIK
NO! I JUST CAN'T!
I CAN'T PLAY FEELING THIS WAY, ESPECIALLY WITH HIM WATCHING...

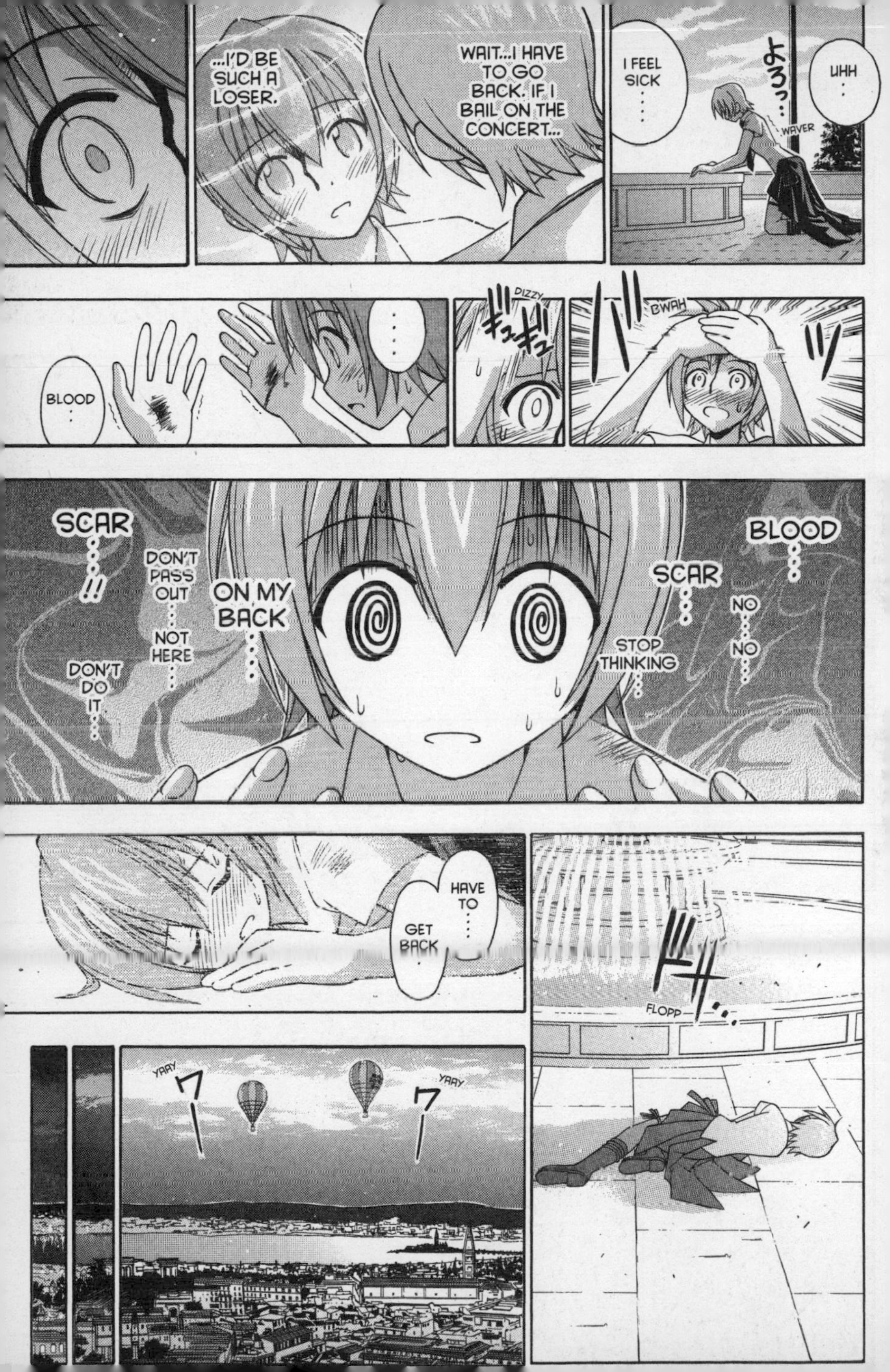
UHH
よろっ…
WAVER
I FEEL SICK
WAIT...I HAVE TO GO BACK. IF I BAIL ON THE CONCERT...
...I'D BE SUCH A LOSER.
バ
ッ
BWAH
ギュギュ
DIZZY
...
BLOOD
BLOOD
NO
NO
SCAR
STOP THINKING
ON MY BACK
DON'T PASS OUT
NOT HERE
DON'T DO IT
SCAR
ドサ
FLOPP
HAVE TO....
GET BACK
ワー
YAAY
ワー
YAAY

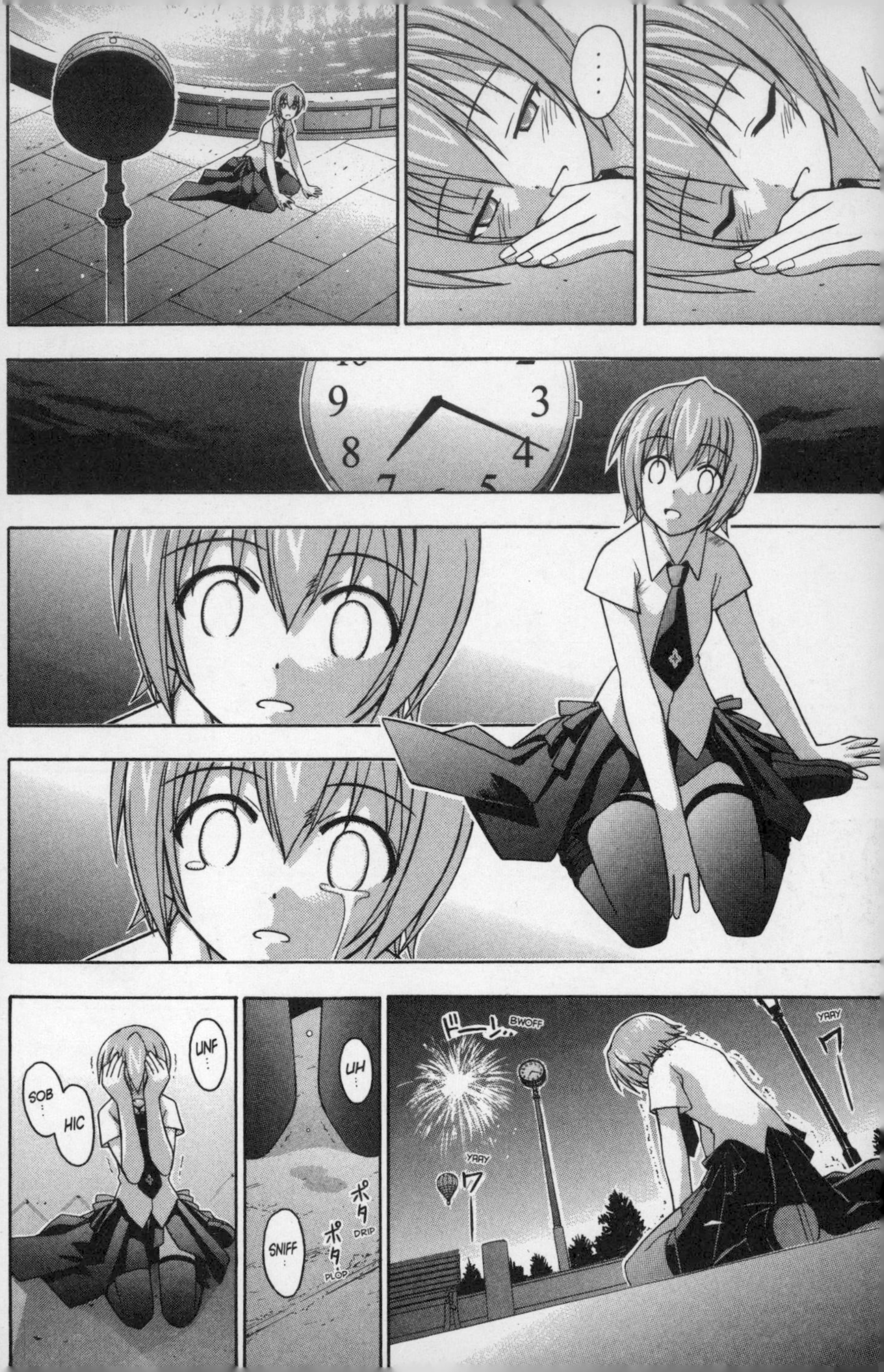

....
YAAY
BWOFF
YAAY
UH...
ポタ DRIP
ポタ PLOP
SNIFF...
UNF...
SOB...
HIC

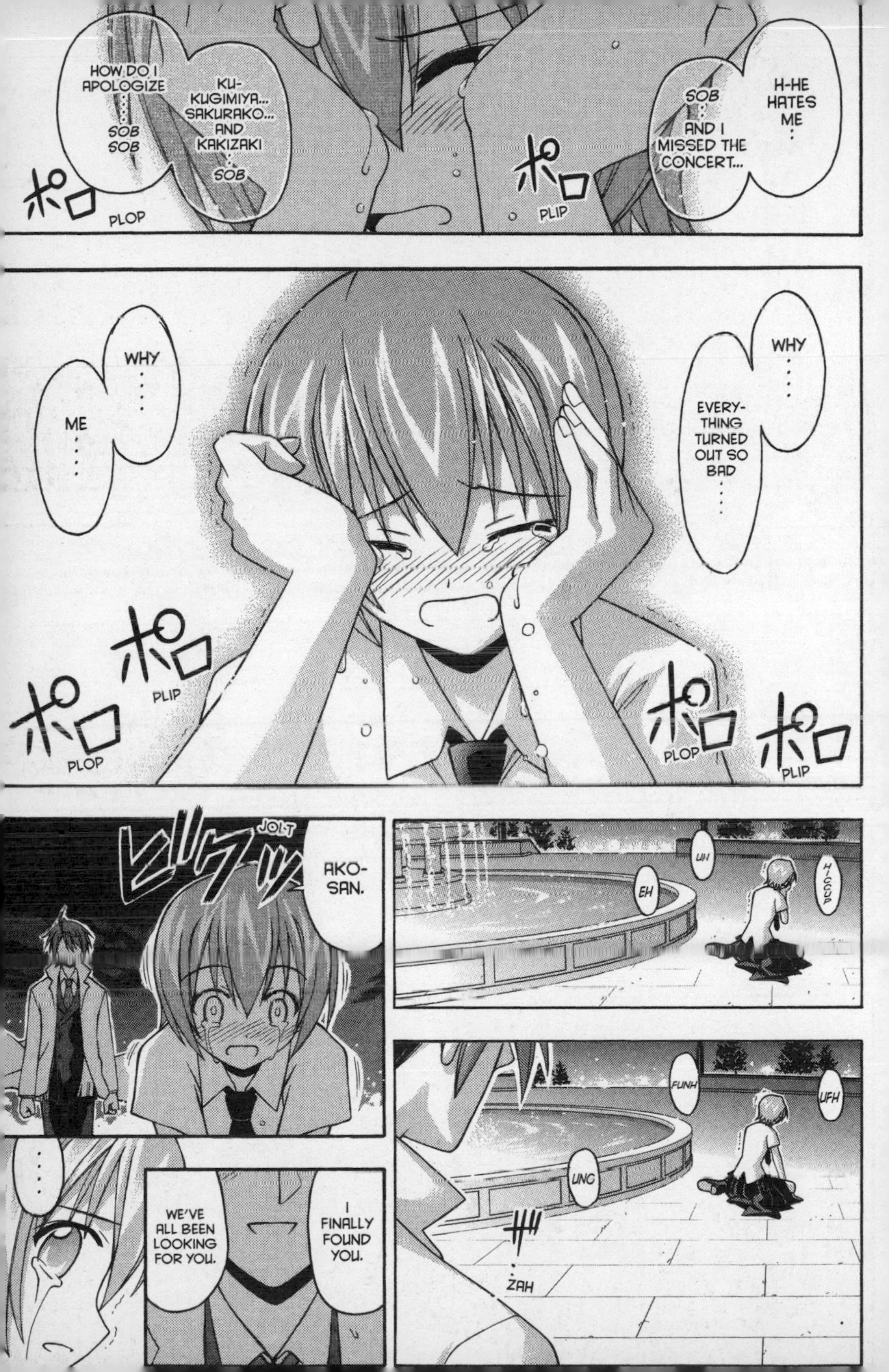
H-HE HATES ME :
SOB : AND I MISSED THE CONCERT...
ポロ
PLIP
KU-KUGIMIYA... SAKURAKO... AND KAKIZAKI : SOB
HOW DO I APOLOGIZE : SOB SOB
ポロ
PLOP
WHY ....
EVERYTHING TURNED OUT SO BAD ....
WHY ....
ME ....
ポロ
PLIP
ポロ
PLOP
ポロ
PLIP
ポロ
PLOP
UH
HICCUP
EH
UFH
FUNH
UNG
ザ
ZAH
AKO-SAN.
ビクッ
JOLT
I FINALLY FOUND YOU.
WE'VE ALL BEEN LOOKING FOR YOU.
....

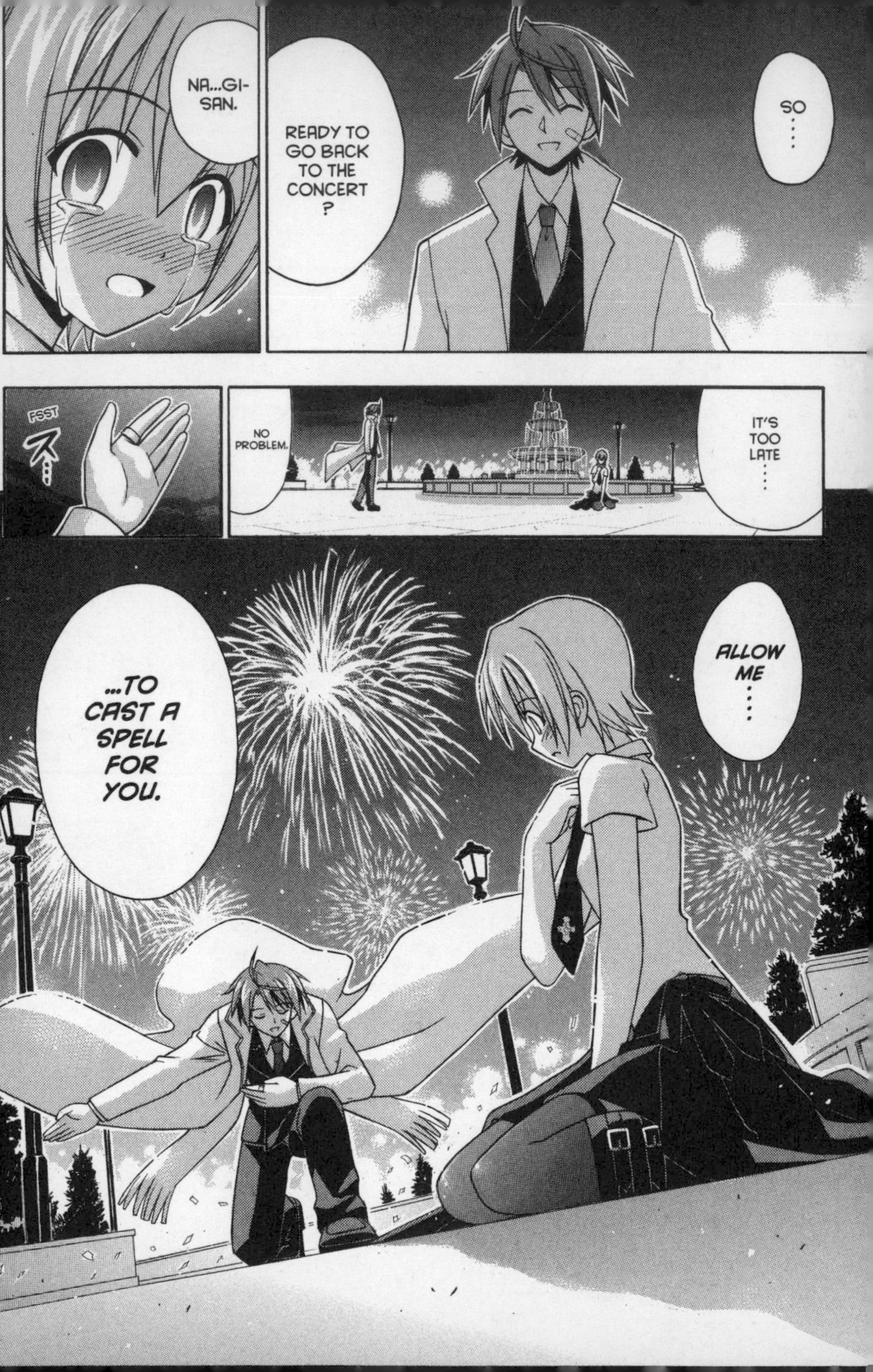
SO....
READY TO GO BACK TO THE CONCERT?
NA...GI-SAN.
IT'S TOO LATE....
NO PROBLEM.
FSST
ス...
ALLOW ME....
...TO CAST A SPELL FOR YOU.

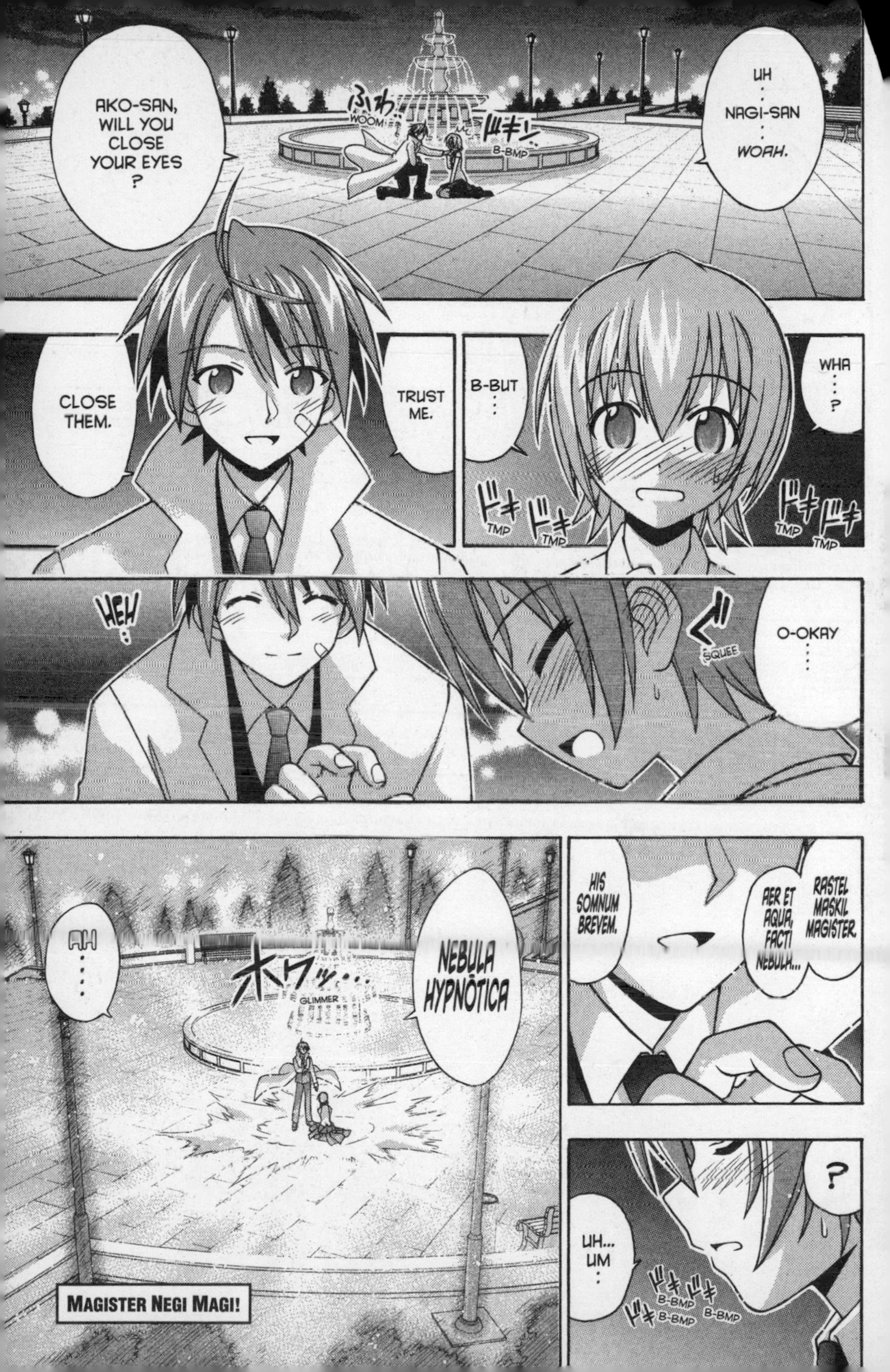

UH... NAGI-SAN... WOAH.
ドキッ
B-BMP
ふわ
WOOM
AKO-SAN, WILL YOU CLOSE YOUR EYES?
WHA...?
B-BUT...
ドキドキ
TMP TMP
TRUST ME.
CLOSE THEM.
ドキドキ
TMP TMP
O-OKAY...
ぐ
SQUEE
HEH.
RASTEL MASKIL MAGISTER.
AER ET AQUA, FACTI NEBULA...
HIS SOMNUM BREVEM.
?
UH... UM...
ドキドキ
B-BMP B-BMP
ドキ
B-BMP
NEBULA HYPNŌTICA
ホワッ...
GLIMMER
AH....
MAGISTER NEGI MAGI!

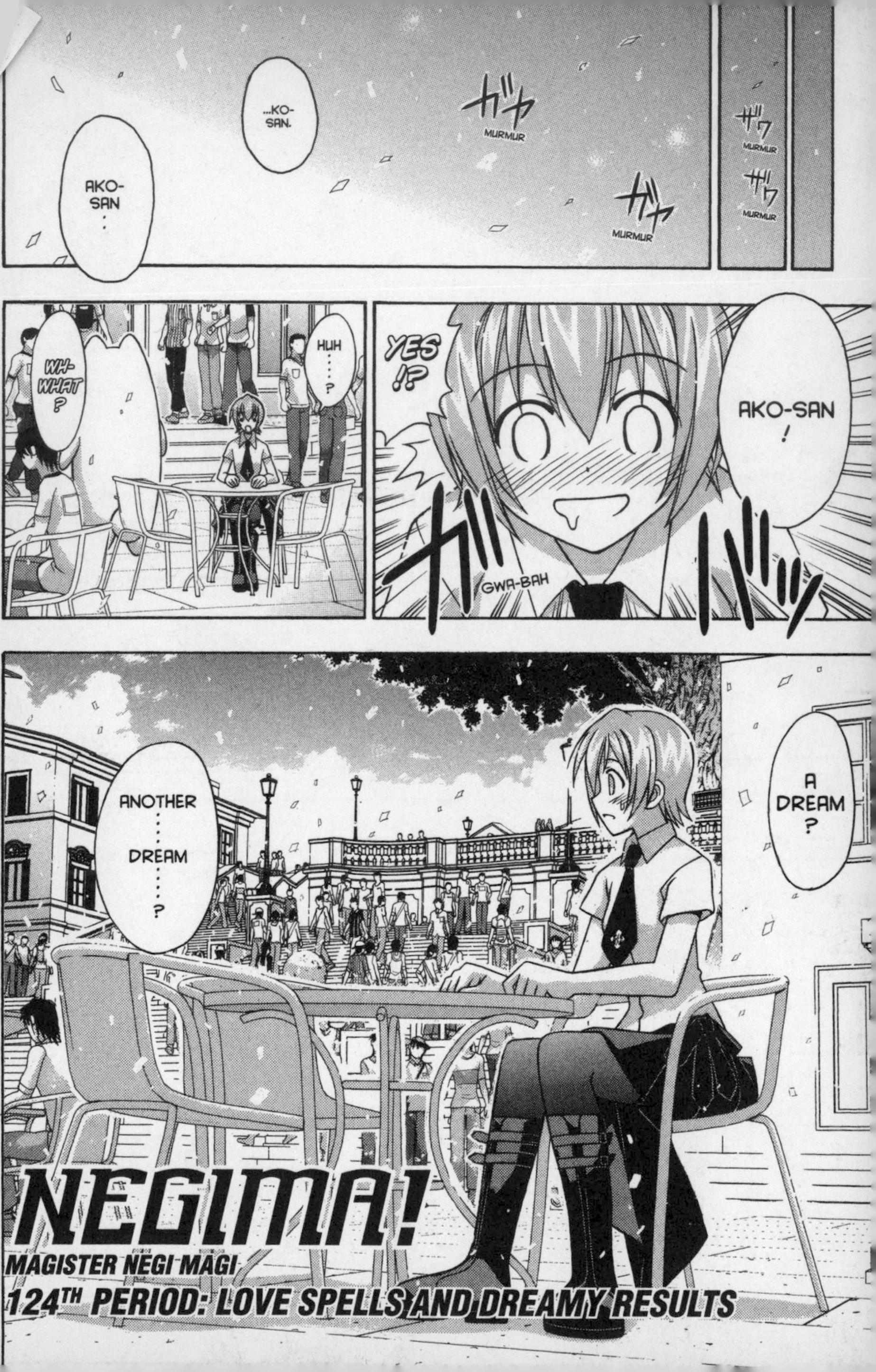

ザワ
MURMUR
ザワ
MURMUR
ガヤ
MURMUR
ガヤ
MURMUR
...KO-SAN.
AKO-SAN . . .
AKO-SAN !
YES !?
ガバッ
GWA-BAH
HUH . . . . ?
WH-WHAT ?
A DREAM ?
ANOTHER . . . . . . DREAM . . . . . . ?
NEGIMA!
MAGISTER NEGI MAGI
124TH PERIOD: LOVE SPELLS AND DREAMY RESULTS

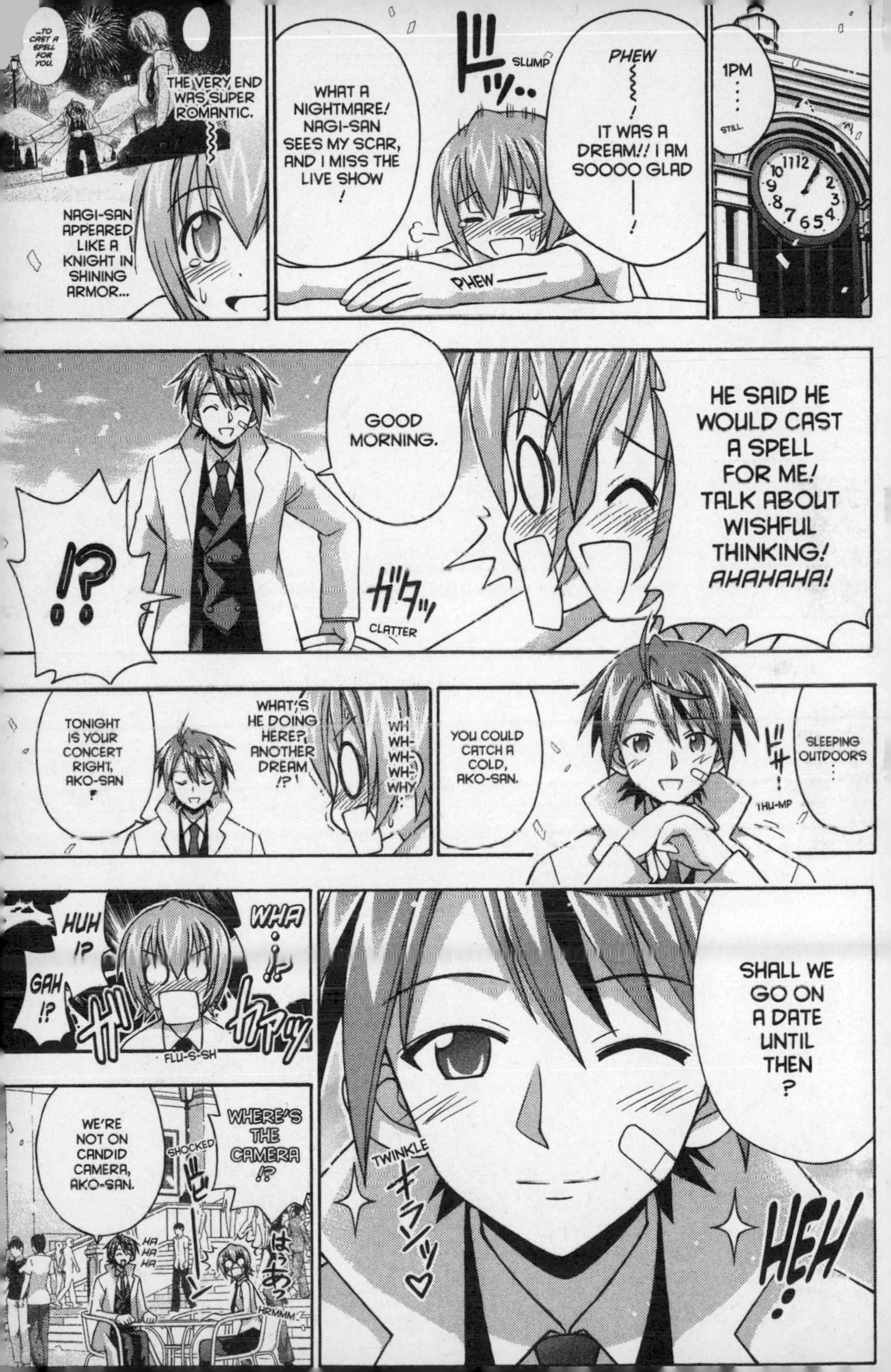
1PM
...
STILL.
PHEW
!
IT WAS A DREAM!! I AM SOOOO GLAD —!
SLUMP
WHAT A NIGHTMARE! NAGI-SAN SEES MY SCAR, AND I MISS THE LIVE SHOW!
PHEW
...TO CAST A SPELL FOR YOU.
THE VERY END WAS SUPER ROMANTIC.
NAGI-SAN APPEARED LIKE A KNIGHT IN SHINING ARMOR...
HE SAID HE WOULD CAST A SPELL FOR ME! TALK ABOUT WISHFUL THINKING! AHAHAHA!
GOOD MORNING.
CLATTER
!?
SLEEPING OUTDOORS...
THU-MP
YOU COULD CATCH A COLD, AKO-SAN.
WH WH- WH- WH- WHY...
WHAT'S HE DOING HERE? ANOTHER DREAM!?
TONIGHT IS YOUR CONCERT RIGHT, AKO-SAN?
SHALL WE GO ON A DATE UNTIL THEN?
TWINKLE
HEH!
WHA...!?
HUH!?
GAH!?
FLU-S-SH
WHERE'S THE CAMERA!?
SHOCKED
WE'RE NOT ON CANDID CAMERA, AKO-SAN.
HA HA HA
HRMMM

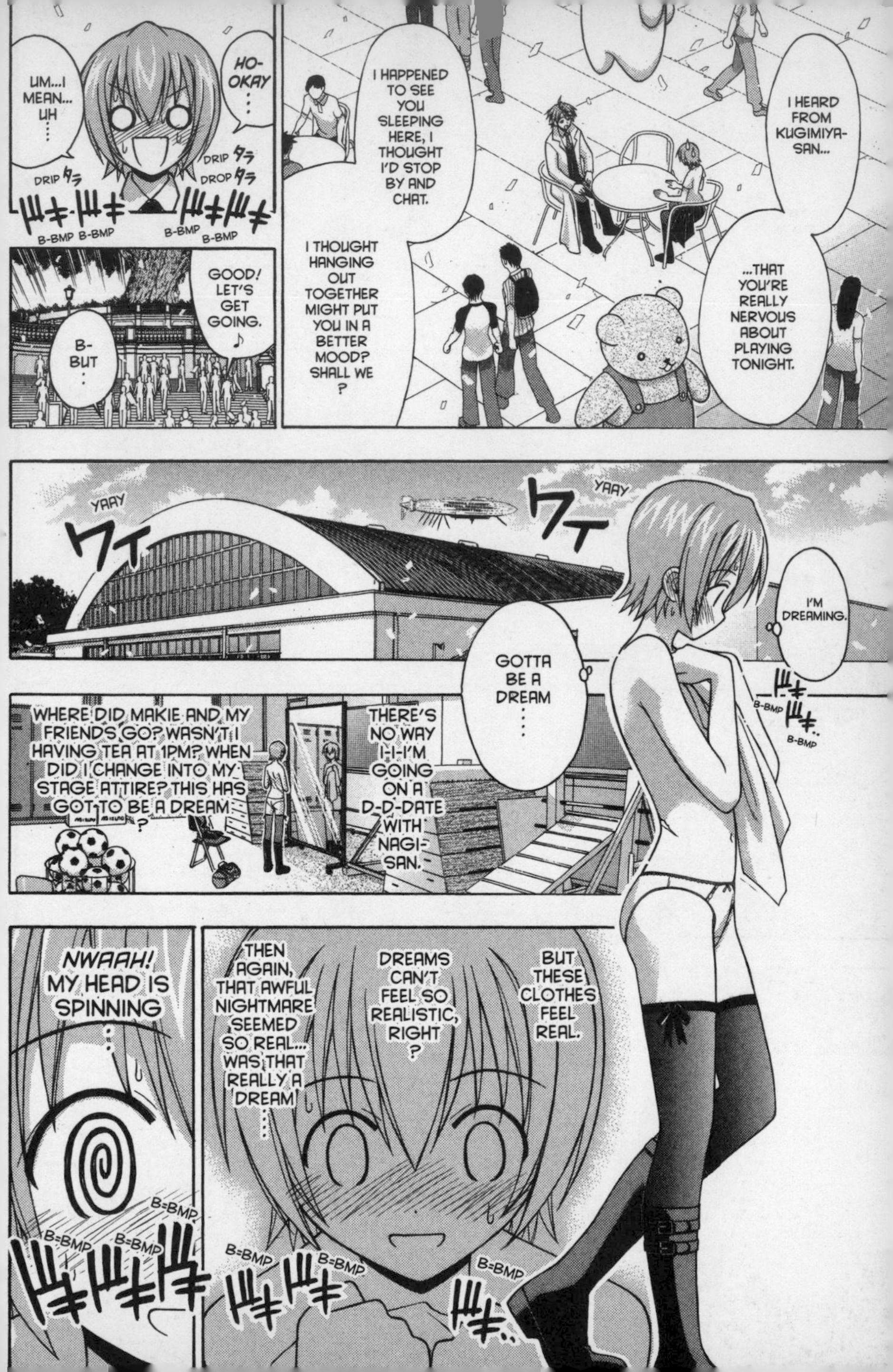
I HEARD FROM KUGIMIYA-SAN...
...THAT YOU'RE REALLY NERVOUS ABOUT PLAYING TONIGHT.
I HAPPENED TO SEE YOU SLEEPING HERE, I THOUGHT I'D STOP BY AND CHAT.
I THOUGHT HANGING OUT TOGETHER MIGHT PUT YOU IN A BETTER MOOD? SHALL WE ?
HO-OKAY ...
UM...I MEAN... UH ...
DRIP
DROP
DRIP
B-BMP B-BMP
B-BMP B-BMP
GOOD! LET'S GET GOING. ♪
B-BUT ...
YAAY
YAAY
I'M DREAMING.
GOTTA BE A DREAM ...
B-BMP
B-BMP
THERE'S NO WAY I-I-I'M GOING ON A D-D-DATE WITH NAGI-SAN.
WHERE DID MAKIE AND MY FRIENDS GO? WASN'T I HAVING TEA AT 1PM? WHEN DID I CHANGE INTO MY STAGE ATTIRE? THIS HAS GOT TO BE A DREAM ?
BUT THESE CLOTHES FEEL REAL.
DREAMS CAN'T FEEL SO REALISTIC, RIGHT ?
THEN AGAIN, THAT AWFUL NIGHTMARE SEEMED SO REAL... WAS THAT REALLY A DREAM ...
B=BMP
B=BMP
B=BMP
NWAAH! MY HEAD IS SPINNING ...
B=BMP
B=BMP
B=BMP

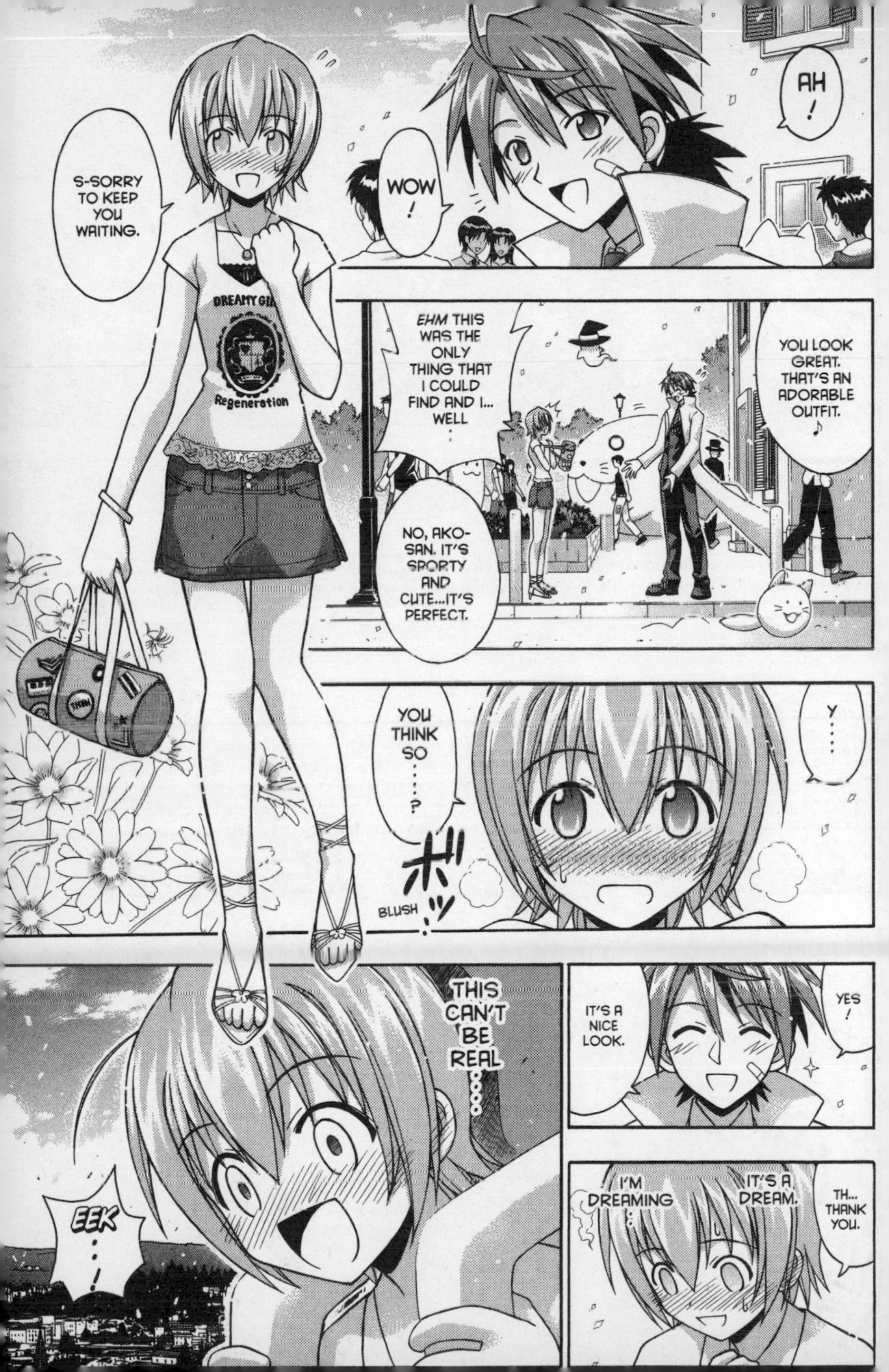
AH!
WOW!
YOU LOOK GREAT. THAT'S AN ADORABLE OUTFIT. ♪
EHM THIS WAS THE ONLY THING THAT I COULD FIND AND I... WELL
NO, AKO-SAN. IT'S SPORTY AND CUTE...IT'S PERFECT.
Y....
YOU THINK SO.....?
BLUSH
S-SORRY TO KEEP YOU WAITING.
Regeneration
YES!
IT'S A NICE LOOK.
TH... THANK YOU.
IT'S A DREAM.
I'M DREAMING...
THIS CAN'T BE REAL....
EEK...!

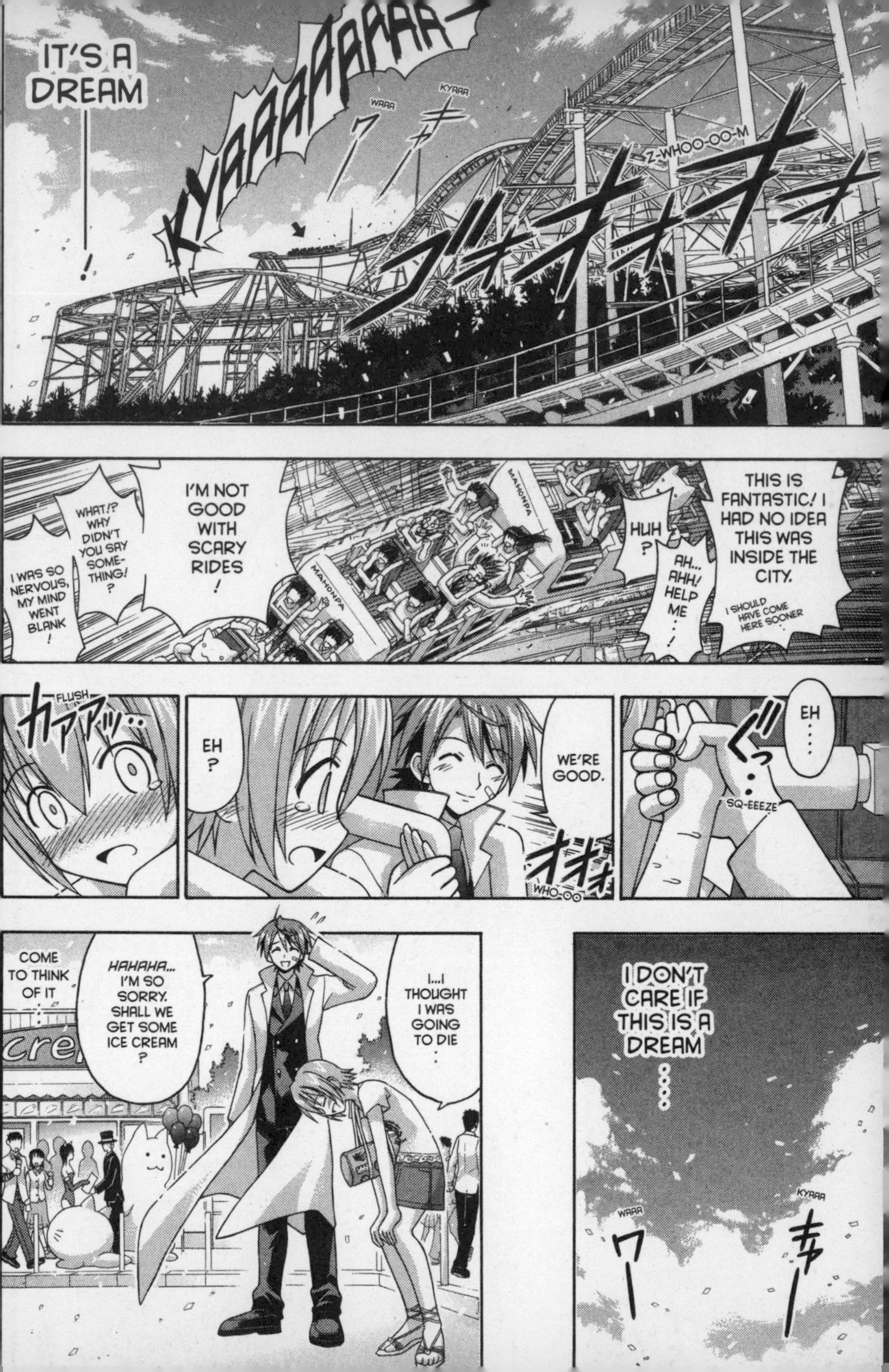

Z-WHOO-OO-M
KYAAA
WAAA
KYAAAAAAAAAA—
IT'S A DREAM —!
THIS IS FANTASTIC! I HAD NO IDEA THIS WAS INSIDE THE CITY.
I SHOULD HAVE COME HERE SOONER...
HUH?
AH... AHH! HELP ME...!
MAHONPA
I'M NOT GOOD WITH SCARY RIDES!
WHAT!? WHY DIDN'T YOU SAY SOME-THING!?
I WAS SO NERVOUS, MY MIND WENT BLANK!
EH.....
SQ-EEEZE
WE'RE GOOD.
EH?
WHO-OO
FLUSH
I DON'T CARE IF THIS IS A DREAM....
KYAAA
WAAA
I...I THOUGHT I WAS GOING TO DIE...
HAHAHA... I'M SO SORRY. SHALL WE GET SOME ICE CREAM?
COME TO THINK OF IT...

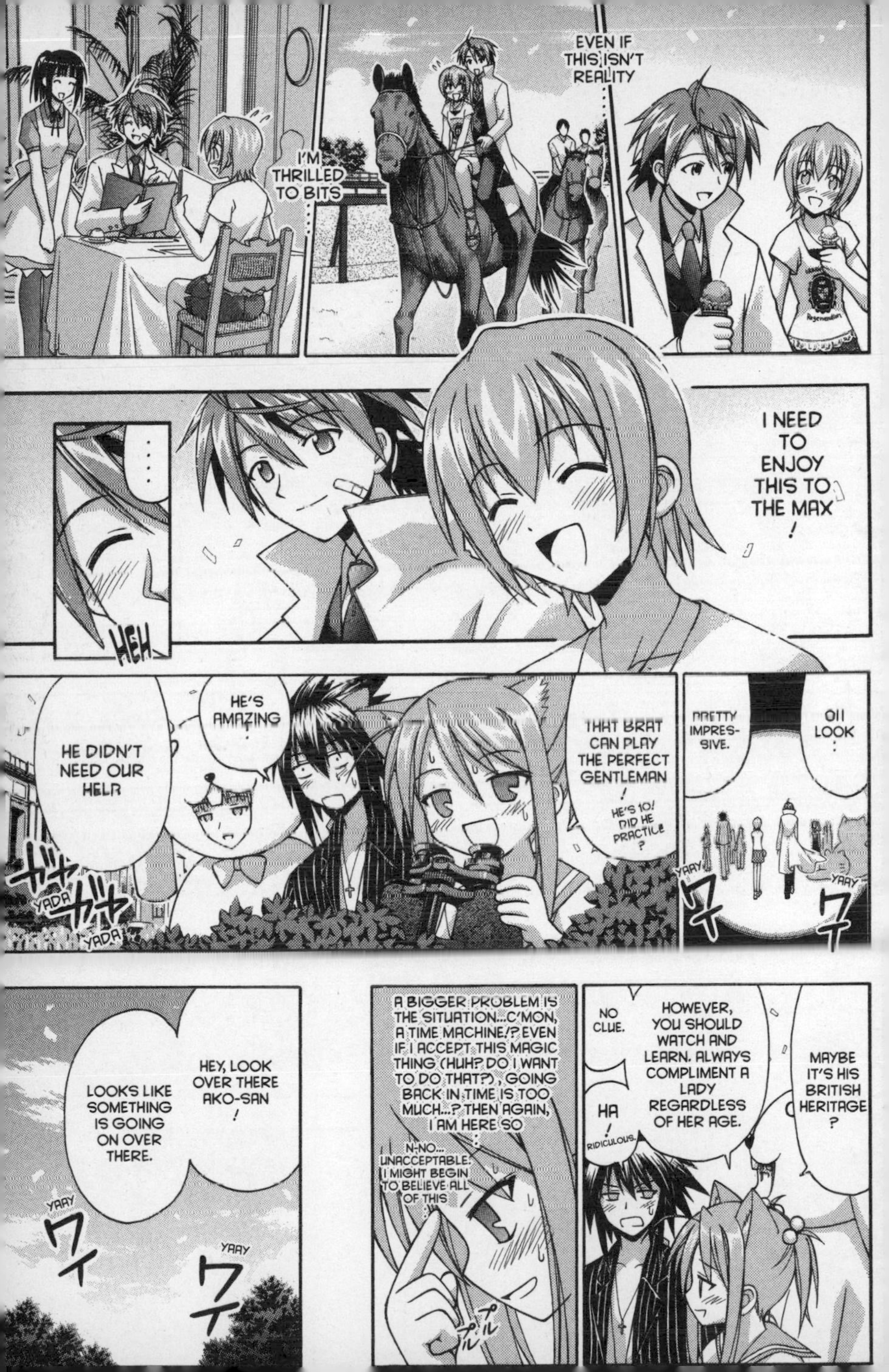
EVEN IF THIS ISN'T REALITY...
I'M THRILLED TO BITS...
I NEED TO ENJOY THIS TO THE MAX!
....
HEH
OI! LOOK:
PRETTY IMPRESSIVE.
YAAY ワイ
YAAY ワイ
THAT BRAT CAN PLAY THE PERFECT GENTLEMAN!
HE'S 10! DID HE PRACTICE?
HE'S AMAZING!
HE DIDN'T NEED OUR HELP
YADA ガヤ YADA ガヤ
MAYBE IT'S HIS BRITISH HERITAGE?
HOWEVER, YOU SHOULD WATCH AND LEARN. ALWAYS COMPLIMENT A LADY REGARDLESS OF HER AGE.
NO CLUE.
HA! RIDICULOUS.
A BIGGER PROBLEM IS THE SITUATION...C'MON, A TIME MACHINE!? EVEN IF I ACCEPT THIS MAGIC THING (HUH? DO I WANT TO DO THAT?), GOING BACK IN TIME IS TOO MUCH...? THEN AGAIN, I AM HERE SO...
N-NO... UNACCEPTABLE! I MIGHT BEGIN TO BELIEVE ALL OF THIS...
プルプル
HEY, LOOK OVER THERE AKO-SAN!
LOOKS LIKE SOMETHING IS GOING ON OVER THERE.
YAAY ワイ
YAAY ワイ

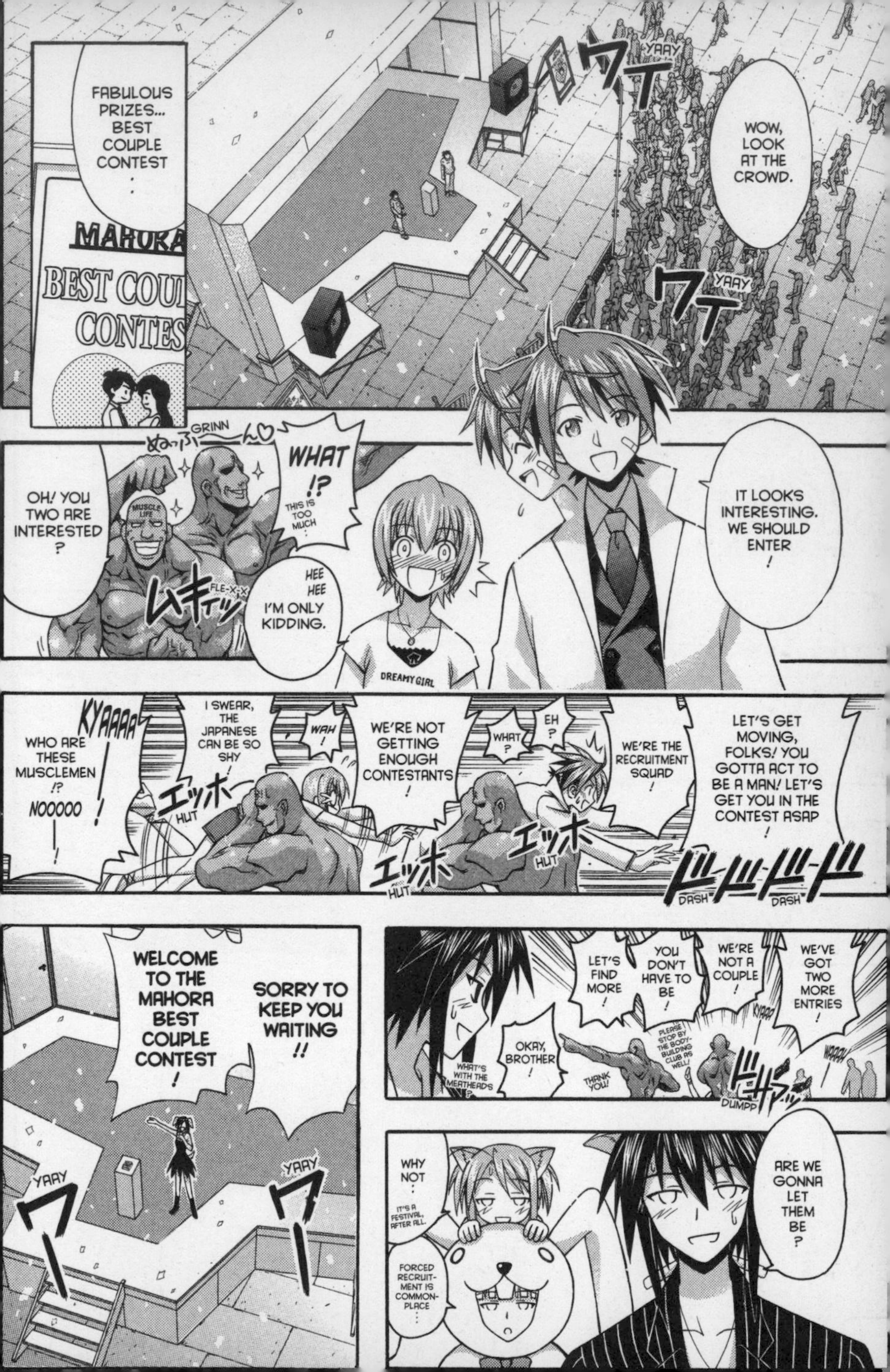
YAAY
WOW, LOOK AT THE CROWD.
YAAY
FABULOUS PRIZES... BEST COUPLE CONTEST...
MAHORA
BEST COUPLE CONTEST
IT LOOKS INTERESTING. WE SHOULD ENTER!
HEE HEE I'M ONLY KIDDING.
DREAMY GIRL
WHAT!? THIS IS TOO MUCH...
GRINN
OH! YOU TWO ARE INTERESTED?
MUSCLE LIFE
FLE-X-X
LET'S GET MOVING, FOLKS! YOU GOTTA ACT TO BE A MAN! LET'S GET YOU IN THE CONTEST ASAP!
DASH DASH
WE'RE THE RECRUITMENT SQUAD!
EH?
WHAT?
HUT
WE'RE NOT GETTING ENOUGH CONTESTANTS!
HUT
WAH!
I SWEAR, THE JAPANESE CAN BE SO SHY!
HUT
KYAAAA
WHO ARE THESE MUSCLEMEN!? NOOOOO!
WE'VE GOT TWO MORE ENTRIES!
WE'RE NOT A COUPLE!
YOU DON'T HAVE TO BE!
LET'S FIND MORE!
KYAAA
WAAAH
DUMPP
PLEASE STOP BY THE BODY-BUILDING CLUB AS WELL!
THANK YOU!
OKAY, BROTHER!
WHAT'S WITH THE MEATHEADS?
ARE WE GONNA LET THEM BE?
WHY NOT...
IT'S A FESTIVAL, AFTER ALL.
FORCED RECRUITMENT IS COMMONPLACE...
WELCOME TO THE MAHORA BEST COUPLE CONTEST!
SORRY TO KEEP YOU WAITING!!
YAAY
YAAY

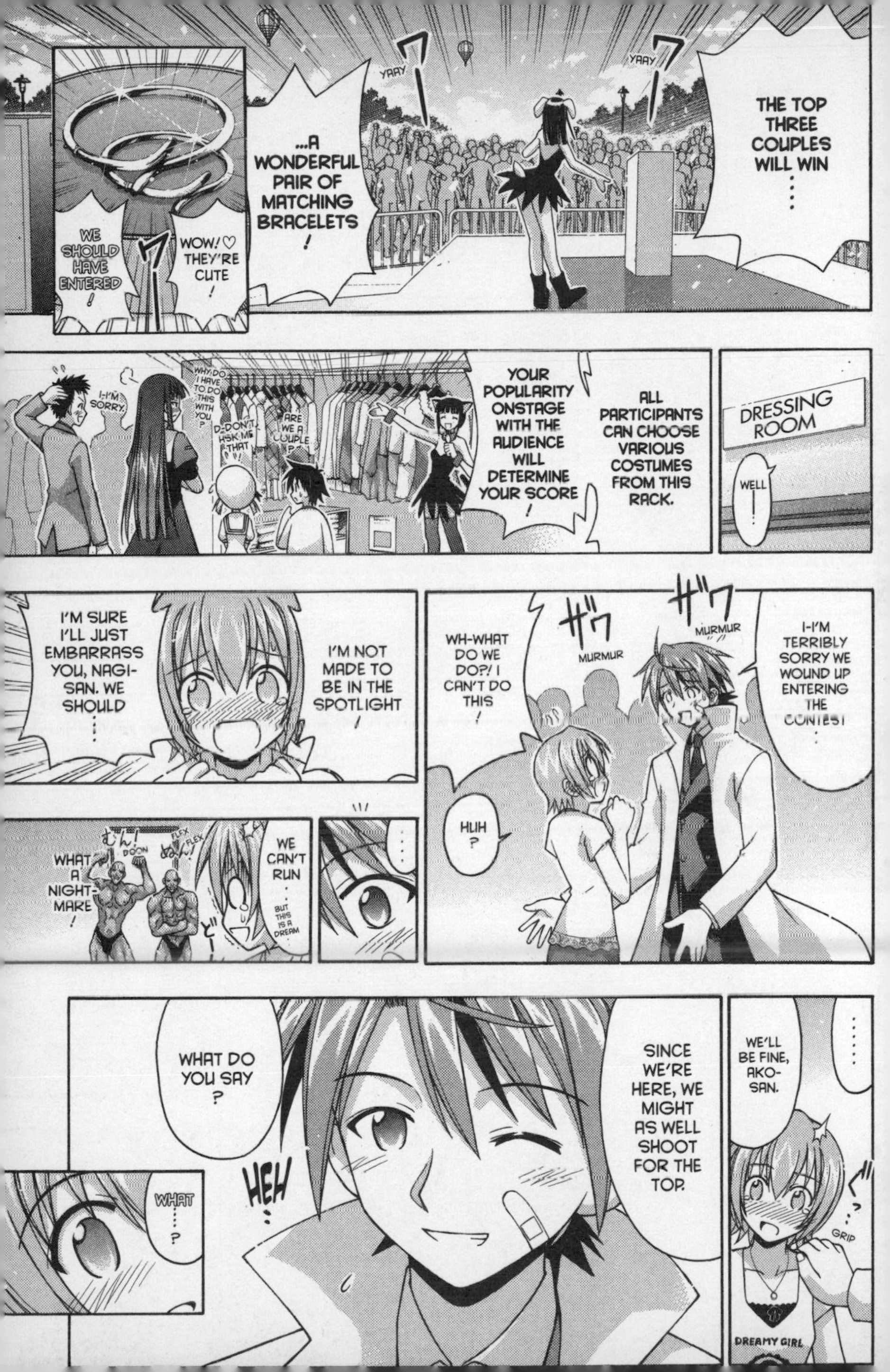
THE TOP THREE COUPLES WILL WIN....
YAAY
YAAY
...A WONDERFUL PAIR OF MATCHING BRACELETS!
WOW! ♡ THEY'RE CUTE!
WE SHOULD HAVE ENTERED!
DRESSING ROOM
WELL!
ALL PARTICIPANTS CAN CHOOSE VARIOUS COSTUMES FROM THIS RACK.
YOUR POPULARITY ONSTAGE WITH THE AUDIENCE WILL DETERMINE YOUR SCORE!
ARE WE A COUPLE?
D-DON'T ASK ME THAT!
WHY DO I HAVE TO DO THIS WITH YOU?
I-I'M SORRY.
I-I'M TERRIBLY SORRY WE WOUND UP ENTERING THE CONTEST...
ザワ MURMUR
ザワ MURMUR
WH-WHAT DO WE DO?! I CAN'T DO THIS!
HUH?
I'M NOT MADE TO BE IN THE SPOTLIGHT!
I'M SURE I'LL JUST EMBARRASS YOU, NAGI-SAN. WE SHOULD...
...
WE CAN'T RUN
BUT THIS IS A DREAM
むん! DOON
ぬん! FLEX FLEX
WHAT A NIGHTMARE!
......
WE'LL BE FINE, AKO-SAN.
?
GRIP
DREAMY GIRL
SINCE WE'RE HERE, WE MIGHT AS WELL SHOOT FOR THE TOP.
WHAT DO YOU SAY?
HEH
WHAT...?

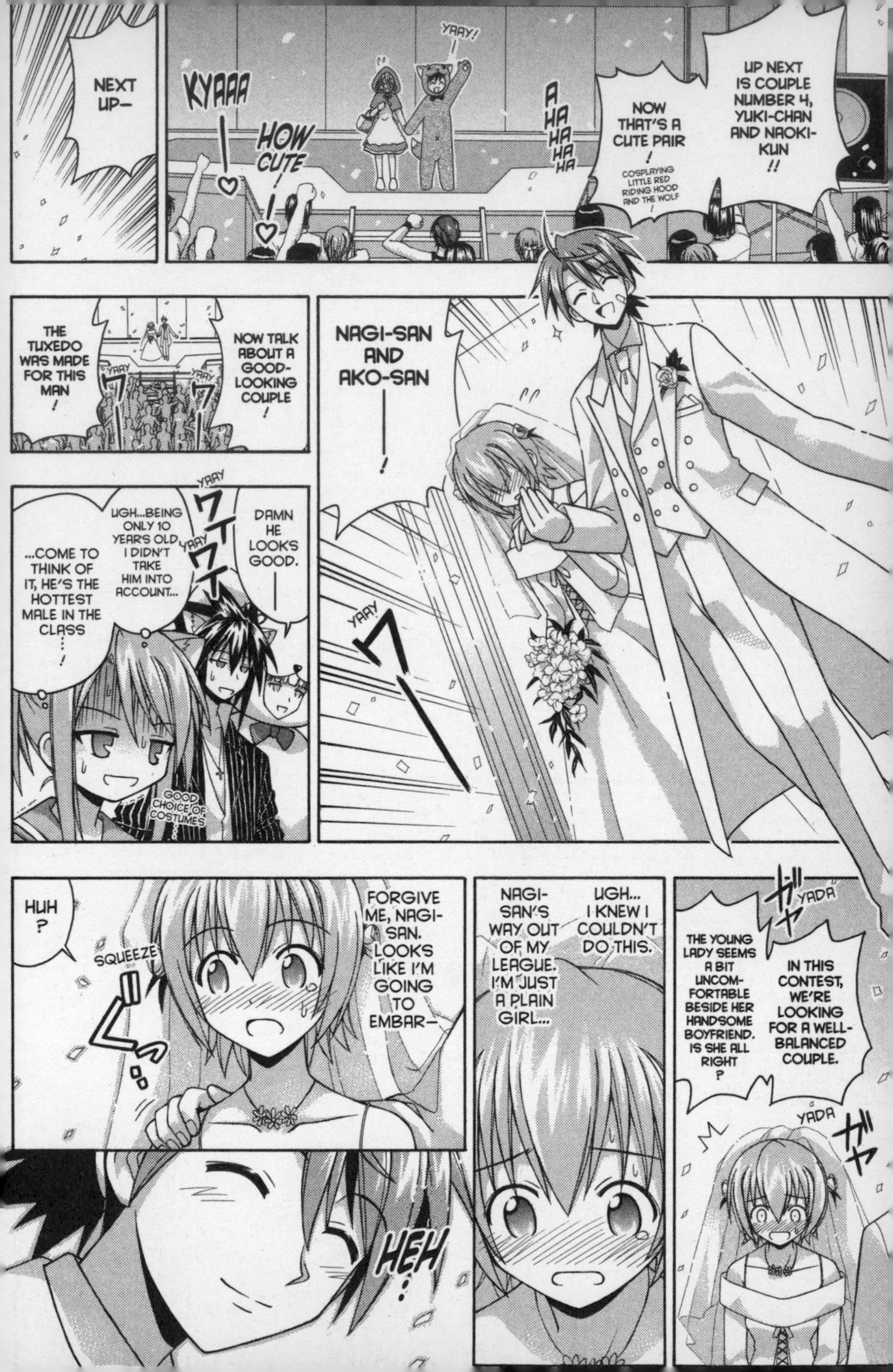
UP NEXT IS COUPLE NUMBER 4, YUKI-CHAN AND NAOKI-KUN!!
NOW THAT'S A CUTE PAIR!
COSPLAYING LITTLE RED RIDING HOOD AND THE WOLF!
A HA HA HA HA HA
YAAY!
KYAAA—♡
HOW CUTE!—♡
NEXT UP—
NAGI-SAN AND AKO-SAN—!
YAAY
NOW TALK ABOUT A GOOD-LOOKING COUPLE!
THE TUXEDO WAS MADE FOR THIS MAN!
YAAY
YAAY
DAMN HE LOOKS GOOD.—
YAAY
YAAY
UGH...BEING ONLY 10 YEAR'S OLD, I DIDN'T TAKE HIM INTO ACCOUNT...
...COME TO THINK OF IT, HE'S THE HOTTEST MALE IN THE CLASS...!
GOOD CHOICE OF COSTUMES
YADA
IN THIS CONTEST, WE'RE LOOKING FOR A WELL-BALANCED COUPLE.
THE YOUNG LADY SEEMS A BIT UNCOMFORTABLE BESIDE HER HANDSOME BOYFRIEND. IS SHE ALL RIGHT?
YADA
UGH... I KNEW I COULDN'T DO THIS.
NAGI-SAN'S WAY OUT OF MY LEAGUE. I'M JUST A PLAIN GIRL...
FORGIVE ME, NAGI-SAN. LOOKS LIKE I'M GOING TO EMBAR—
HUH?
SQUEEZE
HEH...

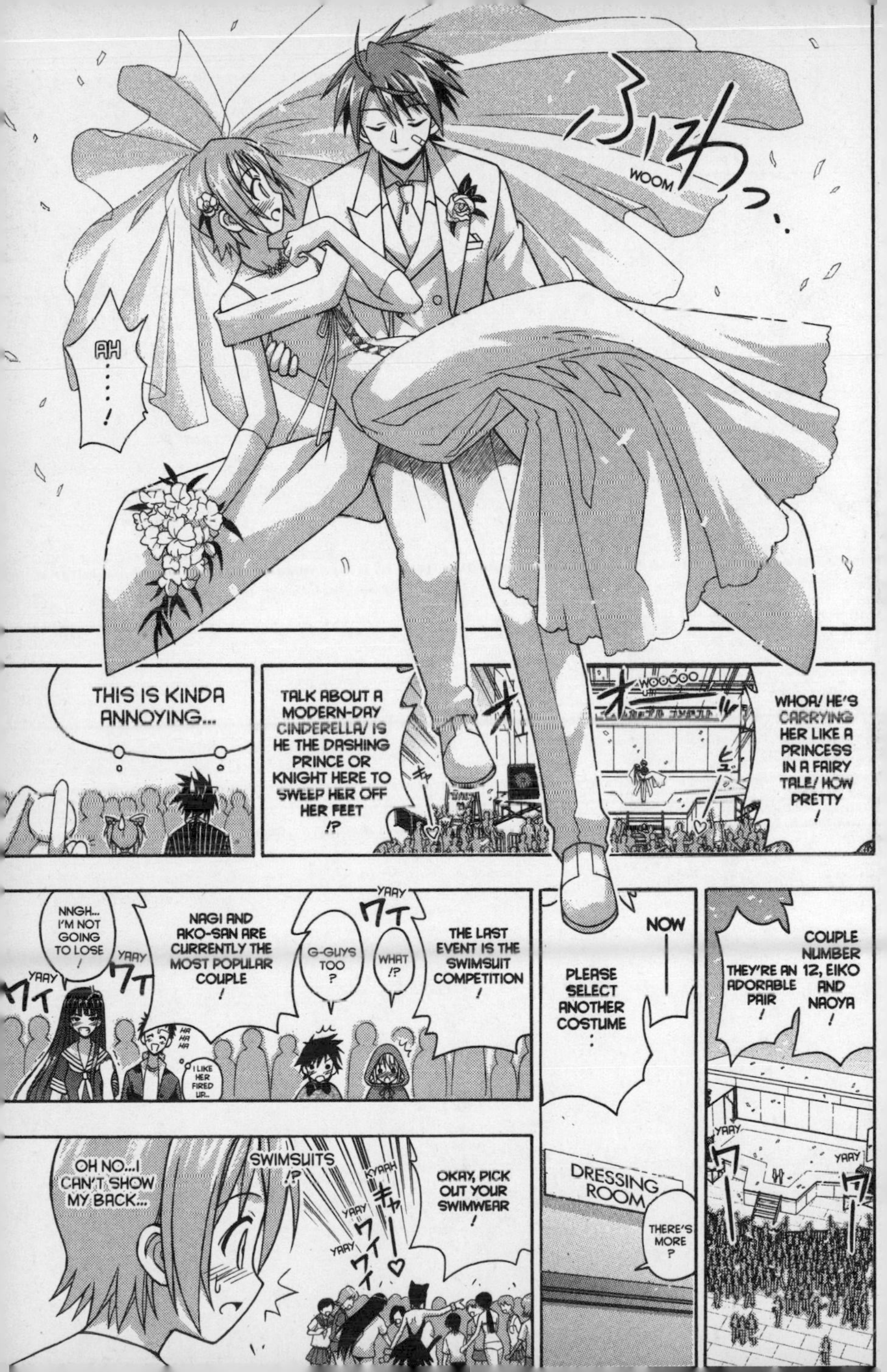
ふわっ
WOOM
AH.....!
WHOA! HE'S CARRYING HER LIKE A PRINCESS IN A FAIRY TALE! HOW PRETTY!
WOOOOO
TALK ABOUT A MODERN-DAY CINDERELLA! IS HE THE DASHING PRINCE OR KNIGHT HERE TO SWEEP HER OFF HER FEET!?
THIS IS KINDA ANNOYING...
COUPLE NUMBER 12, EIKO AND NAOYA!
THEY'RE AN ADORABLE PAIR!
YAAY
YAAY
NOW—
PLEASE SELECT ANOTHER COSTUME...
DRESSING ROOM
THERE'S MORE?
THE LAST EVENT IS THE SWIMSUIT COMPETITION!
WHAT!?
G-GUYS TOO?
YAAY
NAGI AND AKO-SAN ARE CURRENTLY THE MOST POPULAR COUPLE!
YAAY
YAAY
NNGH... I'M NOT GOING TO LOSE!
HA HA HA
I LIKE HER FIRED UP..
OKAY, PICK OUT YOUR SWIMWEAR!
KYAAH
YAAY
YAAY
SWIMSUITS!?
OH NO...I CAN'T SHOW MY BACK...

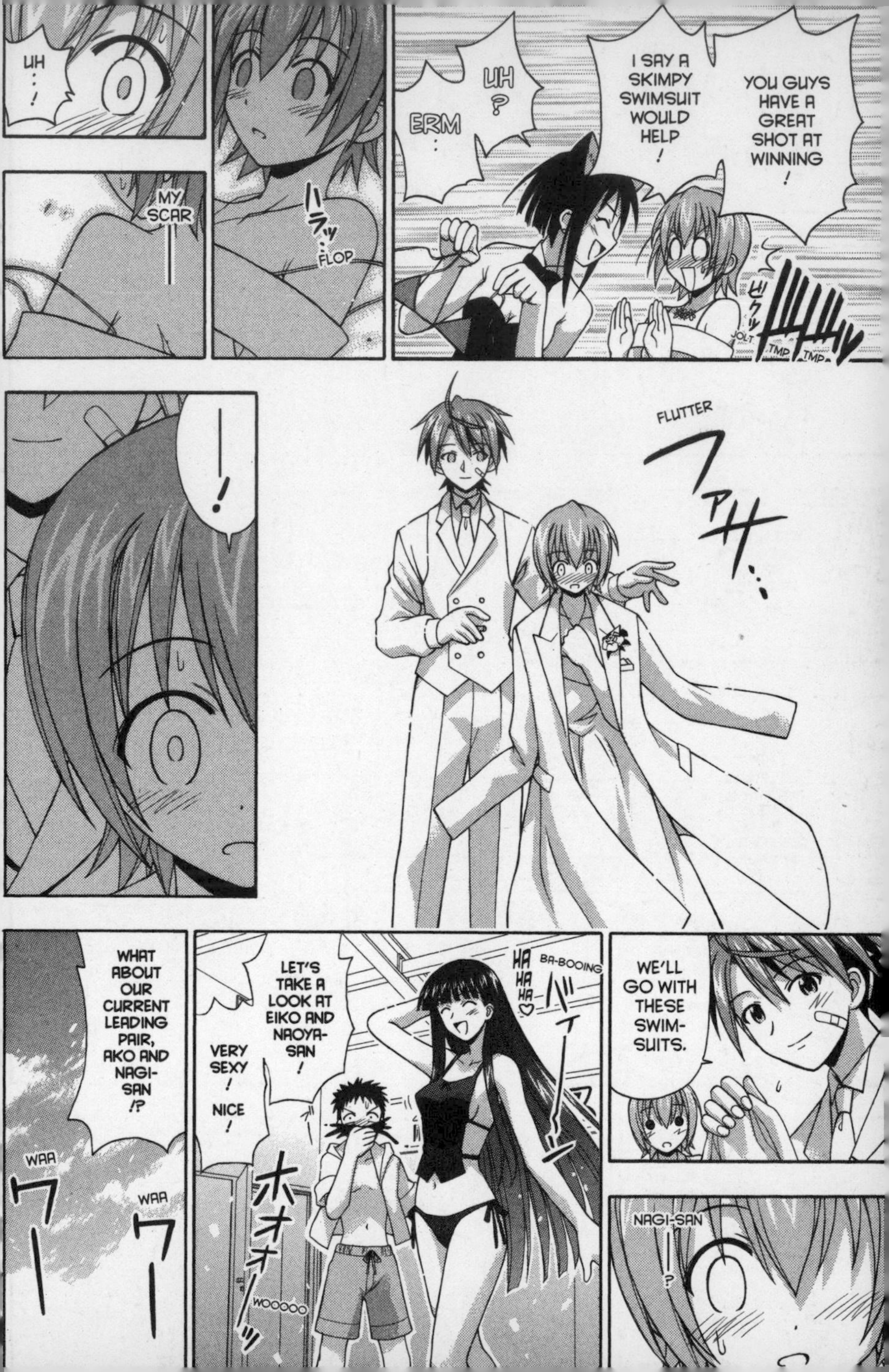
YOU GUYS HAVE A GREAT SHOT AT WINNING!
I SAY A SKIMPY SWIMSUIT WOULD HELP!
UH?
ERM...
JOLT
TMP TMP
FLOP
UH...!
MY SCAR—
FLUTTER
!
WE'LL GO WITH THESE SWIM-SUITS.
NAGI-SAN—?
HA HA HA ♡
BA-BOOING
LET'S TAKE A LOOK AT EIKO AND NAOYA-SAN!
VERY SEXY!
NICE!
WOOOOO
WHAT ABOUT OUR CURRENT LEADING PAIR, AKO AND NAGI-SAN!?
WAA
WAA

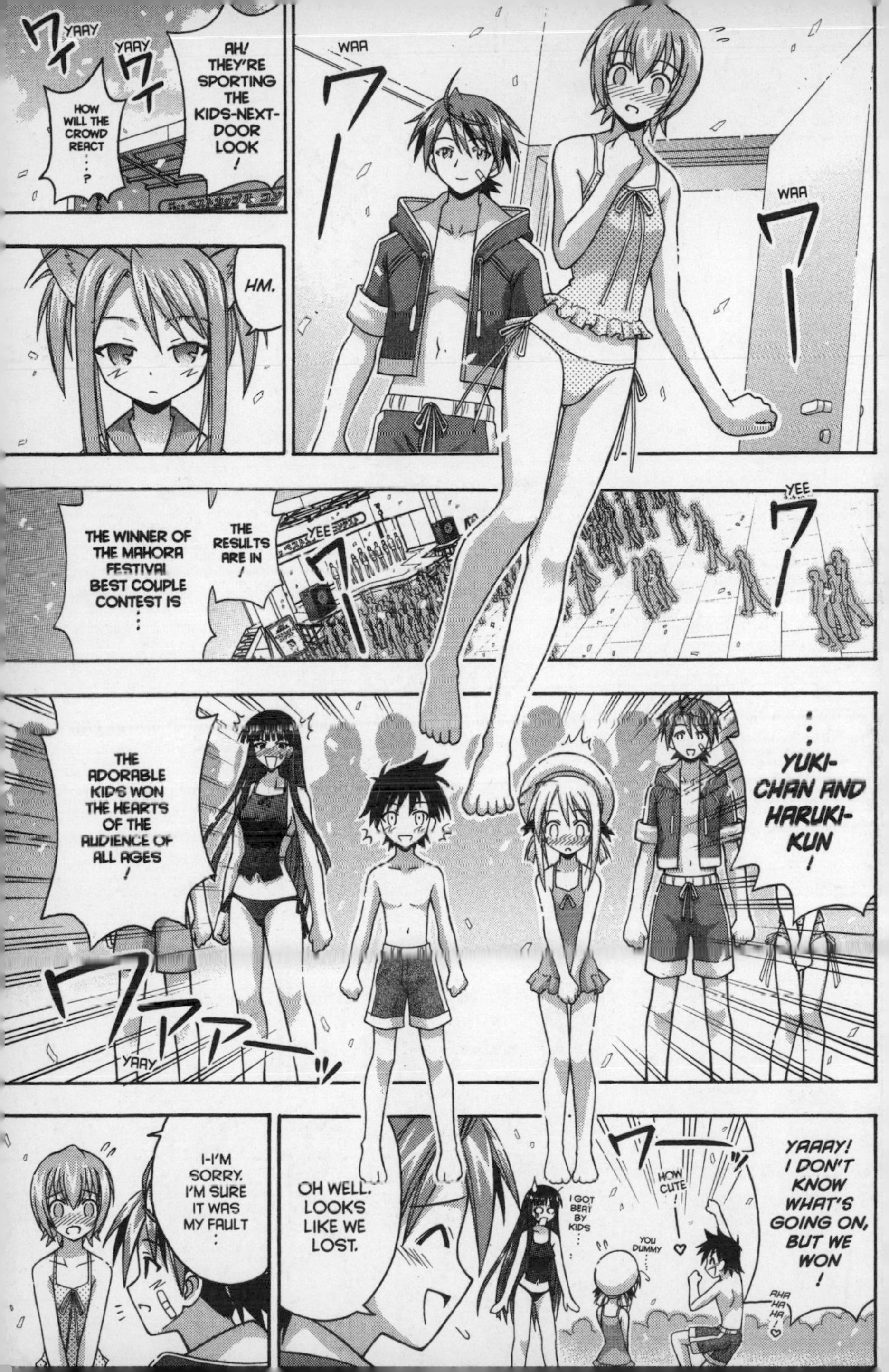
WAA
WAA
YAAY
YAAY
AH! THEY'RE SPORTING THE KIDS-NEXT-DOOR LOOK!
HOW WILL THE CROWD REACT...?
HM.
YEE
THE RESULTS ARE IN!
THE WINNER OF THE MAHORA FESTIVAL BEST COUPLE CONTEST IS...
YEE
...YUKI-CHAN AND HARUKI-KUN!
THE ADORABLE KIDS WON THE HEARTS OF THE AUDIENCE OF ALL AGES!
YAAY
YAAAY! I DON'T KNOW WHAT'S GOING ON, BUT WE WON!
AHA HA HA!
HOW CUTE!
YOU DUMMY...
I GOT BEAT BY KIDS...
OH WELL. LOOKS LIKE WE LOST.
I-I'M SORRY. I'M SURE IT WAS MY FAULT...

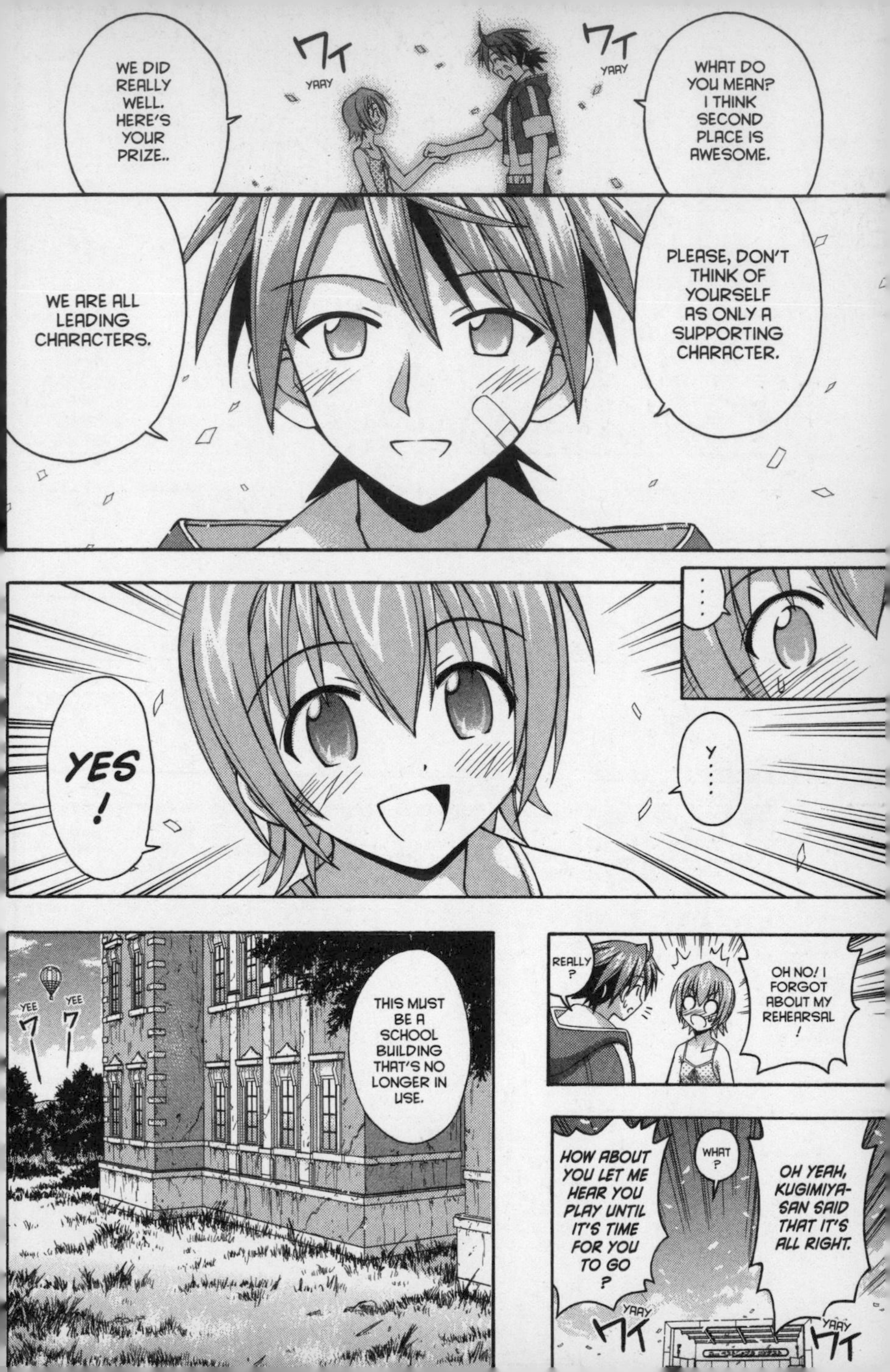
YAAY
WHAT DO YOU MEAN? I THINK SECOND PLACE IS AWESOME.
YAAY
WE DID REALLY WELL. HERE'S YOUR PRIZE..
PLEASE, DON'T THINK OF YOURSELF AS ONLY A SUPPORTING CHARACTER.
WE ARE ALL LEADING CHARACTERS.
....
Y....
YES!
OH NO! I FORGOT ABOUT MY REHEARSAL!
REALLY?
OH YEAH, KUGIMIYA-SAN SAID THAT IT'S ALL RIGHT.
WHAT?
HOW ABOUT YOU LET ME HEAR YOU PLAY UNTIL IT'S TIME FOR YOU TO GO?
YAAY
YAAY
YEE
YEE
THIS MUST BE A SCHOOL BUILDING THAT'S NO LONGER IN USE.

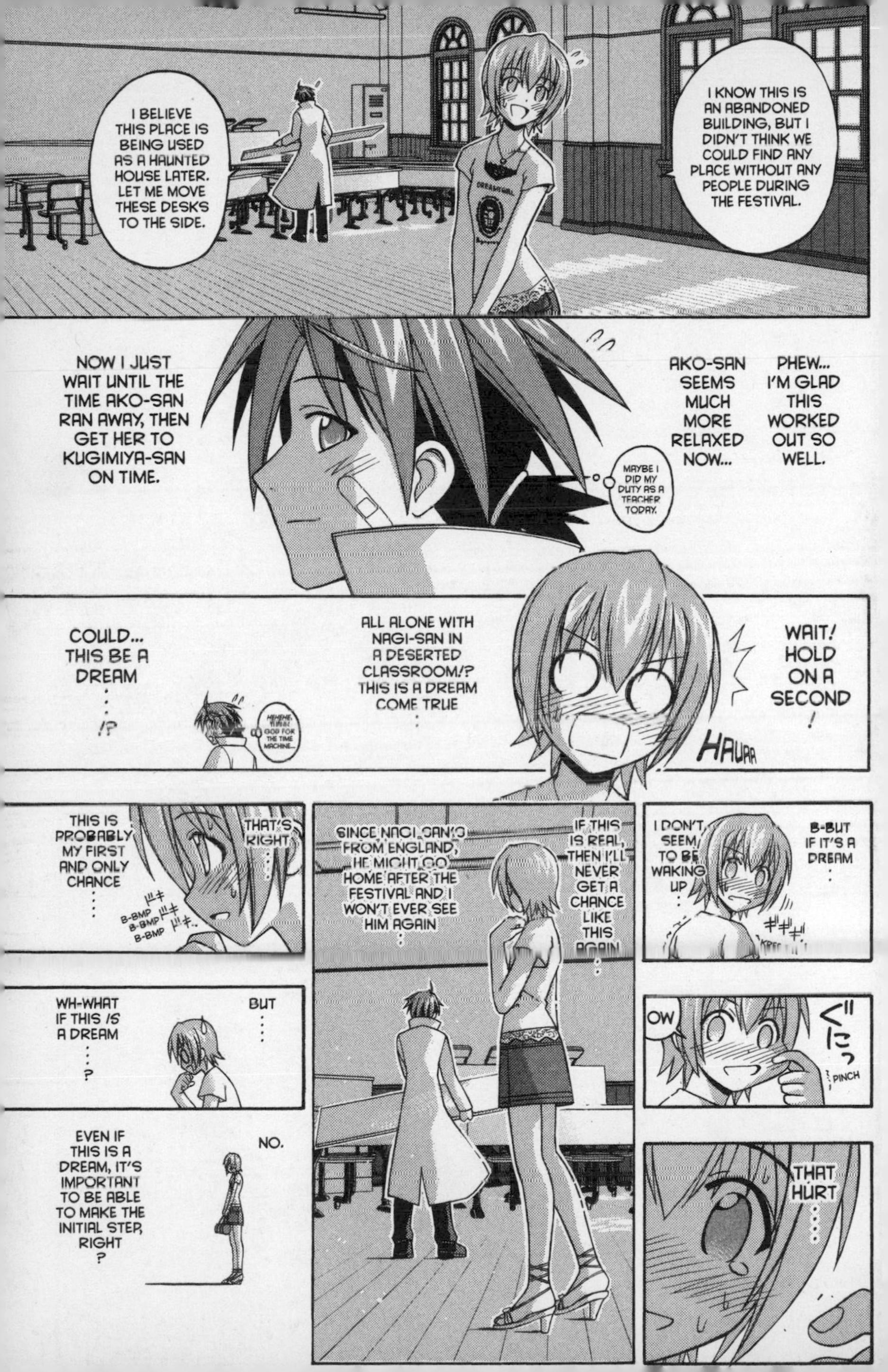
I KNOW THIS IS AN ABANDONED BUILDING, BUT I DIDN'T THINK WE COULD FIND ANY PLACE WITHOUT ANY PEOPLE DURING THE FESTIVAL.
I BELIEVE THIS PLACE IS BEING USED AS A HAUNTED HOUSE LATER. LET ME MOVE THESE DESKS TO THE SIDE.
PHEW... I'M GLAD THIS WORKED OUT SO WELL.
AKO-SAN SEEMS MUCH MORE RELAXED NOW...
MAYBE I DID MY DUTY AS A TEACHER TODAY.
NOW I JUST WAIT UNTIL THE TIME AKO-SAN RAN AWAY, THEN GET HER TO KUGIMIYA-SAN ON TIME.
WAIT! HOLD ON A SECOND!
HAURA
ALL ALONE WITH NAGI-SAN IN A DESERTED CLASSROOM!? THIS IS A DREAM COME TRUE...
HEHEHE, THANK GOD FOR THE TIME MACHINE...
COULD... THIS BE A DREAM...!?
B-BUT IF IT'S A DREAM...
I DON'T SEEM TO BE WAKING UP...
ギギギ
ぐにっ
PINCH
OW
THAT HURT....
IF THIS IS REAL, THEN I'LL NEVER GET A CHANCE LIKE THIS AGAIN...
SINCE NAGI-SAN'S FROM ENGLAND, HE MIGHT GO HOME AFTER THE FESTIVAL AND I WON'T EVER SEE HIM AGAIN...
THAT'S RIGHT...
THIS IS PROBABLY MY FIRST AND ONLY CHANCE...
ドキ ドキ ドキ
B-BMP B-BMP B-BMP
BUT...
WH-WHAT IF THIS IS A DREAM...?
NO.
EVEN IF THIS IS A DREAM, IT'S IMPORTANT TO BE ABLE TO MAKE THE INITIAL STEP, RIGHT?

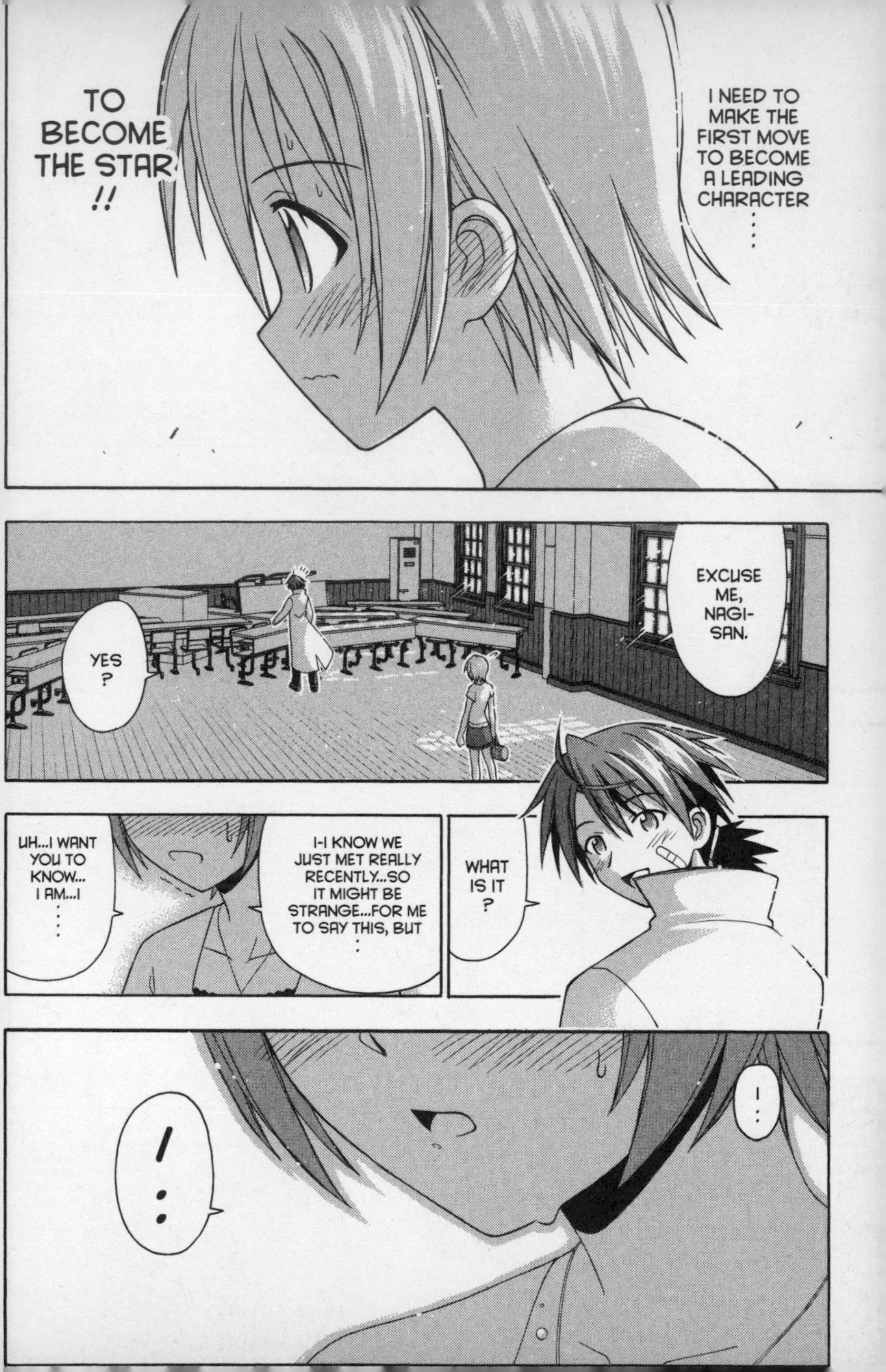
I NEED TO MAKE THE FIRST MOVE TO BECOME A LEADING CHARACTER...
TO BECOME THE STAR!!
EXCUSE ME, NAGI-SAN.
YES?
WHAT IS IT?
I-I KNOW WE JUST MET REALLY RECENTLY...SO IT MIGHT BE STRANGE...FOR ME TO SAY THIS, BUT..
UH...I WANT YOU TO KNOW... I AM...I...
I..
!..

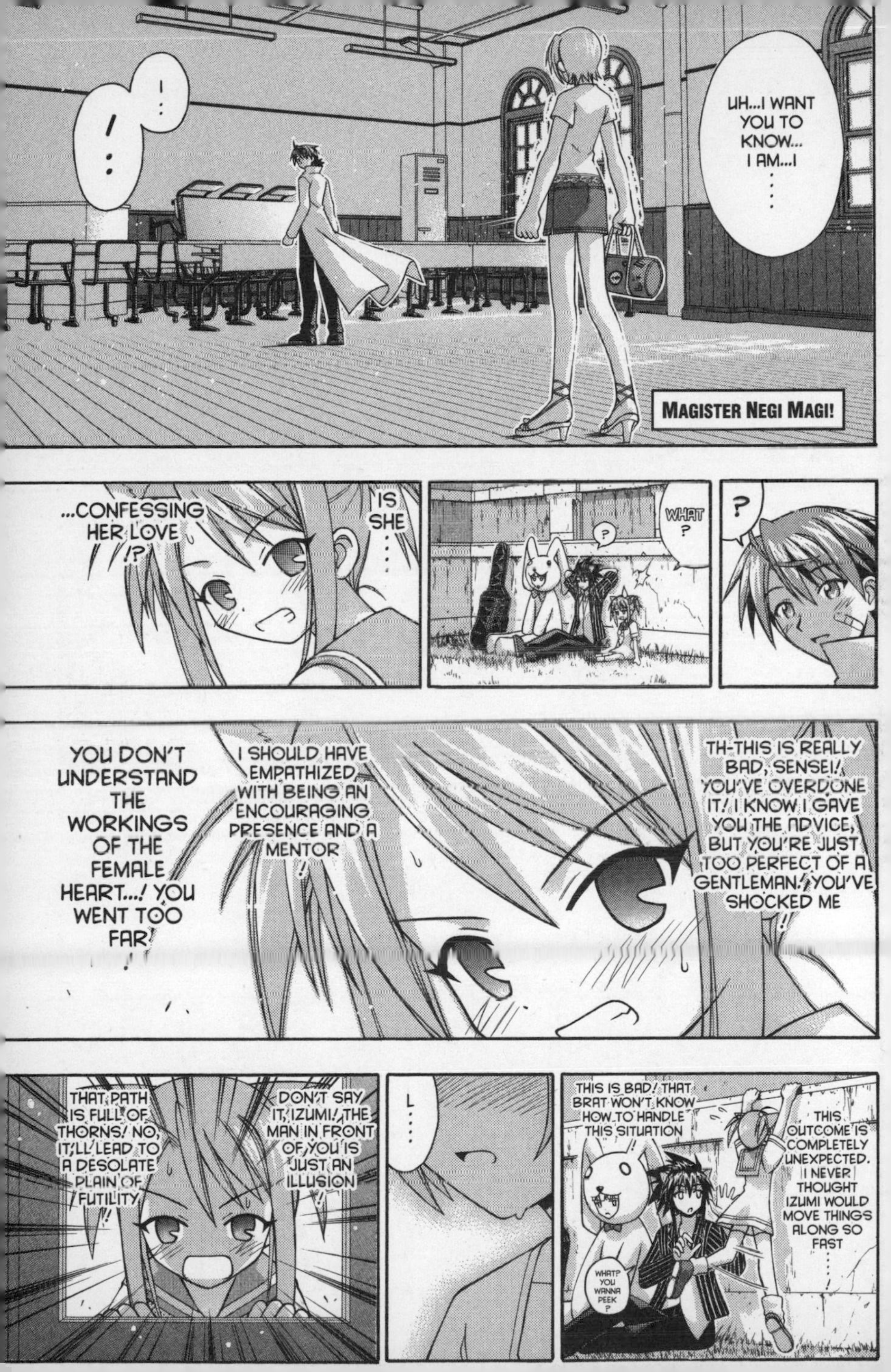
UH...I WANT YOU TO KNOW... I AM...I ......
I...!...
MAGISTER NEGI MAGI!
?
WHAT?
?
IS SHE....
...CONFESSING HER LOVE!?
TH-THIS IS REALLY BAD, SENSEI! YOU'VE OVERDONE IT! I KNOW I GAVE YOU THE ADVICE, BUT YOU'RE JUST TOO PERFECT OF A GENTLEMAN! YOU'VE SHOCKED ME!
I SHOULD HAVE EMPATHIZED WITH BEING AN ENCOURAGING PRESENCE AND A MENTOR!
YOU DON'T UNDERSTAND THE WORKINGS OF THE FEMALE HEART...! YOU WENT TOO FAR!
THIS OUTCOME IS COMPLETELY UNEXPECTED. I NEVER THOUGHT IZUMI WOULD MOVE THINGS ALONG SO FAST....
THIS IS BAD! THAT BRAT WON'T KNOW HOW TO HANDLE THIS SITUATION
WHAT? YOU WANNA PEEK?
L....
DON'T SAY IT, IZUMI! THE MAN IN FRONT OF YOU IS JUST AN ILLUSION!
THAT PATH IS FULL OF THORNS! NO, IT'LL LEAD TO A DESOLATE PLAIN OF FUTILITY!

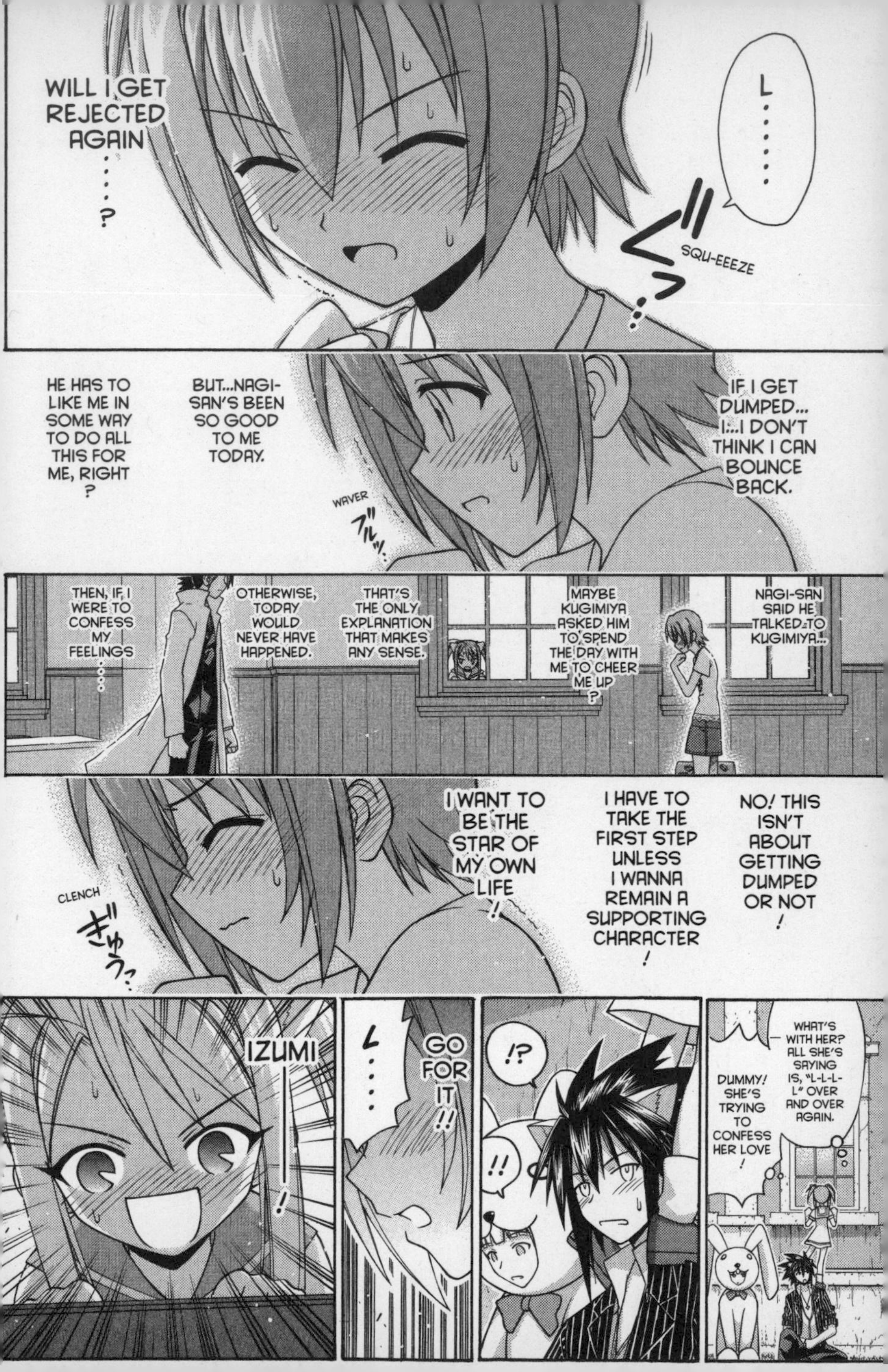
L......
SQU-EEZE
WILL I GET REJECTED AGAIN...?
IF I GET DUMPED... I...I DON'T THINK I CAN BOUNCE BACK.
BUT...NAGI-SAN'S BEEN SO GOOD TO ME TODAY.
HE HAS TO LIKE ME IN SOME WAY TO DO ALL THIS FOR ME, RIGHT?
WAVER
NAGI-SAN SAID HE TALKED TO KUGIMIYA...
MAYBE KUGIMIYA ASKED HIM TO SPEND THE DAY WITH ME TO CHEER ME UP?
THAT'S THE ONLY EXPLANATION THAT MAKES ANY SENSE.
OTHERWISE, TODAY WOULD NEVER HAVE HAPPENED.
THEN, IF I WERE TO CONFESS MY FEELINGS.....
NO! THIS ISN'T ABOUT GETTING DUMPED OR NOT!
I HAVE TO TAKE THE FIRST STEP UNLESS I WANNA REMAIN A SUPPORTING CHARACTER!
I WANT TO BE THE STAR OF MY OWN LIFE!
CLENCH
WHAT'S WITH HER? ALL SHE'S SAYING IS, "L-L-L-L" OVER AND OVER AGAIN.
DUMMY! SHE'S TRYING TO CONFESS HER LOVE!
!?
!!
GO FOR IT!!
L....
IZUMI—!

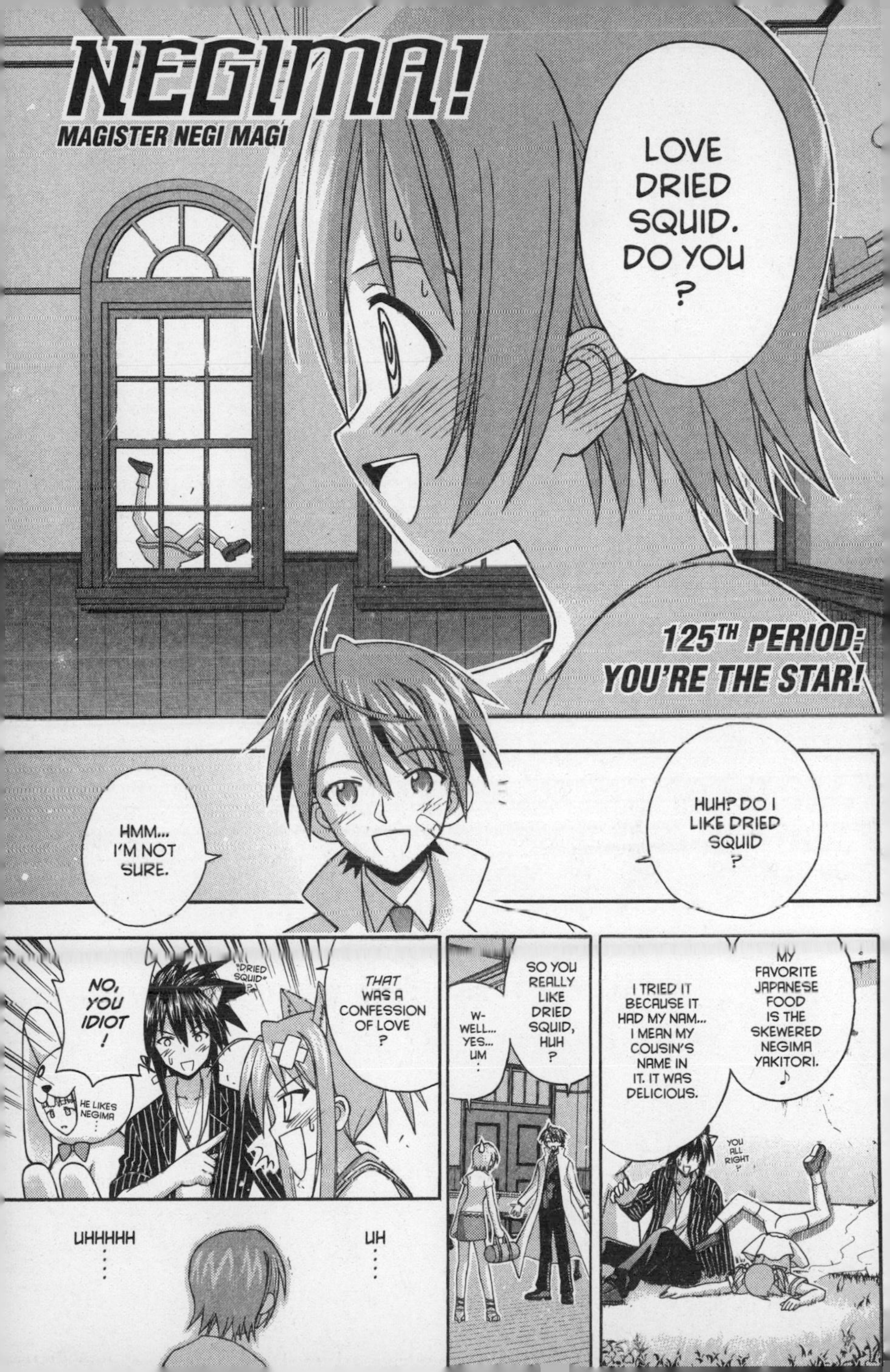
NEGIMA!
MAGISTER NEGI MAGI
LOVE DRIED SQUID. DO YOU ?
125TH PERIOD: YOU'RE THE STAR!
HUH? DO I LIKE DRIED SQUID ?
HMM... I'M NOT SURE.
MY FAVORITE JAPANESE FOOD IS THE SKEWERED NEGIMA YAKITORI. ♪
I TRIED IT BECAUSE IT HAD MY NAM... I MEAN MY COUSIN'S NAME IN IT. IT WAS DELICIOUS.
YOU ALL RIGHT ?
SO YOU REALLY LIKE DRIED SQUID, HUH ?
W-WELL... YES... UM ...
THAT WAS A CONFESSION OF LOVE ?
"DRIED SQUID" ?
NO, YOU IDIOT !
HE LIKES NEGIMA ...
UH ...
UHHHHH ...

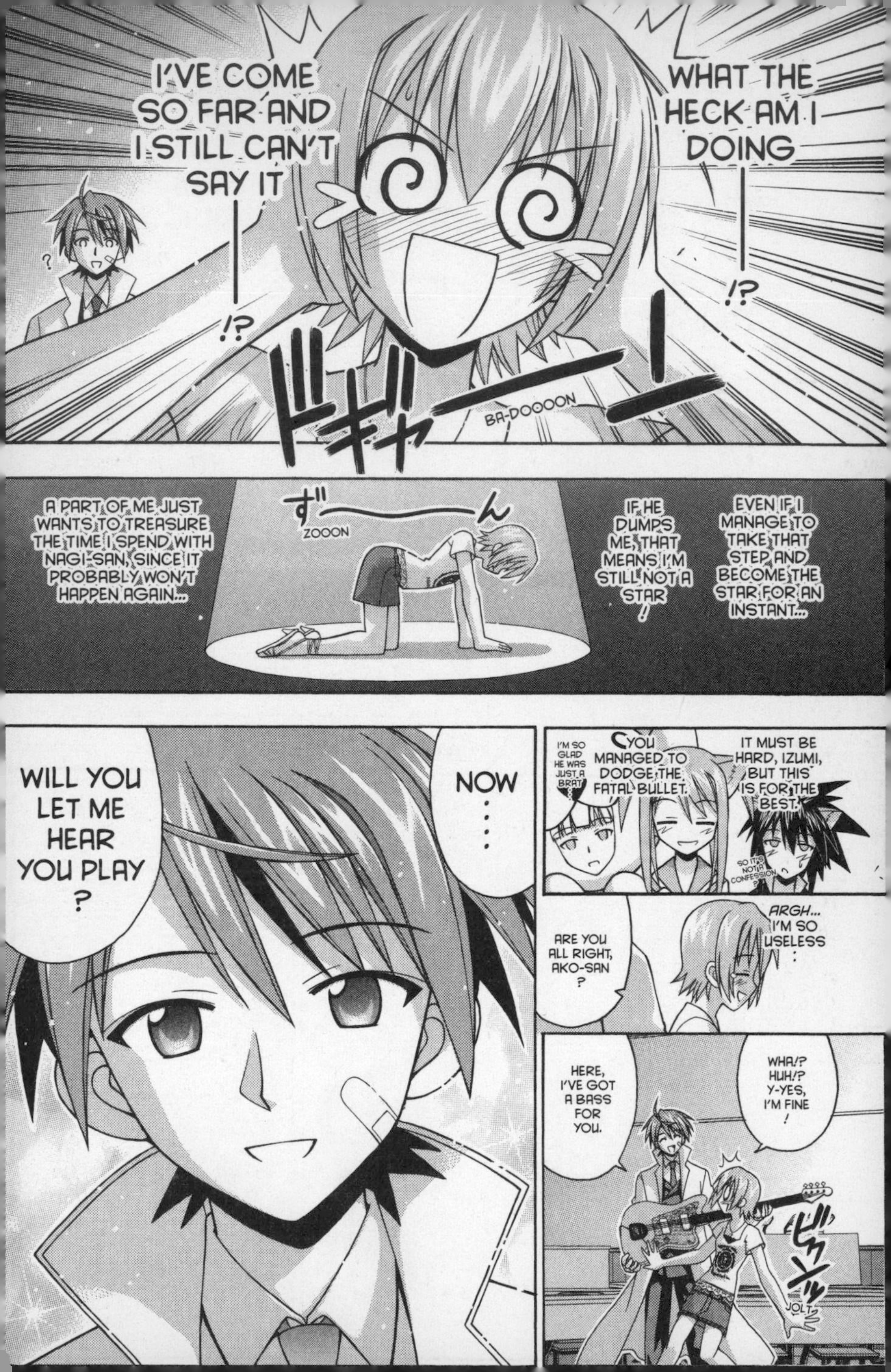
WHAT THE HECK AM I DOING
!?
I'VE COME SO FAR AND I STILL CAN'T SAY IT
!?
?
BA-DOOOON
EVEN IF I MANAGE TO TAKE THAT STEP AND BECOME THE STAR FOR AN INSTANT...
IF HE DUMPS ME, THAT MEANS I'M STILL NOT A STAR!
ZOOON
A PART OF ME JUST WANTS TO TREASURE THE TIME I SPEND WITH NAGI-SAN, SINCE IT PROBABLY WON'T HAPPEN AGAIN...
IT MUST BE HARD, IZUMI, BUT THIS IS FOR THE BEST.
SO IT'S NOT A CONFESSION?
YOU MANAGED TO DODGE THE FATAL BULLET.
I'M SO GLAD HE WAS JUST A BRAT.
ARGH... I'M SO USELESS:
ARE YOU ALL RIGHT, AKO-SAN?
WHA!? HUH!? Y-YES, I'M FINE!
HERE, I'VE GOT A BASS FOR YOU.
JOLT
NOW....
WILL YOU LET ME HEAR YOU PLAY?

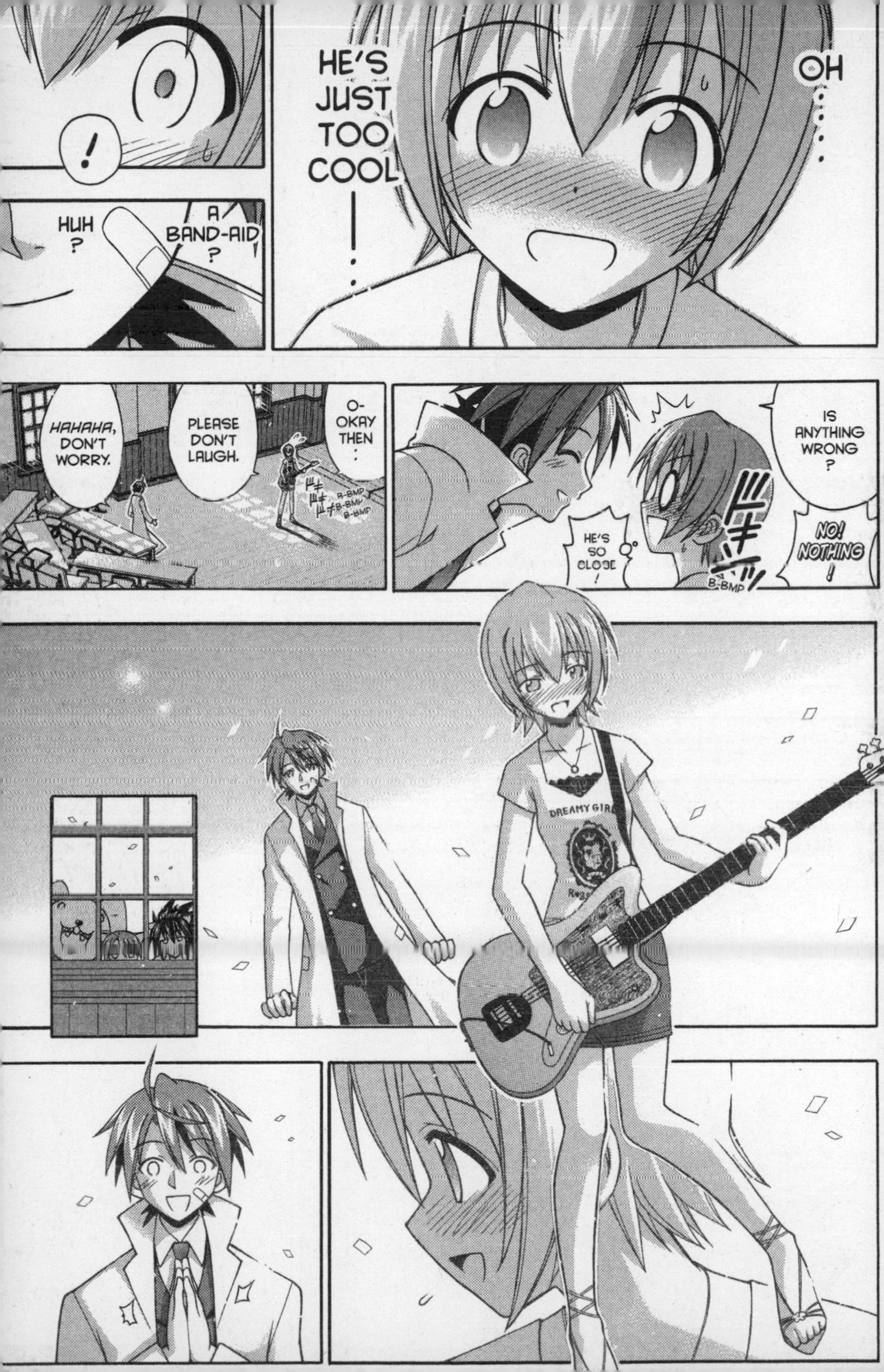
OH......
HE'S JUST TOO COOL......!
!
A BAND-AID?
HUH?
IS ANYTHING WRONG?
NO! NOTHING!
HE'S SO CLOSE!
B-BMP
O-OKAY THEN...
PLEASE DON'T LAUGH.
HAHAHA, DON'T WORRY.
B-BMP
B-BMP
B-BMP

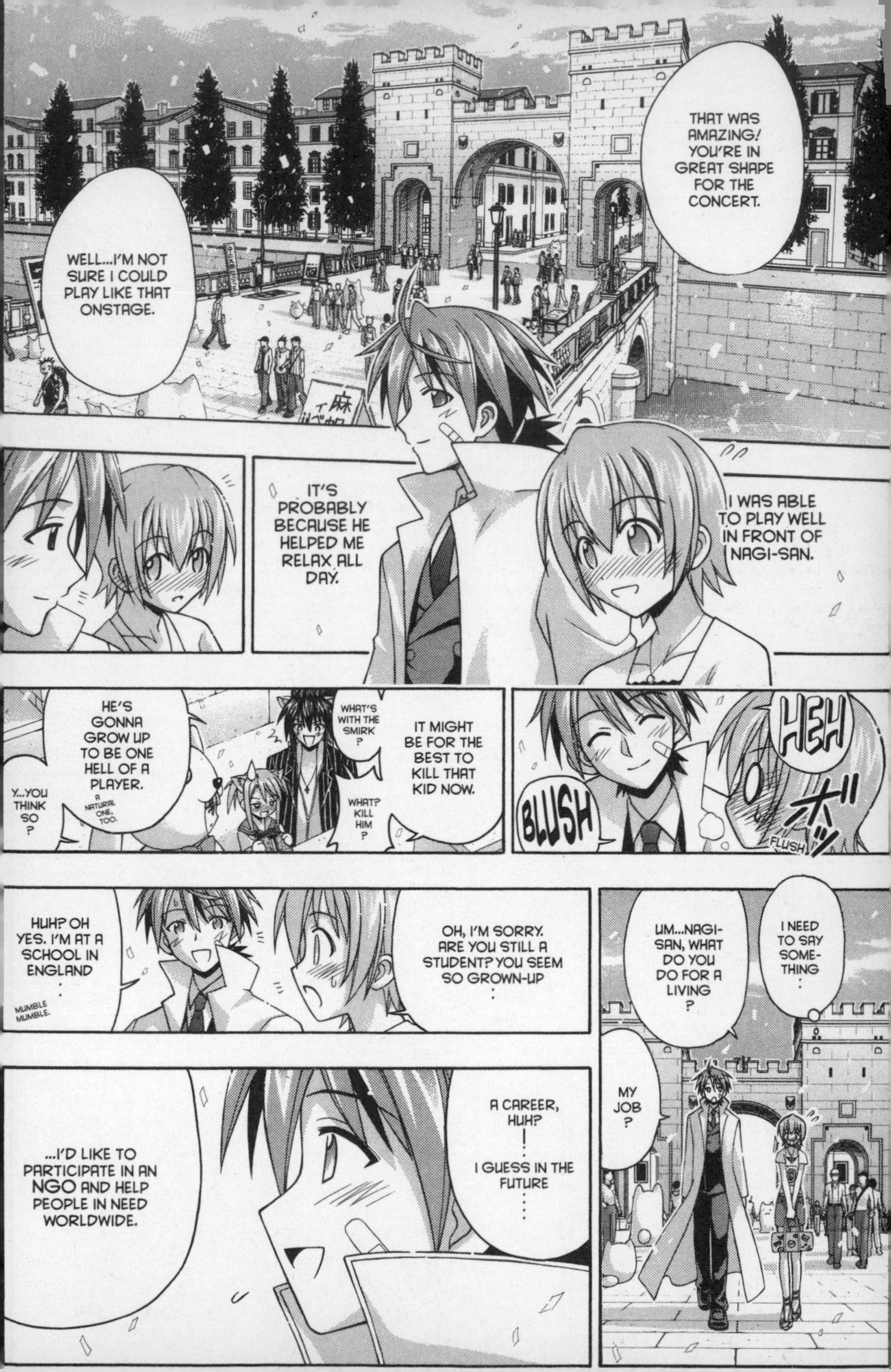
THAT WAS AMAZING! YOU'RE IN GREAT SHAPE FOR THE CONCERT.
WELL...I'M NOT SURE I COULD PLAY LIKE THAT ONSTAGE.
I WAS ABLE TO PLAY WELL IN FRONT OF NAGI-SAN.
IT'S PROBABLY BECAUSE HE HELPED ME RELAX ALL DAY.
HEH
ボッ
FLUSH
BLUSH
IT MIGHT BE FOR THE BEST TO KILL THAT KID NOW.
WHAT'S WITH THE SMIRK?
WHAT? KILL HIM?
HE'S GONNA GROW UP TO BE ONE HELL OF A PLAYER.
A NATURAL ONE, TOO.
Y...YOU THINK SO?
I NEED TO SAY SOMETHING...
UM...NAGI-SAN, WHAT DO YOU DO FOR A LIVING?
MY JOB?
OH, I'M SORRY. ARE YOU STILL A STUDENT? YOU SEEM SO GROWN-UP...
HUH? OH YES. I'M AT A SCHOOL IN ENGLAND...
MUMBLE MUMBLE.
A CAREER, HUH?
!
I GUESS IN THE FUTURE...
...I'D LIKE TO PARTICIPATE IN AN NGO AND HELP PEOPLE IN NEED WORLDWIDE.

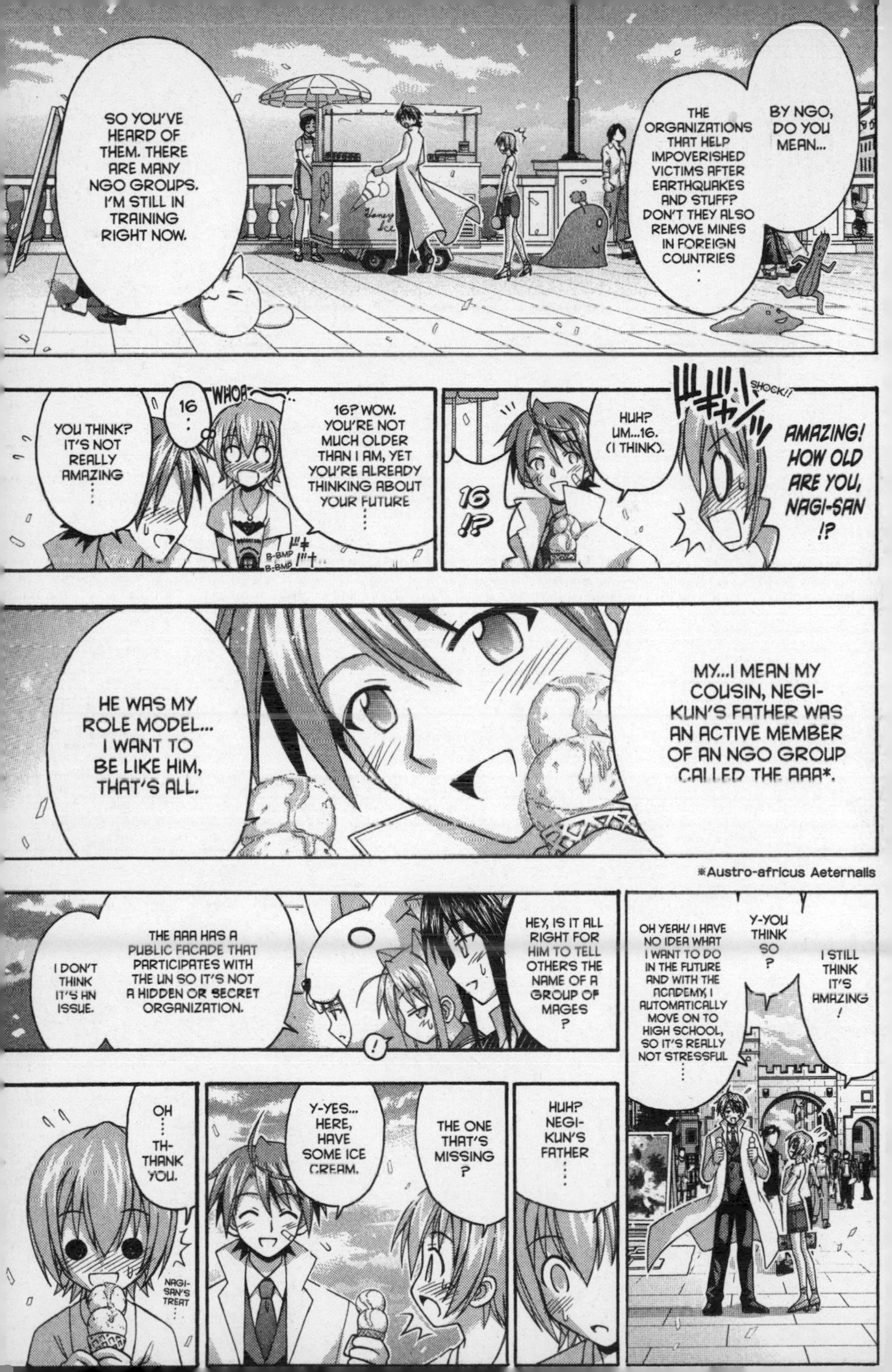
BY NGO, DO YOU MEAN...
THE ORGANIZATIONS THAT HELP IMPOVERISHED VICTIMS AFTER EARTHQUAKES AND STUFF? DON'T THEY ALSO REMOVE MINES IN FOREIGN COUNTRIES ...
SO YOU'VE HEARD OF THEM. THERE ARE MANY NGO GROUPS. I'M STILL IN TRAINING RIGHT NOW.
AMAZING! HOW OLD ARE YOU, NAGI-SAN !?
SHOCK!!
HUH? UM...16. (I THINK).
16 !?
16? WOW. YOU'RE NOT MUCH OLDER THAN I AM, YET YOU'RE ALREADY THINKING ABOUT YOUR FUTURE ...
WHOA
16 ...
YOU THINK? IT'S NOT REALLY AMAZING ...
B-BMP B-BMP
MY...I MEAN MY COUSIN, NEGI-KUN'S FATHER WAS AN ACTIVE MEMBER OF AN NGO GROUP CALLED THE AAA*.
HE WAS MY ROLE MODEL... I WANT TO BE LIKE HIM, THAT'S ALL.
I STILL THINK IT'S AMAZING !
Y-YOU THINK SO ?
OH YEAH! I HAVE NO IDEA WHAT I WANT TO DO IN THE FUTURE AND WITH THE ACADEMY, I AUTOMATICALLY MOVE ON TO HIGH SCHOOL, SO IT'S REALLY NOT STRESSFUL ...
HEY, IS IT ALL RIGHT FOR HIM TO TELL OTHERS THE NAME OF A GROUP OF MAGES ?
!
THE AAA HAS A PUBLIC FACADE THAT PARTICIPATES WITH THE UN SO IT'S NOT A HIDDEN OR SECRET ORGANIZATION.
I DON'T THINK IT'S AN ISSUE.
HUH? NEGI-KUN'S FATHER ...
THE ONE THAT'S MISSING ?
Y-YES... HERE, HAVE SOME ICE CREAM.
OH ... TH-THANK YOU.
NAGI-SAN'S TREAT ...

*Austro-africus Aeternalis

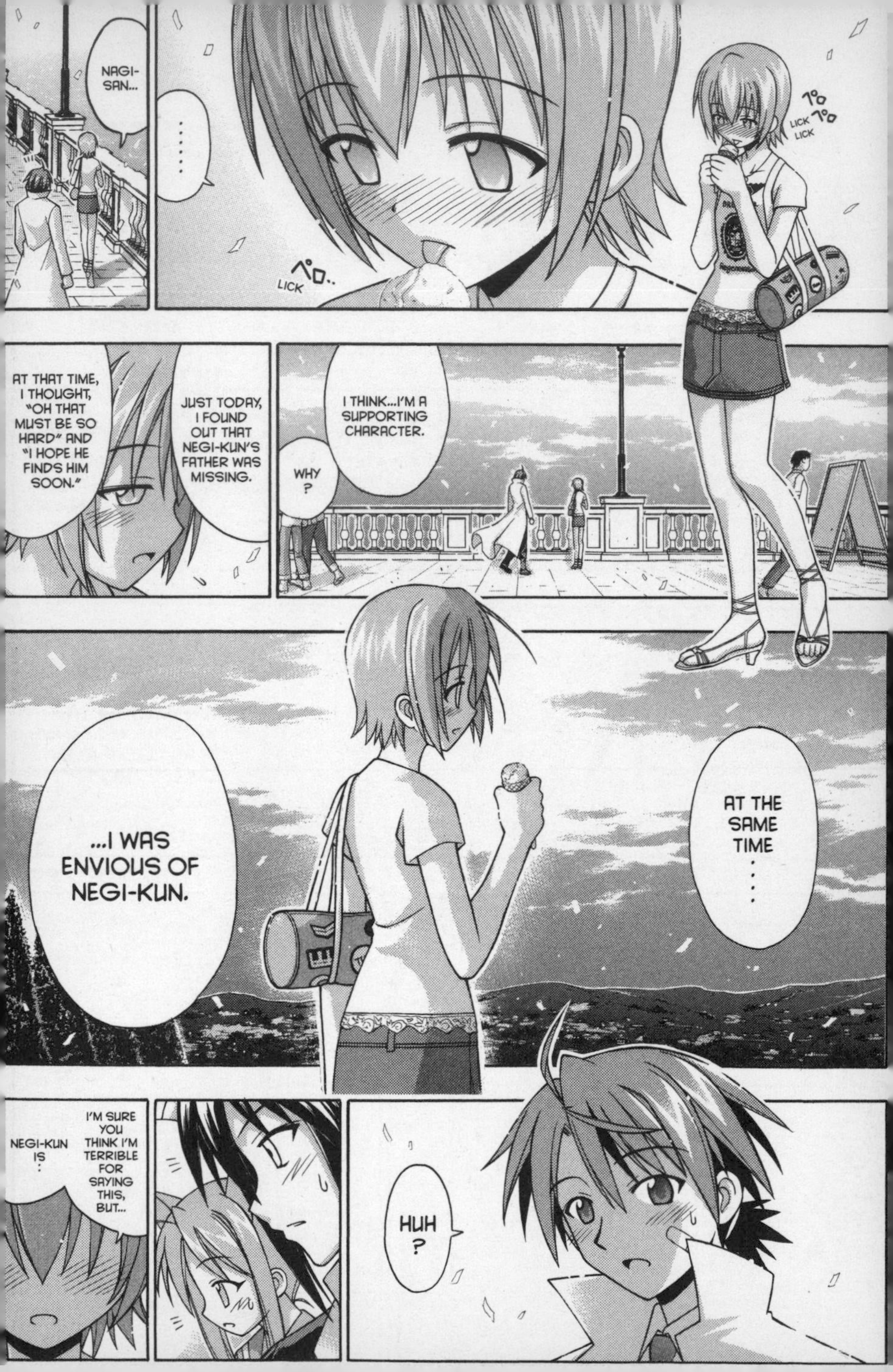

ペロ ペロ
LICK LICK
ペロ..
LICK
NAGI-SAN...
......
I THINK...I'M A SUPPORTING CHARACTER.
WHY?
JUST TODAY, I FOUND OUT THAT NEGI-KUN'S FATHER WAS MISSING.
AT THAT TIME, I THOUGHT, "OH THAT MUST BE SO HARD" AND "I HOPE HE FINDS HIM SOON."
AT THE SAME TIME.....
...I WAS ENVIOUS OF NEGI-KUN.
HUH?
I'M SURE YOU THINK I'M TERRIBLE FOR SAYING THIS, BUT...
NEGI-KUN IS :

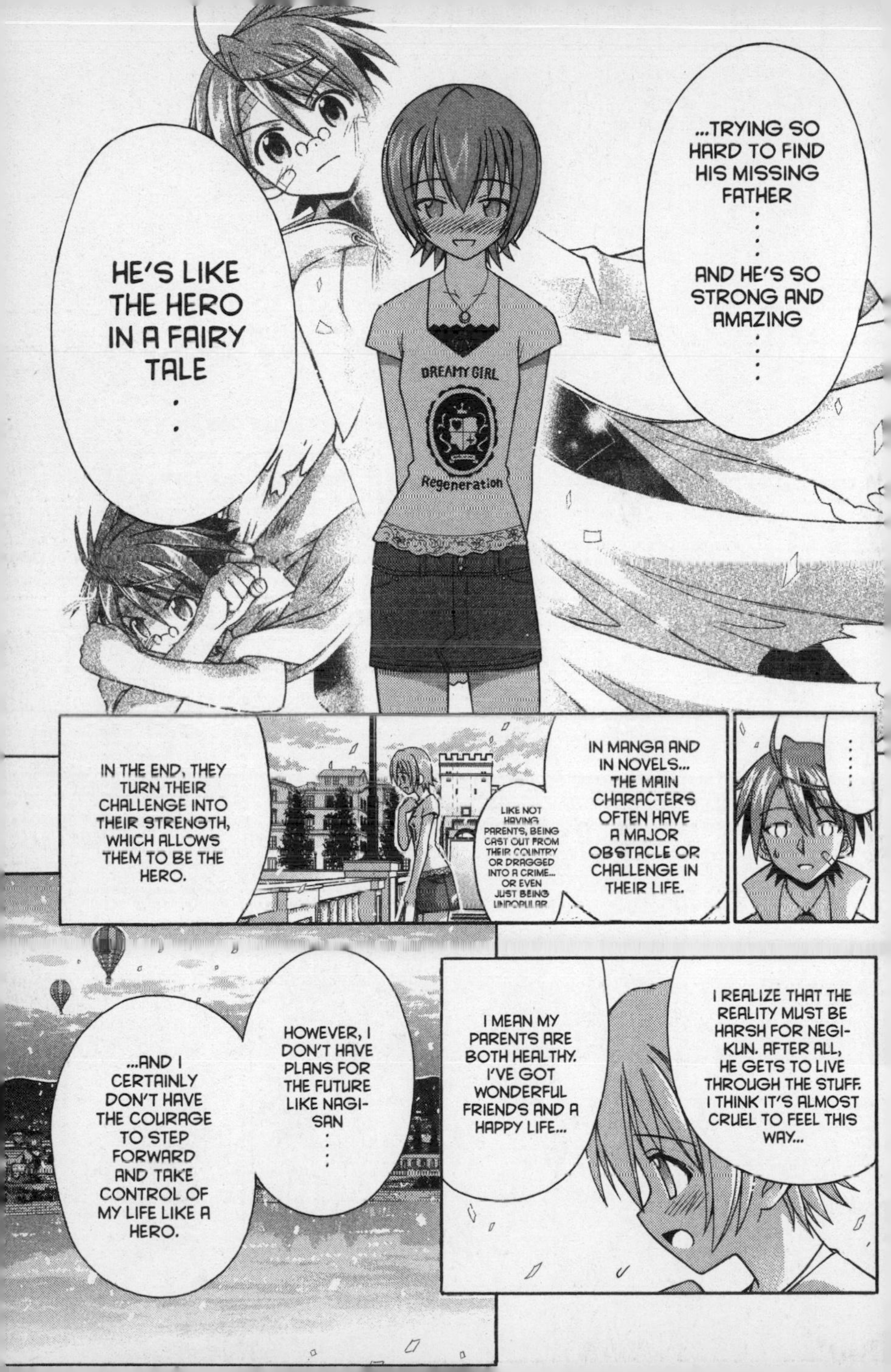
...TRYING SO HARD TO FIND HIS MISSING FATHER . . . AND HE'S SO STRONG AND AMAZING . . . .
DREAMY GIRL
Regeneration
HE'S LIKE THE HERO IN A FAIRY TALE . .
. . . . .
IN MANGA AND IN NOVELS... THE MAIN CHARACTERS OFTEN HAVE A MAJOR OBSTACLE OR CHALLENGE IN THEIR LIFE.
LIKE NOT HAVING PARENTS, BEING CAST OUT FROM THEIR COUNTRY OR DRAGGED INTO A CRIME... OR EVEN JUST BEING UNPOPULAR
IN THE END, THEY TURN THEIR CHALLENGE INTO THEIR STRENGTH, WHICH ALLOWS THEM TO BE THE HERO.
I REALIZE THAT THE REALITY MUST BE HARSH FOR NEGI-KUN. AFTER ALL, HE GETS TO LIVE THROUGH THE STUFF. I THINK IT'S ALMOST CRUEL TO FEEL THIS WAY...
I MEAN MY PARENTS ARE BOTH HEALTHY. I'VE GOT WONDERFUL FRIENDS AND A HAPPY LIFE...
HOWEVER, I DON'T HAVE PLANS FOR THE FUTURE LIKE NAGI-SAN . . . .
...AND I CERTAINLY DON'T HAVE THE COURAGE TO STEP FORWARD AND TAKE CONTROL OF MY LIFE LIKE A HERO.

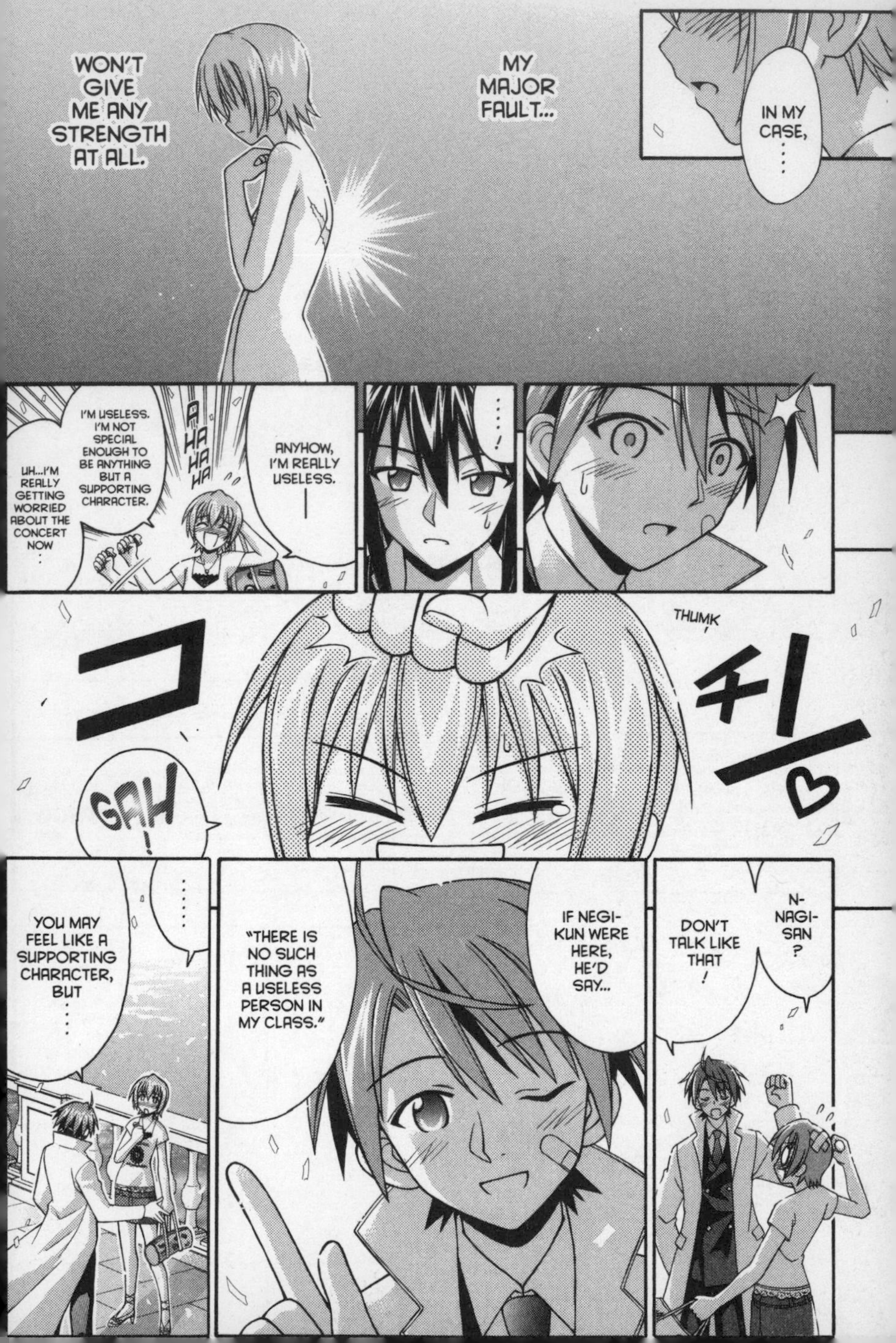

IN MY CASE, ...
MY MAJOR FAULT...
WON'T GIVE ME ANY STRENGTH AT ALL.
...!
ANYHOW, I'M REALLY USELESS.
AHAHAHA
I'M USELESS. I'M NOT SPECIAL ENOUGH TO BE ANYTHING BUT A SUPPORTING CHARACTER.
UH...I'M REALLY GETTING WORRIED ABOUT THE CONCERT NOW...
THUMK
コチン
GAH!
N-NAGI-SAN?
DON'T TALK LIKE THAT!
IF NEGI-KUN WERE HERE, HE'D SAY...
"THERE IS NO SUCH THING AS A USELESS PERSON IN MY CLASS."
......
YOU MAY FEEL LIKE A SUPPORTING CHARACTER, BUT...

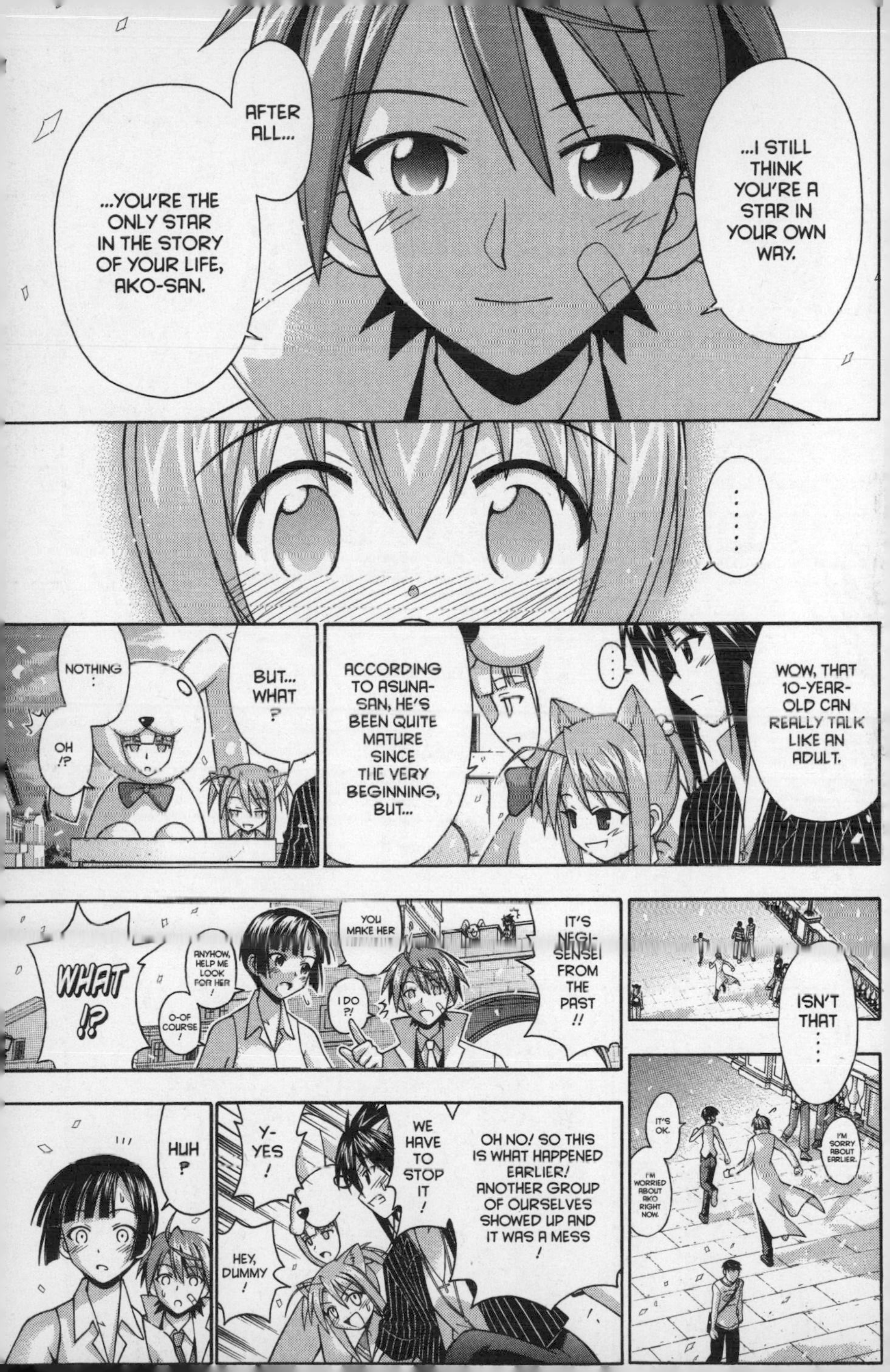
...I STILL THINK YOU'RE A STAR IN YOUR OWN WAY.
AFTER ALL...
...YOU'RE THE ONLY STAR IN THE STORY OF YOUR LIFE, AKO-SAN.
......
WOW, THAT 10-YEAR-OLD CAN REALLY TALK LIKE AN ADULT.
...
ACCORDING TO ASUNA-SAN, HE'S BEEN QUITE MATURE SINCE THE VERY BEGINNING, BUT...
BUT... WHAT?
NOTHING.
OH!?
ISN'T THAT...
IT'S NEGI-SENSEI FROM THE PAST!!
YOU MAKE HER
I DO?!
ANYHOW, HELP ME LOOK FOR HER!
O-OF COURSE!
WHAT!?
I'M SORRY ABOUT EARLIER.
IT'S OK.
I'M WORRIED ABOUT AKO RIGHT NOW.
OH NO! SO THIS IS WHAT HAPPENED EARLIER! ANOTHER GROUP OF OURSELVES SHOWED UP AND IT WAS A MESS!
WE HAVE TO STOP IT!
Y-YES!
HEY, DUMMY!
HUH?

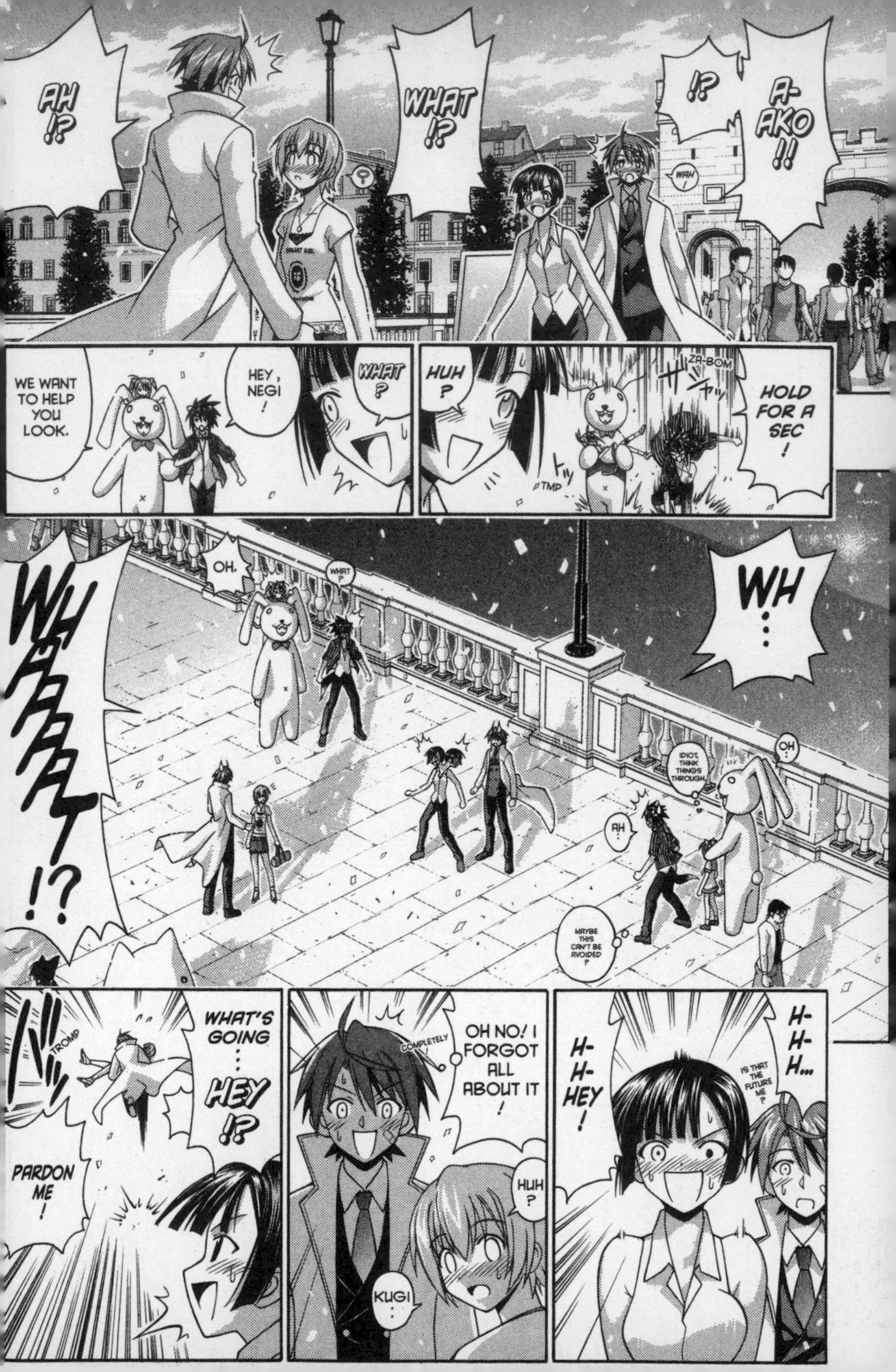
A-AKO!!
!?
WAH!
WHAT!?
?
AH!?
HOLD FOR A SEC!
ZA-BOM
TMP
HUH?
WHAT?
HEY, NEGI!
WE WANT TO HELP YOU LOOK.
WH...
OH
IDIOT, THINK THINGS THROUGH.
AH
MAYBE THIS CAN'T BE AVOIDED?
WHAT?
OH.
WHAAAAAT!?
H-H-H...
IS THAT THE FUTURE ME?
H-H-HEY!
OH NO! I FORGOT ALL ABOUT IT!
COMPLETELY!
HUH?
KUGI...
WHAT'S GOING...
HEY!?
TROMP
PARDON ME!

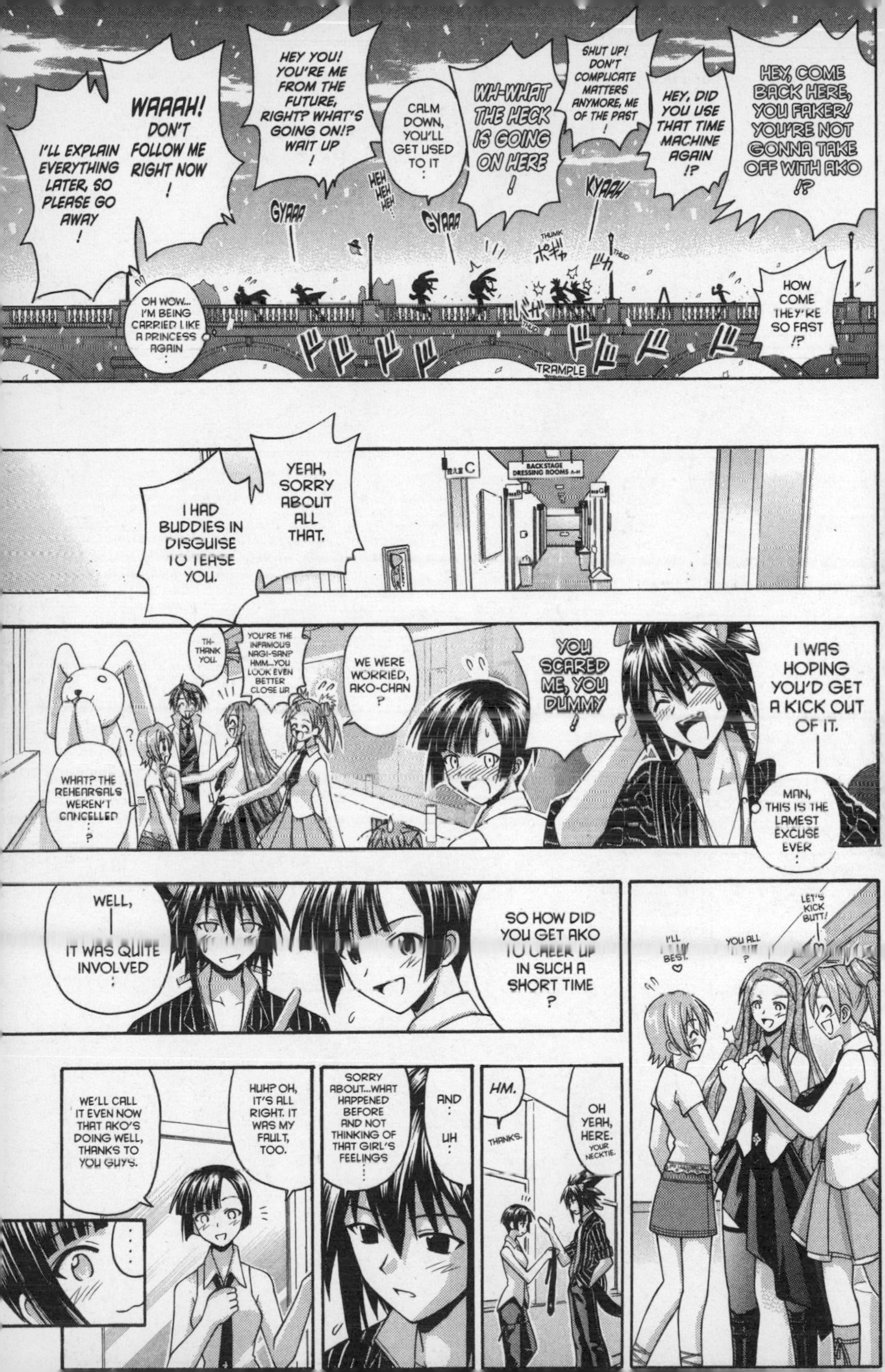
HEY, COME BACK HERE, YOU FAKER! YOU'RE NOT GONNA TAKE OFF WITH AKO !?
HEY, DID YOU USE THAT TIME MACHINE AGAIN !?
SHUT UP! DON'T COMPLICATE MATTERS ANYMORE, ME OF THE PAST !
WH-WHAT THE HECK IS GOING ON HERE !
CALM DOWN, YOU'LL GET USED TO IT ...
HEY YOU! YOU'RE ME FROM THE FUTURE, RIGHT? WHAT'S GOING ON!? WAIT UP !
WAAAH! DON'T FOLLOW ME RIGHT NOW !
I'LL EXPLAIN EVERYTHING LATER, SO PLEASE GO AWAY !
HOW COME THEY'RE SO FAST !?
KYAAH
THUD
THUMK
THUD
GYAAA
HEH HEH HEH
GYAAA
OH WOW... I'M BEING CARRIED LIKE A PRINCESS AGAIN ...
TRAMPLE
YEAH, SORRY ABOUT ALL THAT.
I HAD BUDDIES IN DISGUISE TO TEASE YOU.
BACKSTAGE DRESSING ROOMS
C
I WAS HOPING YOU'D GET A KICK OUT OF IT.
MAN, THIS IS THE LAMEST EXCUSE EVER ...
YOU SCARED ME, YOU DUMMY !
WE WERE WORRIED, AKO-CHAN ?
YOU'RE THE INFAMOUS NAGI-SAN? HMM...YOU LOOK EVEN BETTER CLOSE UP.
TH-THANK YOU.
WHAT? THE REHEARSALS WEREN'T CANCELLED ...?
LET'S KICK BUTT!
YOU ALL ?
I'LL
BEST.
SO HOW DID YOU GET AKO TO CHEER UP IN SUCH A SHORT TIME ?
WELL, IT WAS QUITE INVOLVED ...
OH YEAH, HERE. YOUR NECKTIE.
HM.
THANKS.
AND ... UH ...
SORRY ABOUT...WHAT HAPPENED BEFORE AND NOT THINKING OF THAT GIRL'S FEELINGS ...
HUH? OH, IT'S ALL RIGHT. IT WAS MY FAULT, TOO.
WE'LL CALL IT EVEN NOW THAT AKO'S DOING WELL, THANKS TO YOU GUYS.
....

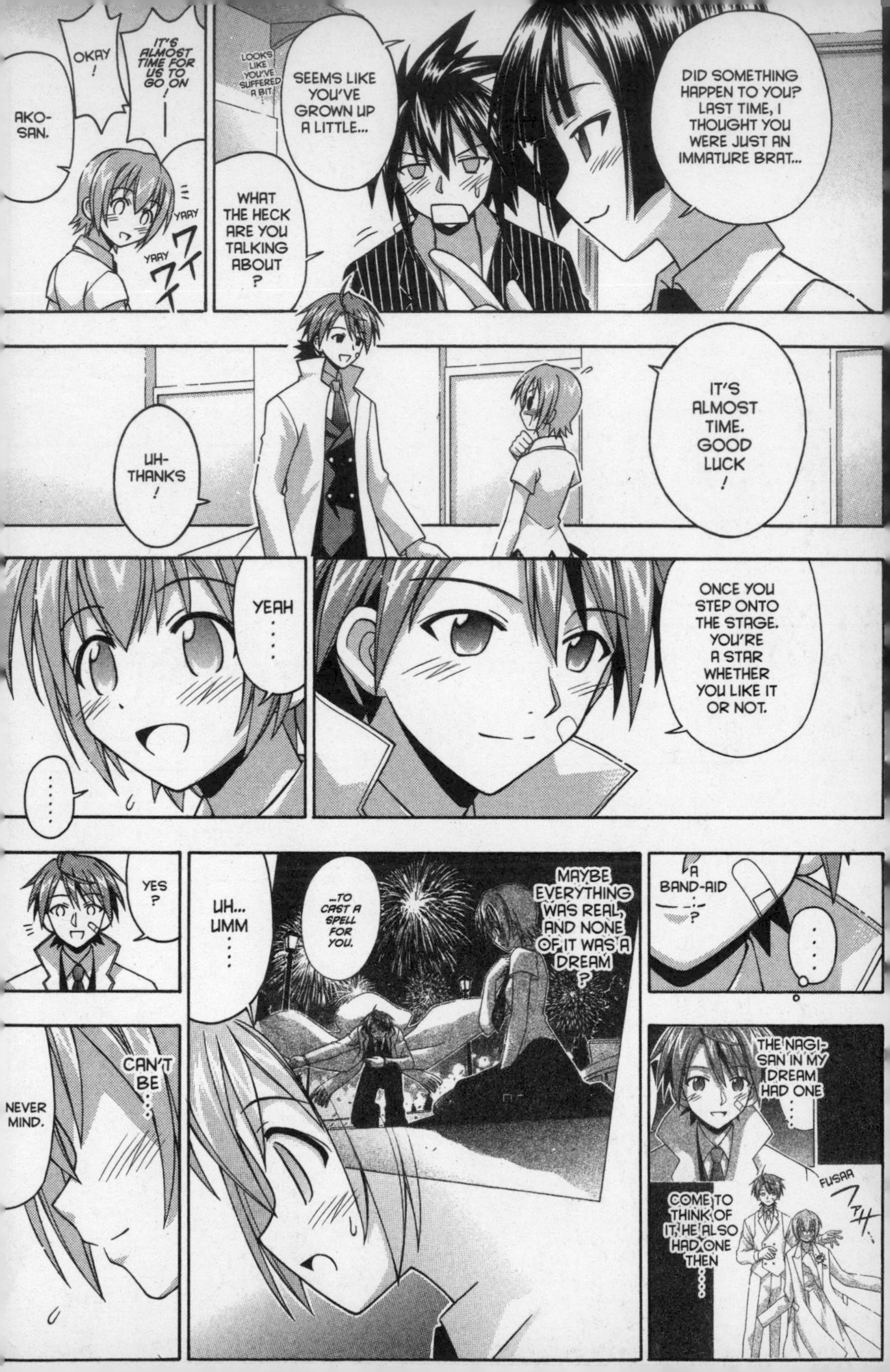
DID SOMETHING HAPPEN TO YOU? LAST TIME, I THOUGHT YOU WERE JUST AN IMMATURE BRAT...
SEEMS LIKE YOU'VE GROWN UP A LITTLE...
LOOKS LIKE YOU'VE SUFFERED A BIT...
WHAT THE HECK ARE YOU TALKING ABOUT?
IT'S ALMOST TIME FOR US TO GO ON!
OKAY!
AKO-SAN.
YAAY
YAAY
IT'S ALMOST TIME. GOOD LUCK!
UH-THANKS!
ONCE YOU STEP ONTO THE STAGE. YOU'RE A STAR WHETHER YOU LIKE IT OR NOT.
YEAH....
......
A BAND-AID...?
.....
MAYBE EVERYTHING WAS REAL, AND NONE OF IT WAS A DREAM?
...TO CAST A SPELL FOR YOU.
UH... UMM...
YES?
THE NAGI-SAN IN MY DREAM HAD ONE....
FUSAA
COME TO THINK OF IT, HE ALSO HAD ONE THEN....
CAN'T BE...
NEVER MIND.

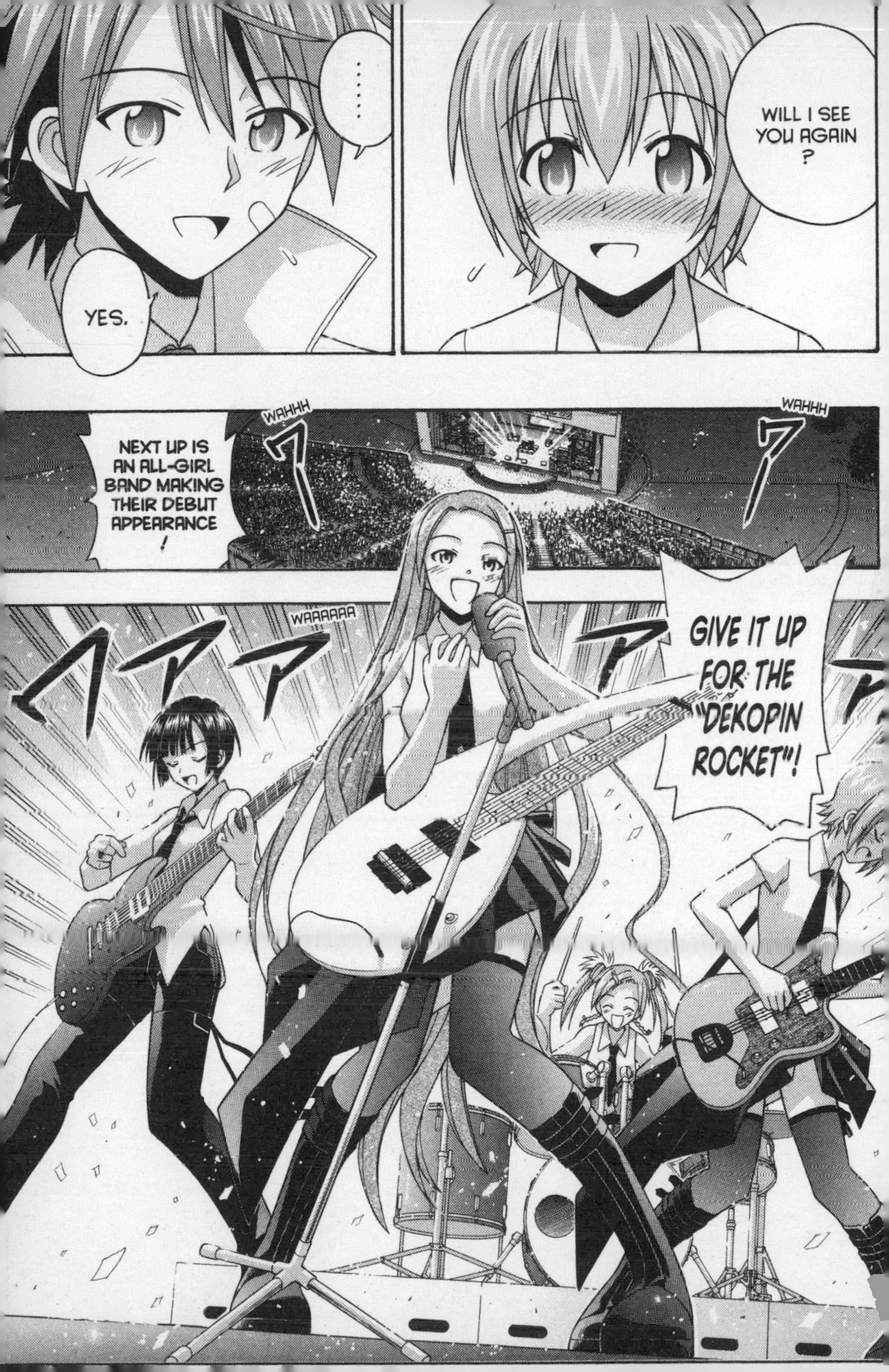
WILL I SEE YOU AGAIN ?
......
YES.
WAHHH
WAHHH
NEXT UP IS AN ALL-GIRL BAND MAKING THEIR DEBUT APPEARANCE !
GIVE IT UP FOR THE "DEKOPIN ROCKET"!
WAAAAAAA

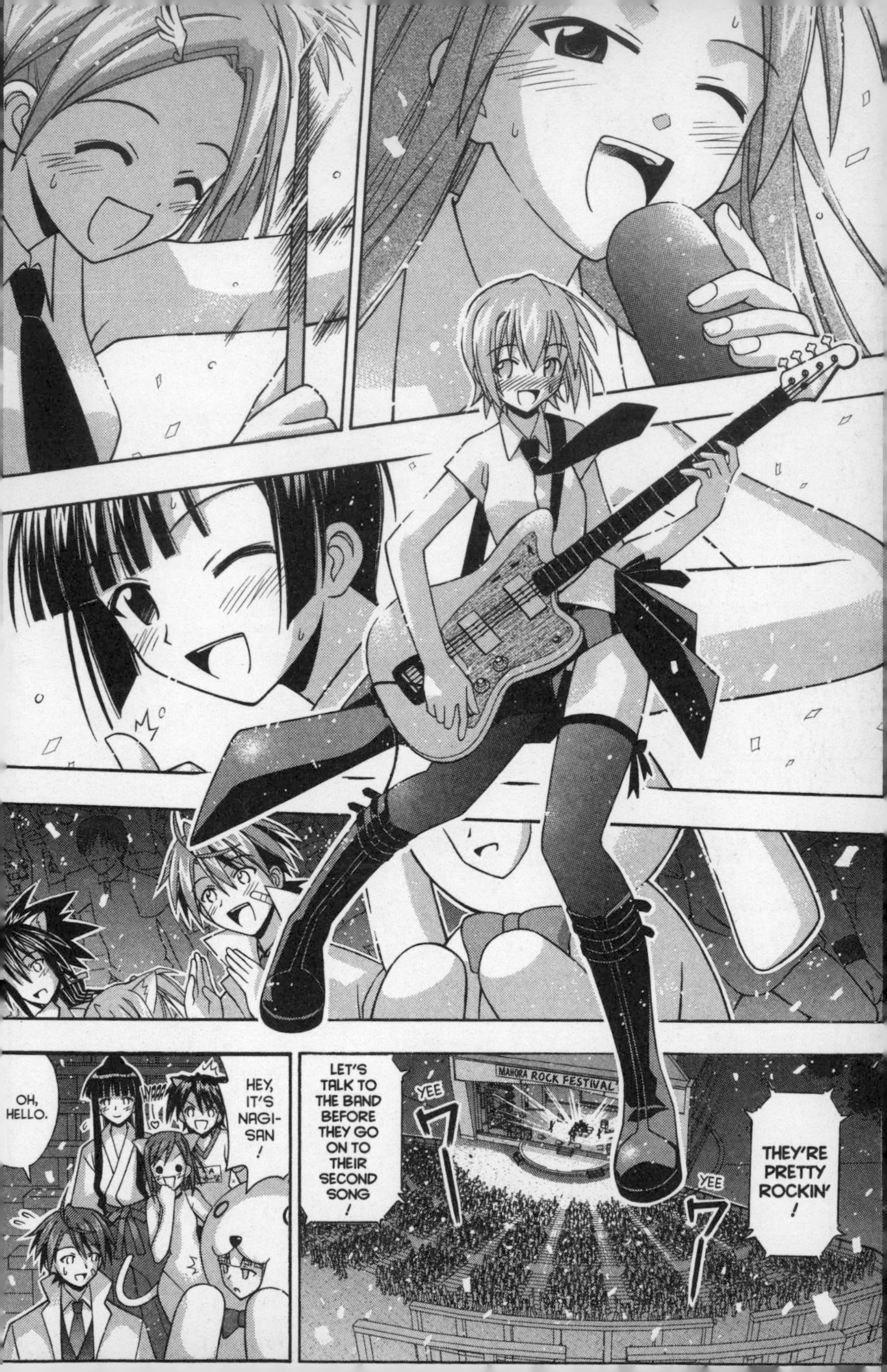
MAHORA ROCK FESTIVAL
THEY'RE PRETTY ROCKIN'!
YEE
YEE
LET'S TALK TO THE BAND BEFORE THEY GO ON TO THEIR SECOND SONG!
HEY, IT'S NAGI-SAN!
OH, HELLO.

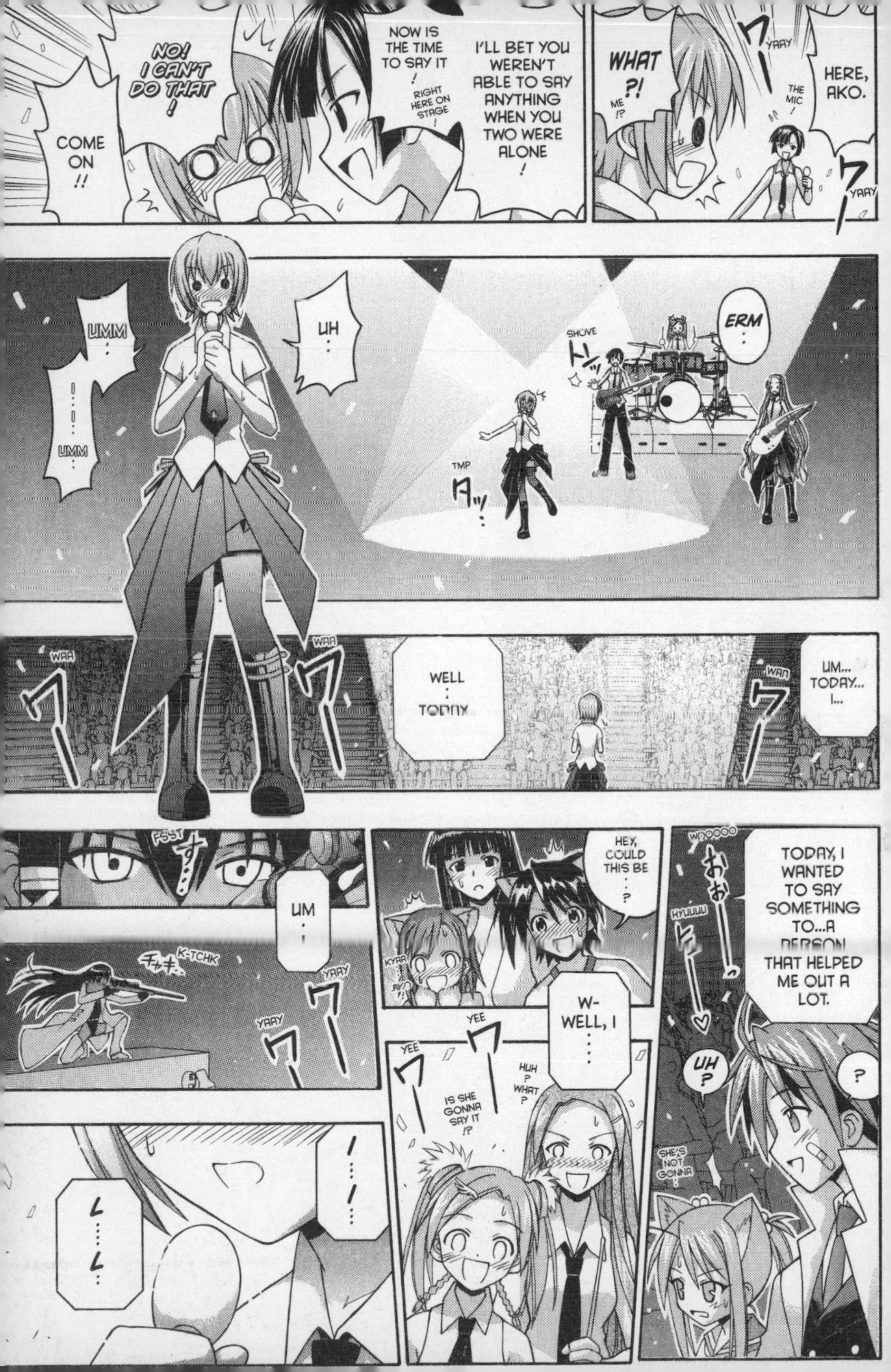
HERE, AKO.
THE MIC!
YAAY
YAAY
WHAT?! ME!?
I'LL BET YOU WEREN'T ABLE TO SAY ANYTHING WHEN YOU TWO WERE ALONE!
NOW IS THE TIME TO SAY IT!
RIGHT HERE ON STAGE!
NO! I CAN'T DO THAT!
COME ON!!
ERM...
SHOVE
TMP
UH...
UMM...
I... I...
UMM...
UM... TODAY... I...
WAA
WELL... TODAY
WAA
WAA
TODAY, I WANTED TO SAY SOMETHING TO...A PERSON THAT HELPED ME OUT A LOT.
WOOOOO
HYUUUU
UH?
?
SHE'S NOT GONNA...
HEY, COULD THIS BE...?
KYAA... AH!!
W-WELL, I...
YEE
YEE
HUH? WHAT?
IS SHE GONNA SAY IT!?
FSST
UM...
K-TCHK
YAAY
YAAY
I... I...
L... L...

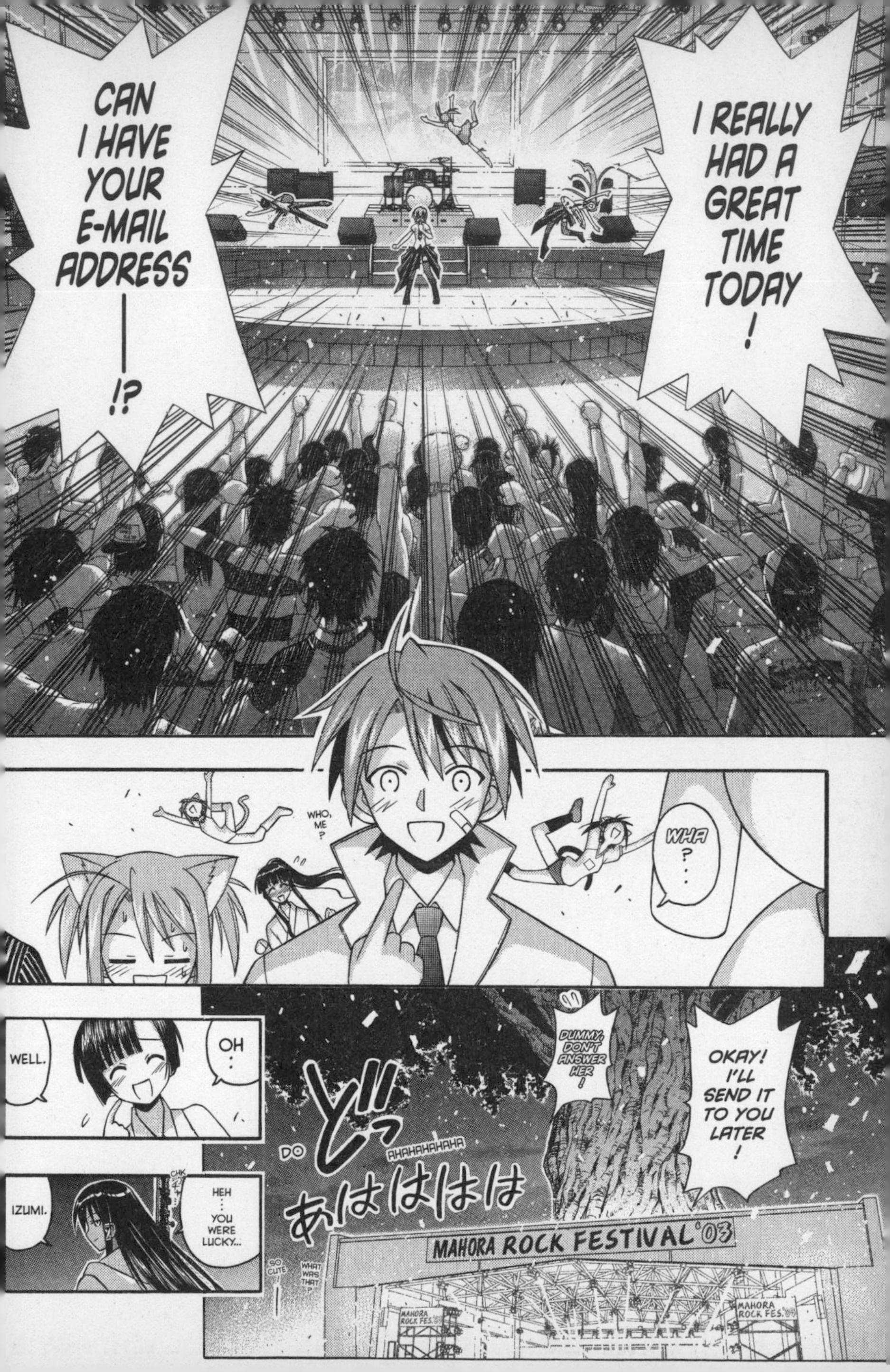
I REALLY HAD A GREAT TIME TODAY!
CAN I HAVE YOUR E-MAIL ADDRESS—!?
WHA?...
WHO, ME?
OKAY! I'LL SEND IT TO YOU LATER!
DUMMY, DON'T ANSWER HER!
どっ
DO
あははははは
AHAHAHAHAHA
MAHORA ROCK FESTIVAL '03
MAHORA ROCK FES. '03
MAHORA ROCK FES.
WHAT WAS THAT?
SO CUTE—
OH...
WELL.
HEH... YOU WERE LUCKY...
CHK
IZUMI.

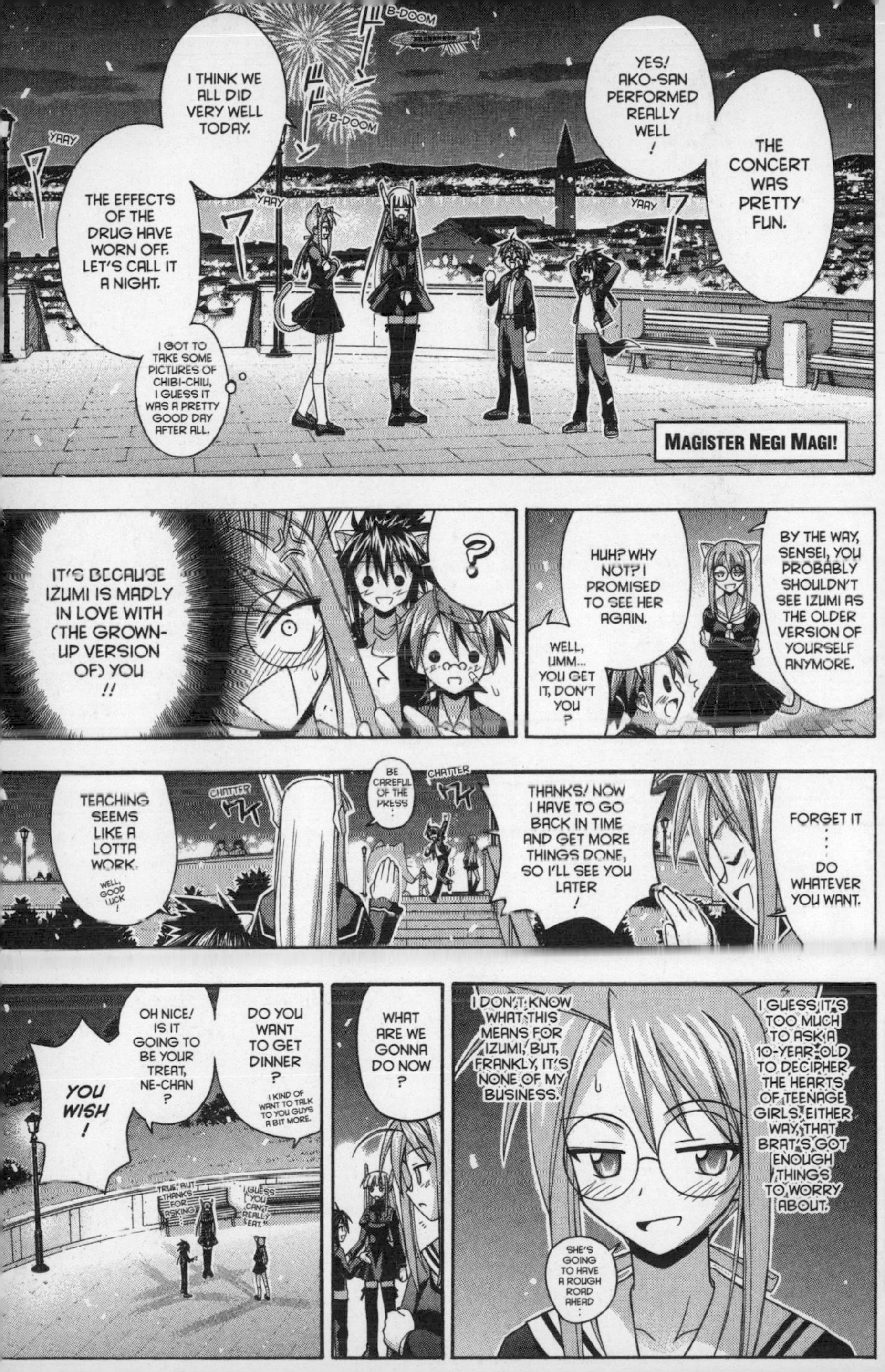
YES! AKO-SAN PERFORMED REALLY WELL!
THE CONCERT WAS PRETTY FUN.
YAAY
B-DOOM
B-DOOM
I THINK WE ALL DID VERY WELL TODAY.
YAAY
THE EFFECTS OF THE DRUG HAVE WORN OFF. LET'S CALL IT A NIGHT.
YAAY
I GOT TO TAKE SOME PICTURES OF CHIBI-CHIU, I GUESS IT WAS A PRETTY GOOD DAY AFTER ALL.
MAGISTER NEGI MAGI!
BY THE WAY, SENSEI, YOU PROBABLY SHOULDN'T SEE IZUMI AS THE OLDER VERSION OF YOURSELF ANYMORE.
HUH? WHY NOT? I PROMISED TO SEE HER AGAIN.
WELL, UMM... YOU GET IT, DON'T YOU?
?
IT'S BECAUSE IZUMI IS MADLY IN LOVE WITH (THE GROWN-UP VERSION OF) YOU!!
FORGET IT... DO WHATEVER YOU WANT.
THANKS! NOW I HAVE TO GO BACK IN TIME AND GET MORE THINGS DONE, SO I'LL SEE YOU LATER!
CHATTER
BE CAREFUL OF THE PRESS...
CHATTER
TEACHING SEEMS LIKE A LOTTA WORK.
WELL, GOOD LUCK!
I GUESS IT'S TOO MUCH TO ASK A 10-YEAR-OLD TO DECIPHER THE HEARTS OF TEENAGE GIRLS. EITHER WAY, THAT BRAT'S GOT ENOUGH THINGS TO WORRY ABOUT.
I DON'T KNOW WHAT THIS MEANS FOR IZUMI, BUT, FRANKLY, IT'S NONE OF MY BUSINESS.
SHE'S GOING TO HAVE A ROUGH ROAD AHEAD...
WHAT ARE WE GONNA DO NOW?
DO YOU WANT TO GET DINNER?
I KIND OF WANT TO TALK TO YOU GUYS A BIT MORE.
OH NICE! IS IT GOING TO BE YOUR TREAT, NE-CHAN?
YOU WISH!
I GUESS YOU CAN'T REALLY EAT.
TRUE, BUT THANKS FOR ASKING.

NEGIMA!
MAGISTER NEGI MAGI

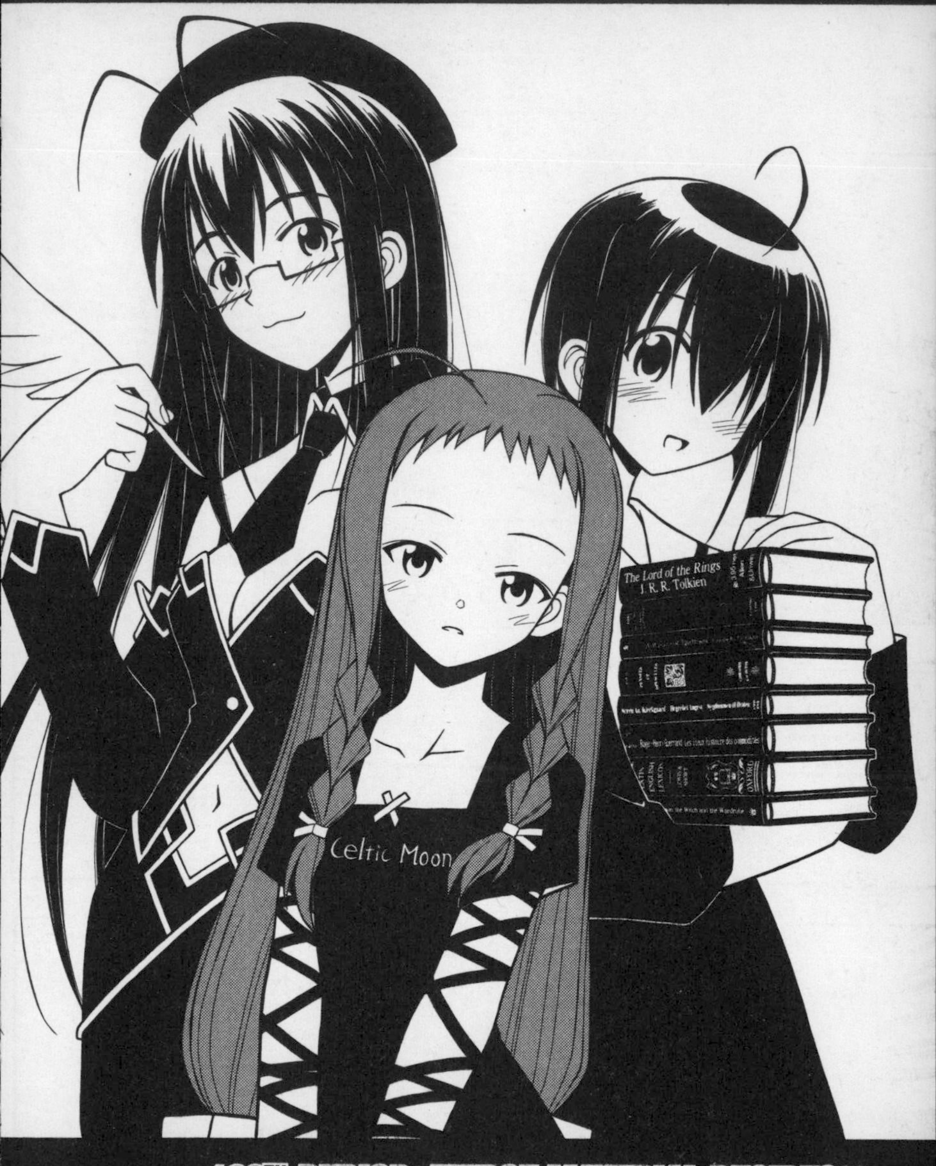
The Lord of the Rings
J. R. R. Tolkien
Celtic Moon

126TH PERIOD: FIERCE MATERIAL DESIRES♡

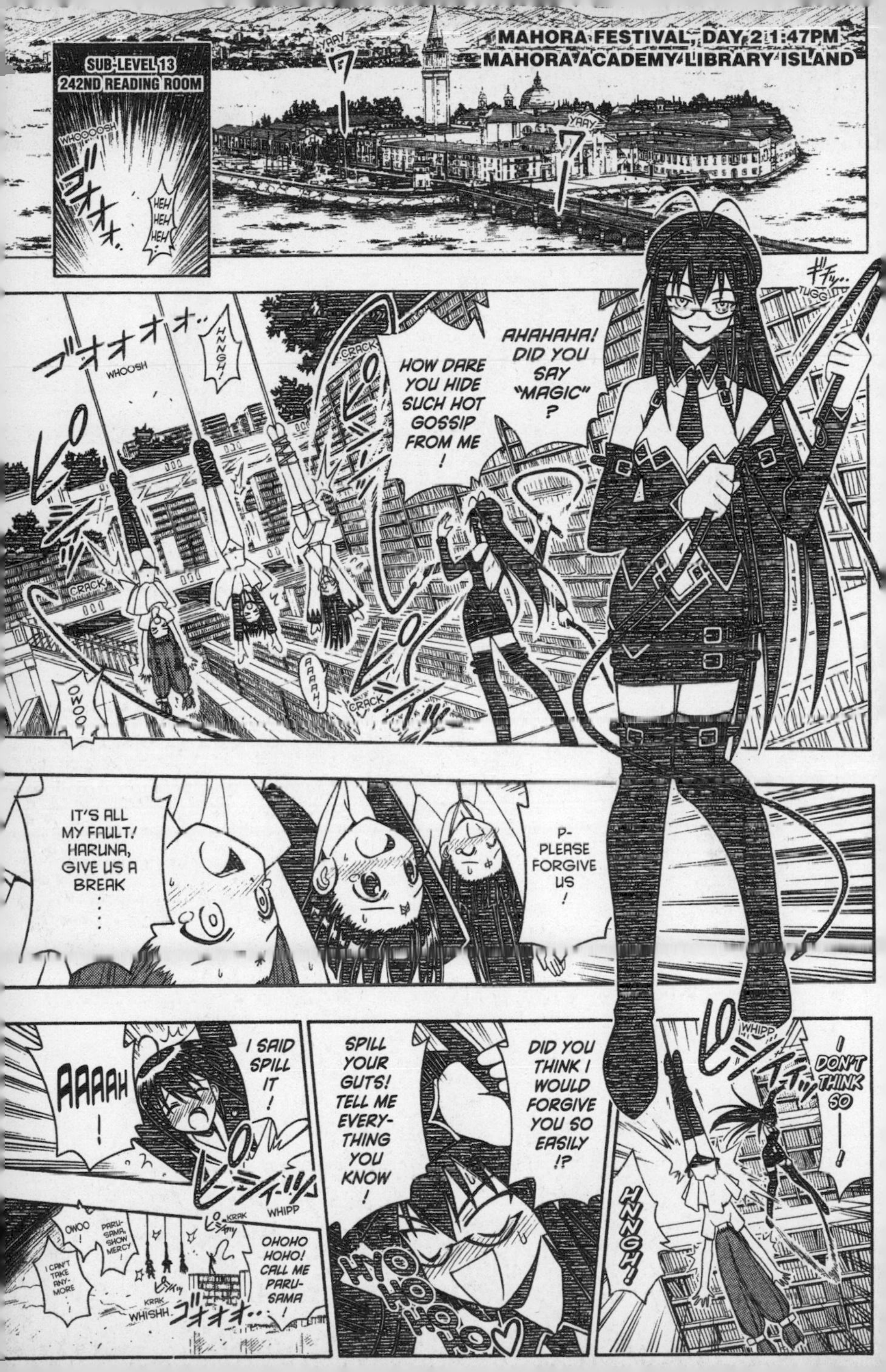
MAHORA FESTIVAL, DAY 2 1:47PM
MAHORA ACADEMY LIBRARY ISLAND
YAAY
YAAY
SUB-LEVEL 13
242ND READING ROOM
WHOOOOSH
HEH HEH HEH
TUGG
AHAHAHA! DID YOU SAY "MAGIC"?
HOW DARE YOU HIDE SUCH HOT GOSSIP FROM ME!
CRACK
HNNGH!
WHOOSH
AAAAH!
CRACK
CRACK
OWOO
P-PLEASE FORGIVE US!
IT'S ALL MY FAULT! HARUNA, GIVE US A BREAK...
I DON'T THINK SO—!
DID YOU THINK I WOULD FORGIVE YOU SO EASILY!?
WHIPP
HNNGH!
SPILL YOUR GUTS! TELL ME EVERY-THING YOU KNOW!
HO HO HO HO
I SAID SPILL IT!
AAAAH!
WHIPP
KRAK
OHOHO HOHO! CALL ME PARU-SAMA!
PARU-SAMA, SHOW MERCY!
OWOO!
I CAN'T TAKE ANY-MORE
KRAK
WHISHH

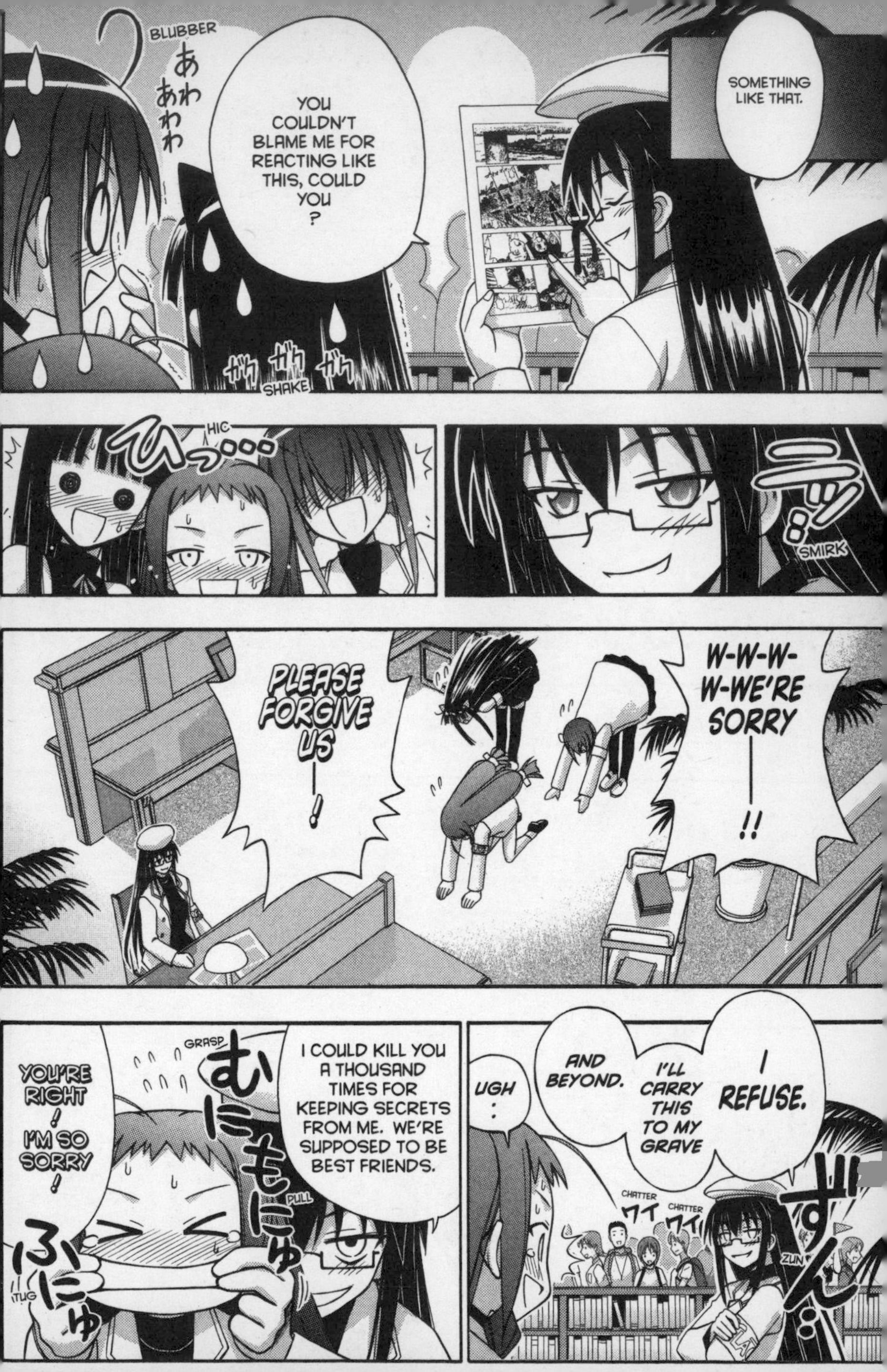
SOMETHING LIKE THAT.
YOU COULDN'T BLAME ME FOR REACTING LIKE THIS, COULD YOU?
BLUBBER
あわあわわ
ガクガクガク
SHAKE
ニッ
SMIRK
ひっ
HIC
W-W-W-W-WE'RE SORRY—!!
PLEASE FORGIVE US—!
I REFUSE.
I'LL CARRY THIS TO MY GRAVE
AND BEYOND.
UGH:
ずん
ZUN
ワイ
CHATTER
ワイ
CHATTER
I COULD KILL YOU A THOUSAND TIMES FOR KEEPING SECRETS FROM ME. WE'RE SUPPOSED TO BE BEST FRIENDS.
GRASP
むにもにゅ
PULL
YOU'RE RIGHT! I'M SO SORRY!
ふにゅ
TUG

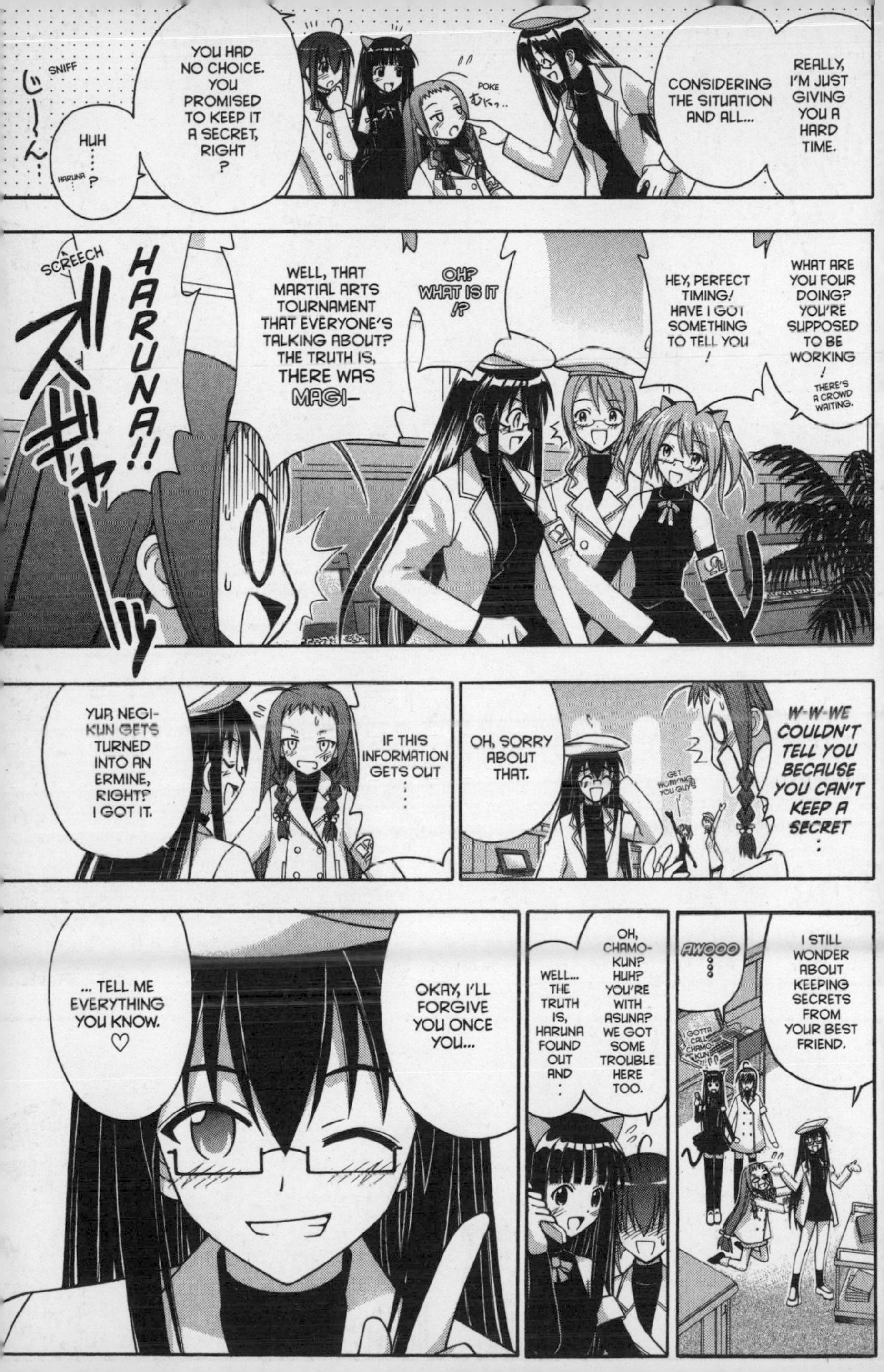
REALLY, I'M JUST GIVING YOU A HARD TIME.
CONSIDERING THE SITUATION AND ALL...
POKE
むにっ...
YOU HAD NO CHOICE. YOU PROMISED TO KEEP IT A SECRET, RIGHT?
HUH...? HARUNA...?
SNIFF
じ~ん...
WHAT ARE YOU FOUR DOING? YOU'RE SUPPOSED TO BE WORKING!
THERE'S A CROWD WAITING.
HEY, PERFECT TIMING! HAVE I GOT SOMETHING TO TELL YOU!
OH? WHAT IS IT!?
WELL, THAT MARTIAL ARTS TOURNAMENT THAT EVERYONE'S TALKING ABOUT? THE TRUTH IS, THERE WAS MAGI–
HARUNA!!
SCREECH
W-W-WE COULDN'T TELL YOU BECAUSE YOU CAN'T KEEP A SECRET...
GET WORKING YOU GUYS!
OH, SORRY ABOUT THAT.
IF THIS INFORMATION GETS OUT...
YUP, NEGI-KUN GETS TURNED INTO AN ERMINE, RIGHT? I GOT IT.
I STILL WONDER ABOUT KEEPING SECRETS FROM YOUR BEST FRIEND.
AWOOO...
I GOTTA CALL CHAMO-KUN!
OH, CHAMO-KUN? HUH? YOU'RE WITH ASUNA? WE GOT SOME TROUBLE HERE TOO.
WELL... THE TRUTH IS, HARUNA FOUND OUT AND...
OKAY, I'LL FORGIVE YOU ONCE YOU...
... TELL ME EVERYTHING YOU KNOW. ♡

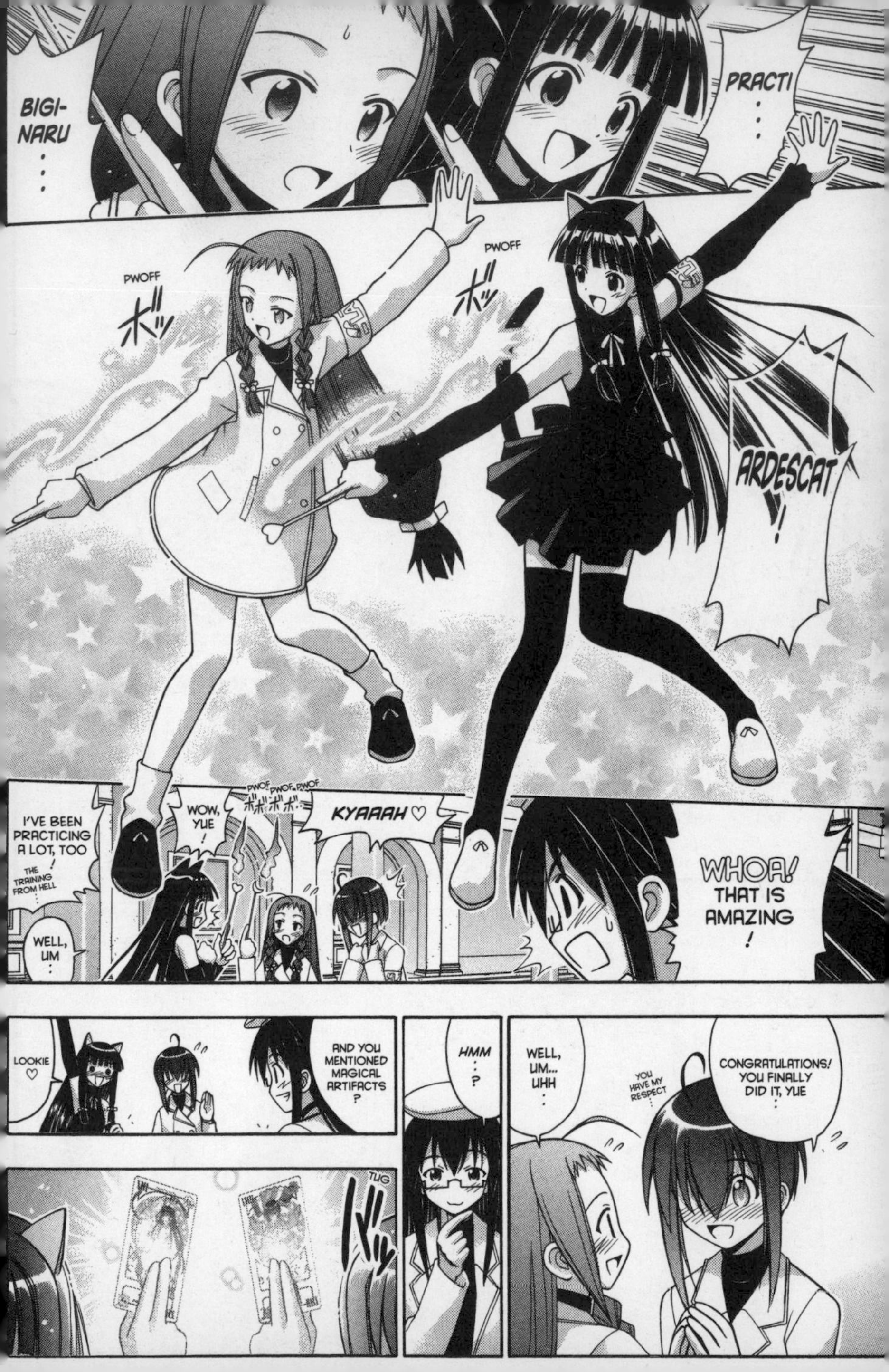
PRACTI...
BIGI-NARU...
ARDESCAT!
PWOFF
PWOFF
WHOA! THAT IS AMAZING!
KYAAAH ♡
PWOF PWOF PWOF
WOW, YUE!
I'VE BEEN PRACTICING A LOT, TOO!
THE TRAINING FROM HELL...
WELL, UM...
CONGRATULATIONS! YOU FINALLY DID IT, YUE...
YOU HAVE MY RESPECT...
WELL, UM... UHH...
HMM...?
AND YOU MENTIONED MAGICAL ARTIFACTS?
LOOKIE ♡
TUG

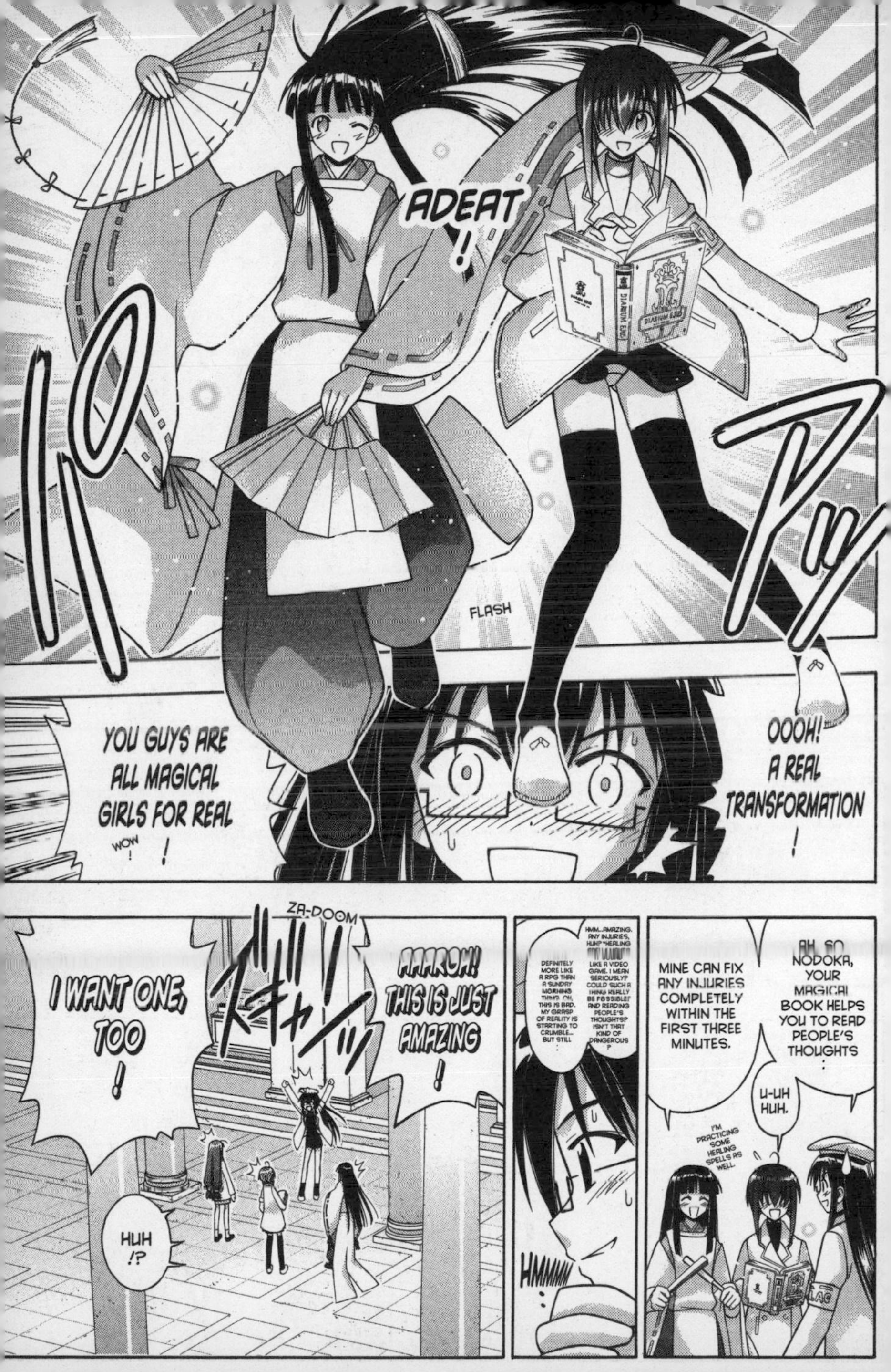
ADEAT!
FLASH
OOOH! A REAL TRANSFORMATION!
YOU GUYS ARE ALL MAGICAL GIRLS FOR REAL!
WOW!
AH, SO NODOKA, YOUR MAGICAL BOOK HELPS YOU TO READ PEOPLE'S THOUGHTS...
U-UH HUH.
MINE CAN FIX ANY INJURIES COMPLETELY WITHIN THE FIRST THREE MINUTES.
I'M PRACTICING SOME HEALING SPELLS AS WELL.
HMM...AMAZING. ANY INJURIES, HUH? *HEALING
LIKE A VIDEO GAME. I MEAN SERIOUSLY? COULD SUCH A THING REALLY BE POSSIBLE? AND READING PEOPLE'S THOUGHTS? ISN'T THAT KIND OF DANGEROUS?
DEFINITELY MORE LIKE A RPG THAN A SUNDAY MORNING THING. OH, THIS IS BAD. MY GRASP OF REALITY IS STARTING TO CRUMBLE... BUT STILL...
HMMM...
ZA-DOOM
AAARGH! THIS IS JUST AMAZING!
I WANT ONE, TOO!
HUH!?

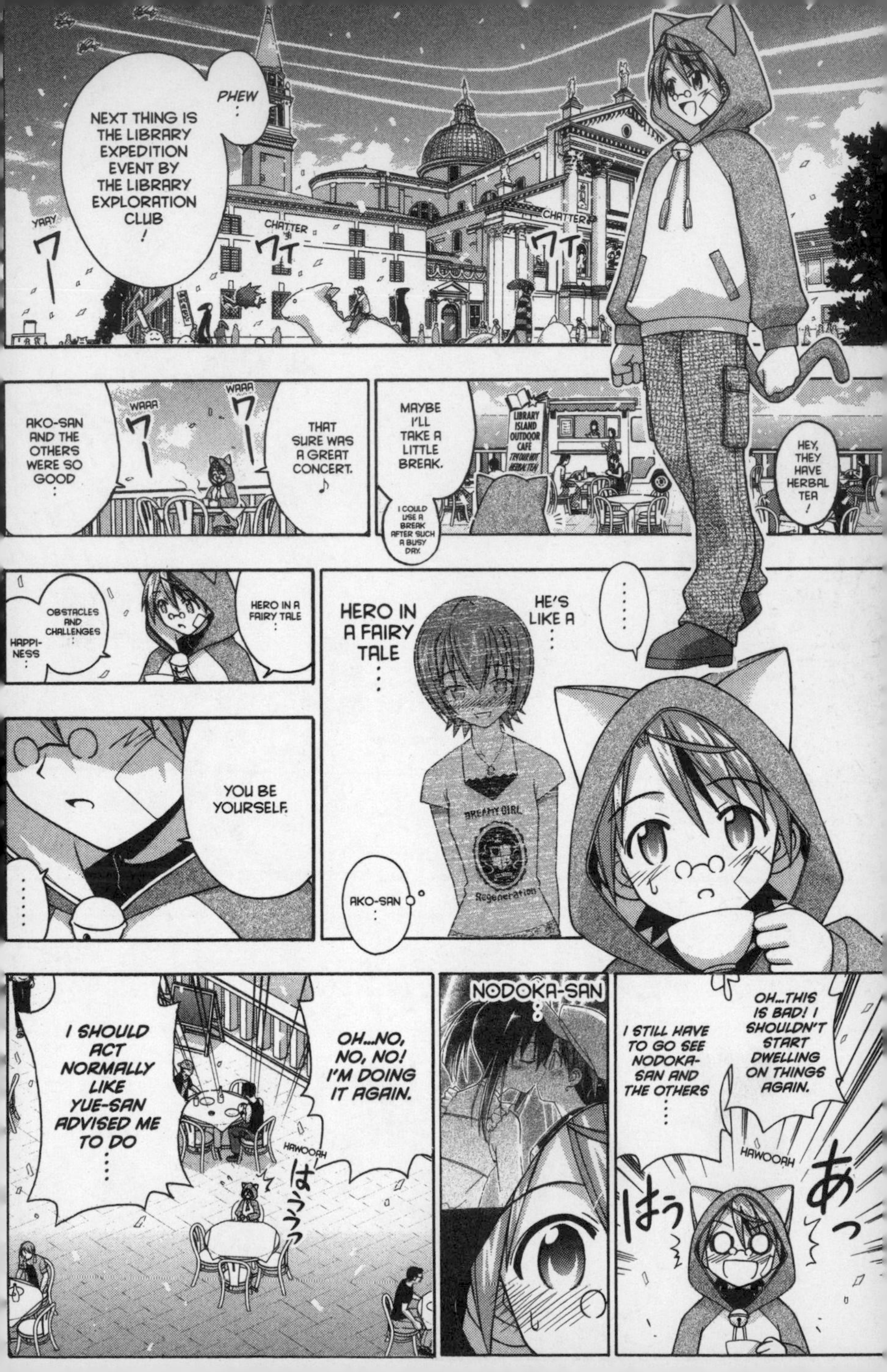
PHEW...
NEXT THING IS THE LIBRARY EXPEDITION EVENT BY THE LIBRARY EXPLORATION CLUB!
CHATTER
CHATTER
YAAY
MAYBE I'LL TAKE A LITTLE BREAK.
HEY, THEY HAVE HERBAL TEA!
LIBRARY ISLAND OUTDOOR CAFE
I COULD USE A BREAK AFTER SUCH A BUSY DAY.
THAT SURE WAS A GREAT CONCERT. ♪
WAAA
WAAA
AKO-SAN AND THE OTHERS WERE SO GOOD...
......
HE'S LIKE A...
HERO IN A FAIRY TALE...
DREAMY GIRL
Regeneration
AKO-SAN...
HERO IN A FAIRY TALE...
OBSTACLES AND CHALLENGES...
HAPPINESS...
YOU BE YOURSELF.
......
OH...THIS IS BAD! I SHOULDN'T START DWELLING ON THINGS AGAIN.
I STILL HAVE TO GO SEE NODOKA-SAN AND THE OTHERS...
HAWOORAH
NODOKA-SAN
OH...NO, NO, NO! I'M DOING IT AGAIN.
I SHOULD ACT NORMALLY LIKE YUE-SAN ADVISED ME TO DO...
HAWOORAH

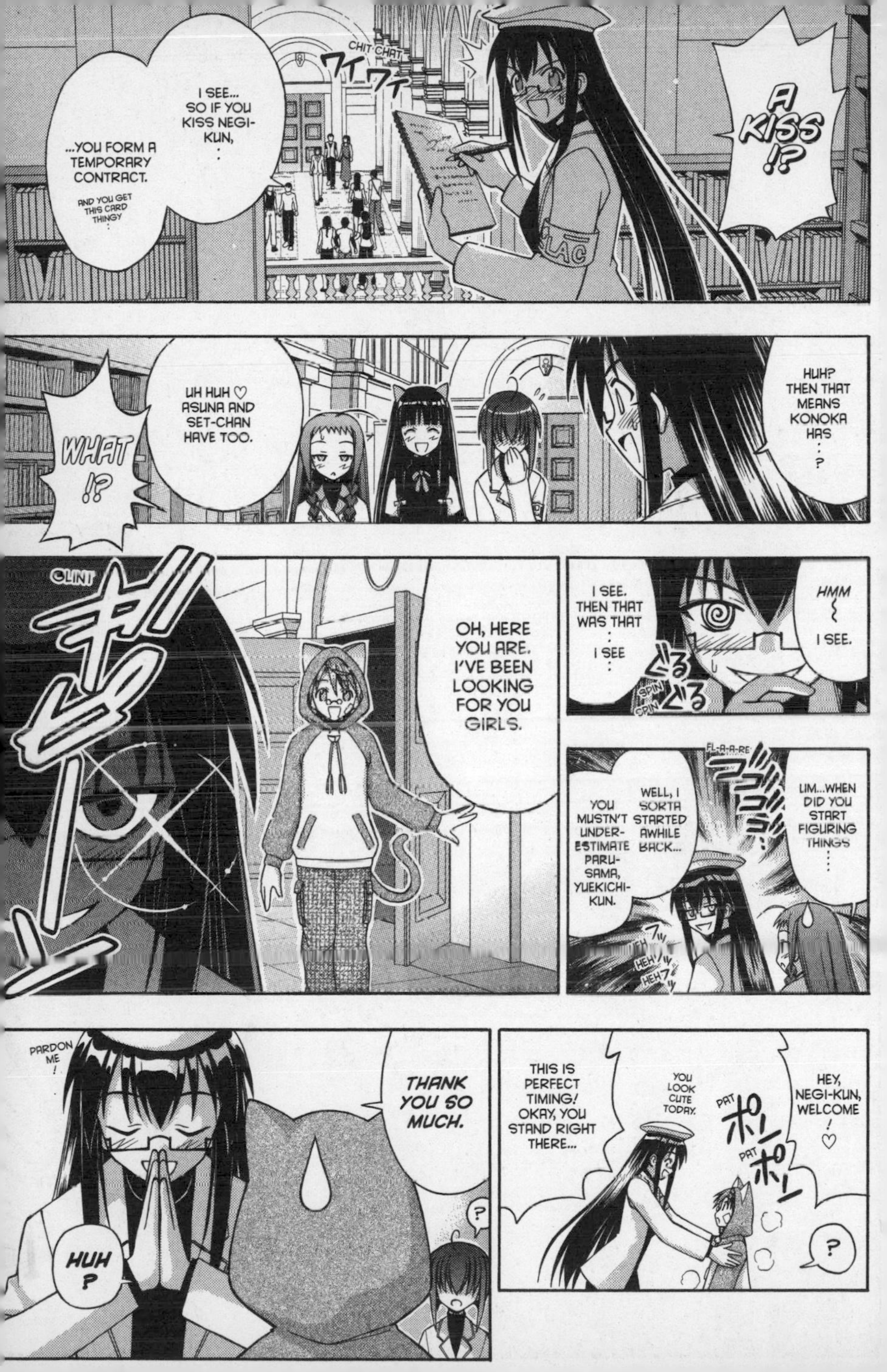
A KISS !?
CHIT CHAT
ワイワイ
I SEE... SO IF YOU KISS NEGI-KUN, . .
...YOU FORM A TEMPORARY CONTRACT.
AND YOU GET THIS CARD THINGY . .
HUH? THEN THAT MEANS KONOKA HAS . . ?
UH HUH ♡ ASUNA AND SET-CHAN HAVE TOO.
WHAT !?
HMM ~ I SEE.
I SEE. THEN THAT WAS THAT . . . I SEE . . .
SPIN SPIN
ぐるぐる
UM...WHEN DID YOU START FIGURING THINGS . . . .
FL-A-A-RE
WELL, I SORTA STARTED AWHILE BACK...
YOU MUSTN'T UNDER-ESTIMATE PARU-SAMA, YUEKICHI-KUN.
HEH HEH HEH
OH, HERE YOU ARE. I'VE BEEN LOOKING FOR YOU GIRLS.
GLINT
HEY, NEGI-KUN, WELCOME ! ♡
PAT PAT
YOU LOOK CUTE TODAY.
THIS IS PERFECT TIMING! OKAY, YOU STAND RIGHT THERE...
?
THANK YOU SO MUCH.
PARDON ME !
?
HUH ?

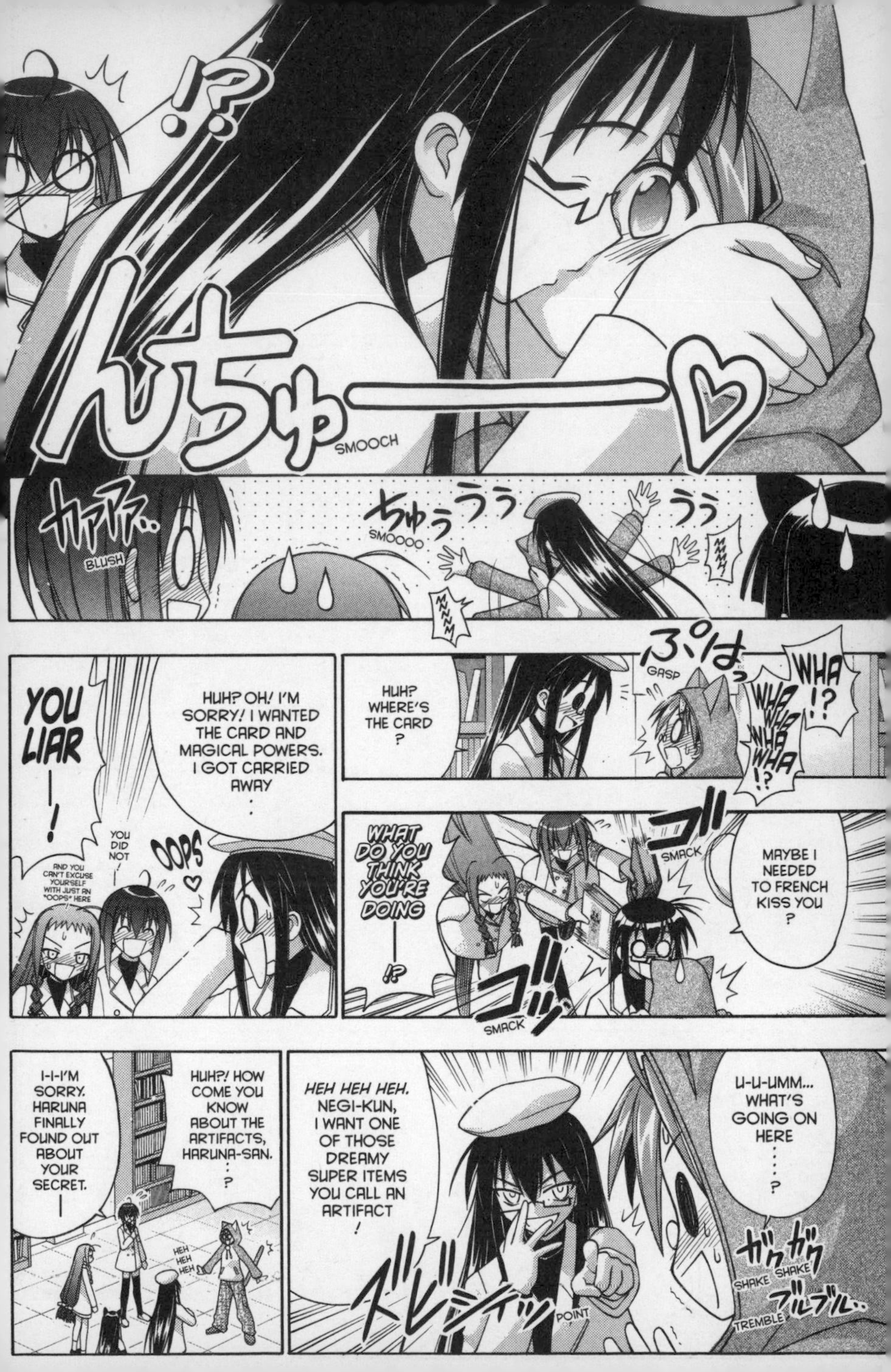
!?
SMOOCH
MMMM!
SMOOOO
MNNNM
BLUSH
WHA!? WHA WHA WHA WHA!?
GASP
HUH? WHERE'S THE CARD?
MAYBE I NEEDED TO FRENCH KISS YOU?
SMACK
WHAT DO YOU THINK YOU'RE DOING—!?
SMACK
HUH? OH! I'M SORRY! I WANTED THE CARD AND MAGICAL POWERS. I GOT CARRIED AWAY...
YOU LIAR—!
OOPS
YOU DID NOT!
AND YOU CAN'T EXCUSE YOURSELF WITH JUST AN "OOPS" HERE
U-U-UMM... WHAT'S GOING ON HERE.....?
HEH HEH HEH. NEGI-KUN, I WANT ONE OF THOSE DREAMY SUPER ITEMS YOU CALL AN ARTIFACT!
POINT
SHAKE SHAKE
TREMBLE
HUH?! HOW COME YOU KNOW ABOUT THE ARTIFACTS, HARUNA-SAN...?
I-I-I'M SORRY. HARUNA FINALLY FOUND OUT ABOUT YOUR SECRET—
HEH HEH HEH

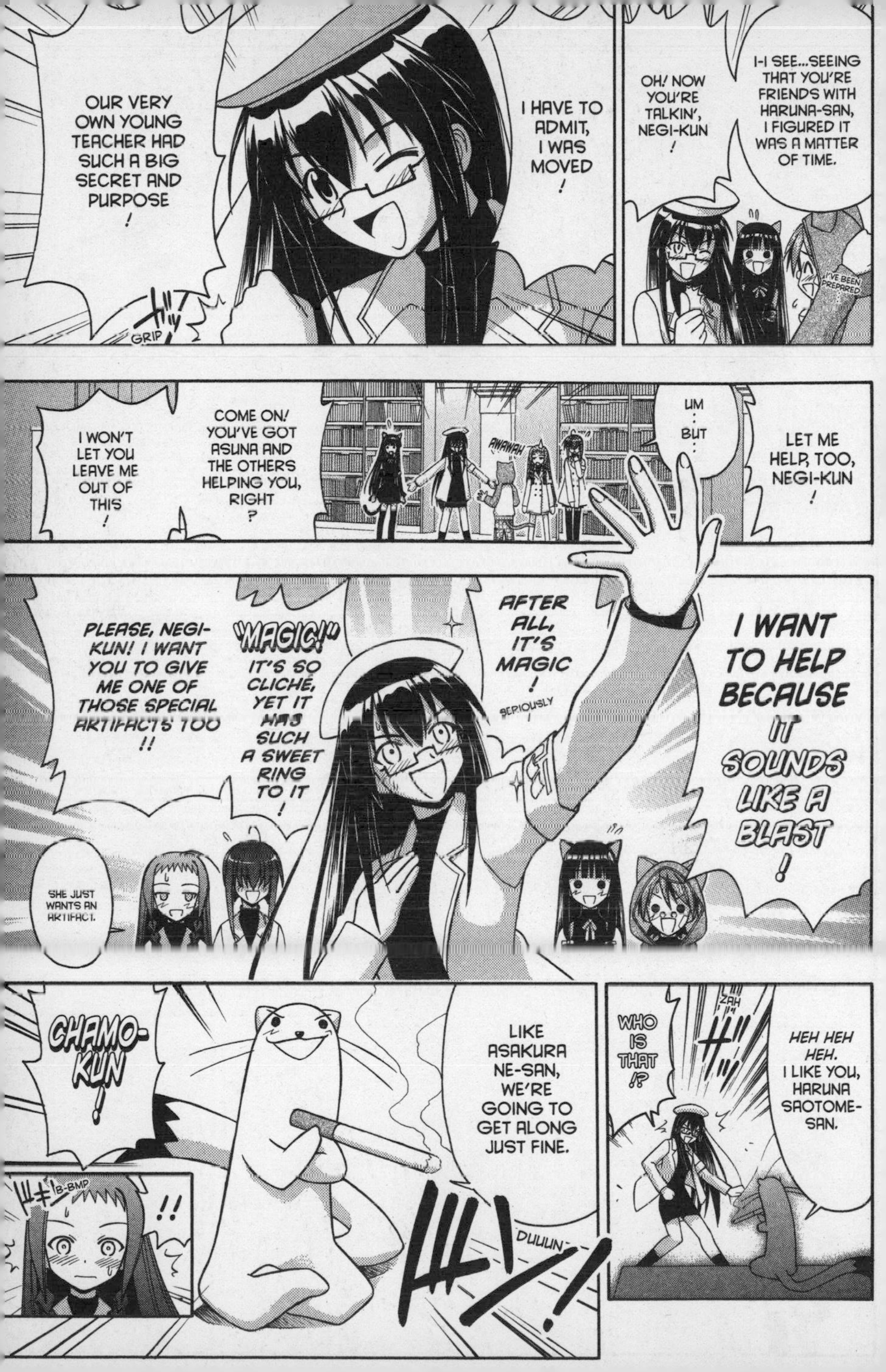

I-I SEE...SEEING THAT YOU'RE FRIENDS WITH HARUNA-SAN, I FIGURED IT WAS A MATTER OF TIME.
OH! NOW YOU'RE TALKIN', NEGI-KUN!
I'VE BEEN PREPARED
I HAVE TO ADMIT, I WAS MOVED!
OUR VERY OWN YOUNG TEACHER HAD SUCH A BIG SECRET AND PURPOSE!
GRIP
LET ME HELP, TOO, NEGI-KUN!
UM... BUT...
AWAWAH
COME ON! YOU'VE GOT ASUNA AND THE OTHERS HELPING YOU, RIGHT?
I WON'T LET YOU LEAVE ME OUT OF THIS!
I WANT TO HELP BECAUSE IT SOUNDS LIKE A BLAST!
AFTER ALL, IT'S MAGIC!
SERIOUSLY!
"MAGIC!" IT'S SO CLICHÉ, YET IT HAS SUCH A SWEET RING TO IT!
PLEASE, NEGI-KUN! I WANT YOU TO GIVE ME ONE OF THOSE SPECIAL ARTIFACTS TOO!!
SHE JUST WANTS AN ARTIFACT.
HEH HEH HEH. I LIKE YOU, HARUNA SAOTOME-SAN.
ZAH
WHO IS THAT!?
LIKE ASAKURA NE-SAN, WE'RE GOING TO GET ALONG JUST FINE.
CHAMO-KUN!
DUUUN
B-BMP
!!

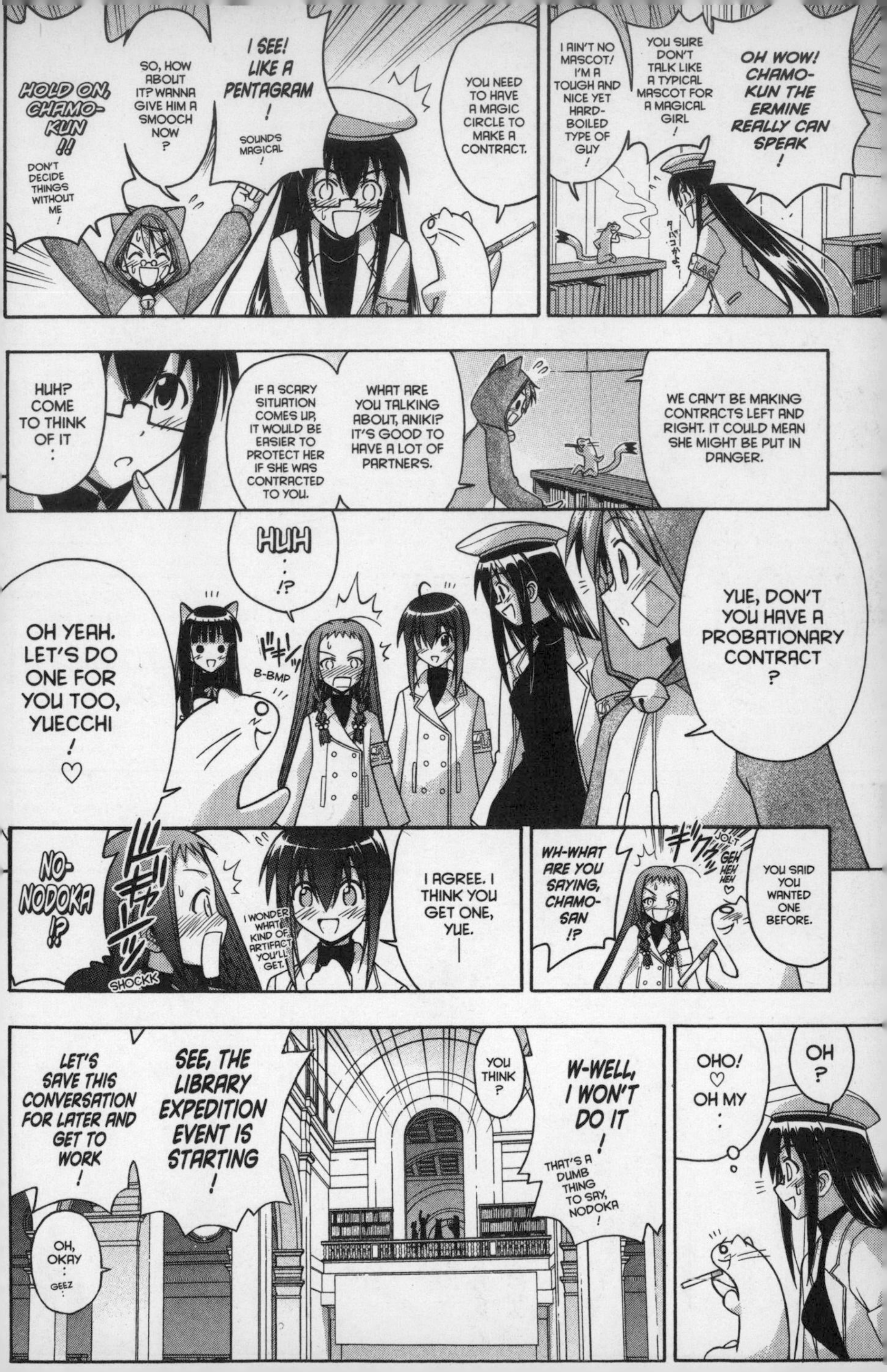
OH WOW! CHAMO-KUN THE ERMINE REALLY CAN SPEAK!
YOU SURE DON'T TALK LIKE A TYPICAL MASCOT FOR A MAGICAL GIRL!
I AIN'T NO MASCOT! I'M A TOUGH AND NICE YET HARD-BOILED TYPE OF GUY!
YOU NEED TO HAVE A MAGIC CIRCLE TO MAKE A CONTRACT.
I SEE! LIKE A PENTAGRAM!
SOUNDS MAGICAL!
SO, HOW ABOUT IT? WANNA GIVE HIM A SMOOCH NOW?
HOLD ON, CHAMO-KUN!!
DON'T DECIDE THINGS WITHOUT ME!
WE CAN'T BE MAKING CONTRACTS LEFT AND RIGHT. IT COULD MEAN SHE MIGHT BE PUT IN DANGER.
WHAT ARE YOU TALKING ABOUT, ANIKI? IT'S GOOD TO HAVE A LOT OF PARTNERS.
IF A SCARY SITUATION COMES UP, IT WOULD BE EASIER TO PROTECT HER IF SHE WAS CONTRACTED TO YOU.
HUH? COME TO THINK OF IT:
YUE, DON'T YOU HAVE A PROBATIONARY CONTRACT?
HUH:!?
B-BMP
OH YEAH. LET'S DO ONE FOR YOU TOO, YUECCHI! ♡
YOU SAID YOU WANTED ONE BEFORE.
JOLT
GEH HEH HEH ♡
WH-WHAT ARE YOU SAYING, CHAMO-SAN!?
I AGREE. I THINK YOU GET ONE, YUE.
I WONDER WHAT KIND OF ARTIFACT YOU'LL GET.
NO-NODOKA!?
SHOCKK
OH?
OHO! ♡ OH MY:
W-WELL, I WON'T DO IT!
YOU THINK?
THAT'S A DUMB THING TO SAY, NODOKA!
SEE, THE LIBRARY EXPEDITION EVENT IS STARTING!
LET'S SAVE THIS CONVERSATION FOR LATER AND GET TO WORK!
OH, OKAY:
GEEZ:

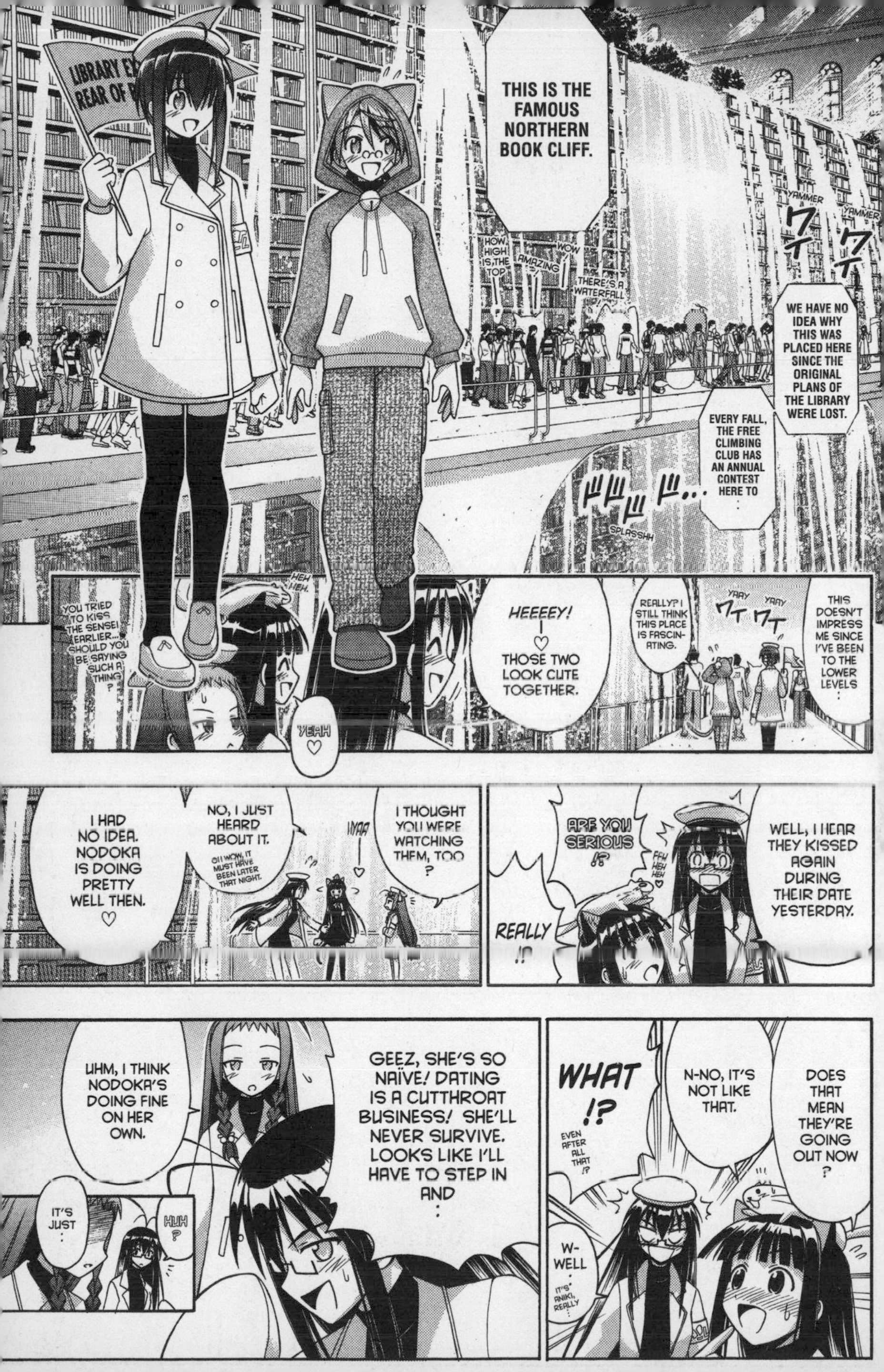

THIS IS THE FAMOUS NORTHERN BOOK CLIFF.
YAMMER YAMMER
WOW!
THERE'S A WATERFALL!
AMAZING!
HOW HIGH IS THE TOP!
WE HAVE NO IDEA WHY THIS WAS PLACED HERE SINCE THE ORIGINAL PLANS OF THE LIBRARY WERE LOST.
EVERY FALL, THE FREE CLIMBING CLUB HAS AN ANNUAL CONTEST HERE TO...
SPLASSHH
THIS DOESN'T IMPRESS ME SINCE I'VE BEEN TO THE LOWER LEVELS...
YAAY YAAY
REALLY?! I STILL THINK THIS PLACE IS FASCINATING.
HEEEEY! ♡ THOSE TWO LOOK CUTE TOGETHER.
HEH HEH.
YOU TRIED TO KISS THE SENSEI EARLIER... SHOULD YOU BE SAYING SUCH A THING?
YEAH ♡
WELL, I HEAR THEY KISSED AGAIN DURING THEIR DATE YESTERDAY.
ARE YOU SERIOUS !?
FFU HEH HEH ♡
REALLY !?
I THOUGHT YOU WERE WATCHING THEM, TOO?
IYAA ♡
NO, I JUST HEARD ABOUT IT.
OH WOW, IT MUST HAVE BEEN LATER THAT NIGHT.
I HAD NO IDEA. NODOKA IS DOING PRETTY WELL THEN. ♡
DOES THAT MEAN THEY'RE GOING OUT NOW?
N-NO, IT'S NOT LIKE THAT.
WHAT !?
EVEN AFTER ALL THAT !?
W-WELL...
IT'S ANIKI, REALLY...
GEEZ, SHE'S SO NAÏVE! DATING IS A CUTTHROAT BUSINESS! SHE'LL NEVER SURVIVE. LOOKS LIKE I'LL HAVE TO STEP IN AND...
UHM, I THINK NODOKA'S DOING FINE ON HER OWN.
HUH?
IT'S JUST...

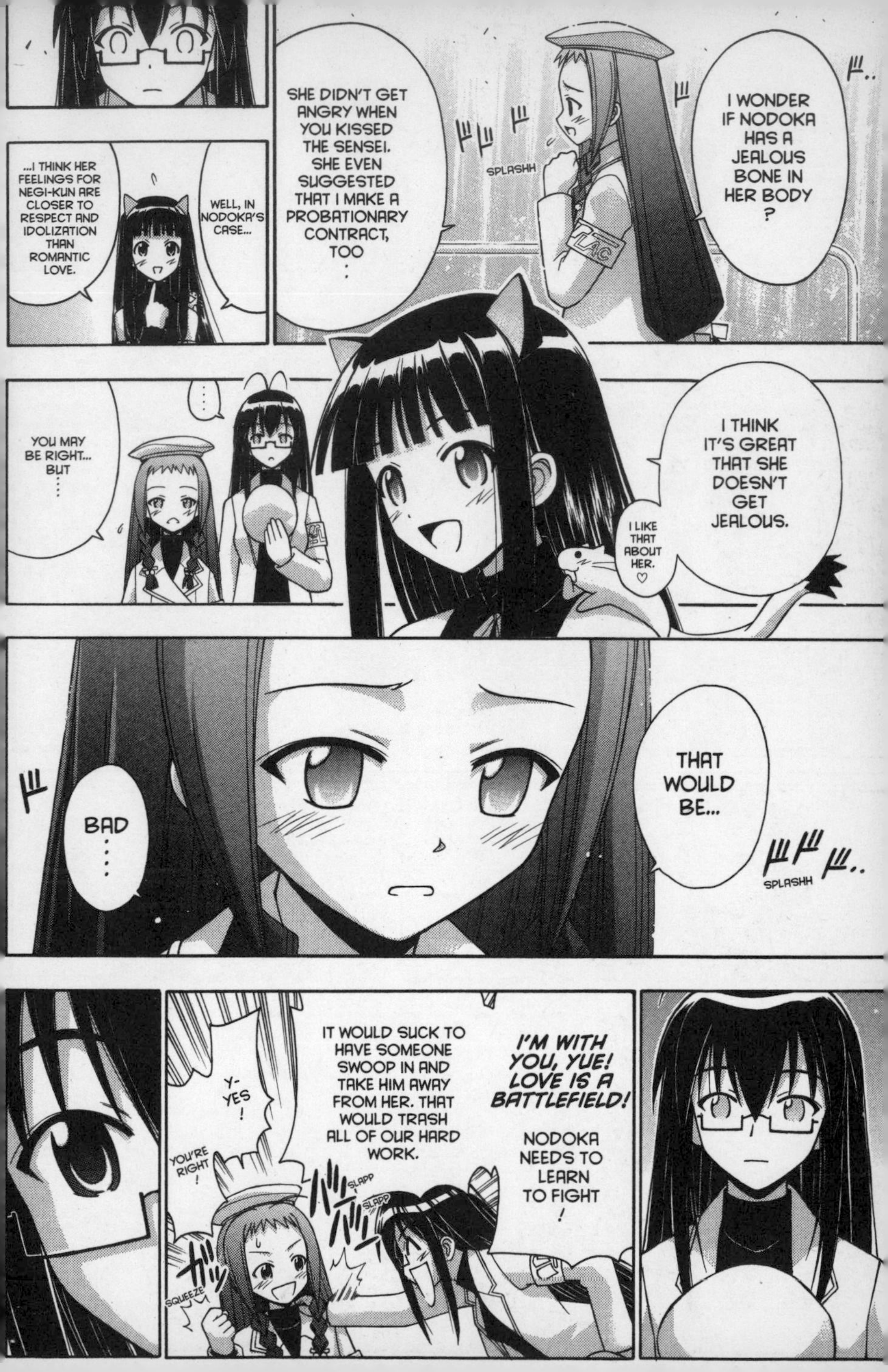
I WONDER IF NODOKA HAS A JEALOUS BONE IN HER BODY?
SPLASHH
SHE DIDN'T GET ANGRY WHEN YOU KISSED THE SENSEI. SHE EVEN SUGGESTED THAT I MAKE A PROBATIONARY CONTRACT, TOO ...
WELL, IN NODOKA'S CASE...
...I THINK HER FEELINGS FOR NEGI-KUN ARE CLOSER TO RESPECT AND IDOLIZATION THAN ROMANTIC LOVE.
I THINK IT'S GREAT THAT SHE DOESN'T GET JEALOUS.
I LIKE THAT ABOUT HER. ♡
....
YOU MAY BE RIGHT... BUT .....
THAT WOULD BE...
SPLASHH
BAD ....
I'M WITH YOU, YUE! LOVE IS A BATTLEFIELD!
NODOKA NEEDS TO LEARN TO FIGHT!
IT WOULD SUCK TO HAVE SOMEONE SWOOP IN AND TAKE HIM AWAY FROM HER. THAT WOULD TRASH ALL OF OUR HARD WORK.
Y-YES!
YOU'RE RIGHT!
SLAPP
SLAPP
SQUEEZE

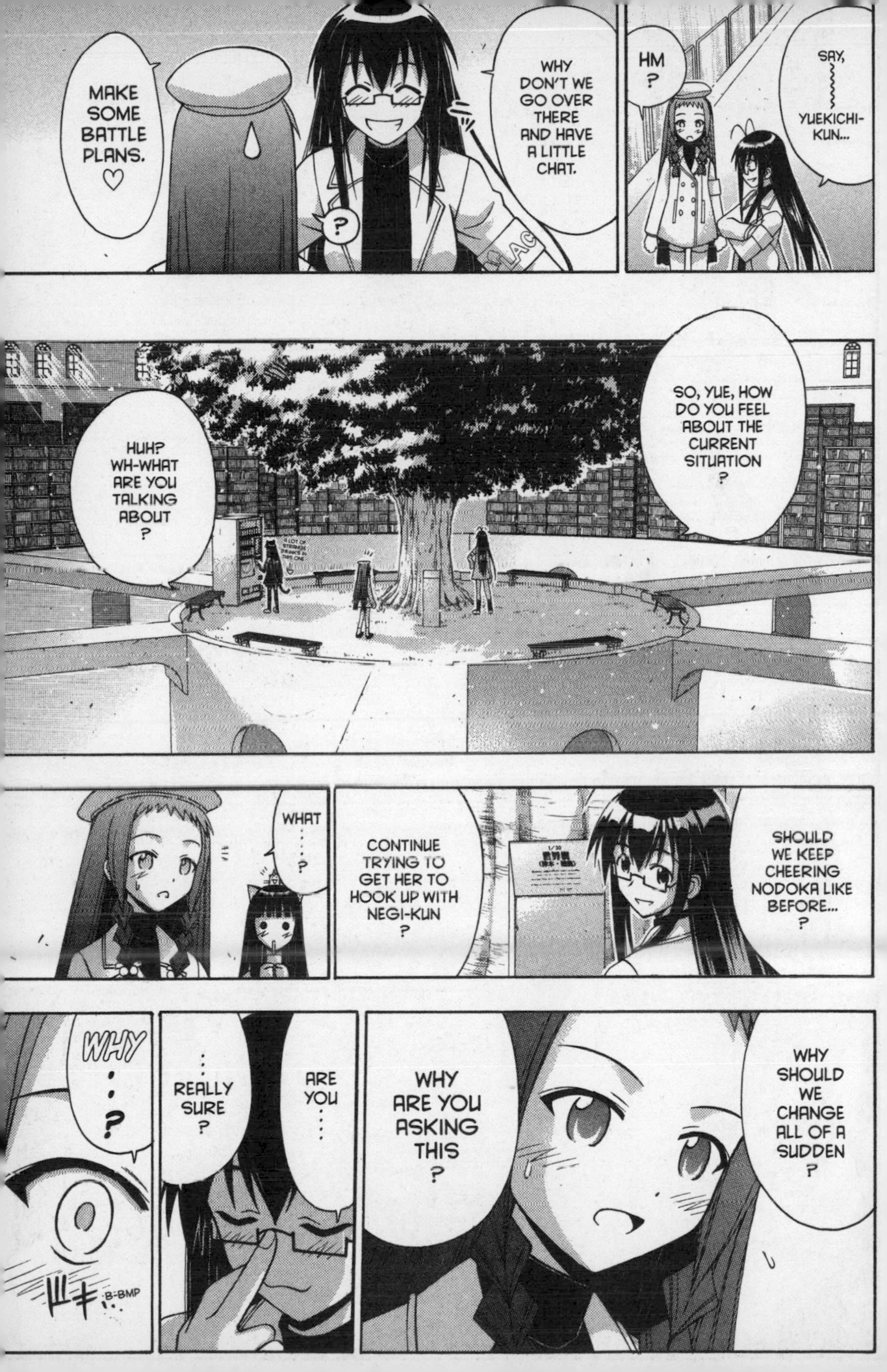
SAY, YUEKICHI-KUN...
HM?
WHY DON'T WE GO OVER THERE AND HAVE A LITTLE CHAT.
?
MAKE SOME BATTLE PLANS. ♡
SO, YUE, HOW DO YOU FEEL ABOUT THE CURRENT SITUATION?
HUH? WH-WHAT ARE YOU TALKING ABOUT?
SHOULD WE KEEP CHEERING NODOKA LIKE BEFORE...?
CONTINUE TRYING TO GET HER TO HOOK UP WITH NEGI-KUN?
WHAT...?
WHY SHOULD WE CHANGE ALL OF A SUDDEN?
WHY ARE YOU ASKING THIS?
ARE YOU....
...REALLY SURE?
WHY..?
B-BMP

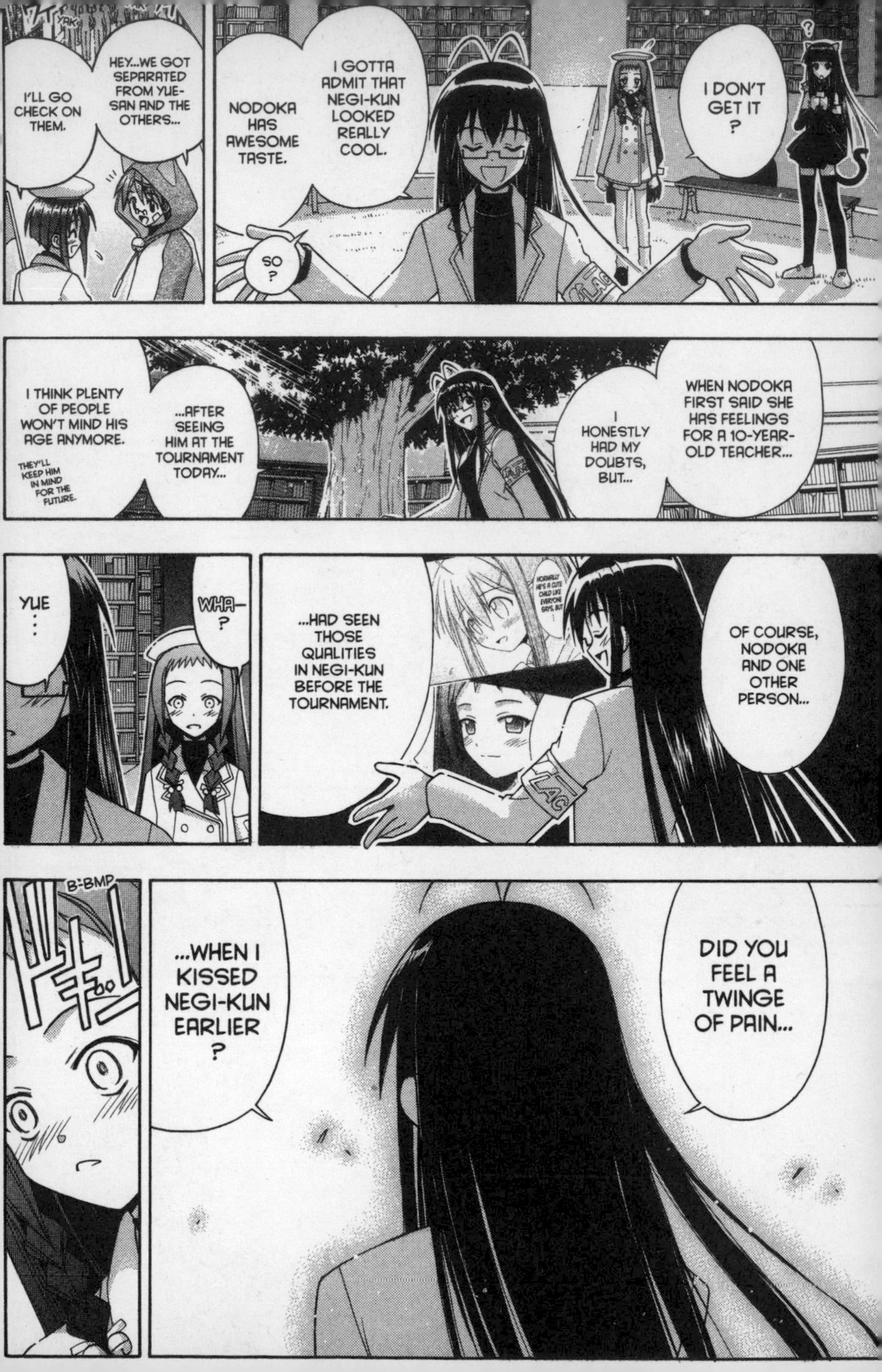
I DON'T GET IT ?
I GOTTA ADMIT THAT NEGI-KUN LOOKED REALLY COOL.
NODOKA HAS AWESOME TASTE.
SO ?
YAK
HEY...WE GOT SEPARATED FROM YUE-SAN AND THE OTHERS...
I'LL GO CHECK ON THEM.
WHEN NODOKA FIRST SAID SHE HAS FEELINGS FOR A 10-YEAR-OLD TEACHER...
I HONESTLY HAD MY DOUBTS, BUT...
...AFTER SEEING HIM AT THE TOURNAMENT TODAY...
I THINK PLENTY OF PEOPLE WON'T MIND HIS AGE ANYMORE.
THEY'LL KEEP HIM IN MIND FOR THE FUTURE.
OF COURSE, NODOKA AND ONE OTHER PERSON...
NORMALLY HE'S A CUTE CHILD LIKE EVERYONE SAYS, BUT
...HAD SEEN THOSE QUALITIES IN NEGI-KUN BEFORE THE TOURNAMENT.
WHA- ?
YUE ...
DID YOU FEEL A TWINGE OF PAIN...
...WHEN I KISSED NEGI-KUN EARLIER ?
B-BMP

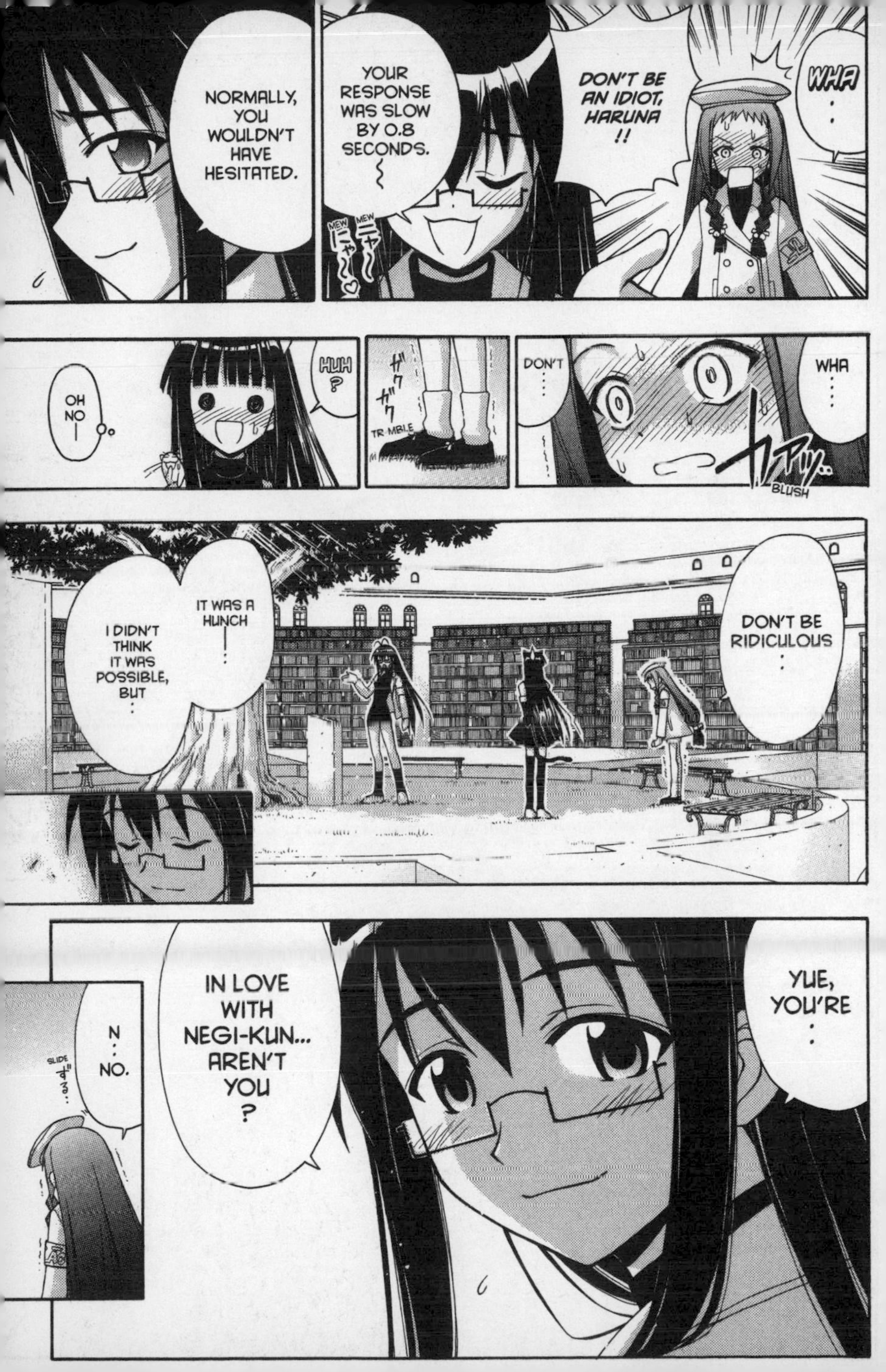
WHA . .
DON'T BE AN IDIOT, HARUNA !!
YOUR RESPONSE WAS SLOW BY 0.8 SECONDS.
MEW ニャ～
MEW にゃ～♡
NORMALLY, YOU WOULDN'T HAVE HESITATED.
WHA ....
DON'T ...
BLUSH
ガク ガク
TR MBLE
HUH ?
OH NO —
DON'T BE RIDICULOUS ...
IT WAS A HUNCH — ...
I DIDN'T THINK IT WAS POSSIBLE, BUT ...
YUE, YOU'RE ...
IN LOVE WITH NEGI-KUN... AREN'T YOU ?
N.. NO.
SLIDE ずる...

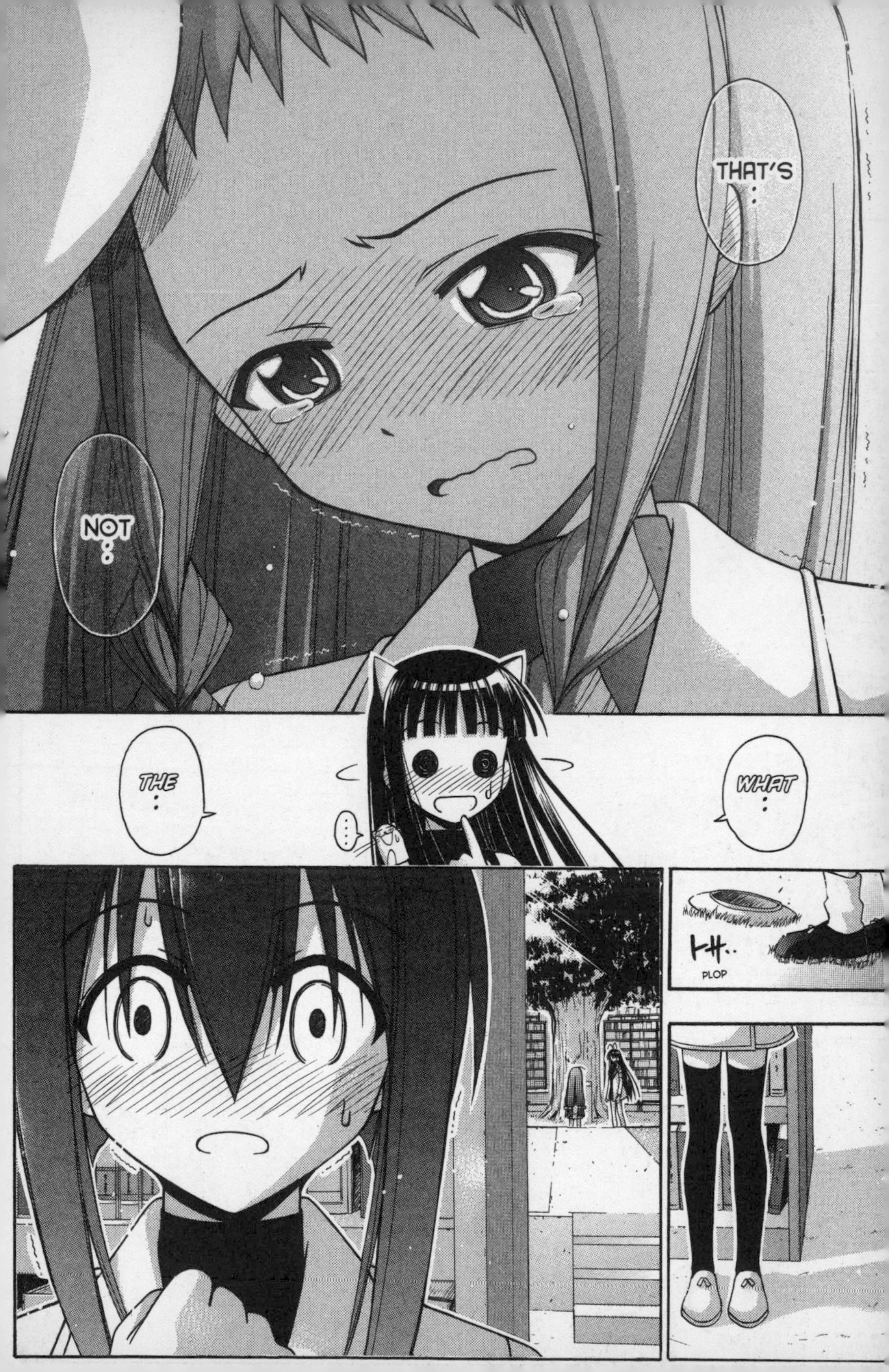
THAT'S ...
NOT ...
WHAT ...
...
THE ...
トサ..
PLOP

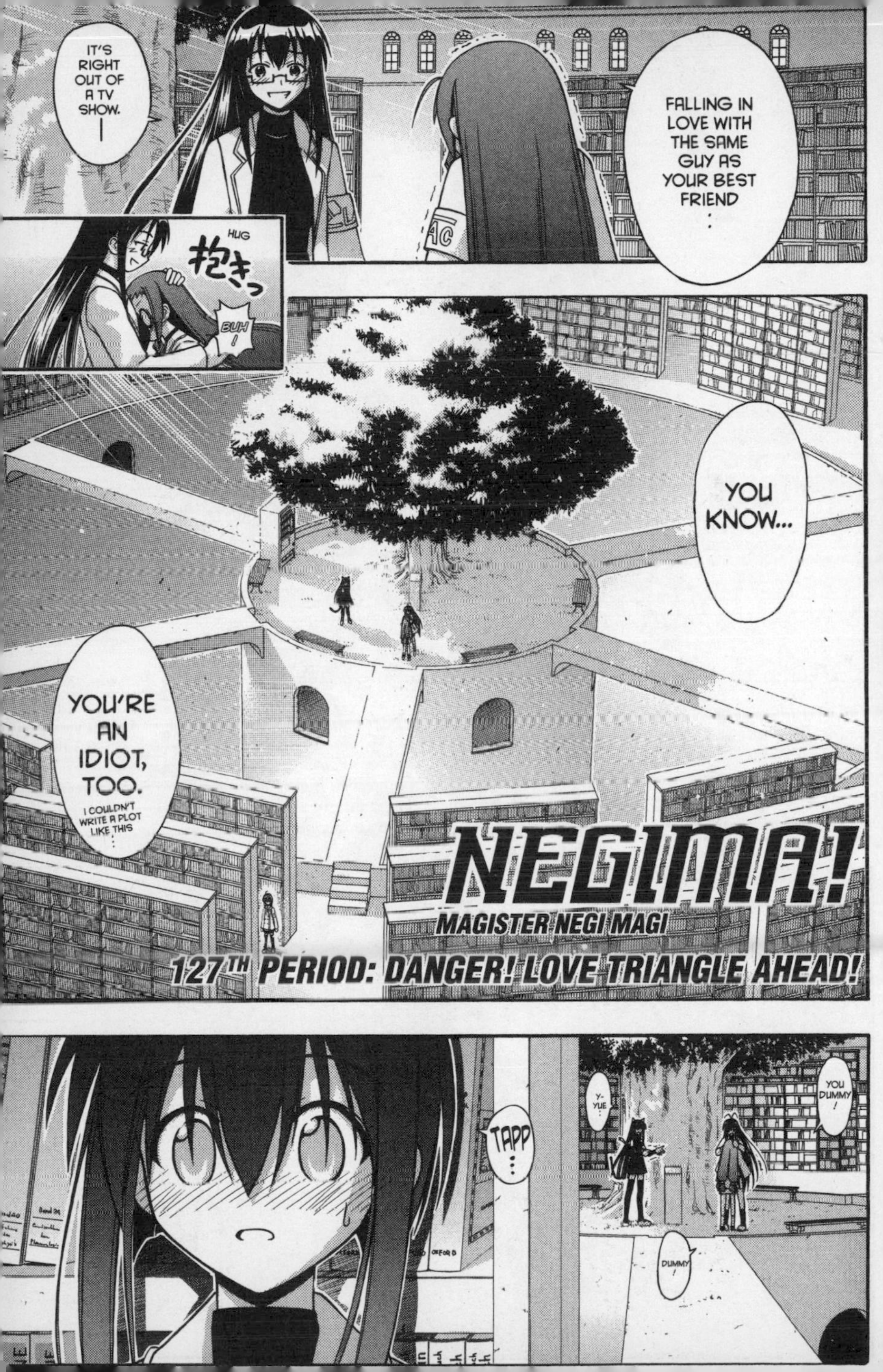

FALLING IN LOVE WITH THE SAME GUY AS YOUR BEST FRIEND :
IT'S RIGHT OUT OF A TV SHOW.
HUG 抱きっ
BUH!
YOU KNOW...
YOU'RE AN IDIOT, TOO.
I COULDN'T WRITE A PLOT LIKE THIS ...
NEGIMA!
MAGISTER NEGI MAGI
127TH PERIOD: DANGER! LOVE TRIANGLE AHEAD!
YOU DUMMY!
Y-YUE...
DUMMY!
TAPP...

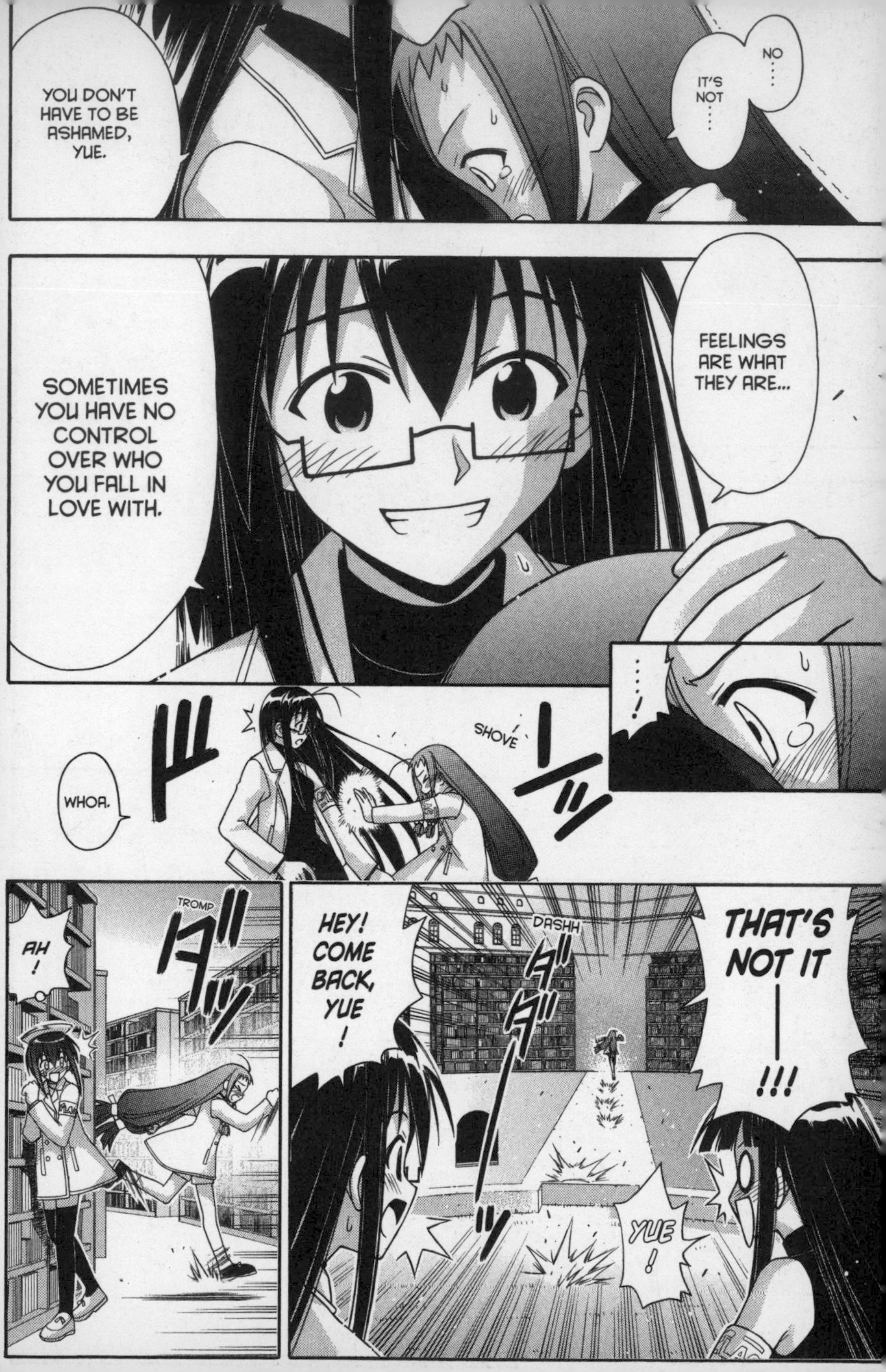
NO..... IT'S NOT.....
YOU DON'T HAVE TO BE ASHAMED, YUE.
FEELINGS ARE WHAT THEY ARE...
SOMETIMES YOU HAVE NO CONTROL OVER WHO YOU FALL IN LOVE WITH.
...!
SHOVE
WHOA.
THAT'S NOT IT —— !!!
YUE!
DASHH
HEY! COME BACK, YUE!
TROMP
AH!

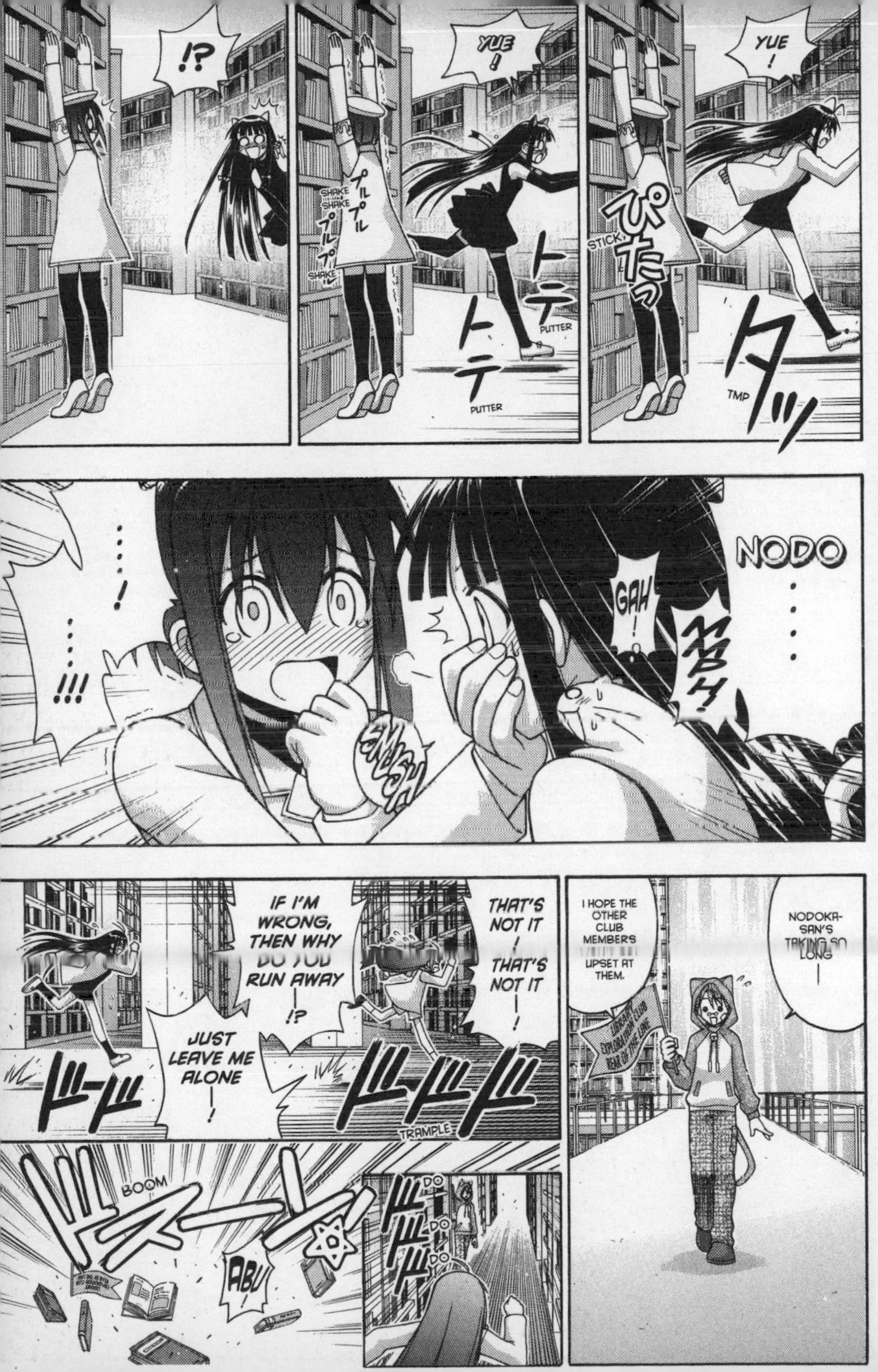

YUE!
STICK
ぴたっ
TMP
タッ
YUE!
SHAKE SHAKE
プルプル
SHAKE
プルプル
トテ
PUTTER
トテ
PUTTER
!?
NODO...
GAH!
MMPH!
SMOOCH
...!
...!!!
NODOKA-SAN'S TAKING SO LONG!
I HOPE THE OTHER CLUB MEMBERS
UPSET AT THEM.
LIBRARY EXPLORATION CLUB REAR OF THE LINE
THAT'S NOT IT! THAT'S NOT IT!
IF I'M WRONG, THEN WHY DO YOU RUN AWAY!?
JUST LEAVE ME ALONE!
TRAMPLE
DO DO DO
BOOM
ABU!

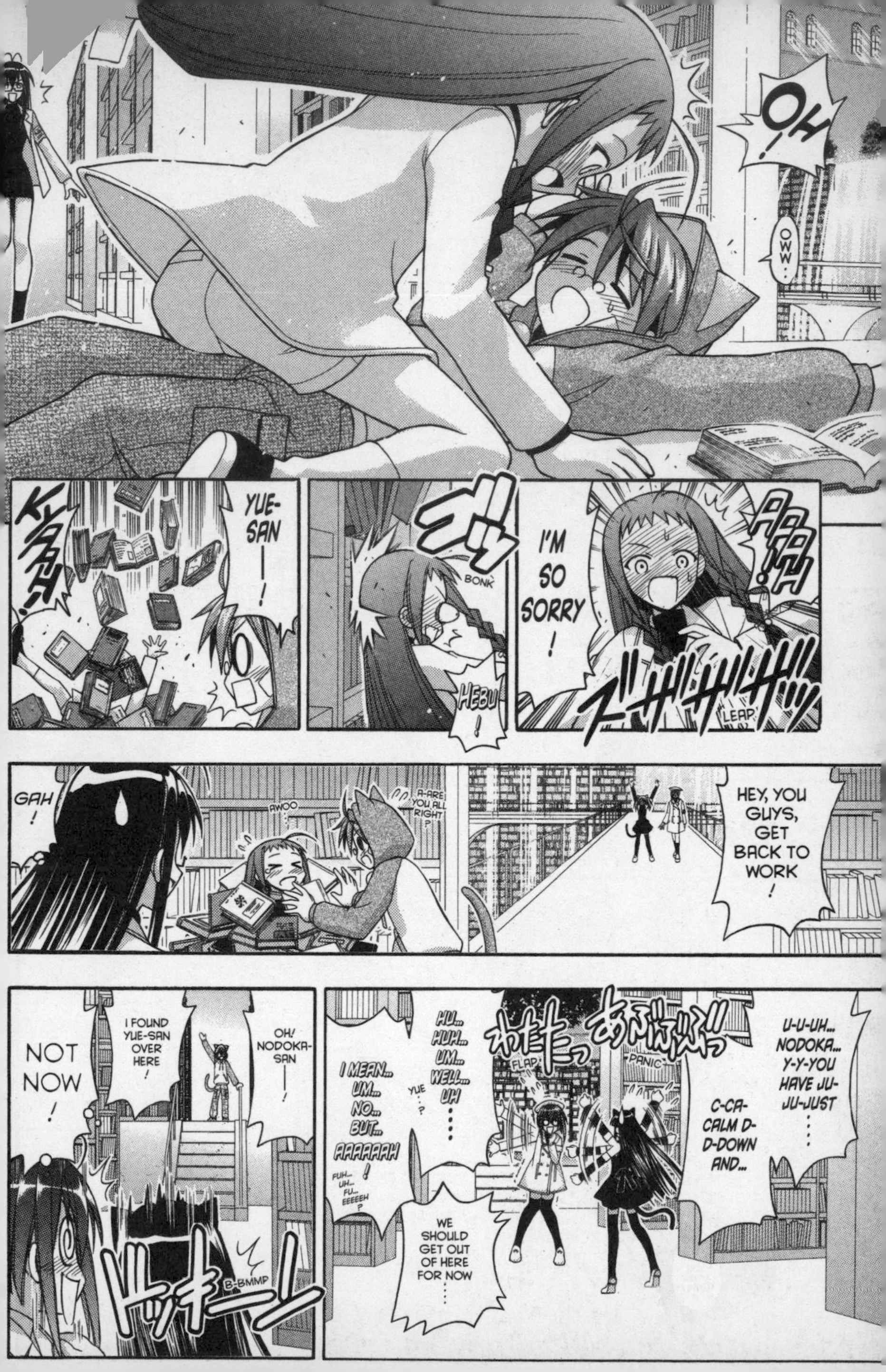
OH!
OWW...
I'M SO SORRY!
LEAP
BONK
HEBU!
YUE-SAN—!
HEY, YOU GUYS, GET BACK TO WORK!
A-ARE YOU ALL RIGHT?
AWOO
GAH!
U-U-UH... NODOKA... Y-Y-YOU HAVE JU-JU-JUST....
C-CA-CALM D-D-DOWN AND...
PANIC
FLAP
HU... HUH... UM... WELL... UH....
YUE...?
I MEAN... UM... NO... BUT... AAAAAAH!
FUH... UH... FU... EEEEEH?
WE SHOULD GET OUT OF HERE FOR NOW....
OH! NODOKA-SAN—!
I FOUND YUE-SAN OVER HERE!
NOT NOW!
B-BMMP

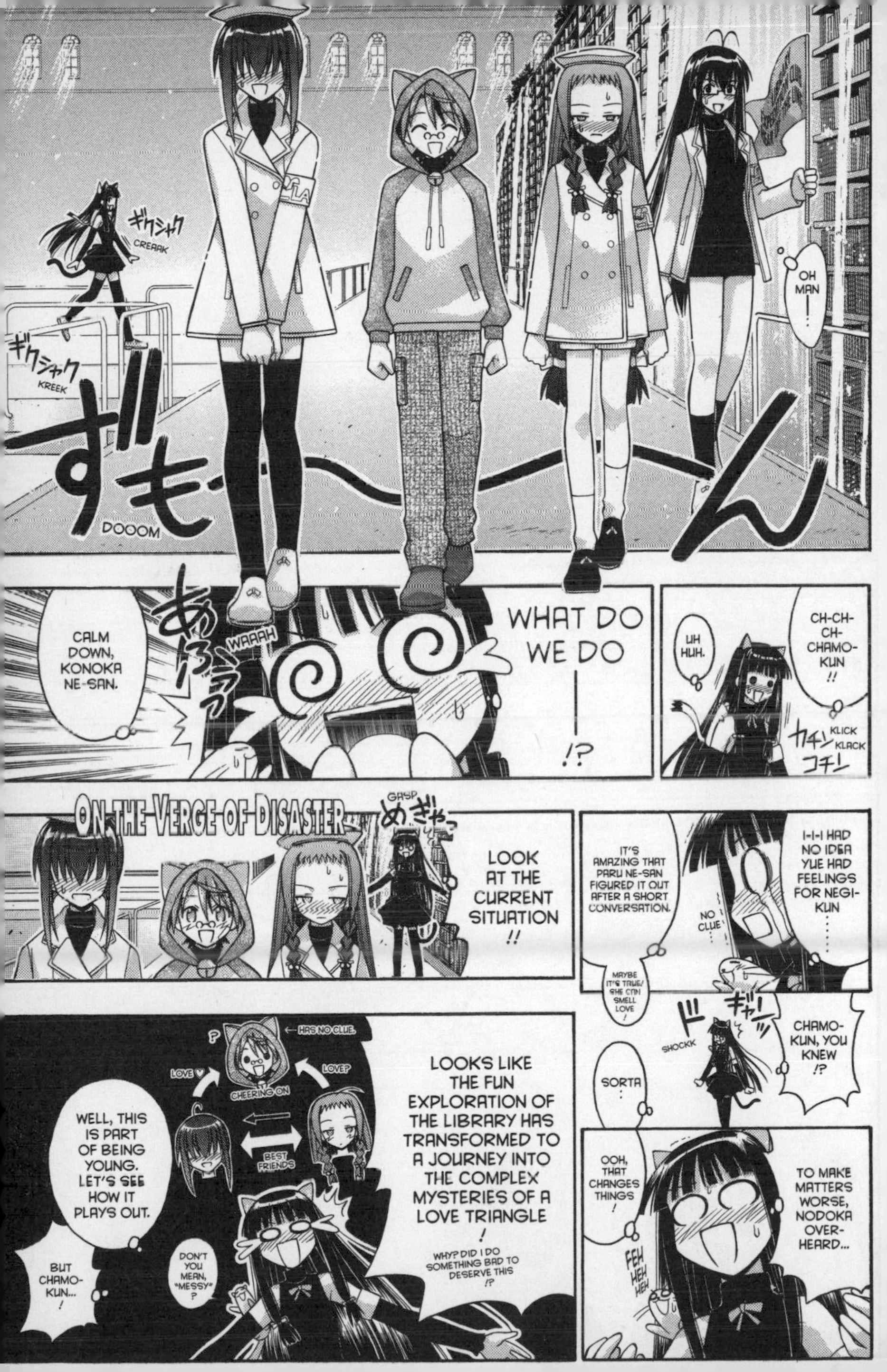
OH MAN ...!
ギクシャク
CREAAK
ギクシャク
KREEK
ずも〜〜ん
DOOOM
CH-CH-CHAMO-KUN !!
UH HUH.
カチン KLICK
コチン KLACK
WHAT DO WE DO —!?
WAAAH
CALM DOWN, KONOKA NE-SAN.
On the Verge of Disaster
I-I-I HAD NO IDEA YUE HAD FEELINGS FOR NEGI-KUN ....
IT'S AMAZING THAT PARU NE-SAN FIGURED IT OUT AFTER A SHORT CONVERSATION.
NO CLUE ...
MAYBE IT'S TRUE/ SHE CAN SMELL LOVE !
GASP めぎゃっ
LOOK AT THE CURRENT SITUATION !!
CHAMO-KUN, YOU KNEW !?
SHOCKK
SORTA ...
TO MAKE MATTERS WORSE, NODOKA OVER-HEARD...
OOH, THAT CHANGES THINGS !
FEH HEH HEH
LOOKS LIKE THE FUN EXPLORATION OF THE LIBRARY HAS TRANSFORMED TO A JOURNEY INTO THE COMPLEX MYSTERIES OF A LOVE TRIANGLE !
WHY? DID I DO SOMETHING BAD TO DESERVE THIS !?
← HAS NO CLUE.
?
LOVE ♡
LOVE?
CHEERING ON
BEST FRIENDS
WELL, THIS IS PART OF BEING YOUNG. LET'S SEE HOW IT PLAYS OUT.
DON'T YOU MEAN, "MESSY" ?
BUT CHAMO-KUN... !

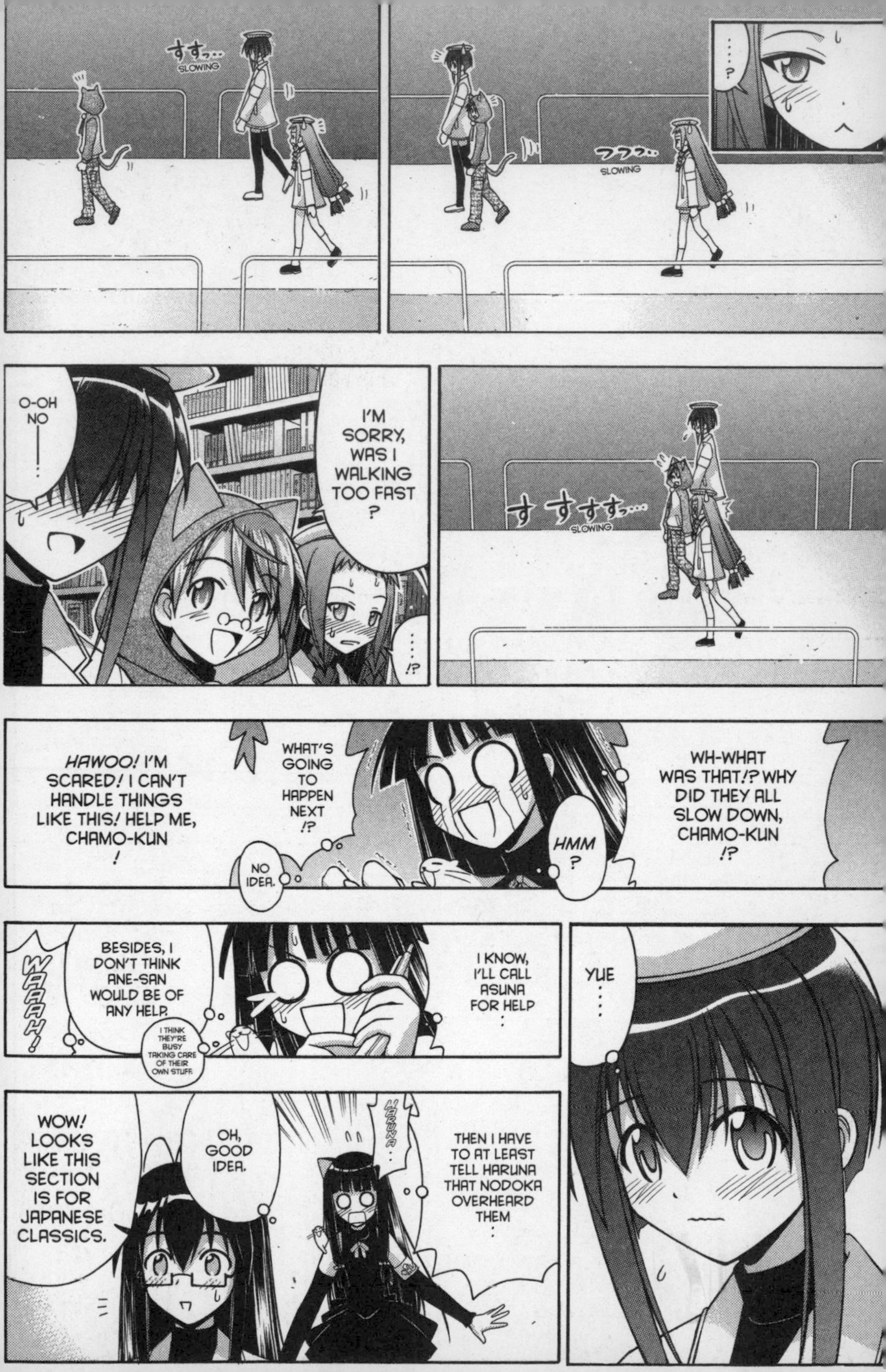

...?
フフフ...
SLOWING
すすっ...
SLOWING
すすすす...
SLOWING
I'M SORRY, WAS I WALKING TOO FAST?
O-OH NO—...
...!?
WH-WHAT WAS THAT!? WHY DID THEY ALL SLOW DOWN, CHAMO-KUN!?
HMM?
WHAT'S GOING TO HAPPEN NEXT!?
NO IDEA.
HAWOO! I'M SCARED! I CAN'T HANDLE THINGS LIKE THIS! HELP ME, CHAMO-KUN!
YUE...
I KNOW, I'LL CALL ASUNA FOR HELP...
BESIDES, I DON'T THINK ANE-SAN WOULD BE OF ANY HELP.
I THINK THEY'RE BUSY TAKING CARE OF THEIR OWN STUFF.
WAAAAH!
THEN I HAVE TO AT LEAST TELL HARUNA THAT NODOKA OVERHEARD THEM...
HARUNA...
OH, GOOD IDEA.
WOW! LOOKS LIKE THIS SECTION IS FOR JAPANESE CLASSICS.

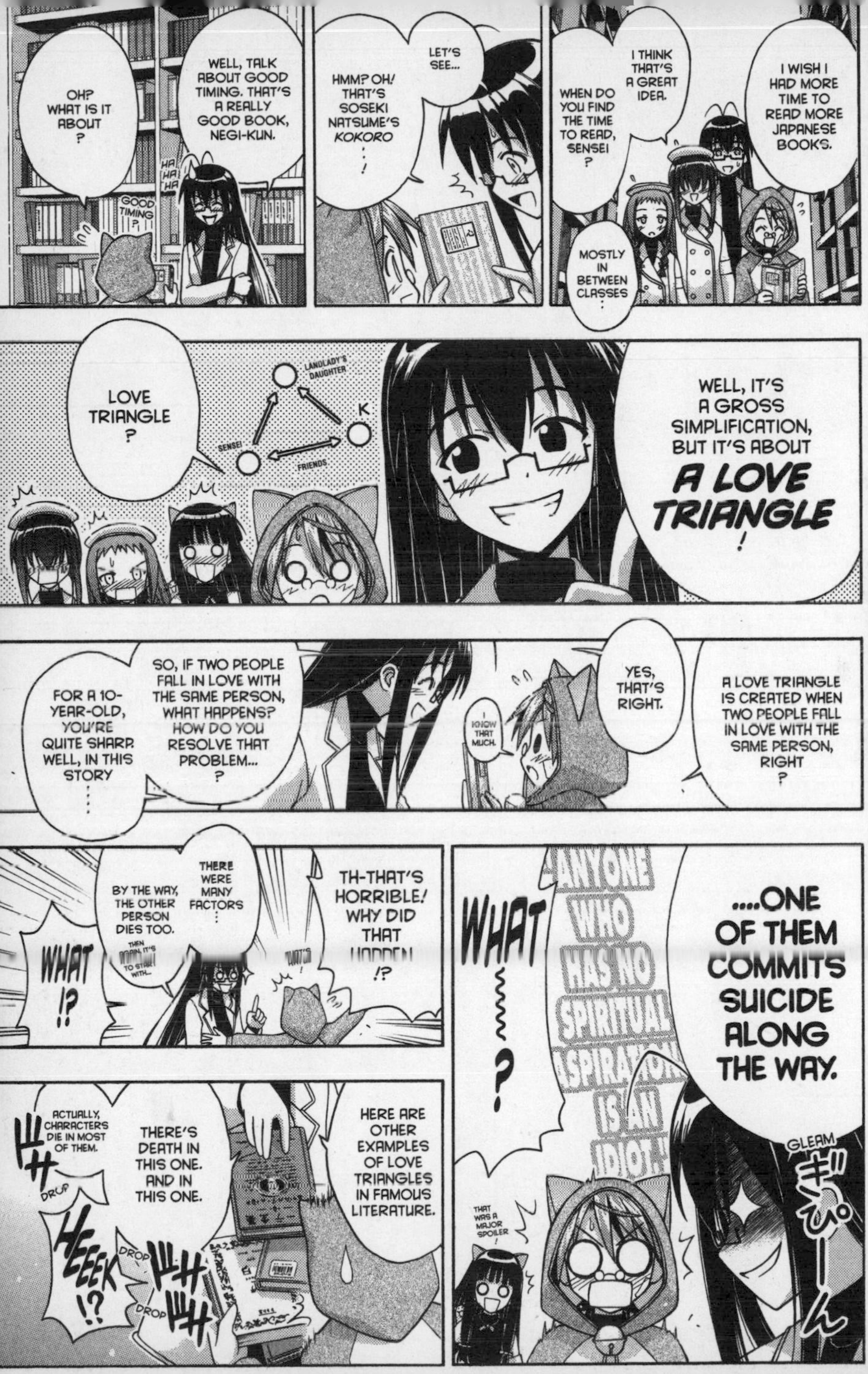
I WISH I HAD MORE TIME TO READ MORE JAPANESE BOOKS.
I THINK THAT'S A GREAT IDEA.
WHEN DO YOU FIND THE TIME TO READ, SENSEI?
MOSTLY IN BETWEEN CLASSES...
LET'S SEE...
HMM? OH! THAT'S SOSEKI NATSUME'S *KOKORO*...!
WELL, TALK ABOUT GOOD TIMING. THAT'S A REALLY GOOD BOOK, NEGI-KUN.
OH? WHAT IS IT ABOUT?
HA HA HA
GOOD TIMING?
WELL, IT'S A GROSS SIMPLIFICATION, BUT IT'S ABOUT **A LOVE TRIANGLE**!
LOVE TRIANGLE?
LANDLADY'S DAUGHTER
K
SENSEI
FRIENDS
A LOVE TRIANGLE IS CREATED WHEN TWO PEOPLE FALL IN LOVE WITH THE SAME PERSON, RIGHT?
YES, THAT'S RIGHT.
I KNOW THAT MUCH.
SO, IF TWO PEOPLE FALL IN LOVE WITH THE SAME PERSON, WHAT HAPPENS? HOW DO YOU RESOLVE THAT PROBLEM...?
FOR A 10-YEAR-OLD, YOU'RE QUITE SHARP. WELL, IN THIS STORY......
....ONE OF THEM COMMITS SUICIDE ALONG THE WAY.
WHAT~~?
ANYONE WHO HAS NO SPIRITUAL ASPIRATION IS AN IDIOT!
GLEAM
THAT WAS A MAJOR SPOILER!
TH-THAT'S HORRIBLE! WHY DID THAT HAPPEN!?
THERE WERE MANY FACTORS...
BY THE WAY, THE OTHER PERSON DIES TOO.
THEN AGAIN, IT'S TO START WITH...
THAT'S!
WHAT!?
HERE ARE OTHER EXAMPLES OF LOVE TRIANGLES IN FAMOUS LITERATURE.
THERE'S DEATH IN THIS ONE. AND IN THIS ONE.
ACTUALLY, CHARACTERS DIE IN MOST OF THEM.
DROP
HEEEK!?
DROP
DROP

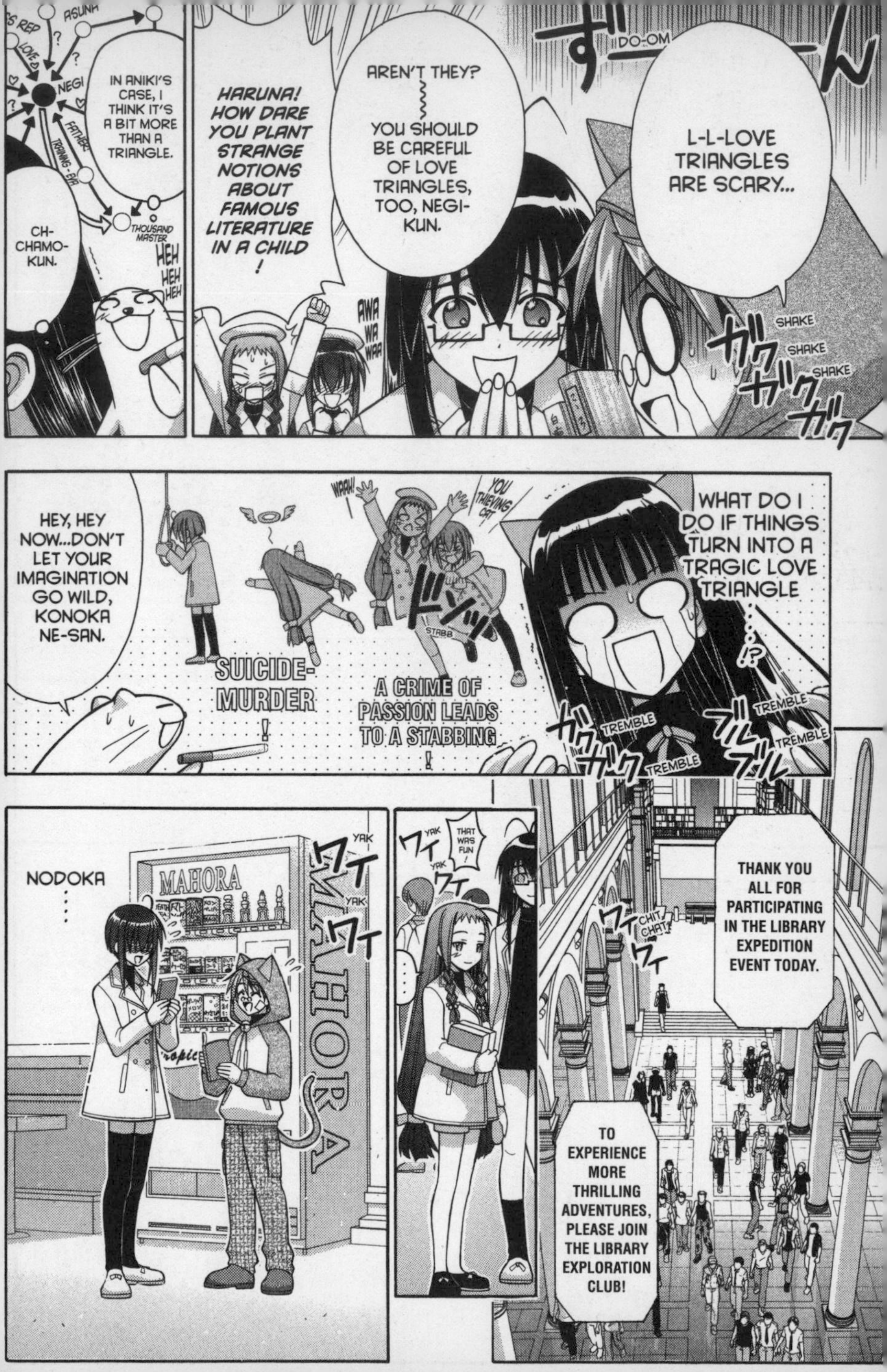
DO-OM
L-L-LOVE TRIANGLES ARE SCARY...
SHAKE
SHAKE
SHAKE
AREN'T THEY? YOU SHOULD BE CAREFUL OF LOVE TRIANGLES, TOO, NEGI-KUN.
HARUNA! HOW DARE YOU PLANT STRANGE NOTIONS ABOUT FAMOUS LITERATURE IN A CHILD!
AWA WA WAA
ASUNA
LOVE
NEGI
FATHER
TRAINING - EVA
THOUSAND MASTER
IN ANIKI'S CASE, I THINK IT'S A BIT MORE THAN A TRIANGLE.
CH-CHAMO-KUN.
HEH HEH HEH
WHAT DO I DO IF THINGS TURN INTO A TRAGIC LOVE TRIANGLE......!?
TREMBLE
TREMBLE
TREMBLE
TREMBLE
YOU THIEVING CAT
WAAH!
STABB
A CRIME OF PASSION LEADS TO A STABBING!
SUICIDE-MURDER!
HEY, HEY NOW...DON'T LET YOUR IMAGINATION GO WILD, KONOKA NE-SAN.
THANK YOU ALL FOR PARTICIPATING IN THE LIBRARY EXPEDITION EVENT TODAY.
CHIT CHAT
TO EXPERIENCE MORE THRILLING ADVENTURES, PLEASE JOIN THE LIBRARY EXPLORATION CLUB!
YAK
YAK
THAT WAS FUN!
YAK
YAK
MAHORA
NODOKA...

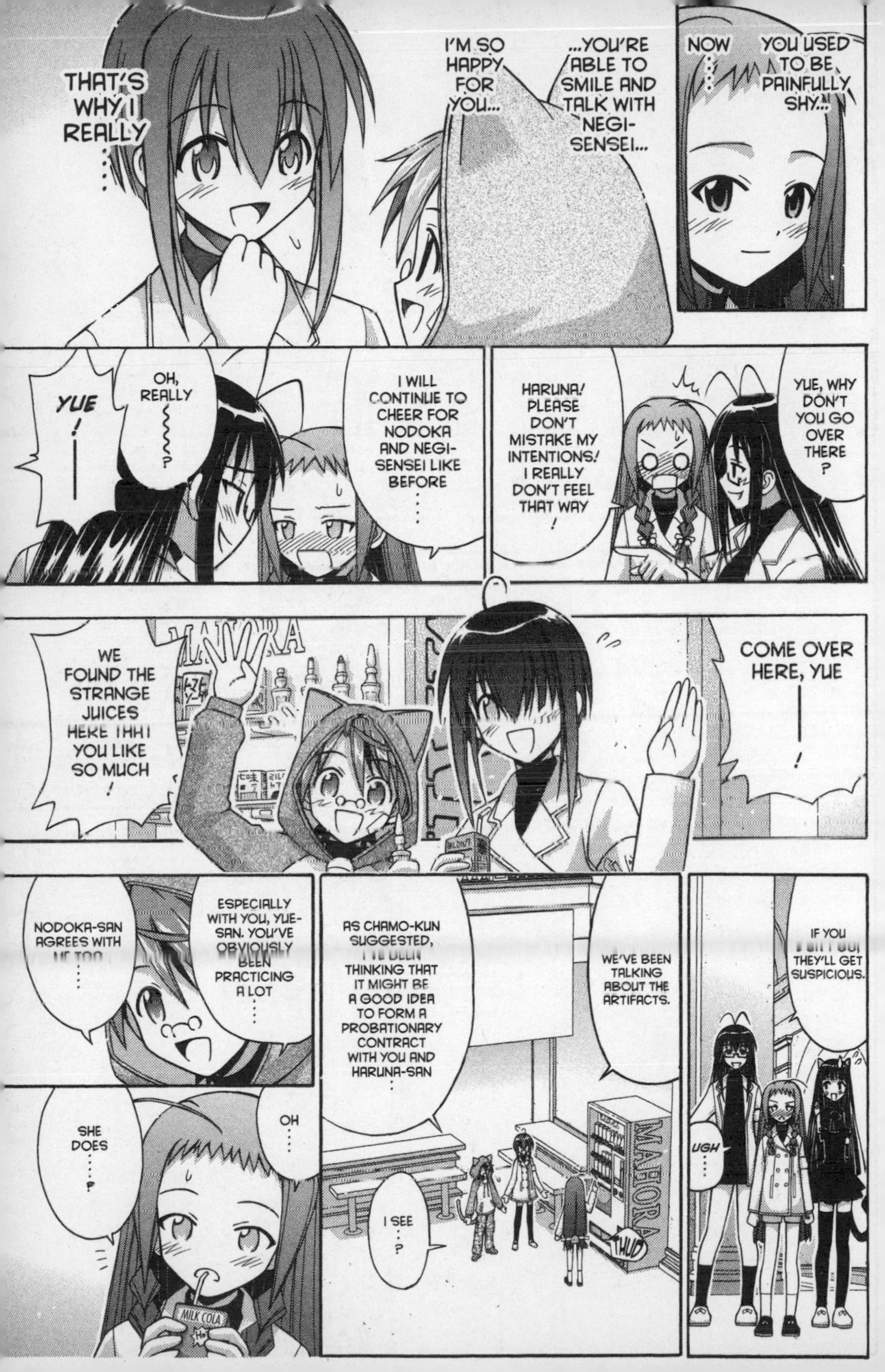
YOU USED TO BE PAINFULLY SHY...
NOW...
...YOU'RE ABLE TO SMILE AND TALK WITH NEGI-SENSEI...
I'M SO HAPPY FOR YOU...
THAT'S WHY I REALLY...
YUE, WHY DON'T YOU GO OVER THERE?
HARUNA! PLEASE DON'T MISTAKE MY INTENTIONS! I REALLY DON'T FEEL THAT WAY!
I WILL CONTINUE TO CHEER FOR NODOKA AND NEGI-SENSEI LIKE BEFORE...
OH, REALLY~?
YUE!—
COME OVER HERE, YUE—!
WE FOUND THE STRANGE JUICES HERE THAT YOU LIKE SO MUCH!
MAHORA
IF YOU
THEY'LL GET SUSPICIOUS.
UGH
WE'VE BEEN TALKING ABOUT THE ARTIFACTS.
AS CHAMO-KUN SUGGESTED,
THINKING THAT IT MIGHT BE A GOOD IDEA TO FORM A PROBATIONARY CONTRACT WITH YOU AND HARUNA-SAN...
I SEE...?
THUD
MAHORA
ESPECIALLY WITH YOU, YUE-SAN. YOU'VE OBVIOUSLY BEEN PRACTICING A LOT...
NODOKA-SAN AGREES WITH
...
OH...
SHE DOES...?
MILK COLA

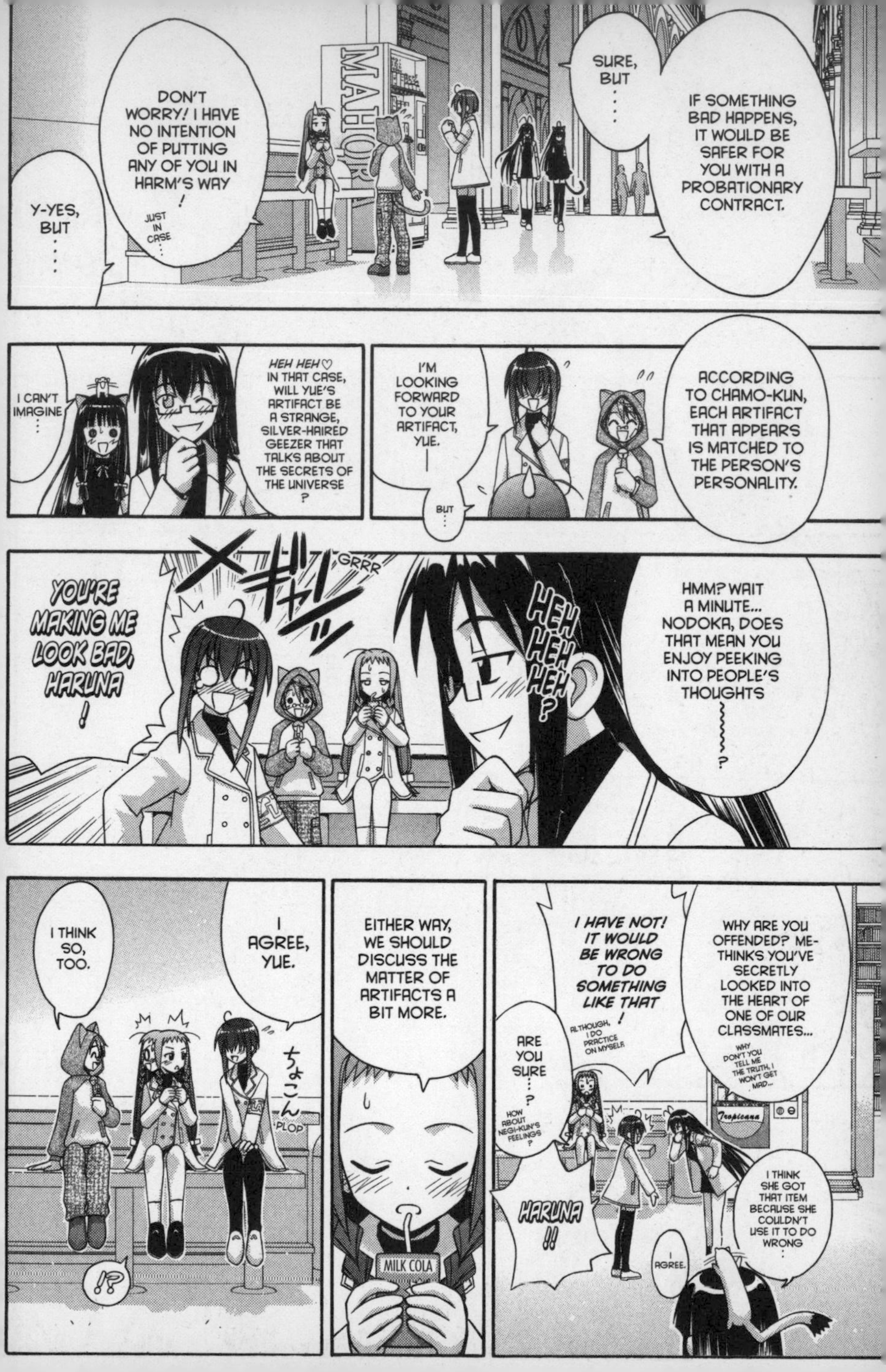
SURE, BUT....
IF SOMETHING BAD HAPPENS, IT WOULD BE SAFER FOR YOU WITH A PROBATIONARY CONTRACT.
DON'T WORRY! I HAVE NO INTENTION OF PUTTING ANY OF YOU IN HARM'S WAY!
JUST IN CASE...
Y-YES, BUT....
ACCORDING TO CHAMO-KUN, EACH ARTIFACT THAT APPEARS IS MATCHED TO THE PERSON'S PERSONALITY.
I'M LOOKING FORWARD TO YOUR ARTIFACT, YUE.
BUT...
HEH HEH♡ IN THAT CASE, WILL YUE'S ARTIFACT BE A STRANGE, SILVER-HAIRED GEEZER THAT TALKS ABOUT THE SECRETS OF THE UNIVERSE?
I CAN'T IMAGINE...
HMM? WAIT A MINUTE... NODOKA, DOES THAT MEAN YOU ENJOY PEEKING INTO PEOPLE'S THOUGHTS~?
HEH HEH HEH?
GRRR
YOU'RE MAKING ME LOOK BAD, HARUNA!
WHY ARE YOU OFFENDED? ME-THINKS YOU'VE SECRETLY LOOKED INTO THE HEART OF ONE OF OUR CLASSMATES...
WHY DON'T YOU TELL ME THE TRUTH, I WON'T GET MAD...
I HAVE NOT! IT WOULD BE WRONG TO DO SOMETHING LIKE THAT!
ALTHOUGH, I DO PRACTICE ON MYSELF.
ARE YOU SURE...?
HOW ABOUT NEGI-KUN'S FEELINGS?
HARUNA!!
Tropicana
I THINK SHE GOT THAT ITEM BECAUSE SHE COULDN'T USE IT TO DO WRONG.
I AGREE.
EITHER WAY, WE SHOULD DISCUSS THE MATTER OF ARTIFACTS A BIT MORE.
MILK COLA
I AGREE, YUE.
I THINK SO, TOO.
ちょこん
PLOP
!?

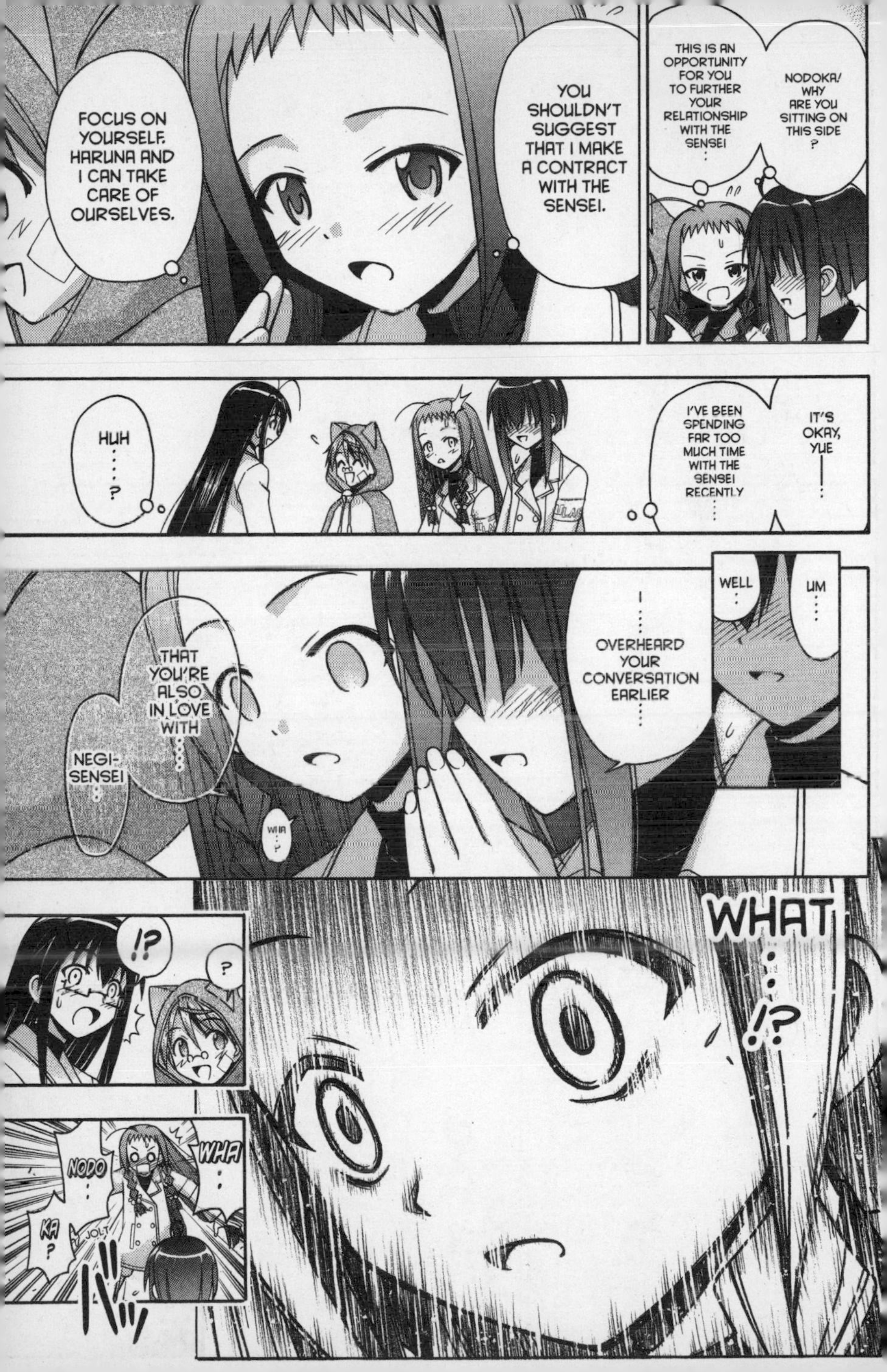
NODOKA! WHY ARE YOU SITTING ON THIS SIDE?
THIS IS AN OPPORTUNITY FOR YOU TO FURTHER YOUR RELATIONSHIP WITH THE SENSEI...
YOU SHOULDN'T SUGGEST THAT I MAKE A CONTRACT WITH THE SENSEI.
FOCUS ON YOURSELF. HARUNA AND I CAN TAKE CARE OF OURSELVES.
IT'S OKAY, YUE—...
I'VE BEEN SPENDING FAR TOO MUCH TIME WITH THE SENSEI RECENTLY...
HUH...?
UM...
WELL...
I... OVERHEARD YOUR CONVERSATION EARLIER...
THAT YOU'RE ALSO IN LOVE WITH...
NEGI-SENSEI...
WHA...?
WHAT...!?
!?
?
WHA...
NODO...KA?
JOLT

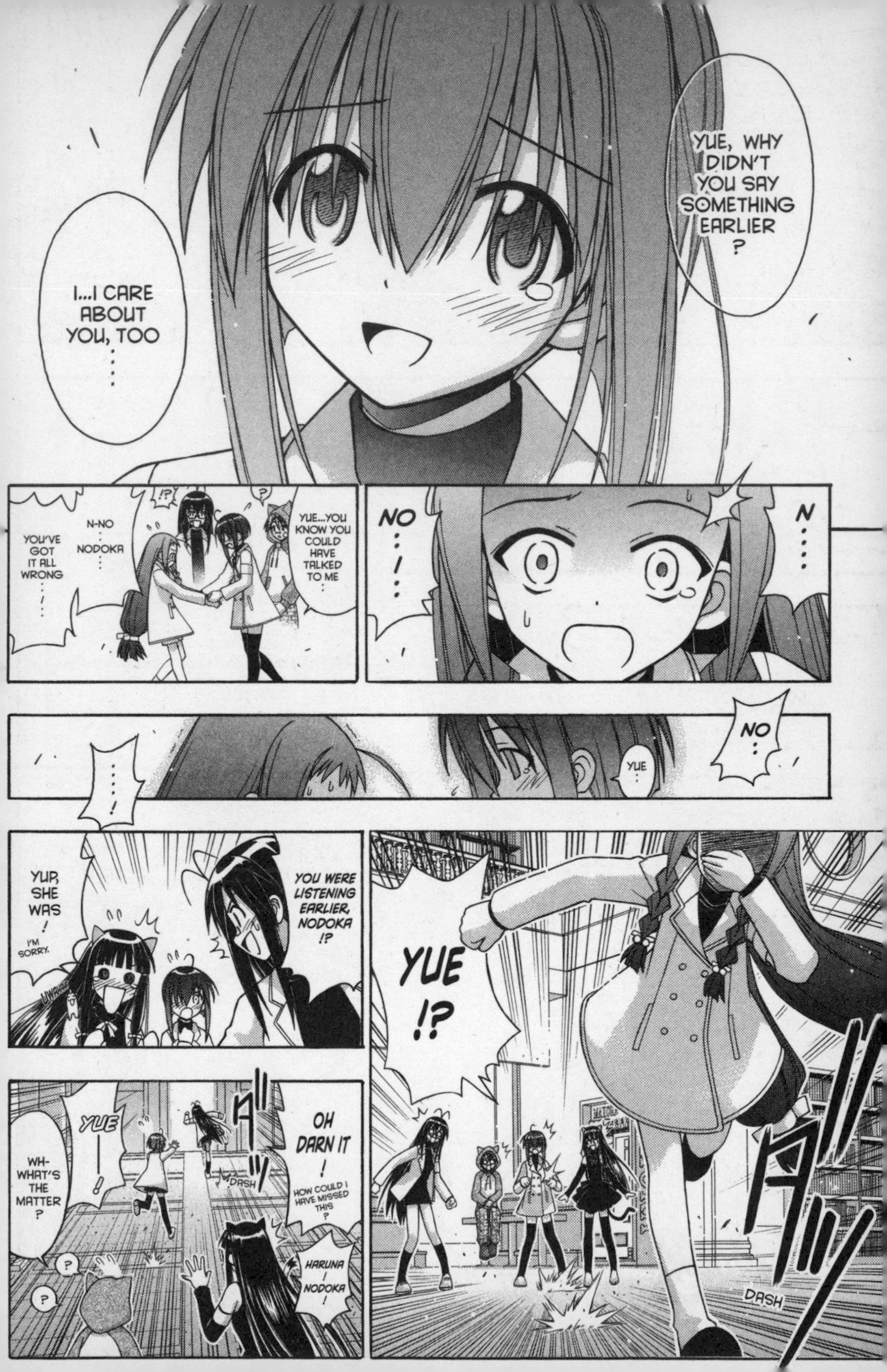
YUE, WHY DIDN'T YOU SAY SOMETHING EARLIER ?
I...I CARE ABOUT YOU, TOO ...
N...
NO...!...
YUE...YOU KNOW YOU COULD HAVE TALKED TO ME...
!?
?
N-NO... NODOKA...
YOU'VE GOT IT ALL WRONG...!...
NO...
YUE...
...!
YUE !?
YOU WERE LISTENING EARLIER, NODOKA !?
YUP, SHE WAS !
I'M SORRY.
DASH
OH DARN IT !
HOW COULD I HAVE MISSED THIS ?
DASH
YUE—!
WH-WHAT'S THE MATTER ?
HARUNA ! NODOKA !
?
?

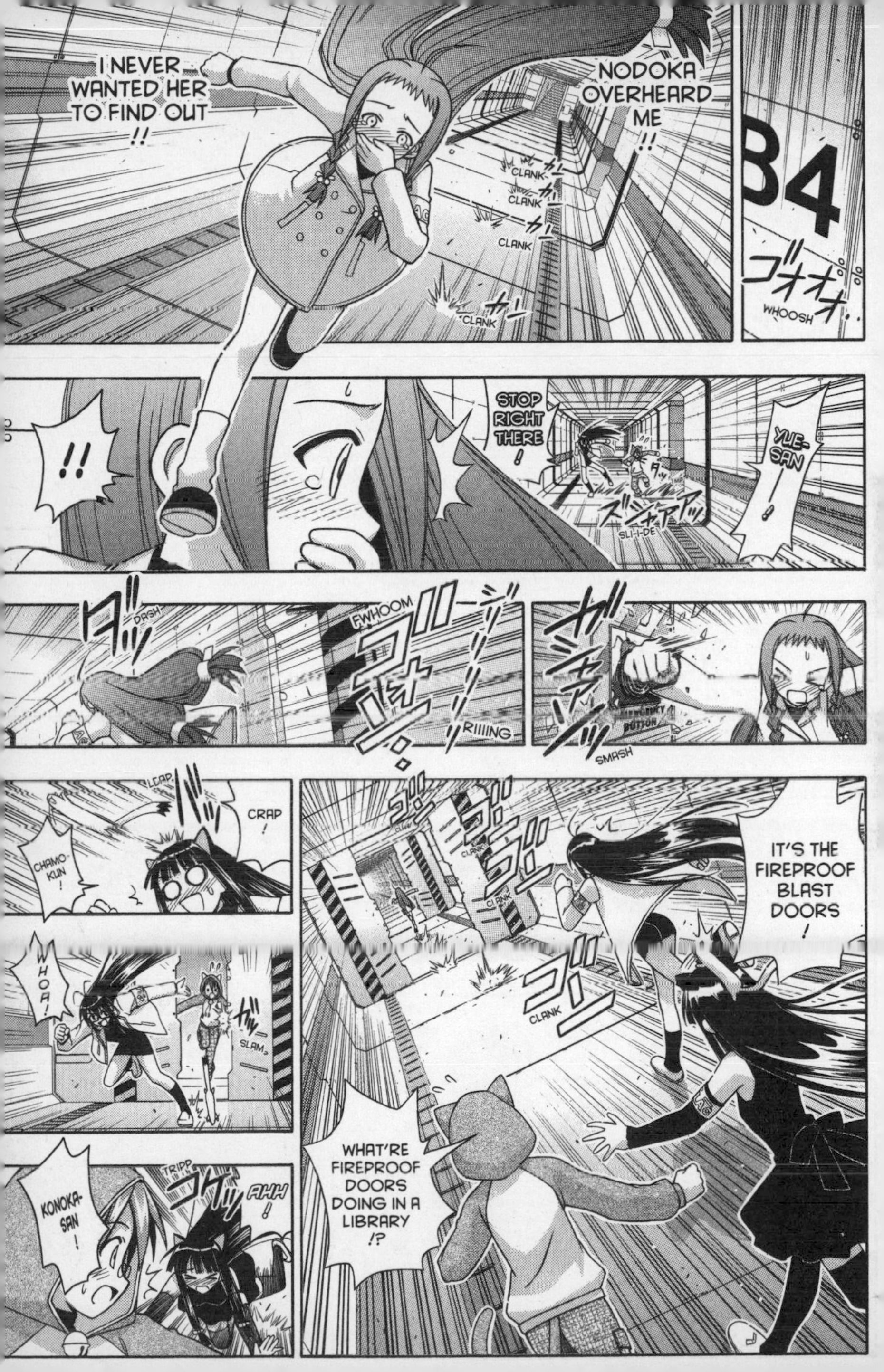
34
WHOOSH
NODOKA OVERHEARD ME !!
CLANK
CLANK
CLANK
CLANK
I NEVER WANTED HER TO FIND OUT !!
YUE-SAN !
STOP RIGHT THERE !
SLI-I-DE
!!
SMASH
RIIING
FWHOOM
DASH
IT'S THE FIREPROOF BLAST DOORS !
CLANK
CLANK
CLANK
WHAT'RE FIREPROOF DOORS DOING IN A LIBRARY !?
LEAP
CRAP !
CHAMO-KUN !
SLAM
WHOA !
AHH !
TRIPP
KONOKA-SAN !

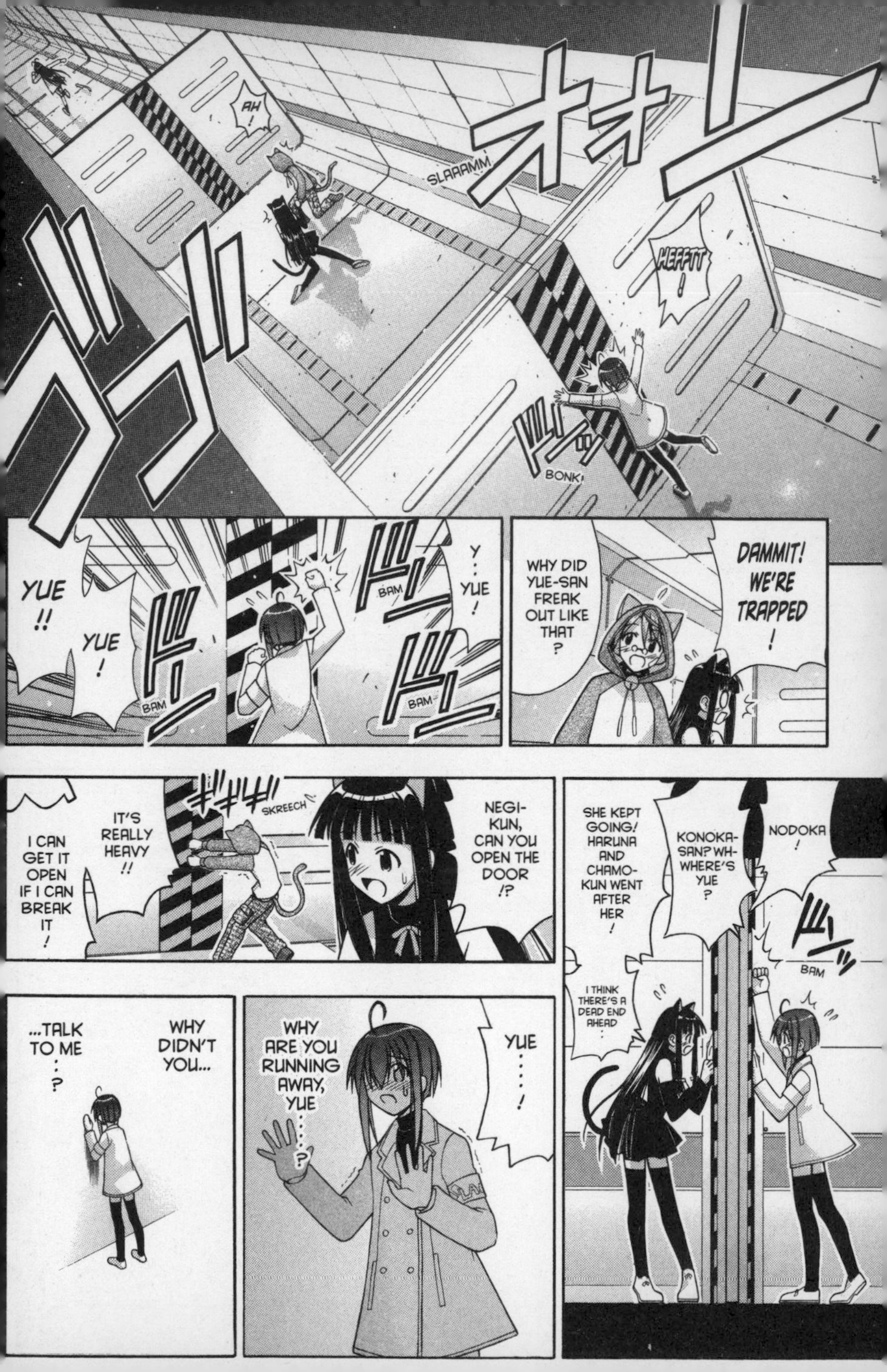
AH!
SLAAAMM
HEFFTT!
BONK
DAMMIT! WE'RE TRAPPED!
WHY DID YUE-SAN FREAK OUT LIKE THAT?
Y... YUE!
BAM
BAM
YUE!!
YUE!
BAM
NODOKA!
KONOKA-SAN? WH-WHERE'S YUE?
SHE KEPT GOING! HARUNA AND CHAMO-KUN WENT AFTER HER!
BAM
I THINK THERE'S A DEAD END AHEAD...
NEGI-KUN, CAN YOU OPEN THE DOOR!?
SKREECH
IT'S REALLY HEAVY!!
I CAN GET IT OPEN IF I CAN BREAK IT!
YUE...!
WHY ARE YOU RUNNING AWAY, YUE...?
WHY DIDN'T YOU...
...TALK TO ME...?

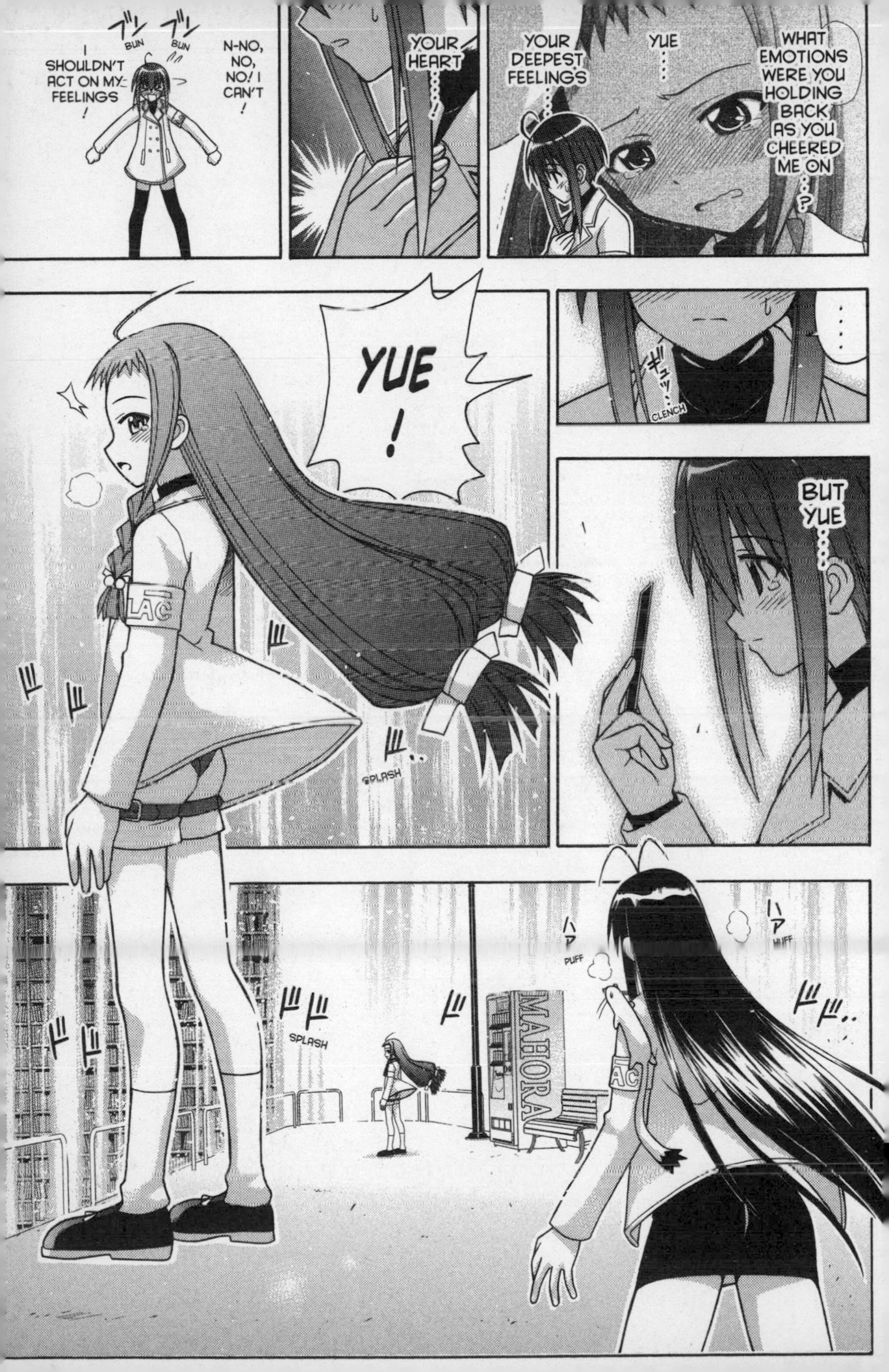

WHAT EMOTIONS WERE YOU HOLDING BACK AS YOU CHEERED ME ON ...?
YUE ...
YOUR DEEPEST FEELINGS
YOUR HEART ...
N-NO, NO, NO! I CAN'T!
ブン ブン
BUN BUN
I SHOULDN'T ACT ON MY FEELINGS!
....
ギュッ
CLENCH
BUT YUE ...
YUE!
SPLASH
ハァ
HUFF
ハァ
PUFF
SPLASH
MAHORA

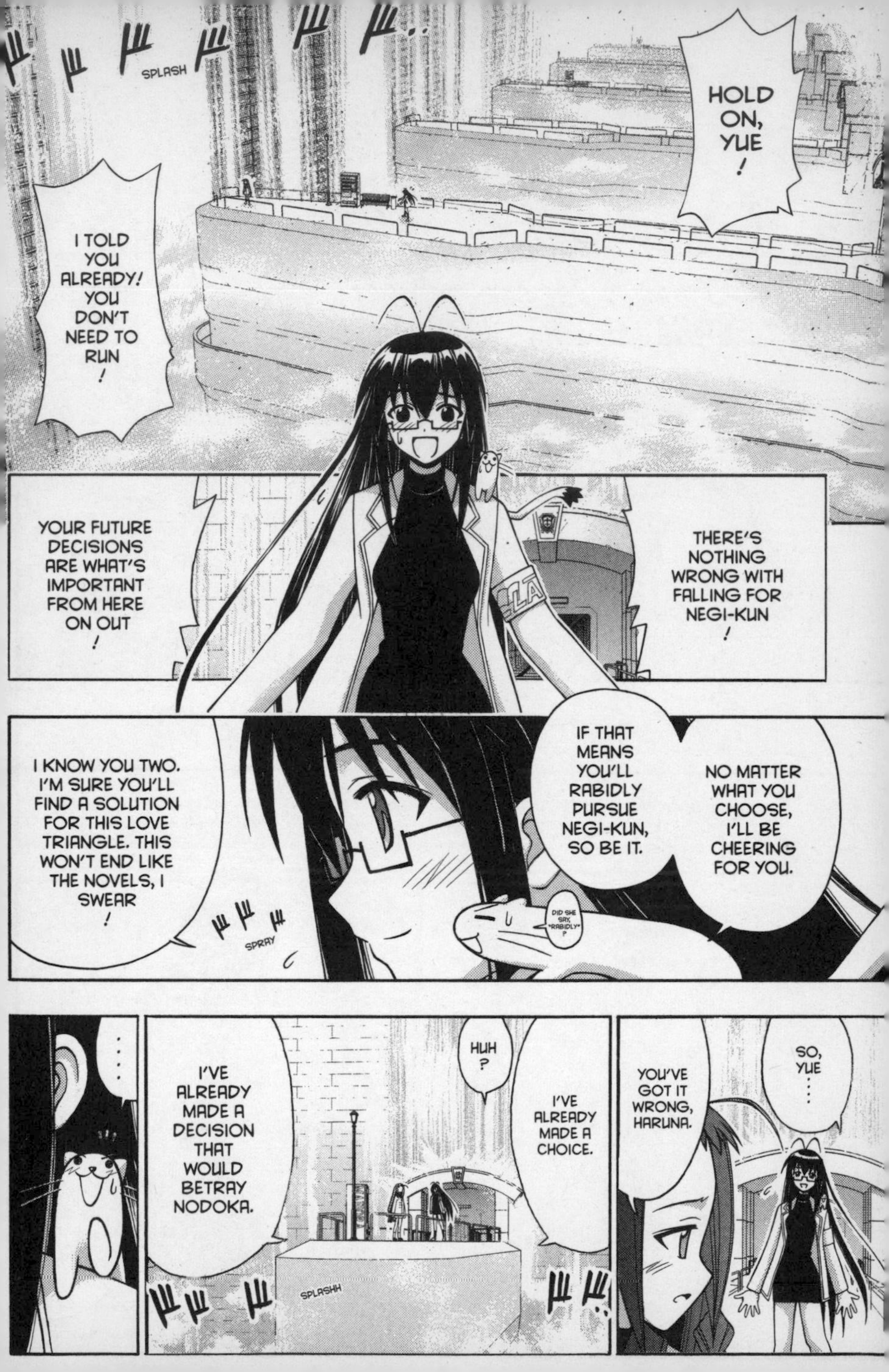
SPLASH
HOLD ON, YUE!
I TOLD YOU ALREADY! YOU DON'T NEED TO RUN!
THERE'S NOTHING WRONG WITH FALLING FOR NEGI-KUN!
YOUR FUTURE DECISIONS ARE WHAT'S IMPORTANT FROM HERE ON OUT!
NO MATTER WHAT YOU CHOOSE, I'LL BE CHEERING FOR YOU.
IF THAT MEANS YOU'LL RABIDLY PURSUE NEGI-KUN, SO BE IT.
DID SHE SAY, "RABIDLY"?
I KNOW YOU TWO. I'M SURE YOU'LL FIND A SOLUTION FOR THIS LOVE TRIANGLE. THIS WON'T END LIKE THE NOVELS, I SWEAR!
SPRAY
SO, YUE....
YOU'VE GOT IT WRONG, HARUNA.
HUH?
I'VE ALREADY MADE A CHOICE.
I'VE ALREADY MADE A DECISION THAT WOULD BETRAY NODOKA.
SPLASHH
....

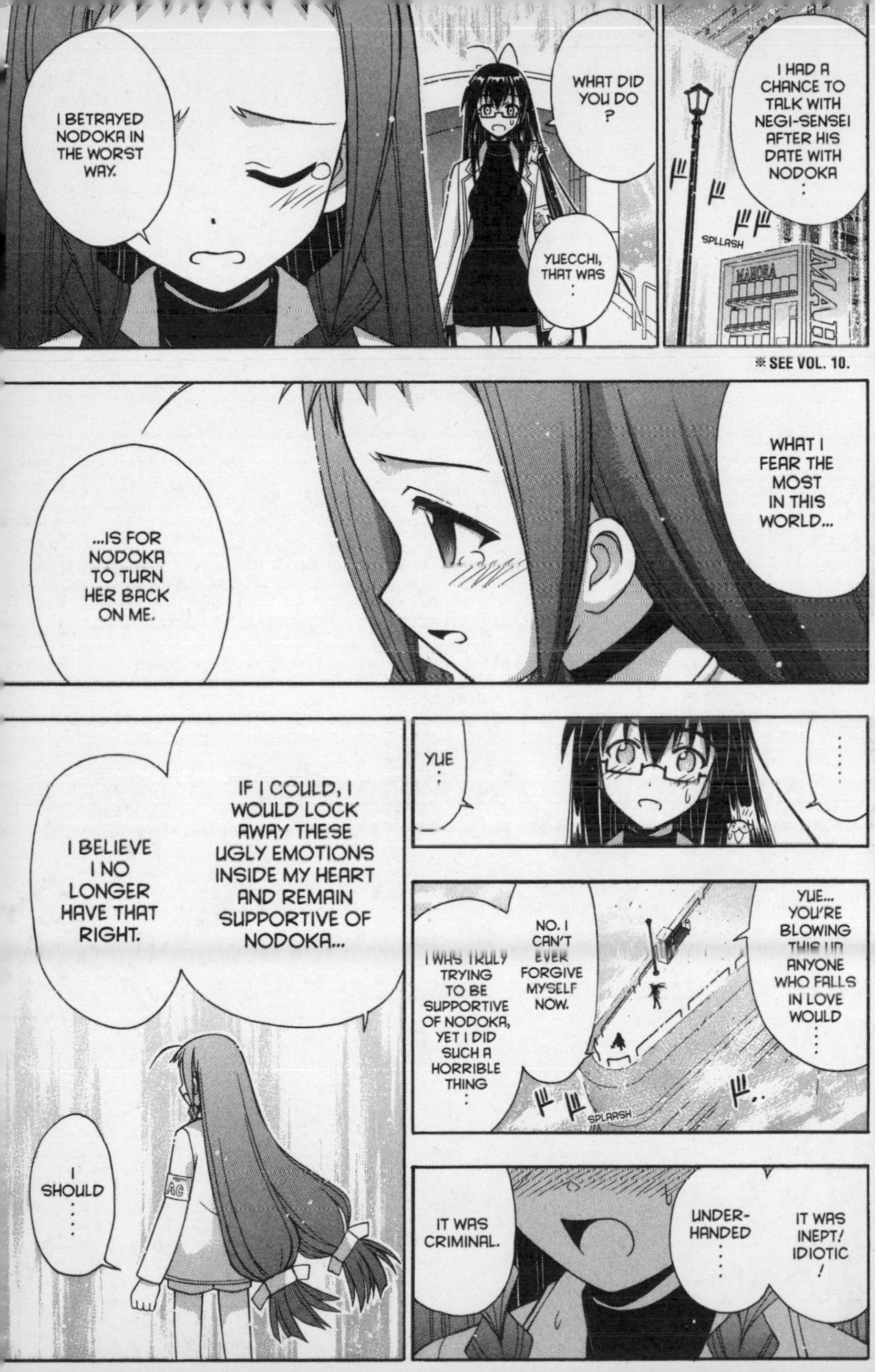
I HAD A CHANCE TO TALK WITH NEGI-SENSEI AFTER HIS DATE WITH NODOKA :
ドドドド
SPLLASH
MAHORA
WHAT DID YOU DO ?
YUECCHI, THAT WAS :
I BETRAYED NODOKA IN THE WORST WAY.
※ SEE VOL. 10.
WHAT I FEAR THE MOST IN THIS WORLD...
...IS FOR NODOKA TO TURN HER BACK ON ME.
.....
YUE :
YUE... YOU'RE BLOWING THIS UP ANYONE WHO FALLS IN LOVE WOULD ....
NO. I CAN'T EVER FORGIVE MYSELF NOW.
I WAS TRULY TRYING TO BE SUPPORTIVE OF NODOKA, YET I DID SUCH A HORRIBLE THING :
ドドド..
SPLAASH
IT WAS INEPT! IDIOTIC !
UNDER-HANDED ....
IT WAS CRIMINAL.
IF I COULD, I WOULD LOCK AWAY THESE UGLY EMOTIONS INSIDE MY HEART AND REMAIN SUPPORTIVE OF NODOKA...
I BELIEVE I NO LONGER HAVE THAT RIGHT.
AC
I SHOULD ....

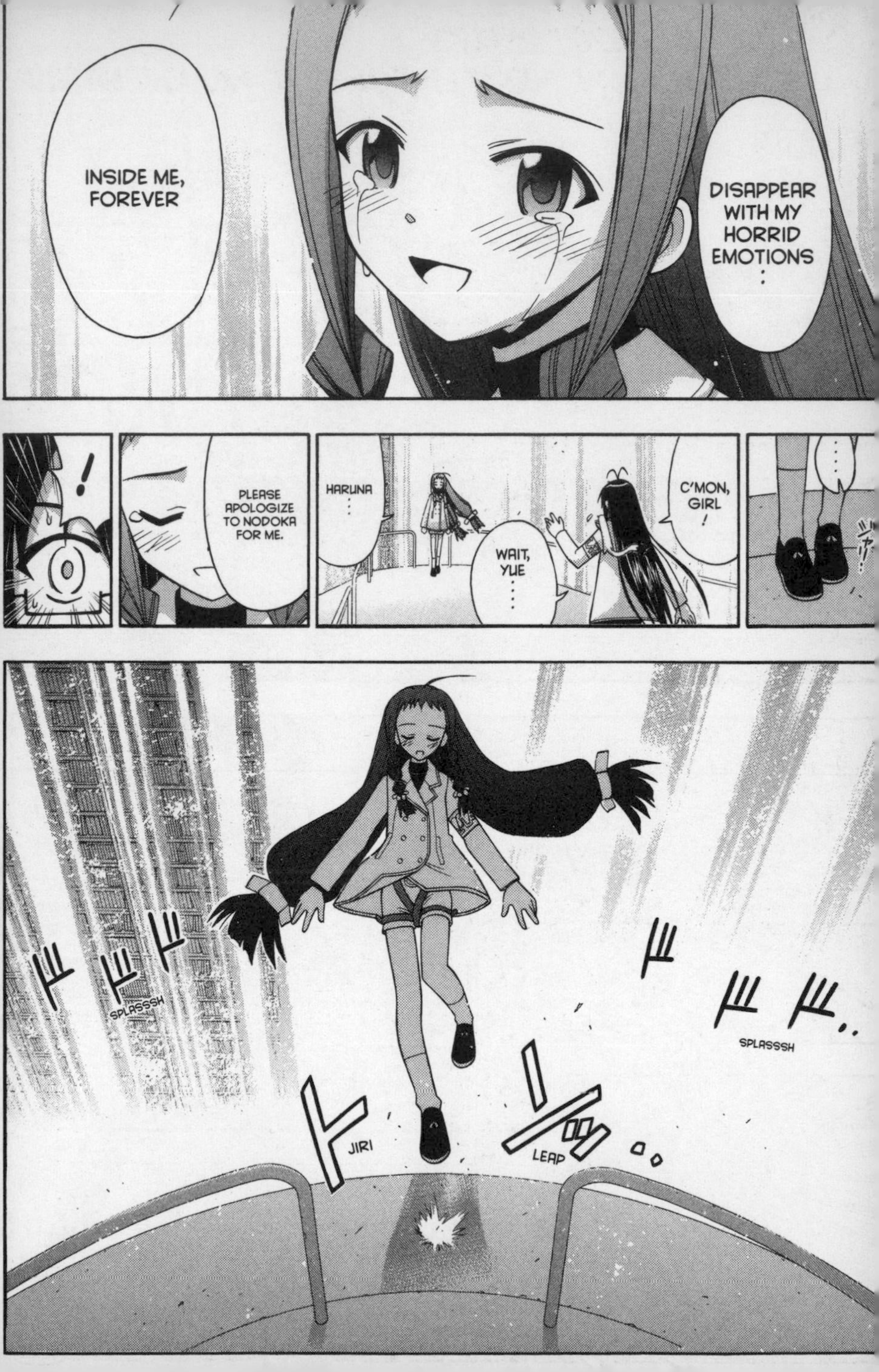
DISAPPEAR WITH MY HORRID EMOTIONS
...
INSIDE ME, FOREVER
...
ジャリ...
C'MON, GIRL!
WAIT, YUE...
HARUNA...
PLEASE APOLOGIZE TO NODOKA FOR ME.
!
ドドド..
SPLASSSH
ドドド
SPLASSSH
ト
JIRI
ーンッ。。
LEAP

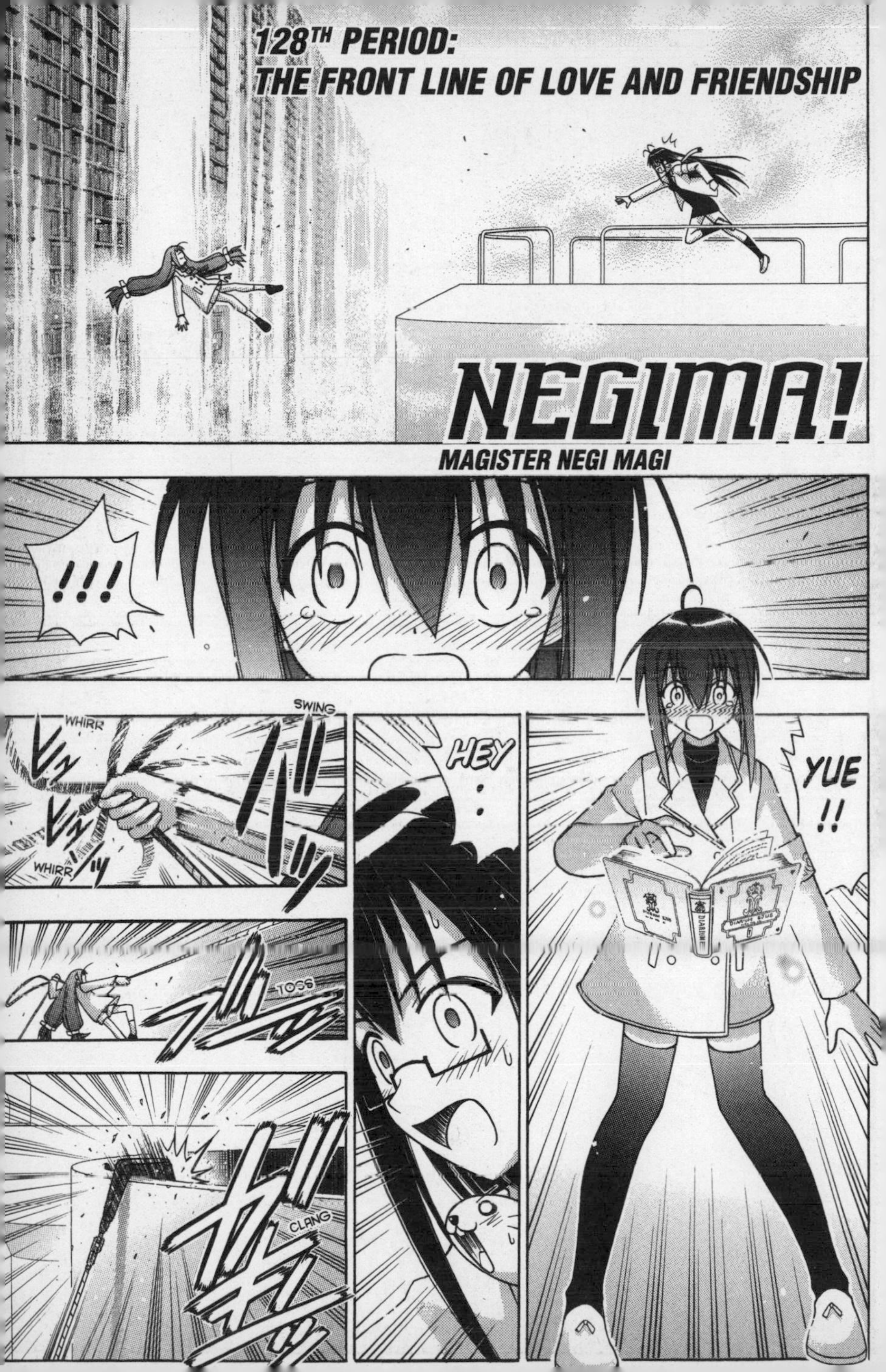
128TH PERIOD:
THE FRONT LINE OF LOVE AND FRIENDSHIP
NEGIMA!
MAGISTER NEGI MAGI
!!!
YUE !!
HEY
...
SWING
WHIRR
WHIRR
TOSS
CLANG

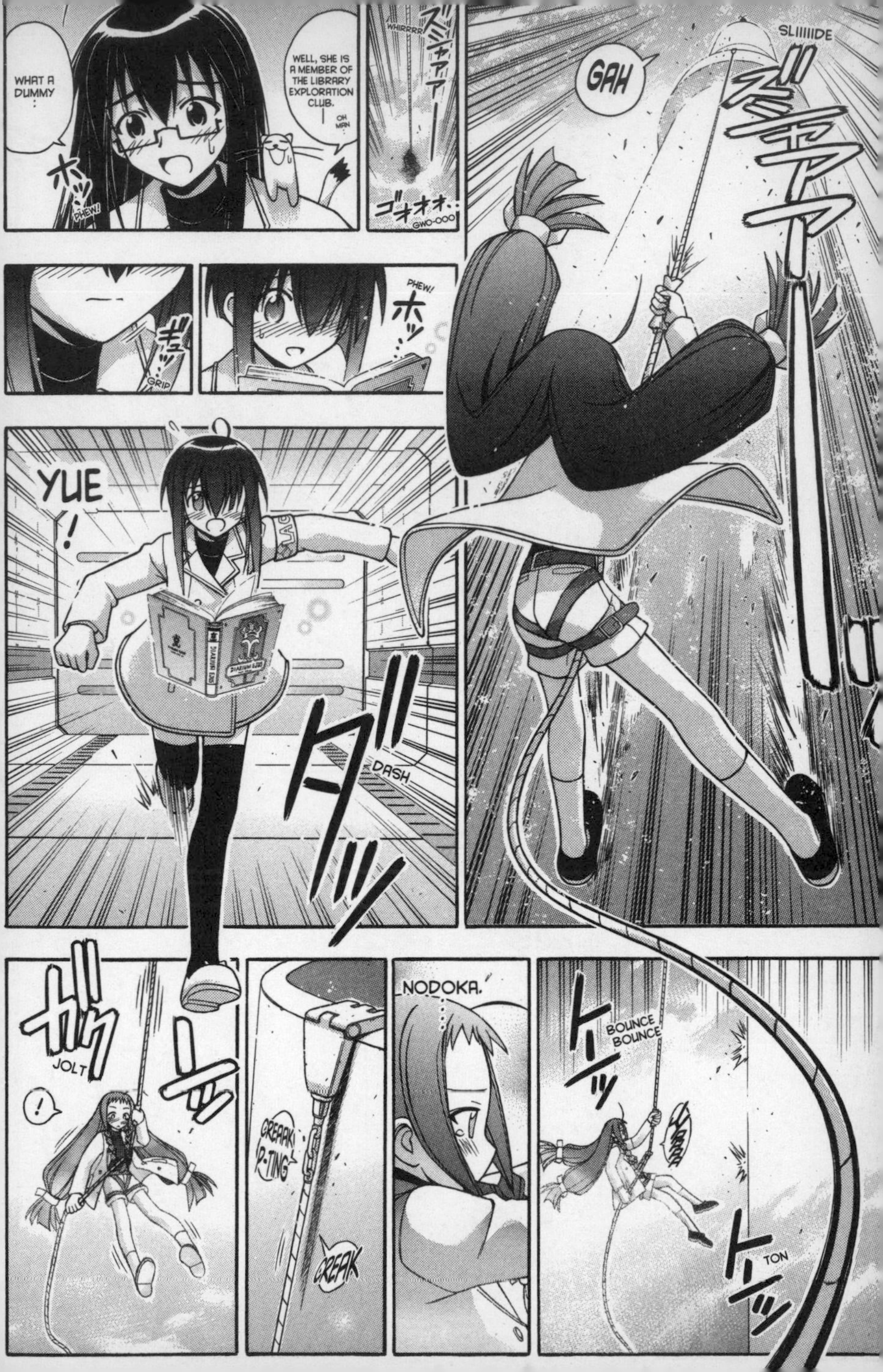
GAH
SLIIIIIDE
WHIRRRR
GWO-OOO
WELL, SHE IS A MEMBER OF THE LIBRARY EXPLORATION CLUB.
OH MAN
WHAT A DUMMY
PHEW!
PHEW!
GRIP
YUE!
DASH
BOUNCE BOUNCE
TON
NODOKA.
CREAK! P-TING
CREAK
JOLT
!

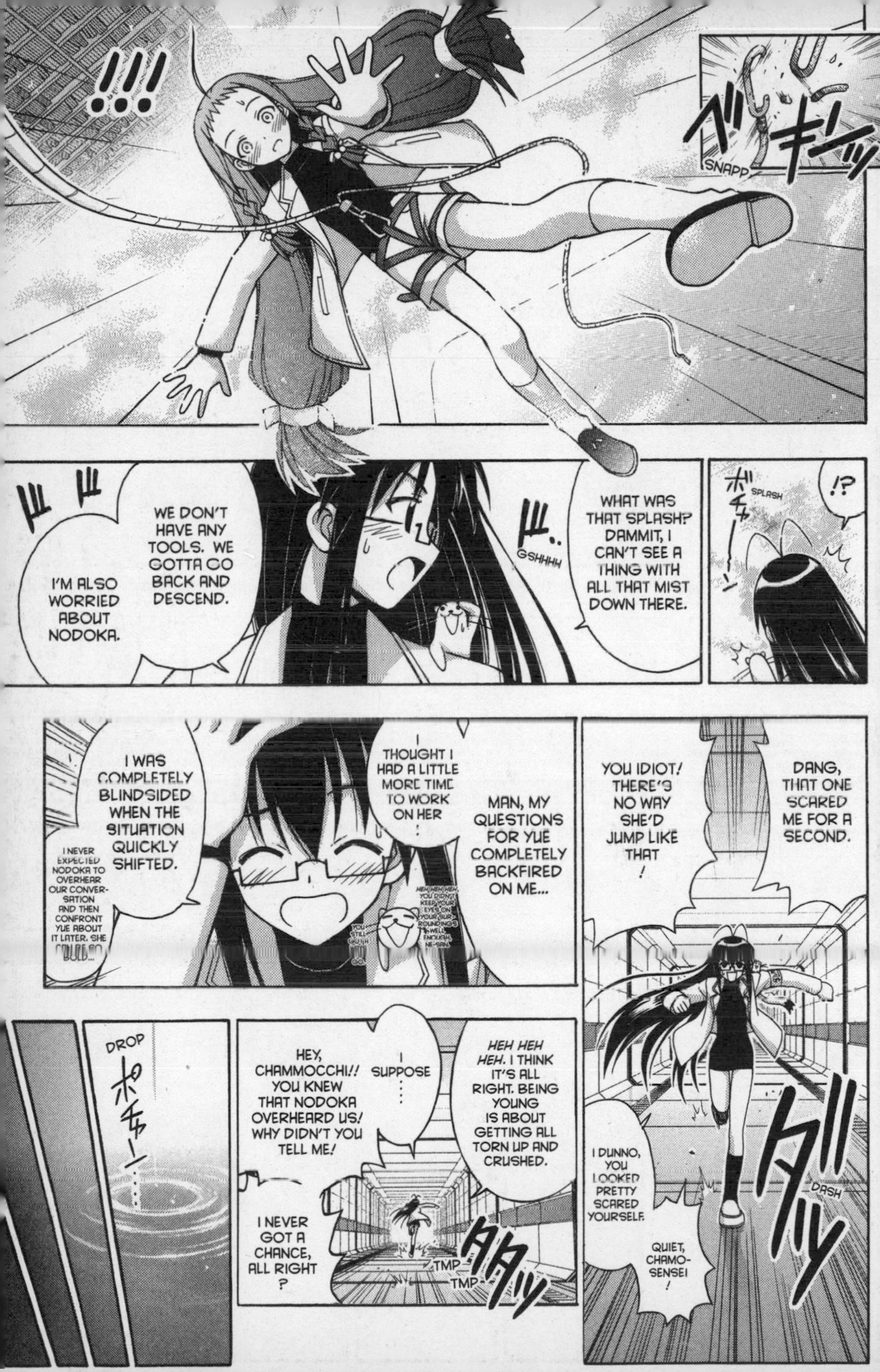
SNAPP
!!!
SPLASH
!?
WHAT WAS THAT SPLASH? DAMMIT, I CAN'T SEE A THING WITH ALL THAT MIST DOWN THERE.
GSHHHH
WE DON'T HAVE ANY TOOLS. WE GOTTA GO BACK AND DESCEND.
I'M ALSO WORRIED ABOUT NODOKA.
DANG, THAT ONE SCARED ME FOR A SECOND.
YOU IDIOT! THERE'S NO WAY SHE'D JUMP LIKE THAT!
DASH
I DUNNO, YOU LOOKED PRETTY SCARED YOURSELF.
QUIET, CHAMO-SENSEI!
MAN, MY QUESTIONS FOR YUE COMPLETELY BACKFIRED ON ME...
I THOUGHT I HAD A LITTLE MORE TIME TO WORK ON HER!
HEH HEH HEH, YOU DIDN'T KEEP YOUR EYES ON YOUR SURROUNDINGS WELL ENOUGH, NE-SAN.
YOU STILL
I WAS COMPLETELY BLINDSIDED WHEN THE SITUATION QUICKLY SHIFTED.
I NEVER EXPECTED NODOKA TO OVERHEAR OUR CONVERSATION AND THEN CONFRONT YUE ABOUT IT LATER. SHE
HEH HEH HEH. I THINK IT'S ALL RIGHT. BEING YOUNG IS ABOUT GETTING ALL TORN UP AND CRUSHED.
I SUPPOSE....
HEY, CHAMMOCCHI!! YOU KNEW THAT NODOKA OVERHEARD US! WHY DIDN'T YOU TELL ME!
I NEVER GOT A CHANCE, ALL RIGHT?
TMP TMP
DROP

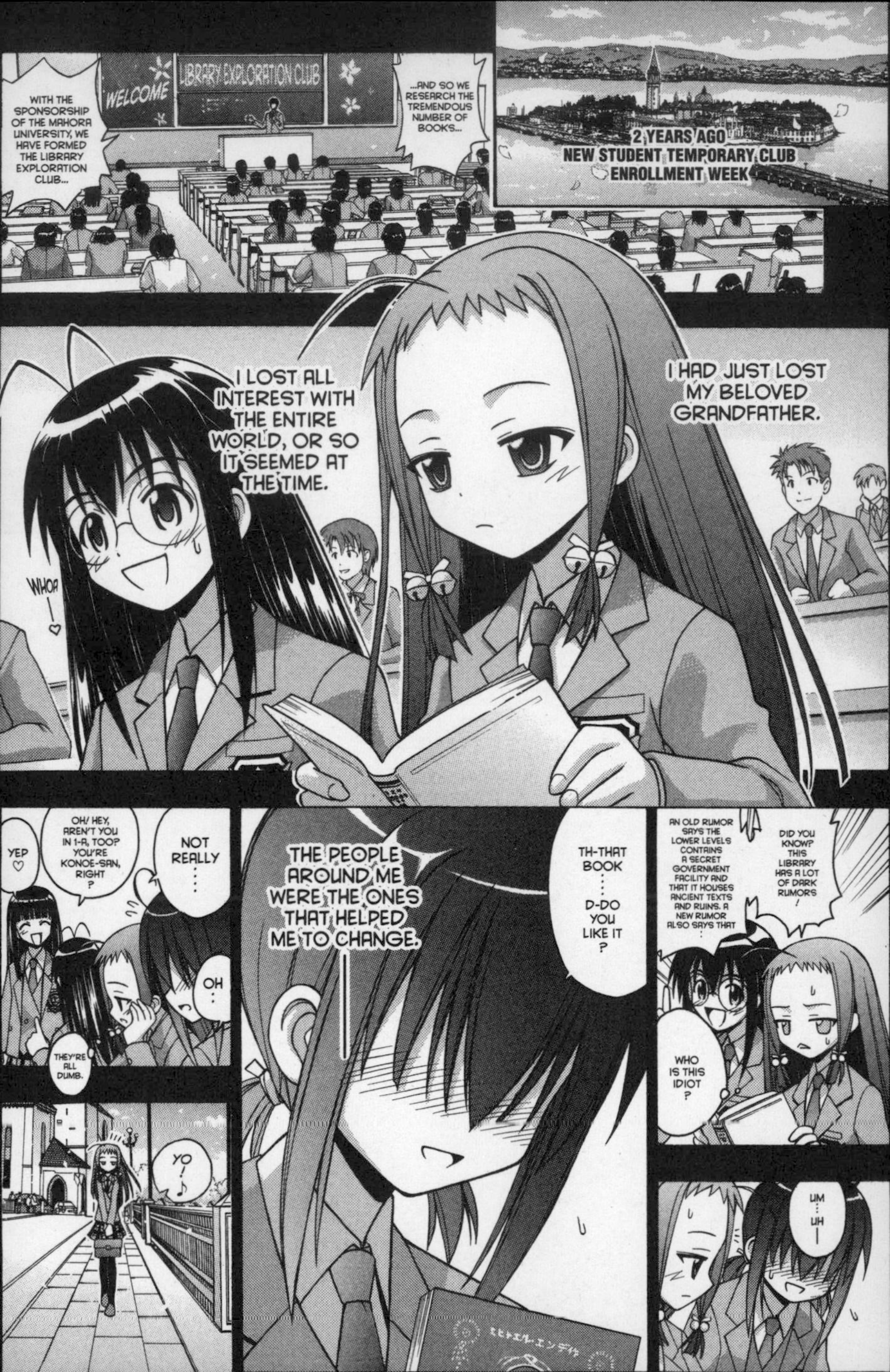

2 YEARS AGO
NEW STUDENT TEMPORARY CLUB ENROLLMENT WEEK
LIBRARY EXPLORATION CLUB
WELCOME
...AND SO WE RESEARCH THE TREMENDOUS NUMBER OF BOOKS...
WITH THE SPONSORSHIP OF THE MAHORA UNIVERSITY, WE HAVE FORMED THE LIBRARY EXPLORATION CLUB...
I HAD JUST LOST MY BELOVED GRANDFATHER.
I LOST ALL INTEREST WITH THE ENTIRE WORLD, OR SO IT SEEMED AT THE TIME.
WHOA—♡
DID YOU KNOW? THIS LIBRARY HAS A LOT OF DARK RUMORS!
AN OLD RUMOR SAYS THE LOWER LEVELS CONTAINS A SECRET GOVERNMENT FACILITY AND THAT IT HOUSES ANCIENT TEXTS AND RUINS. A NEW RUMOR ALSO SAYS THAT...
WHO IS THIS IDIOT?
UM... UH—
TH-THAT BOOK... D-DO YOU LIKE IT?
THE PEOPLE AROUND ME WERE THE ONES THAT HELPED ME TO CHANGE.
NOT REALLY...
OH! HEY, AREN'T YOU IN 1-A, TOO? YOU'RE KONOE-SAN, RIGHT?
YEP ♡
OH...
THEY'RE ALL DUMB.
YO! ♪

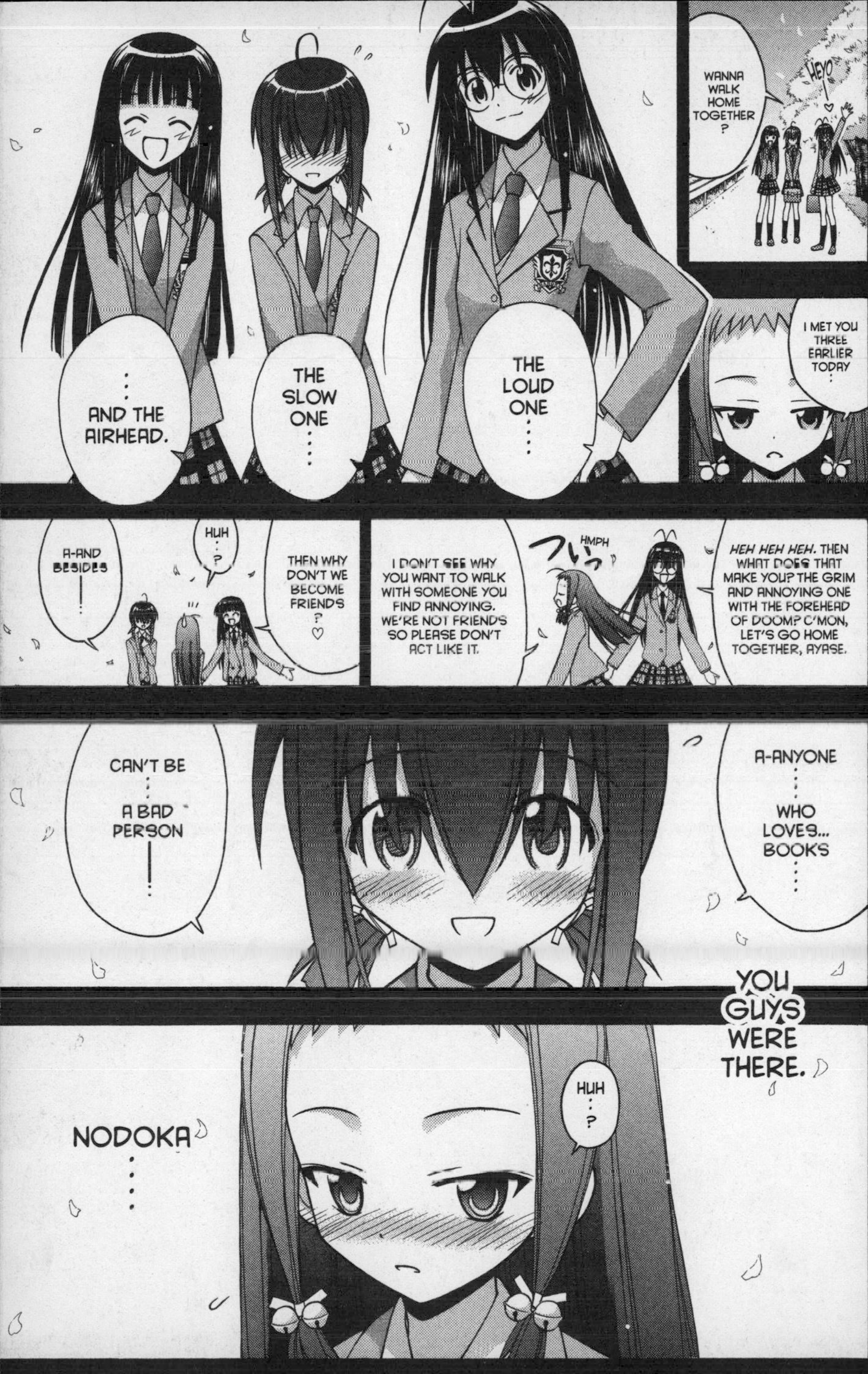
WANNA WALK HOME TOGETHER?
HEYO ♥
I MET YOU THREE EARLIER TODAY...
THE LOUD ONE....
THE SLOW ONE....
...AND THE AIRHEAD.
HEH HEH HEH. THEN WHAT DOES THAT MAKE YOU? THE GRIM AND ANNOYING ONE WITH THE FOREHEAD OF DOOM? C'MON, LET'S GO HOME TOGETHER, AYASE.
HMPH
I DON'T SEE WHY YOU WANT TO WALK WITH SOMEONE YOU FIND ANNOYING. WE'RE NOT FRIENDS SO PLEASE DON'T ACT LIKE IT.
THEN WHY DON'T WE BECOME FRIENDS? ♡
HUH..?
A-AND BESIDES—!
A-ANYONE... WHO LOVES... BOOKS...
CAN'T BE... A BAD PERSON—!
YOU GUYS WERE THERE.
HUH..?
NODOKA....

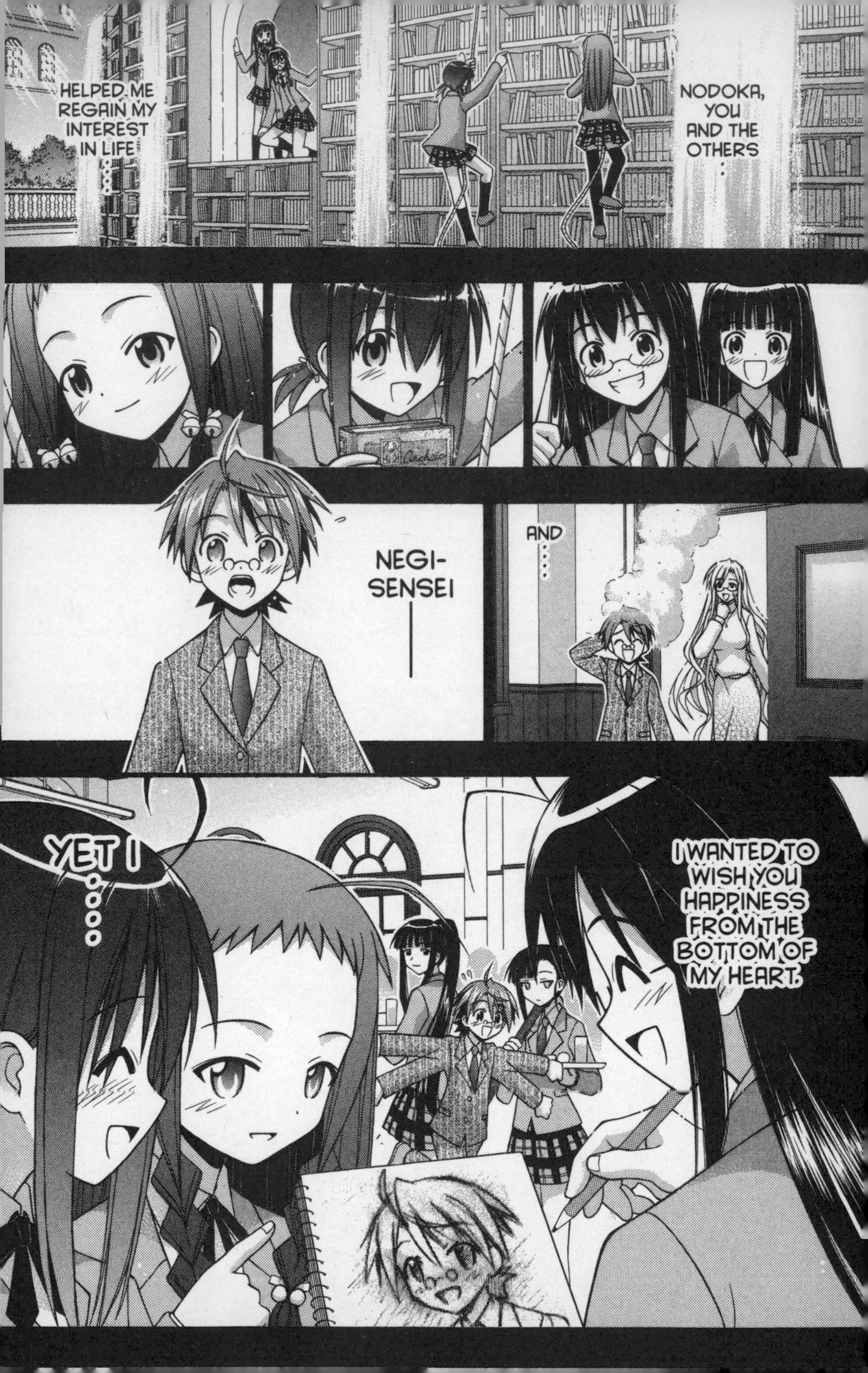
NODOKA, YOU AND THE OTHERS...
HELPED ME REGAIN MY INTEREST IN LIFE...
AND...
NEGI-SENSEI—
I WANTED TO WISH YOU HAPPINESS FROM THE BOTTOM OF MY HEART.
YET I....

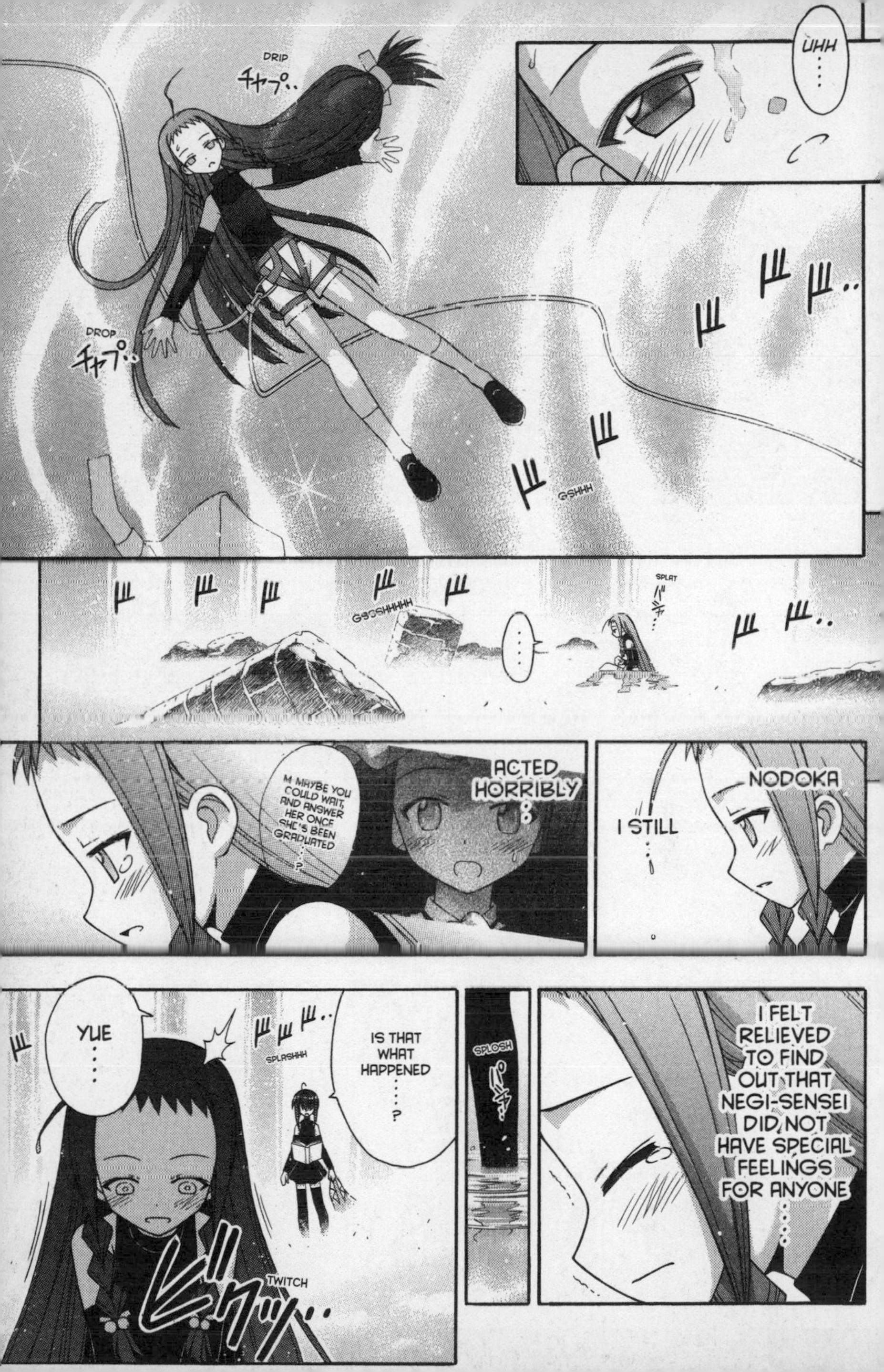
UHH ....
DRIP
チャプ..
DROP
チャプ..
ザ ザ ザ..
ザ ザ ザ
GSHHH
SPLAT
バチャ
ザ ザ..
....
GSSSHHHH
ザ ザ ザ ザ ザ
NODOKA
I STILL ...
ACTED HORRIBLY..
M MAYBE YOU COULD WAIT, AND ANSWER HER ONCE SHE'S BEEN GRADUATED ....?
I FELT RELIEVED TO FIND OUT THAT NEGI-SENSEI DID NOT HAVE SPECIAL FEELINGS FOR ANYONE ....
SPLOSH
ザザザ..
SPLASHHH
IS THAT WHAT HAPPENED ....?
YUE ....
ザ
TWITCH
ビクッ..

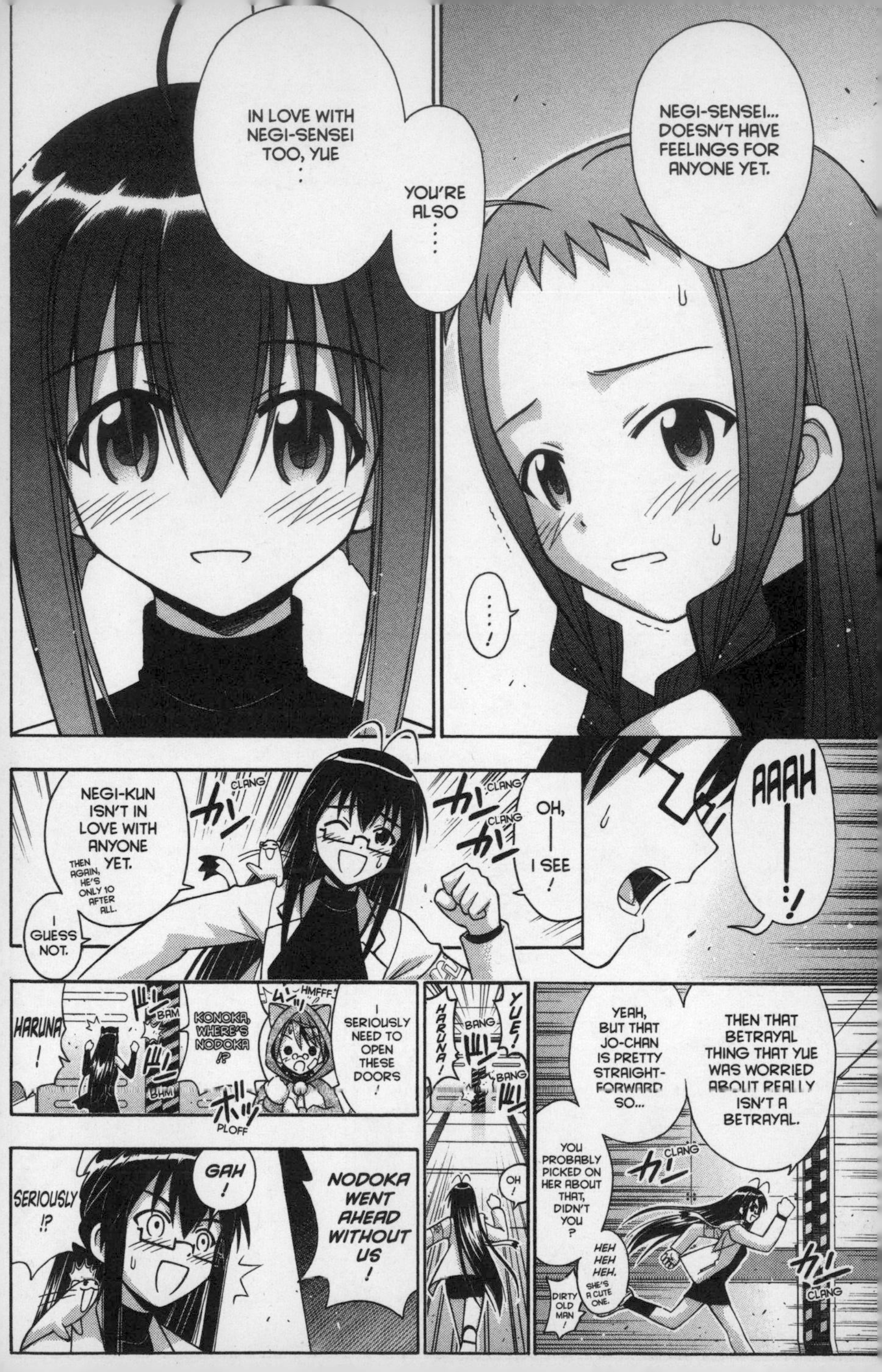
NEGI-SENSEI... DOESN'T HAVE FEELINGS FOR ANYONE YET.
....!
YOU'RE ALSO ....
IN LOVE WITH NEGI-SENSEI TOO, YUE ...
AAAH !!
OH, I SEE!
CLANG
CLANG
CLANG
NEGI-KUN ISN'T IN LOVE WITH ANYONE YET.
THEN AGAIN, HE'S ONLY 10 AFTER ALL.
I GUESS NOT.
THEN THAT BETRAYAL THING THAT YUE WAS WORRIED ABOUT REALLY ISN'T A BETRAYAL.
YEAH, BUT THAT JO-CHAN IS PRETTY STRAIGHT-FORWARD SO...
YOU PROBABLY PICKED ON HER ABOUT THAT, DIDN'T YOU?
CLANG
HEH HEH HEH.
SHE'S A CUTE ONE.
DIRTY OLD MAN!
CLANG
YUE!
HARUNA!
BANG
BANG
OH!
I SERIOUSLY NEED TO OPEN THESE DOORS!
HMFFF
KONOKA, WHERE'S NODOKA!?
PLOFF
BAM
HARUNA!
BAM
NODOKA WENT AHEAD WITHOUT US!
GAH!
SERIOUSLY!?

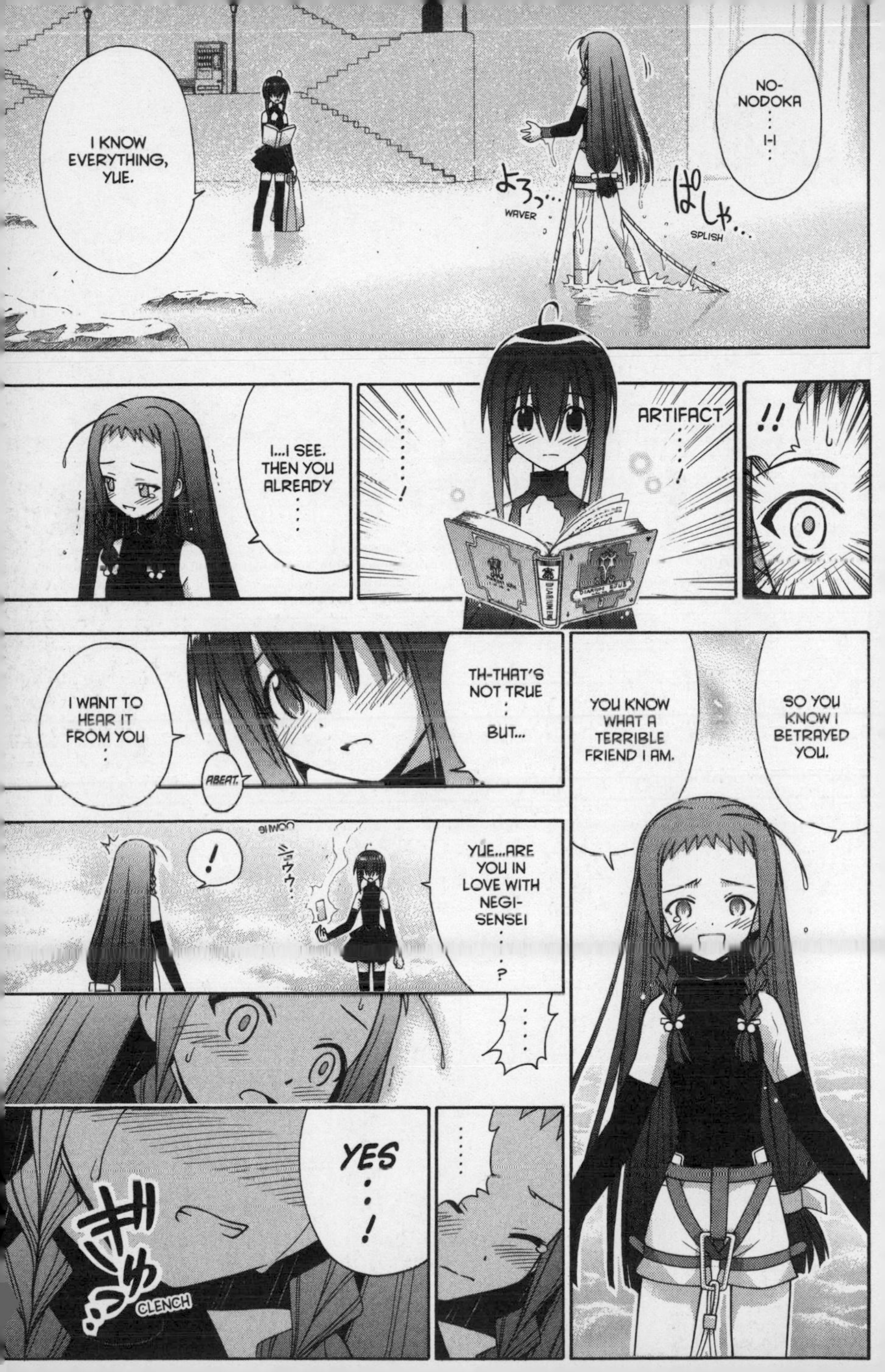
NO-NODOKA... I-I...
ぱしゃ...
SPLISH
よろっ...
WAVER
I KNOW EVERYTHING, YUE.
!!
ARTIFACT...!
......!
I...I SEE. THEN YOU ALREADY...
SO YOU KNOW I BETRAYED YOU.
YOU KNOW WHAT A TERRIBLE FRIEND I AM.
TH-THAT'S NOT TRUE... BUT...
ABEAT.
I WANT TO HEAR IT FROM YOU...
YUE...ARE YOU IN LOVE WITH NEGI-SENSEI...?
シュウ...
!
....
......
YES...!
ぎゅっ
CLENCH

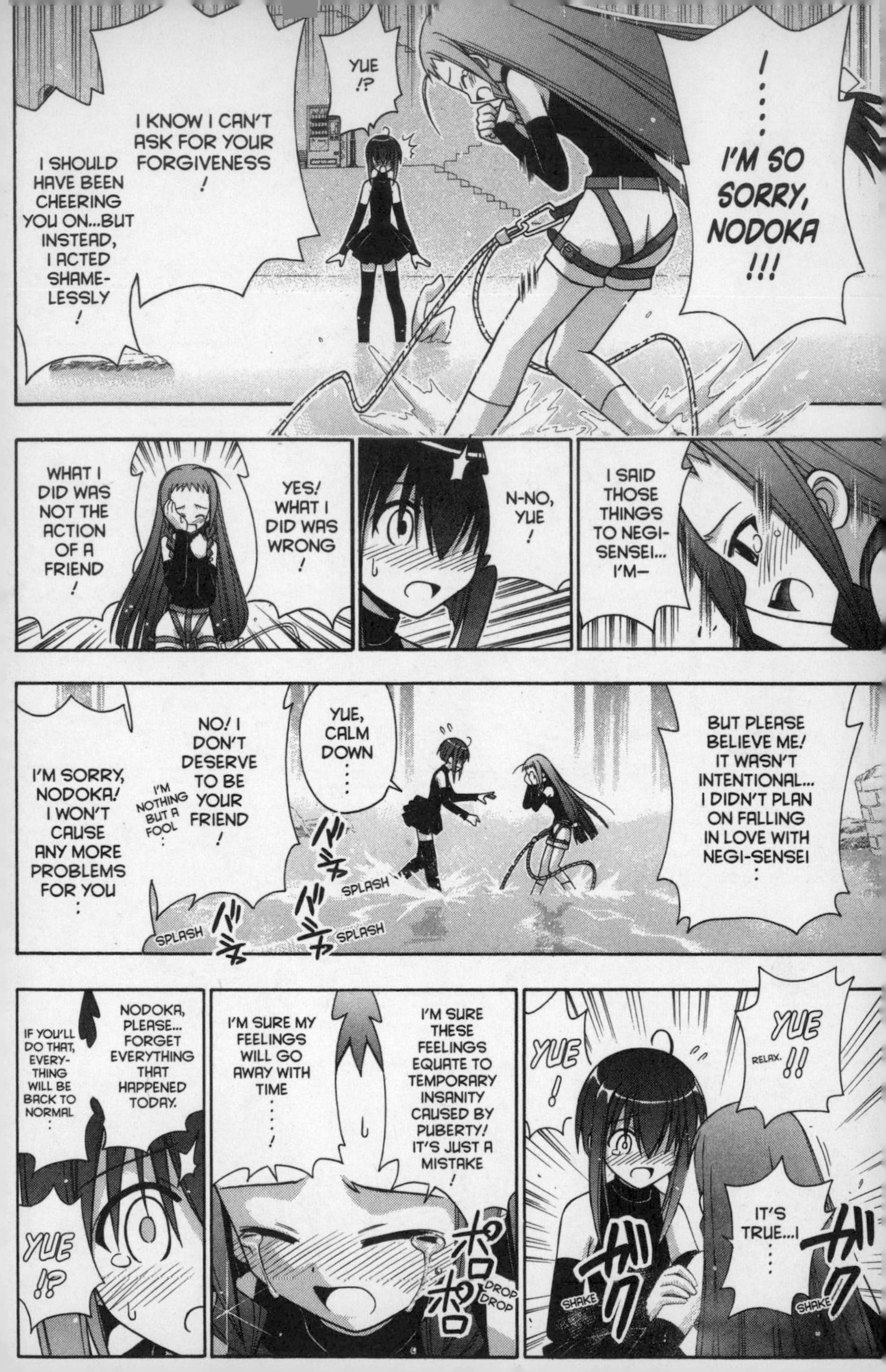
I'M SO SORRY, NODOKA !!!
YUE !?
I KNOW I CAN'T ASK FOR YOUR FORGIVENESS !
I SHOULD HAVE BEEN CHEERING YOU ON...BUT INSTEAD, I ACTED SHAMELESSLY !
I SAID THOSE THINGS TO NEGI-SENSEI... I'M—
N-NO, YUE !
YES! WHAT I DID WAS WRONG !
WHAT I DID WAS NOT THE ACTION OF A FRIEND !
BUT PLEASE BELIEVE ME! IT WASN'T INTENTIONAL... I DIDN'T PLAN ON FALLING IN LOVE WITH NEGI-SENSEI :
YUE, CALM DOWN ....
NO! I DON'T DESERVE TO BE YOUR FRIEND !
I'M NOTHING BUT A FOOL :
I'M SORRY, NODOKA! I WON'T CAUSE ANY MORE PROBLEMS FOR YOU :
SPLASH
SPLASH
SPLASH
YUE !!
RELAX.
YUE !
IT'S TRUE...I ....
SHAKE
SHAKE
I'M SURE THESE FEELINGS EQUATE TO TEMPORARY INSANITY CAUSED BY PUBERTY! IT'S JUST A MISTAKE !
I'M SURE MY FEELINGS WILL GO AWAY WITH TIME .... !
DROP DROP
NODOKA, PLEASE... FORGET EVERYTHING THAT HAPPENED TODAY.
IF YOU'LL DO THAT, EVERYTHING WILL BE BACK TO NORMAL :
YUE !?

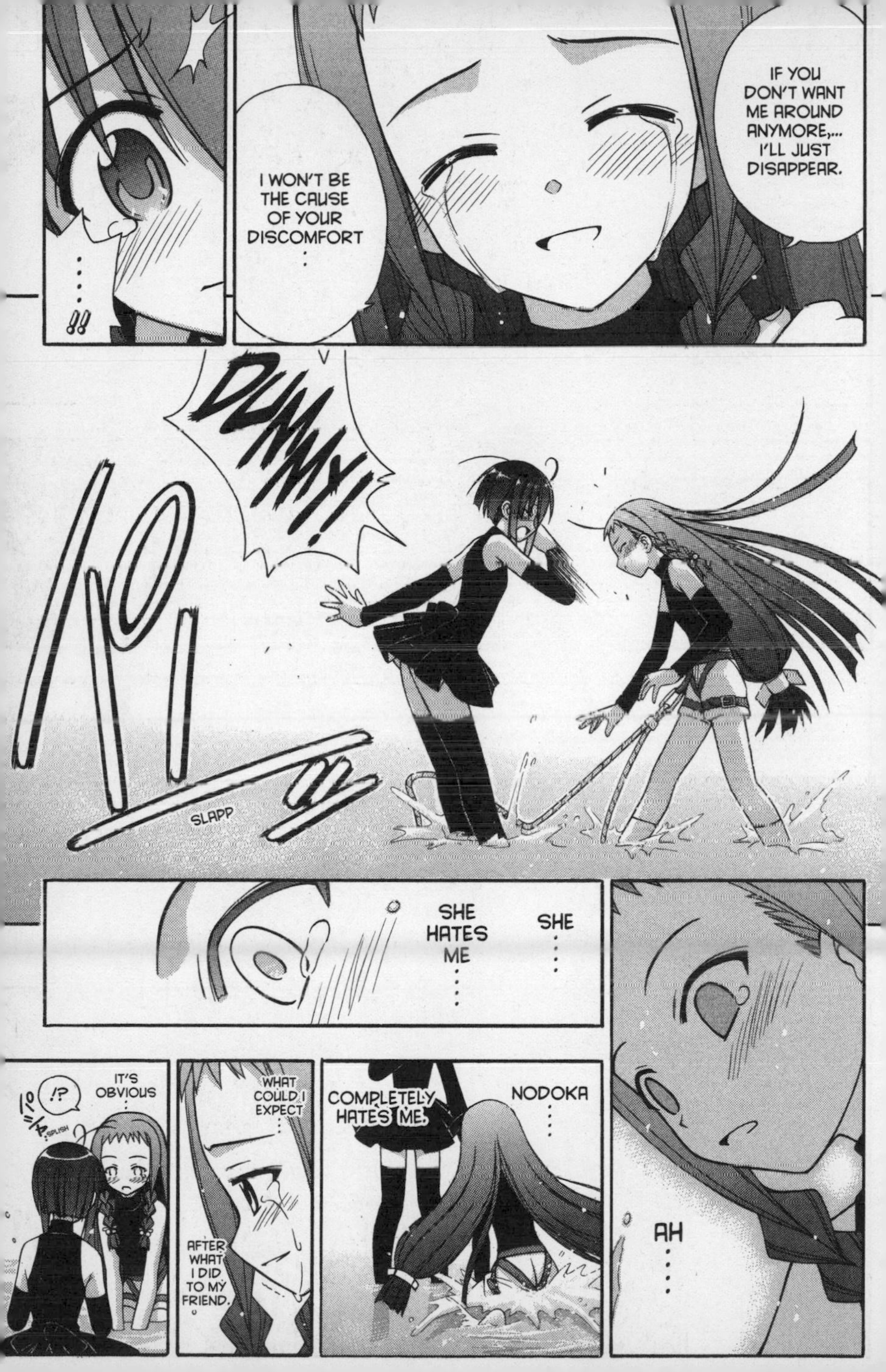
IF YOU DON'T WANT ME AROUND ANYMORE,... I'LL JUST DISAPPEAR.
I WON'T BE THE CAUSE OF YOUR DISCOMFORT ...
...!!
DUMMY!
SLAPP
AH ...
SHE ...
SHE HATES ME ...
NODOKA ...
COMPLETELY HATES ME.
WHAT COULD I EXPECT ...
AFTER WHAT I DID TO MY FRIEND.
IT'S OBVIOUS ...
!?
SPLISH

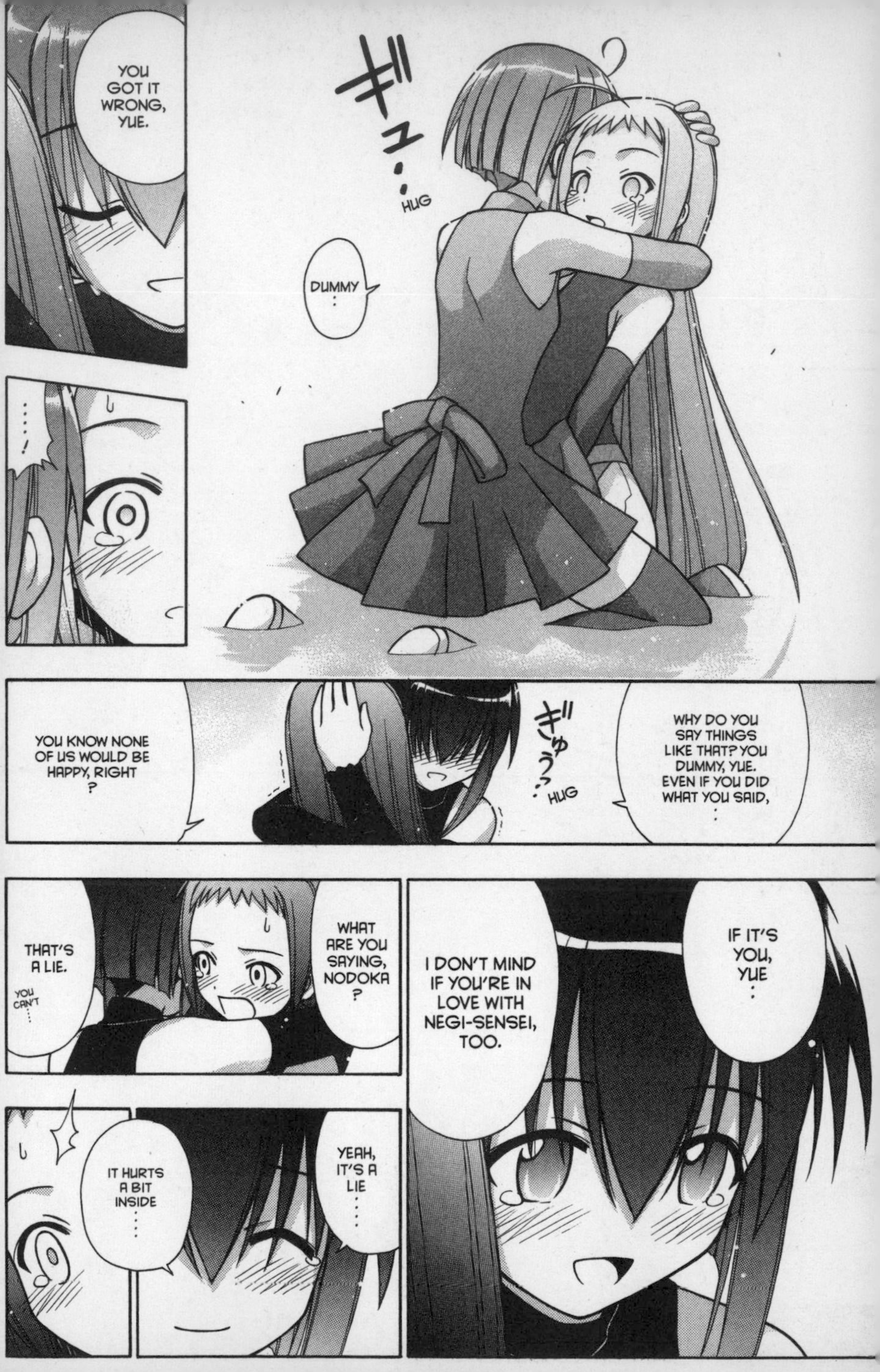
ギュ…
HUG
DUMMY…
YOU GOT IT WRONG, YUE.
…!
WHY DO YOU SAY THINGS LIKE THAT? YOU DUMMY, YUE. EVEN IF YOU DID WHAT YOU SAID, …
ぎゅう…
HUG
YOU KNOW NONE OF US WOULD BE HAPPY, RIGHT?
IF IT'S YOU, YUE…
I DON'T MIND IF YOU'RE IN LOVE WITH NEGI-SENSEI, TOO.
WHAT ARE YOU SAYING, NODOKA?
THAT'S A LIE.
YOU CAN'T…
YEAH, IT'S A LIE…
IT HURTS A BIT INSIDE…

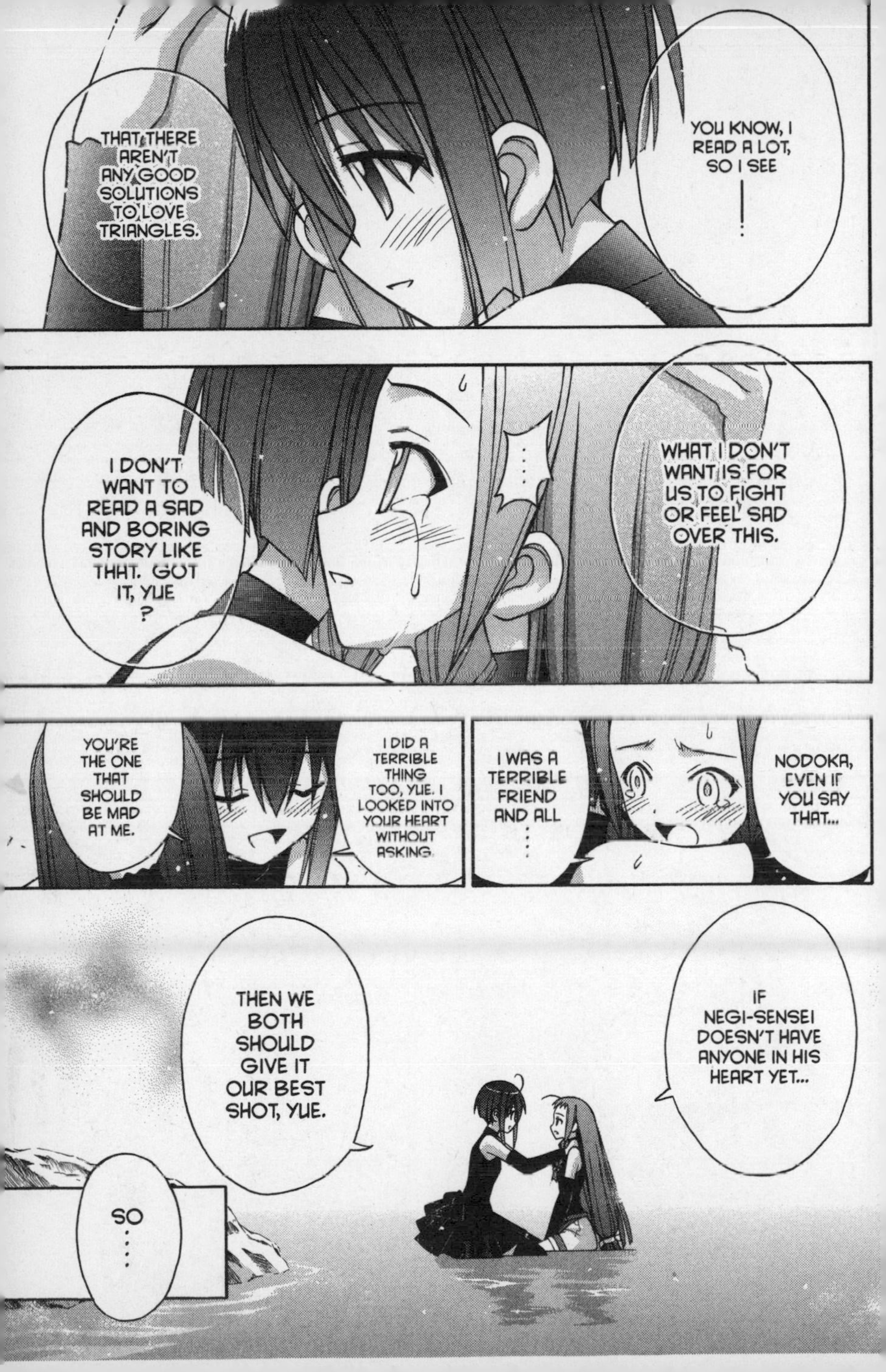
YOU KNOW, I READ A LOT, SO I SEE —
THAT THERE AREN'T ANY GOOD SOLUTIONS TO LOVE TRIANGLES.
WHAT I DON'T WANT IS FOR US TO FIGHT OR FEEL SAD OVER THIS.
...
I DON'T WANT TO READ A SAD AND BORING STORY LIKE THAT. GOT IT, YUE?
NODOKA, EVEN IF YOU SAY THAT...
I WAS A TERRIBLE FRIEND AND ALL...
I DID A TERRIBLE THING TOO, YUE. I LOOKED INTO YOUR HEART WITHOUT ASKING.
YOU'RE THE ONE THAT SHOULD BE MAD AT ME.
IF NEGI-SENSEI DOESN'T HAVE ANYONE IN HIS HEART YET...
THEN WE BOTH SHOULD GIVE IT OUR BEST SHOT, YUE.
SO....

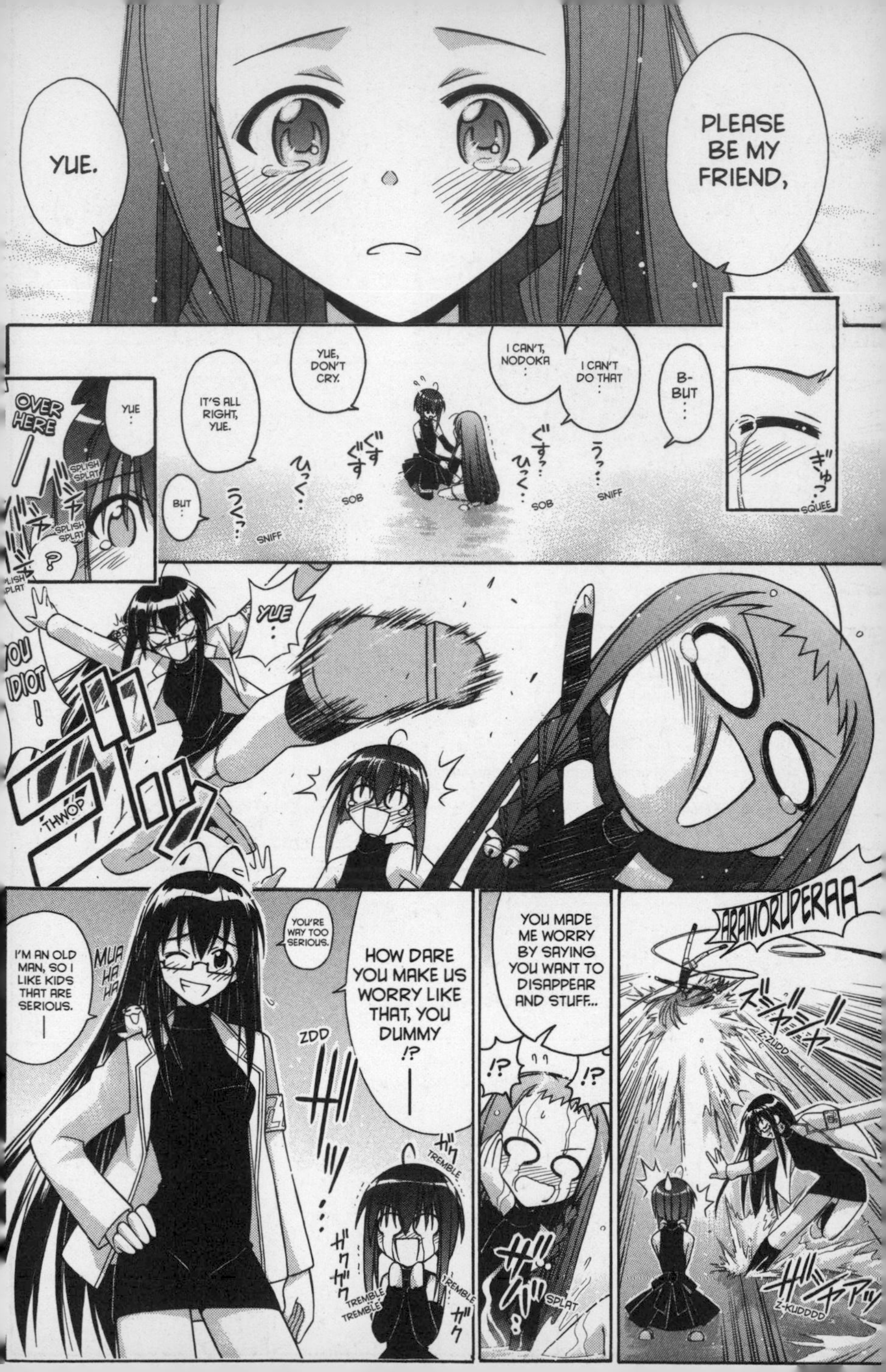
PLEASE BE MY FRIEND,
YUE.
SQUEE
B- BUT . . .
I CAN'T DO THAT . . .
I CAN'T, NODOKA . . .
SNIFF
SOB
YUE, DON'T CRY.
SOB
IT'S ALL RIGHT, YUE.
BUT . . .
SNIFF
YUE . . .
OVER HERE
SPLISH SPLAT
SPLISH SPLAT
?
SPLISH SPLAT
YUE . . .
YOU IDIOT!
THWOP
ARAMORUPERAA
Z-ZUDD
Z-KUDDDD
YOU MADE ME WORRY BY SAYING YOU WANT TO DISAPPEAR AND STUFF...
!?
!?
SPLAT
HOW DARE YOU MAKE US WORRY LIKE THAT, YOU DUMMY !?
ZDD
TREMBLE
TREMBLE TREMBLE
TREMBLE
YOU'RE WAY TOO SERIOUS.
I'M AN OLD MAN, SO I LIKE KIDS THAT ARE SERIOUS.
MUA HA HA

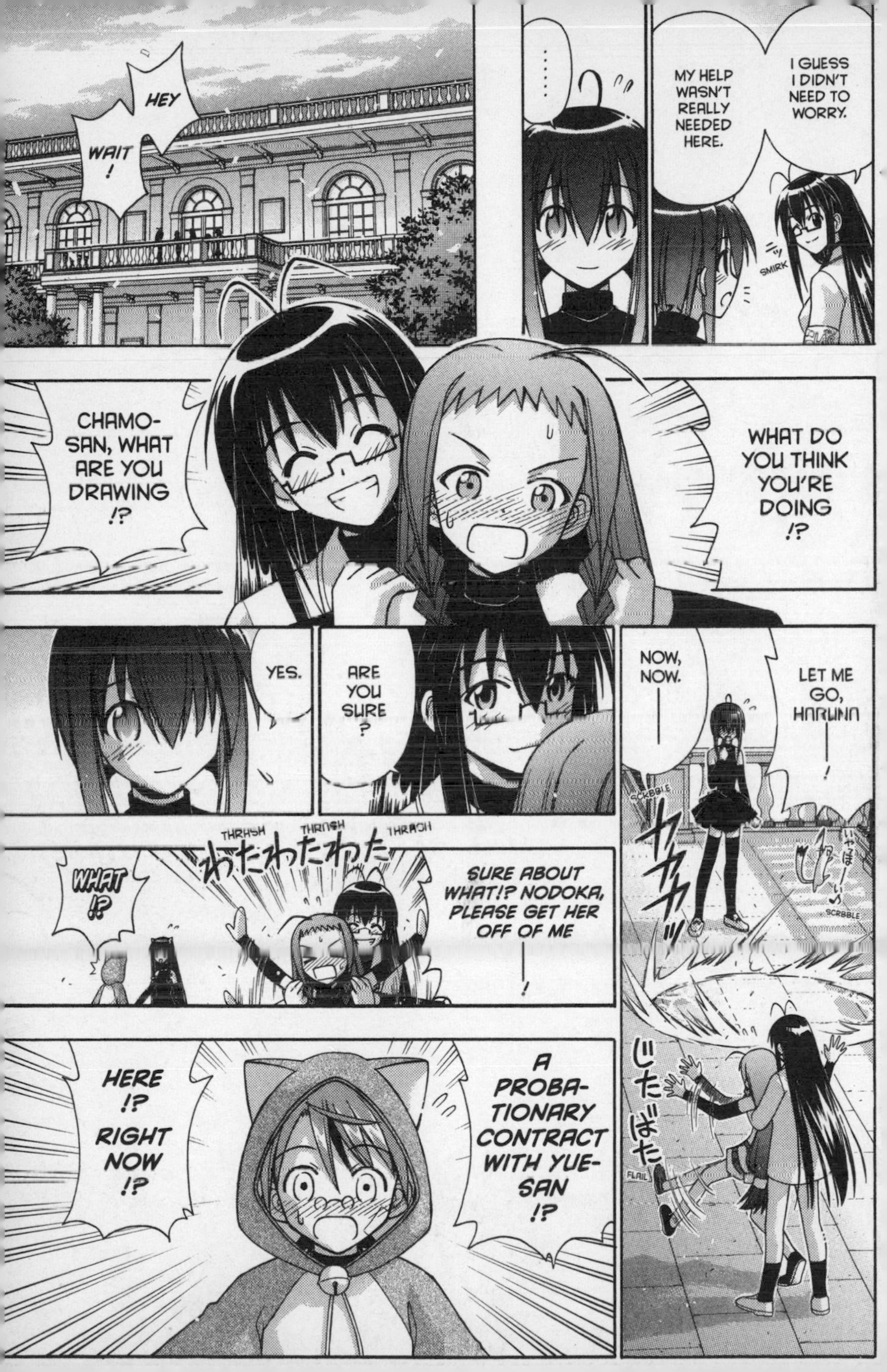
I GUESS I DIDN'T NEED TO WORRY.
MY HELP WASN'T REALLY NEEDED HERE.
SMIRK
......
HEY
WAIT!
WHAT DO YOU THINK YOU'RE DOING!?
CHAMO-SAN, WHAT ARE YOU DRAWING!?
LET ME GO, HARUNA!
NOW, NOW.
SCRBBLE
SCRBBLE
じたばた
FLAIL
ARE YOU SURE?
YES.
SURE ABOUT WHAT!? NODOKA, PLEASE GET HER OFF OF ME!
THRASH THRASH THRASH
わたわたわた
WHAT!?
A PROBATIONARY CONTRACT WITH YUE-SAN!?
HERE!? RIGHT NOW!?

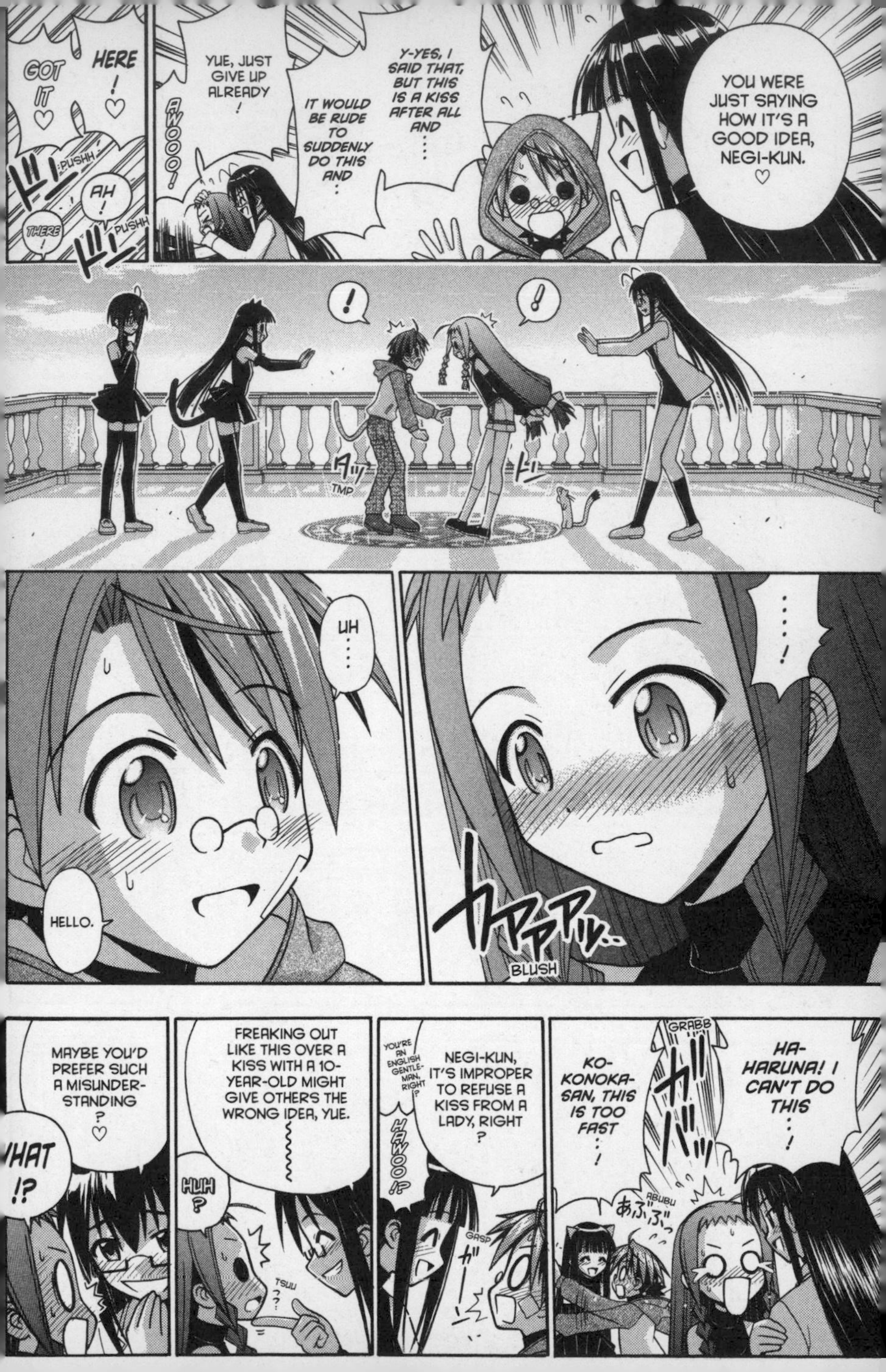

YOU WERE JUST SAYING HOW IT'S A GOOD IDEA, NEGI-KUN. ♡
Y-YES, I SAID THAT, BUT THIS IS A KISS AFTER ALL AND ...
IT WOULD BE RUDE TO SUDDENLY DO THIS AND ...
YUE, JUST GIVE UP ALREADY!
AWOOOO!
HERE! ♡
GOT IT ♡
PUSHH
AH!
THERE!
PUSHH
!
!
TMP
...!
BLUSH
UH...
HELLO.
HA-HARUNA! I CAN'T DO THIS...!
GRABB
KO-KONOKA-SAN, THIS IS TOO FAST...!
ABUBU
NEGI-KUN, IT'S IMPROPER TO REFUSE A KISS FROM A LADY, RIGHT?
YOU'RE AN ENGLISH GENTLE-MAN, RIGHT?
HAWOO!?
GASP
FREAKING OUT LIKE THIS OVER A KISS WITH A 10-YEAR-OLD MIGHT GIVE OTHERS THE WRONG IDEA, YUE.
HUH?
TSUU
MAYBE YOU'D PREFER SUCH A MISUNDER-STANDING? ♡
HAT!?

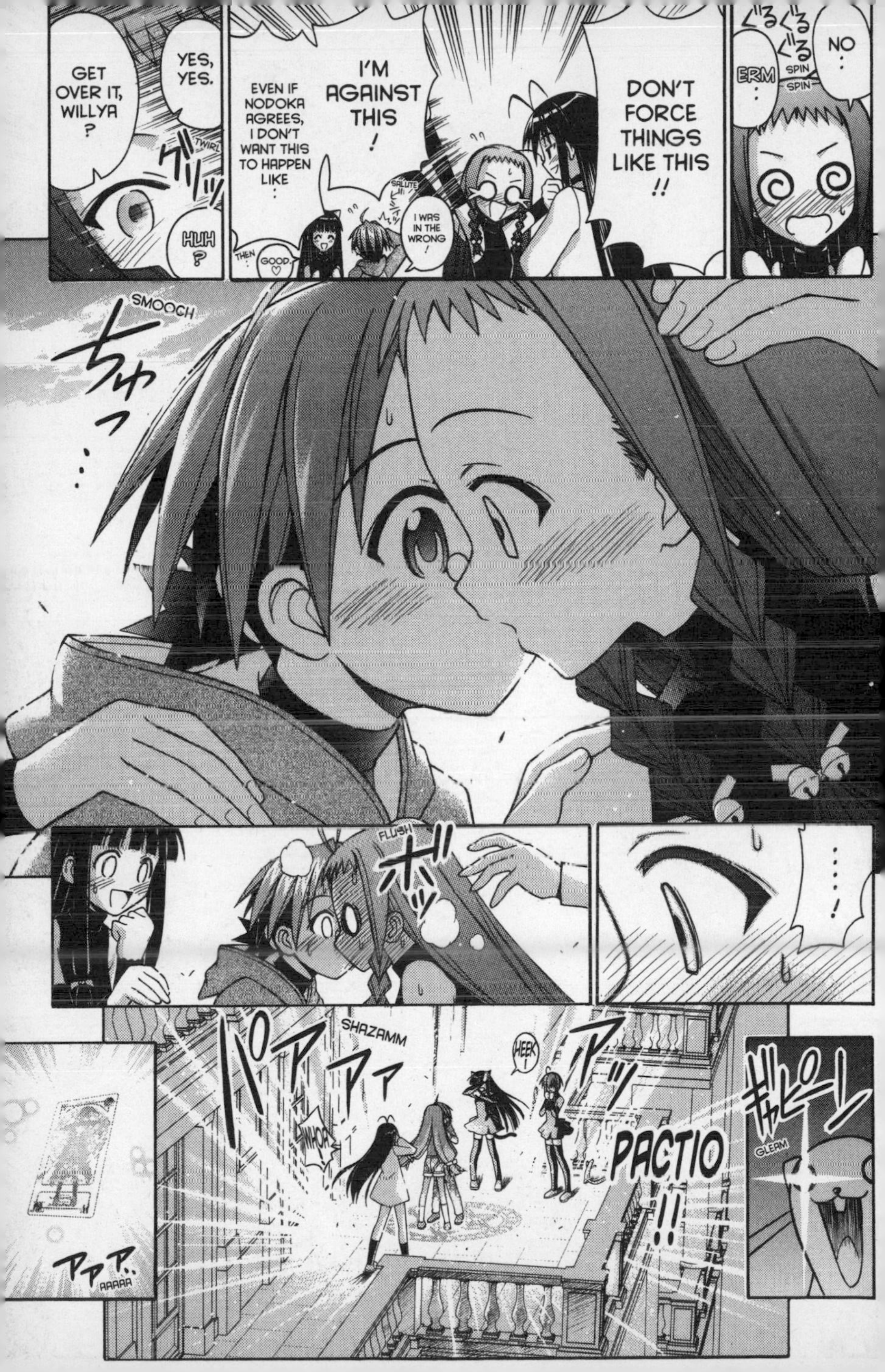
NO ...
ERM ...
SPIN SPIN
DON'T FORCE THINGS LIKE THIS !!
I'M AGAINST THIS !
EVEN IF NODOKA AGREES, I DON'T WANT THIS TO HAPPEN LIKE
I WAS IN THE WRONG !
SALUTE
GOOD.♡
THEN
YES, YES.
GET OVER IT, WILLYA ?
TWIRL
HUH ?
SMOOCH
...
...!
FLUSH
GLEAM
SHAZAMM
HEEK !
WHOA
PACTIO !!
AAAAA

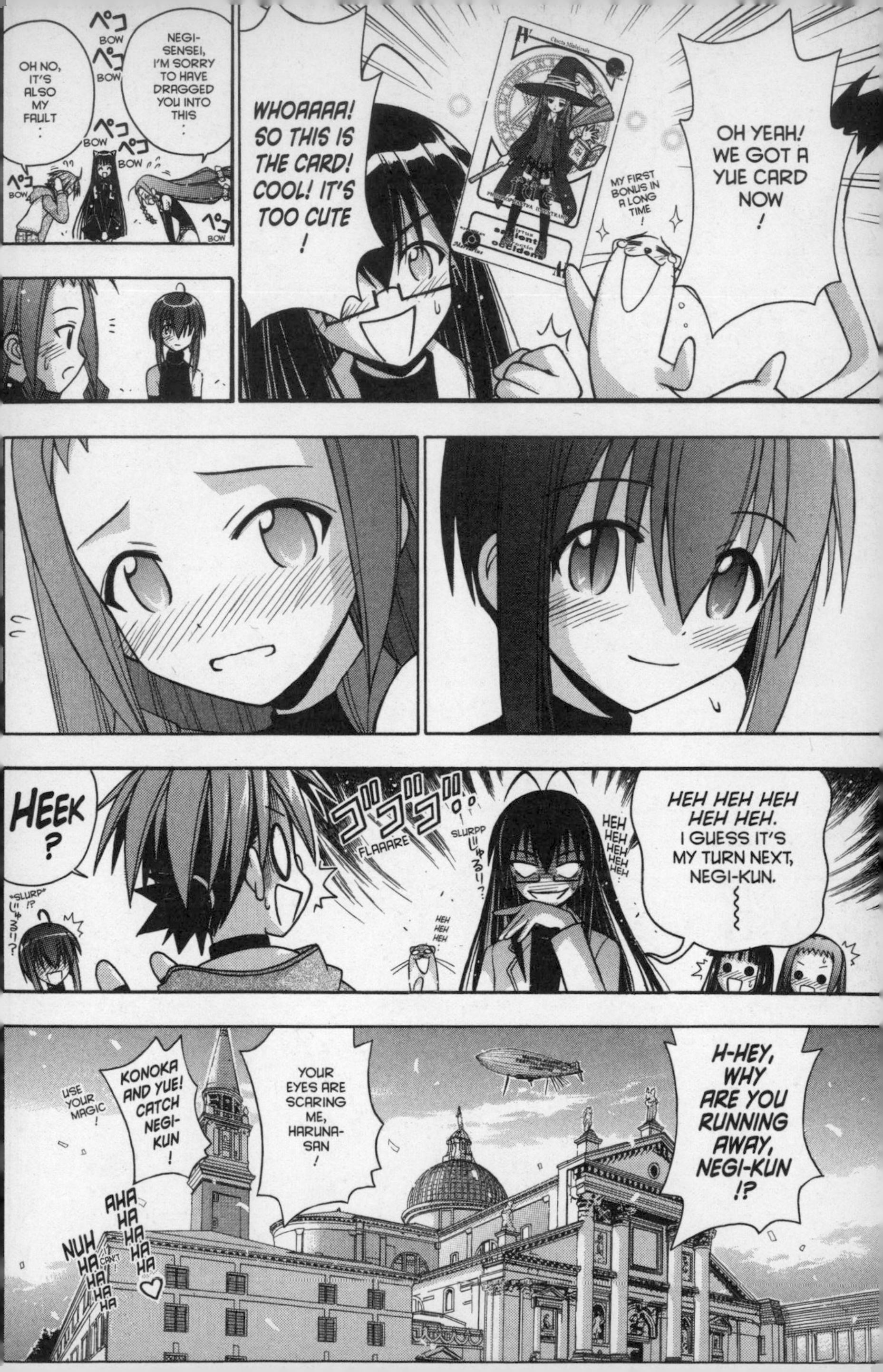

OH YEAH! WE GOT A YUE CARD NOW!
MY FIRST BONUS IN A LONG TIME!
WHOAAAA! SO THIS IS THE CARD! COOL! IT'S TOO CUTE!
ペコ BOW
ペコ BOW
NEGI-SENSEI, I'M SORRY TO HAVE DRAGGED YOU INTO THIS...
ペコ BOW
ペコ BOW
OH NO, IT'S ALSO MY FAULT...
ペコ BOW
ペコ BOW
HEH HEH HEH HEH HEH. I GUESS IT'S MY TURN NEXT, NEGI-KUN...
HEH HEH HEH HEH HEH
SLURPP
FLAAARE
HEH HEH HEH
HEEK?
SLURP
H-HEY, WHY ARE YOU RUNNING AWAY, NEGI-KUN!?
YOUR EYES ARE SCARING ME, HARUNA-SAN!
KONOKA AND YUE! CATCH NEGI-KUN!
USE YOUR MAGIC!
AHA HA HA HA HA ♥
NUH HA HA HA HA
CAN'T!

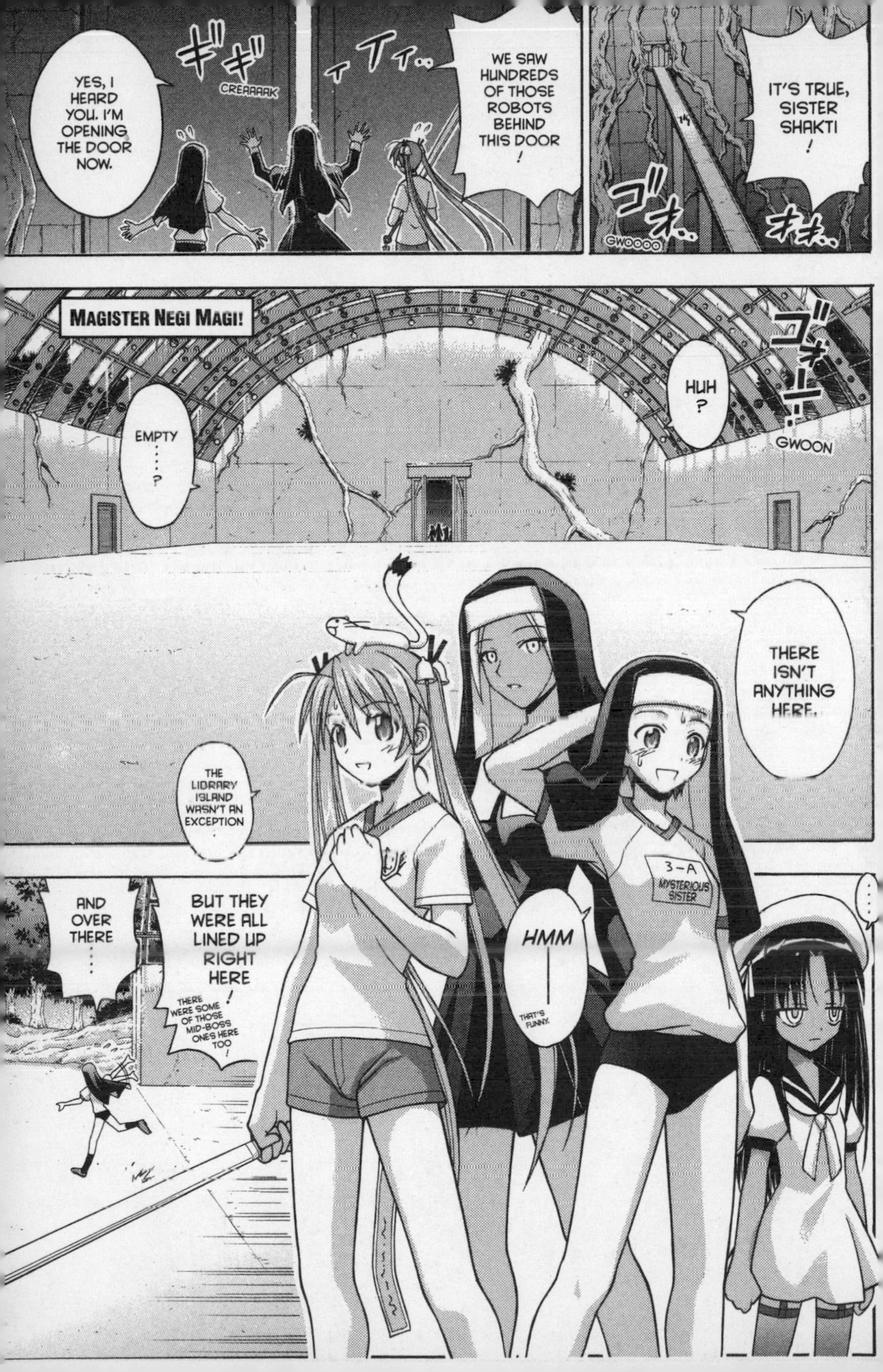
IT'S TRUE, SISTER SHAKTI!
GWOOOO
WE SAW HUNDREDS OF THOSE ROBOTS BEHIND THIS DOOR!
CREAAAAK
YES, I HEARD YOU. I'M OPENING THE DOOR NOW.
MAGISTER NEGI MAGI!
GWOON
HUH?
EMPTY...?
THERE ISN'T ANYTHING HERE.
THE LIBRARY ISLAND WASN'T AN EXCEPTION.
...
3-A MYSTERIOUS SISTER
HMM— THAT'S FUNNY.
BUT THEY WERE ALL LINED UP RIGHT HERE!
THERE WERE SOME OF THOSE MID-BOSS ONES HERE TOO!
AND OVER THERE...

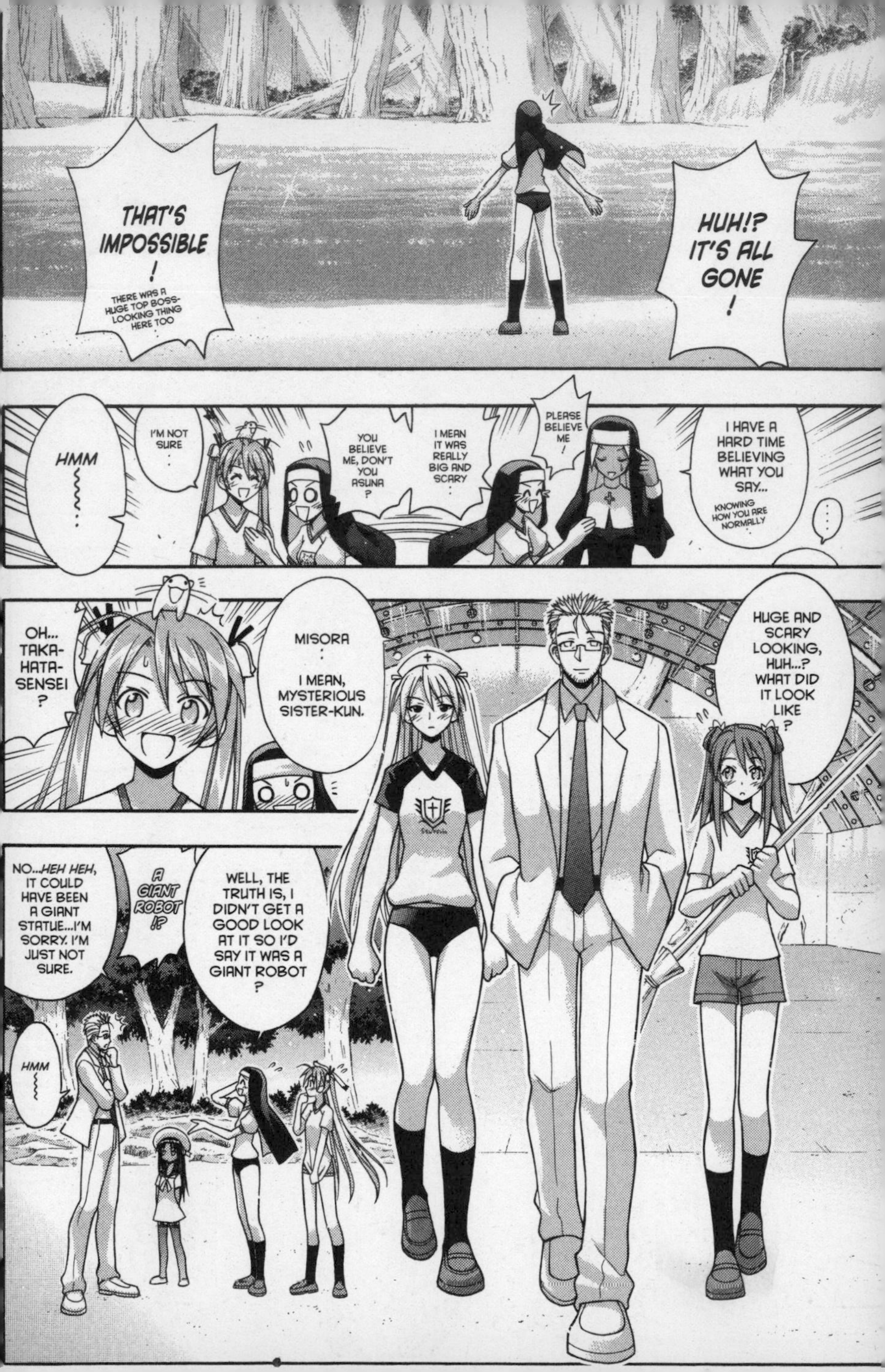
HUH!? IT'S ALL GONE!
THAT'S IMPOSSIBLE!
THERE WAS A HUGE TOP BOSS-LOOKING THING HERE TOO...
I HAVE A HARD TIME BELIEVING WHAT YOU SAY...
KNOWING HOW YOU ARE NORMALLY...
...
PLEASE BELIEVE ME!
I MEAN IT WAS REALLY BIG AND SCARY...
YOU BELIEVE ME, DON'T YOU ASUNA?
I'M NOT SURE...
HMM
HUGE AND SCARY LOOKING, HUH...? WHAT DID IT LOOK LIKE?
MISORA... I MEAN, MYSTERIOUS SISTER-KUN.
OH... TAKA-HATA-SENSEI?
WELL, THE TRUTH IS, I DIDN'T GET A GOOD LOOK AT IT SO I'D SAY IT WAS A GIANT ROBOT?
A GIANT ROBOT!?
NO...HEH HEH, IT COULD HAVE BEEN A GIANT STATUE...I'M SORRY. I'M JUST NOT SURE.
HMM

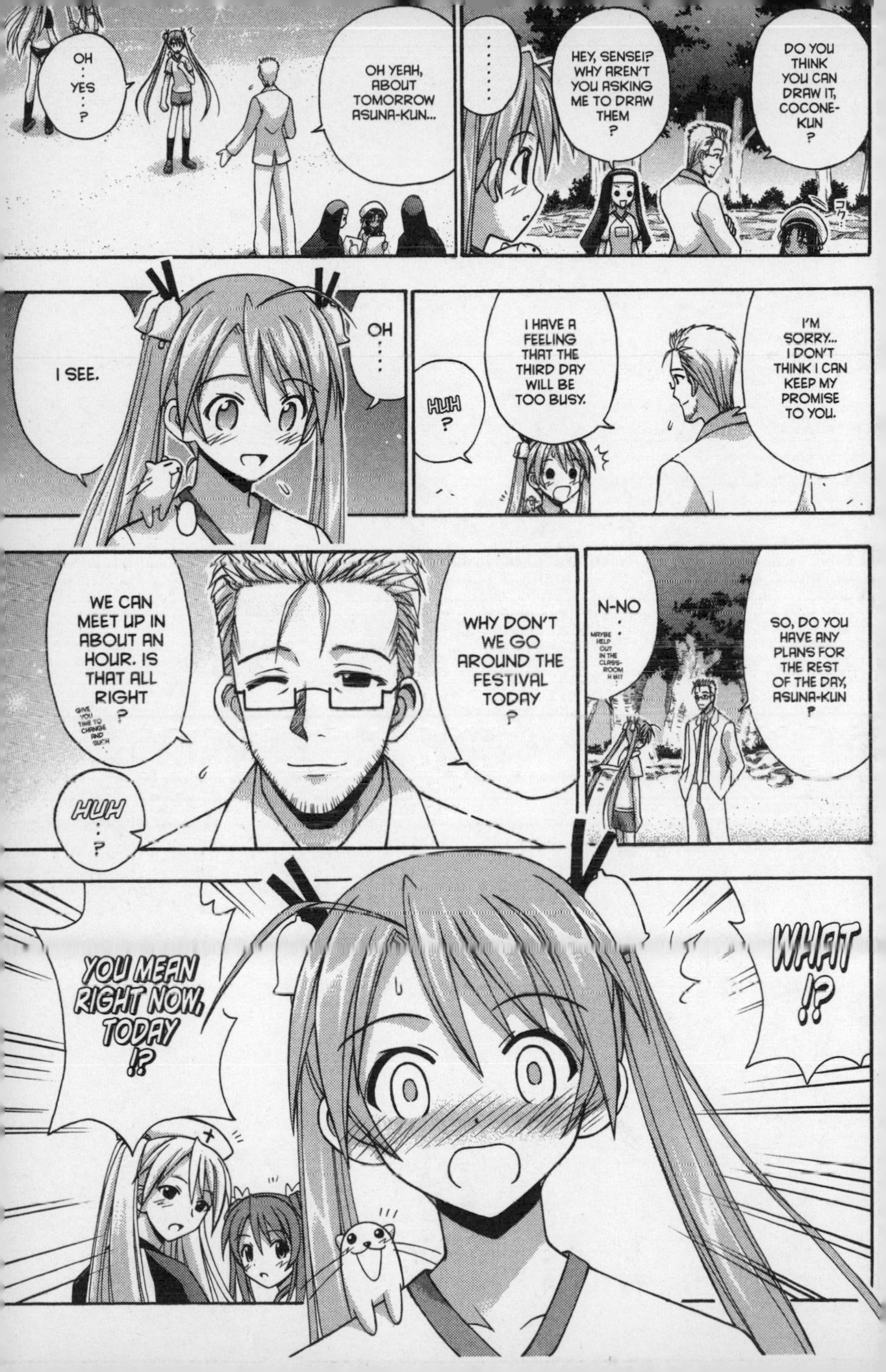
DO YOU THINK YOU CAN DRAW IT, COCONE-KUN?
HEY, SENSEI? WHY AREN'T YOU ASKING ME TO DRAW THEM?
......
OH YEAH, ABOUT TOMORROW ASUNA-KUN...
OH... YES...?
I'M SORRY... I DON'T THINK I CAN KEEP MY PROMISE TO YOU.
I HAVE A FEELING THAT THE THIRD DAY WILL BE TOO BUSY.
HUH?
OH...
I SEE.
SO, DO YOU HAVE ANY PLANS FOR THE REST OF THE DAY, ASUNA-KUN?
N-NO...
MAYBE HELP OUT IN THE CLASS-ROOM A BIT...
WHY DON'T WE GO AROUND THE FESTIVAL TODAY?
WE CAN MEET UP IN ABOUT AN HOUR. IS THAT ALL RIGHT?
GIVE YOU TIME TO CHANGE AND SUCH...
HUH...?
WHAT!?
YOU MEAN RIGHT NOW, TODAY!?

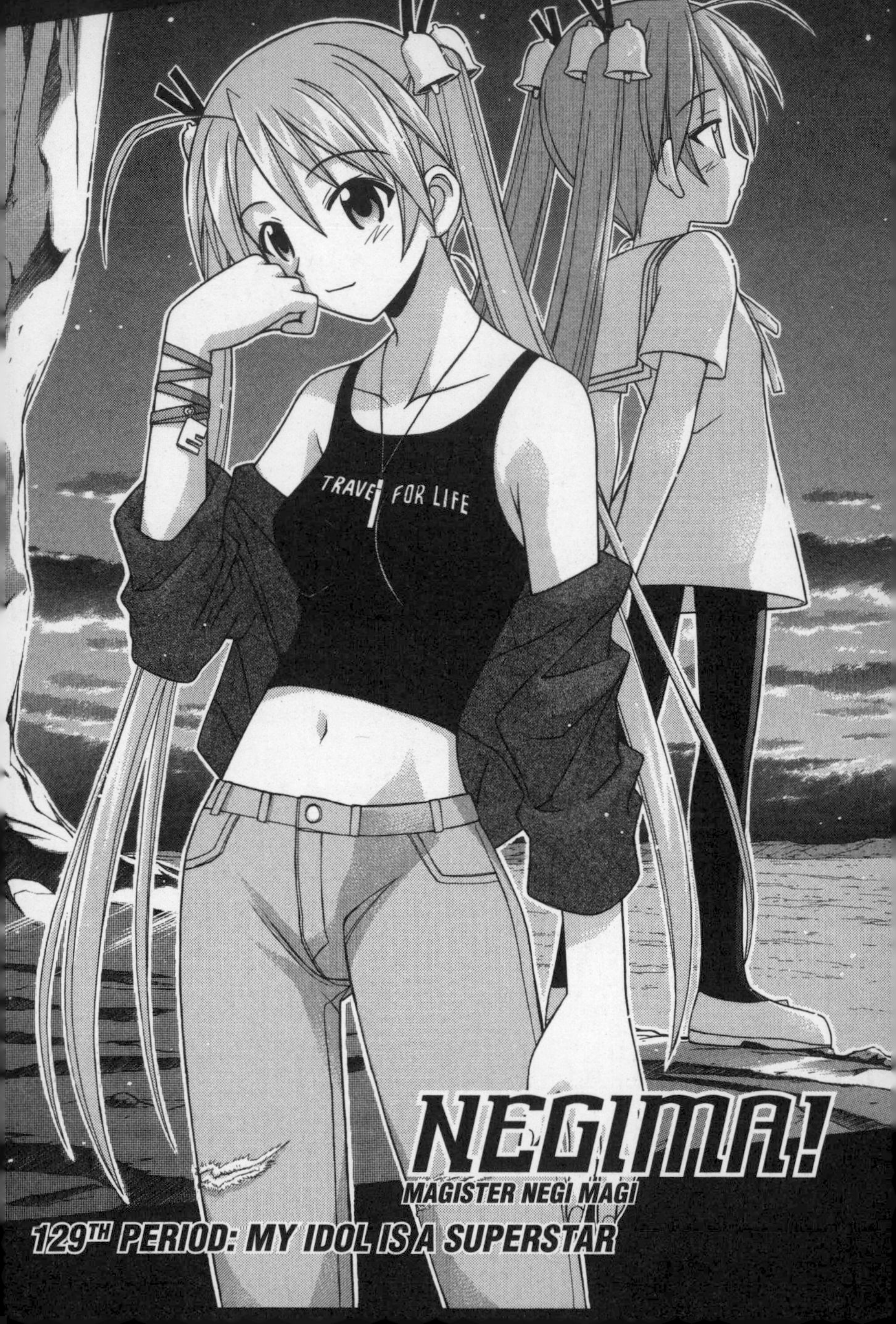
TRAVE FOR LIFE
NEGIMA!
MAGISTER NEGI MAGI
129TH PERIOD: MY IDOL IS A SUPERSTAR

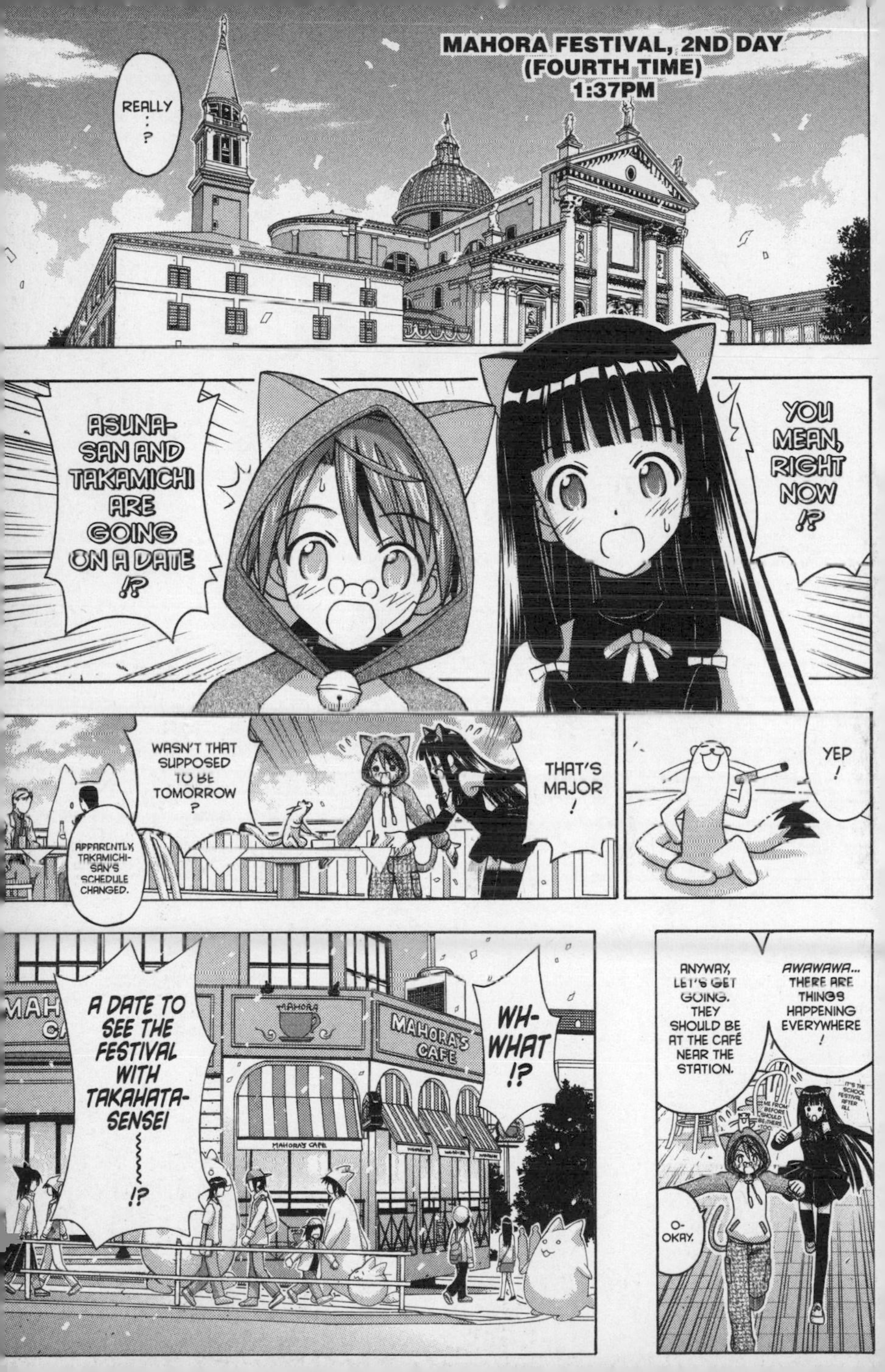
MAHORA FESTIVAL, 2ND DAY (FOURTH TIME) 1:37PM
REALLY...?
YOU MEAN, RIGHT NOW!?
ASUNA-SAN AND TAKAMICHI ARE GOING ON A DATE!?
YEP!
THAT'S MAJOR!
WASN'T THAT SUPPOSED TO BE TOMORROW?
APPARENTLY, TAKAMICHI-SAN'S SCHEDULE CHANGED.
AWAWAWA... THERE ARE THINGS HAPPENING EVERYWHERE!
ANYWAY, LET'S GET GOING. THEY SHOULD BE AT THE CAFÉ NEAR THE STATION.
IT'S THE SCHOOL FESTIVAL, AFTER ALL
ME FROM BEFORE SHOULD BE THERE TOO.
O-OKAY.
WH-WHAT!?
MAHORA
MAHORA'S CAFE
MAHORA'S CAFE
A DATE TO SEE THE FESTIVAL WITH TAKAHATA-SENSEI~~~~!?

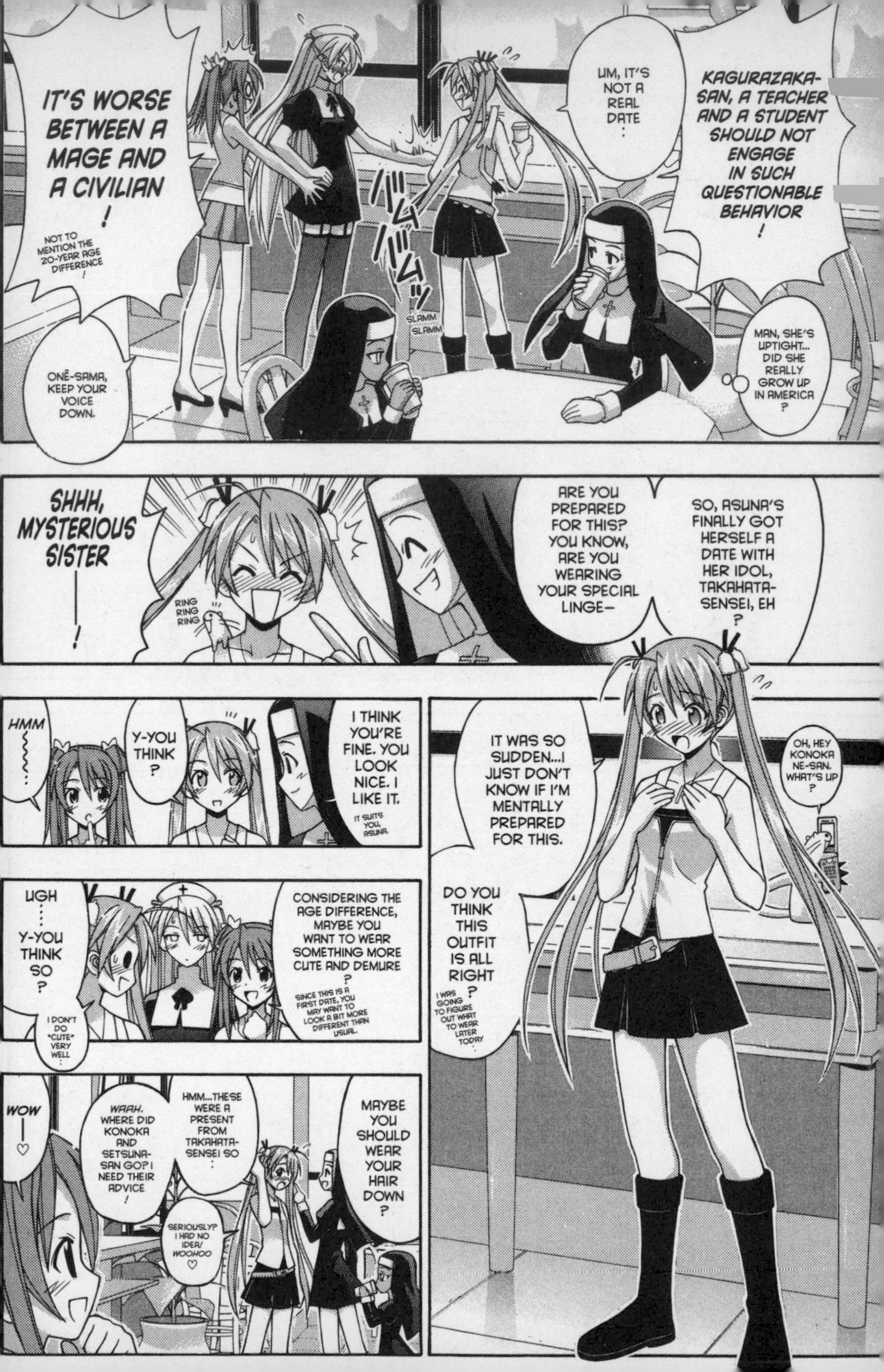
KAGURAZAKA-SAN, A TEACHER AND A STUDENT SHOULD NOT ENGAGE IN SUCH QUESTIONABLE BEHAVIOR!
UM, IT'S NOT A REAL DATE...
IT'S WORSE BETWEEN A MAGE AND A CIVILIAN!
NOT TO MENTION THE 20-YEAR AGE DIFFERENCE!
SLAMM SLAMM
MAN, SHE'S UPTIGHT... DID SHE REALLY GROW UP IN AMERICA?
ONĒ-SAMA, KEEP YOUR VOICE DOWN.
SO, ASUNA'S FINALLY GOT HERSELF A DATE WITH HER IDOL, TAKAHATA-SENSEI, EH?
ARE YOU PREPARED FOR THIS? YOU KNOW, ARE YOU WEARING YOUR SPECIAL LINGE—
SHHH, MYSTERIOUS SISTER—!
RING RING RING
OH, HEY KONOKA NE-SAN. WHAT'S UP?
IT WAS SO SUDDEN...I JUST DON'T KNOW IF I'M MENTALLY PREPARED FOR THIS.
DO YOU THINK THIS OUTFIT IS ALL RIGHT?
I WAS GOING TO FIGURE OUT WHAT TO WEAR LATER TODAY...
I THINK YOU'RE FINE. YOU LOOK NICE. I LIKE IT.
IT SUITS YOU, ASUNA.
Y-YOU THINK?
HMM~~...
CONSIDERING THE AGE DIFFERENCE, MAYBE YOU WANT TO WEAR SOMETHING MORE CUTE AND DEMURE?
SINCE THIS IS A FIRST DATE, YOU MAY WANT TO LOOK A BIT MORE DIFFERENT THAN USUAL.
UGH... Y-YOU THINK SO?
I DON'T DO "CUTE" VERY WELL...
MAYBE YOU SHOULD WEAR YOUR HAIR DOWN?
HMM...THESE WERE A PRESENT FROM TAKAHATA-SENSEI SO...
WAAH. WHERE DID KONOKA AND SETSUNA-SAN GO?! I NEED THEIR ADVICE!
SERIOUSLY?! I HAD NO IDEA! WOOHOO ♡
WOW—♡

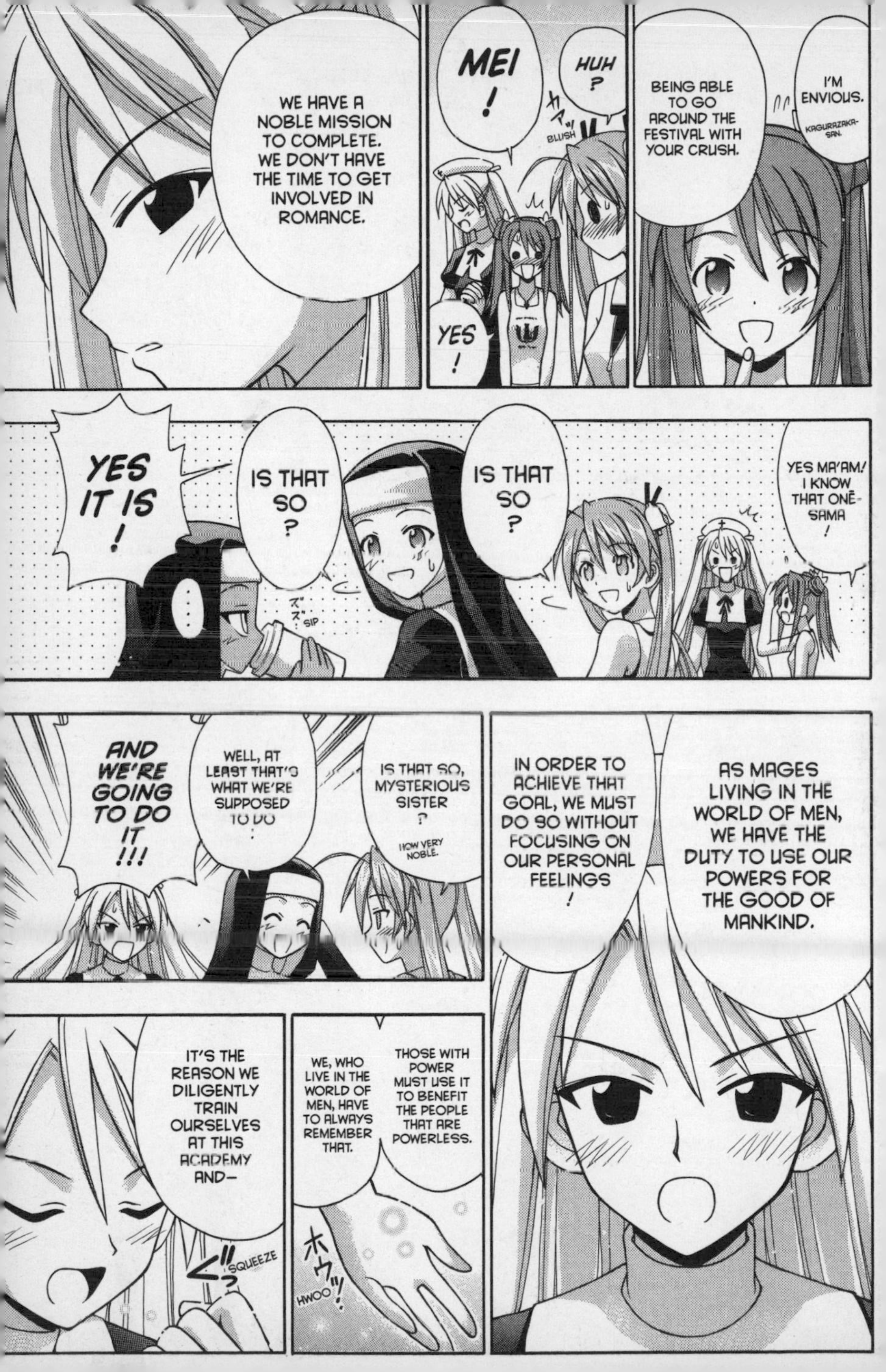
I'M ENVIOUS.
KAGURAZAKA-SAN.
BEING ABLE TO GO AROUND THE FESTIVAL WITH YOUR CRUSH.
HUH?
BLUSH
MEI!
YES!
WE HAVE A NOBLE MISSION TO COMPLETE. WE DON'T HAVE THE TIME TO GET INVOLVED IN ROMANCE.
YES MA'AM! I KNOW THAT ONĒ-SAMA!
IS THAT SO?
IS THAT SO?
SIP
YES IT IS!
AS MAGES LIVING IN THE WORLD OF MEN, WE HAVE THE DUTY TO USE OUR POWERS FOR THE GOOD OF MANKIND.
IN ORDER TO ACHIEVE THAT GOAL, WE MUST DO SO WITHOUT FOCUSING ON OUR PERSONAL FEELINGS!
IS THAT SO, MYSTERIOUS SISTER?
HOW VERY NOBLE.
WELL, AT LEAST THAT'S WHAT WE'RE SUPPOSED TO DO...
AND WE'RE GOING TO DO IT!!!
THOSE WITH POWER MUST USE IT TO BENEFIT THE PEOPLE THAT ARE POWERLESS.
WE, WHO LIVE IN THE WORLD OF MEN, HAVE TO ALWAYS REMEMBER THAT.
HWOO
IT'S THE REASON WE DILIGENTLY TRAIN OURSELVES AT THIS ACADEMY AND–
SQUEEZE

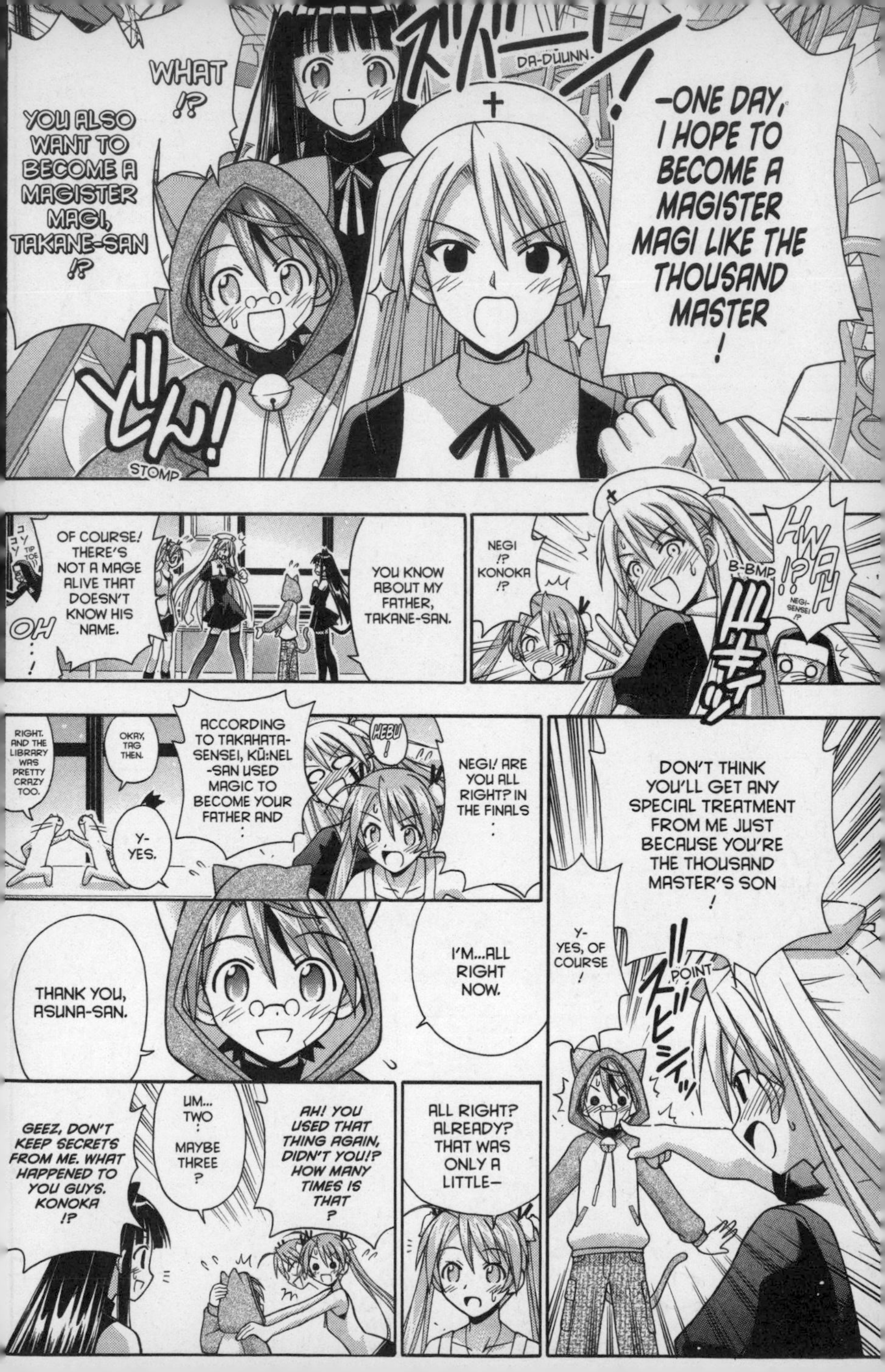

—ONE DAY, I HOPE TO BECOME A MAGISTER MAGI LIKE THE THOUSAND MASTER!
DA-DUUNN.
WHAT!?
YOU ALSO WANT TO BECOME A MAGISTER MAGI, TAKANE-SAN!?
STOMP
HWAAH!?
B-BMP
NEGI-SENSEI!?
NEGI!? KONOKA!?
YOU KNOW ABOUT MY FATHER, TAKANE-SAN.
OF COURSE! THERE'S NOT A MAGE ALIVE THAT DOESN'T KNOW HIS NAME.
TIP TOE
OH...
DON'T THINK YOU'LL GET ANY SPECIAL TREATMENT FROM ME JUST BECAUSE YOU'RE THE THOUSAND MASTER'S SON!
Y-YES, OF COURSE!
POINT
HEBU!
NEGI! ARE YOU ALL RIGHT? IN THE FINALS...
ACCORDING TO TAKAHATA-SENSEI, KŪ:NEL-SAN USED MAGIC TO BECOME YOUR FATHER AND...
Y-YES.
OKAY, TAG THEN.
RIGHT. AND THE LIBRARY WAS PRETTY CRAZY TOO.
I'M...ALL RIGHT NOW.
THANK YOU, ASUNA-SAN.
ALL RIGHT? ALREADY? THAT WAS ONLY A LITTLE—
AH! YOU USED THAT THING AGAIN, DIDN'T YOU!? HOW MANY TIMES IS THAT?
UM... TWO... MAYBE THREE?
GEEZ, DON'T KEEP SECRETS FROM ME. WHAT HAPPENED TO YOU GUYS. KONOKA!?

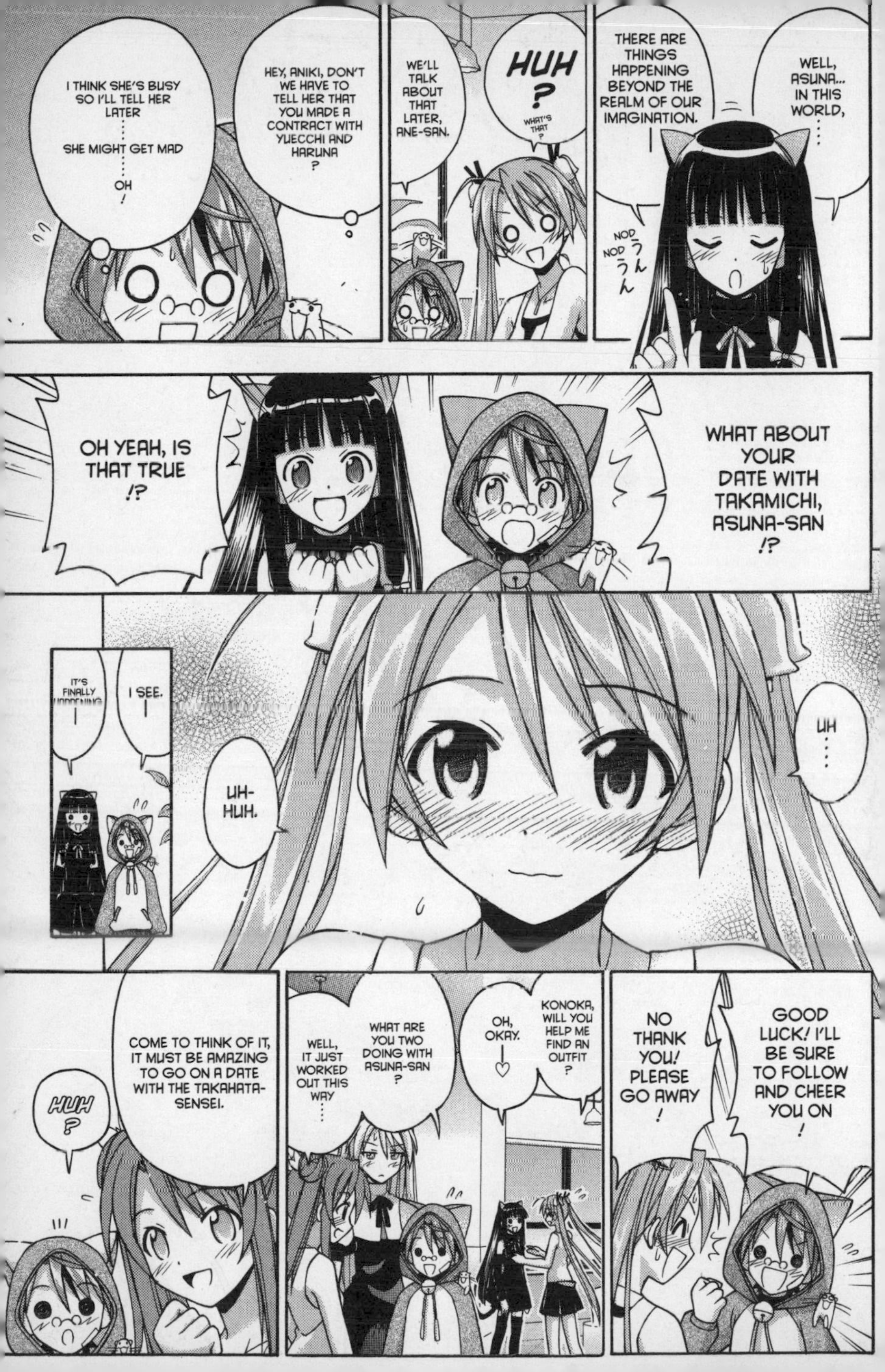
WELL, ASUNA... IN THIS WORLD, ...
THERE ARE THINGS HAPPENING BEYOND THE REALM OF OUR IMAGINATION.
NOD NOD うん うん
HUH ?
WHAT'S THAT ?
WE'LL TALK ABOUT THAT LATER, ANE-SAN.
HEY, ANIKI, DON'T WE HAVE TO TELL HER THAT YOU MADE A CONTRACT WITH YUECCHI AND HARUNA ?
I THINK SHE'S BUSY SO I'LL TELL HER LATER ... SHE MIGHT GET MAD ... OH !
WHAT ABOUT YOUR DATE WITH TAKAMICHI, ASUNA-SAN !?
OH YEAH, IS THAT TRUE !?
UH ...
UH-HUH.
I SEE.
IT'S FINALLY HAPPENING
GOOD LUCK! I'LL BE SURE TO FOLLOW AND CHEER YOU ON !
NO THANK YOU! PLEASE GO AWAY !
KONOKA, WILL YOU HELP ME FIND AN OUTFIT ?
OH, OKAY. ♡
WHAT ARE YOU TWO DOING WITH ASUNA-SAN ?
WELL, IT JUST WORKED OUT THIS WAY ...
COME TO THINK OF IT, IT MUST BE AMAZING TO GO ON A DATE WITH THE TAKAHATA-SENSEI.
HUH ?

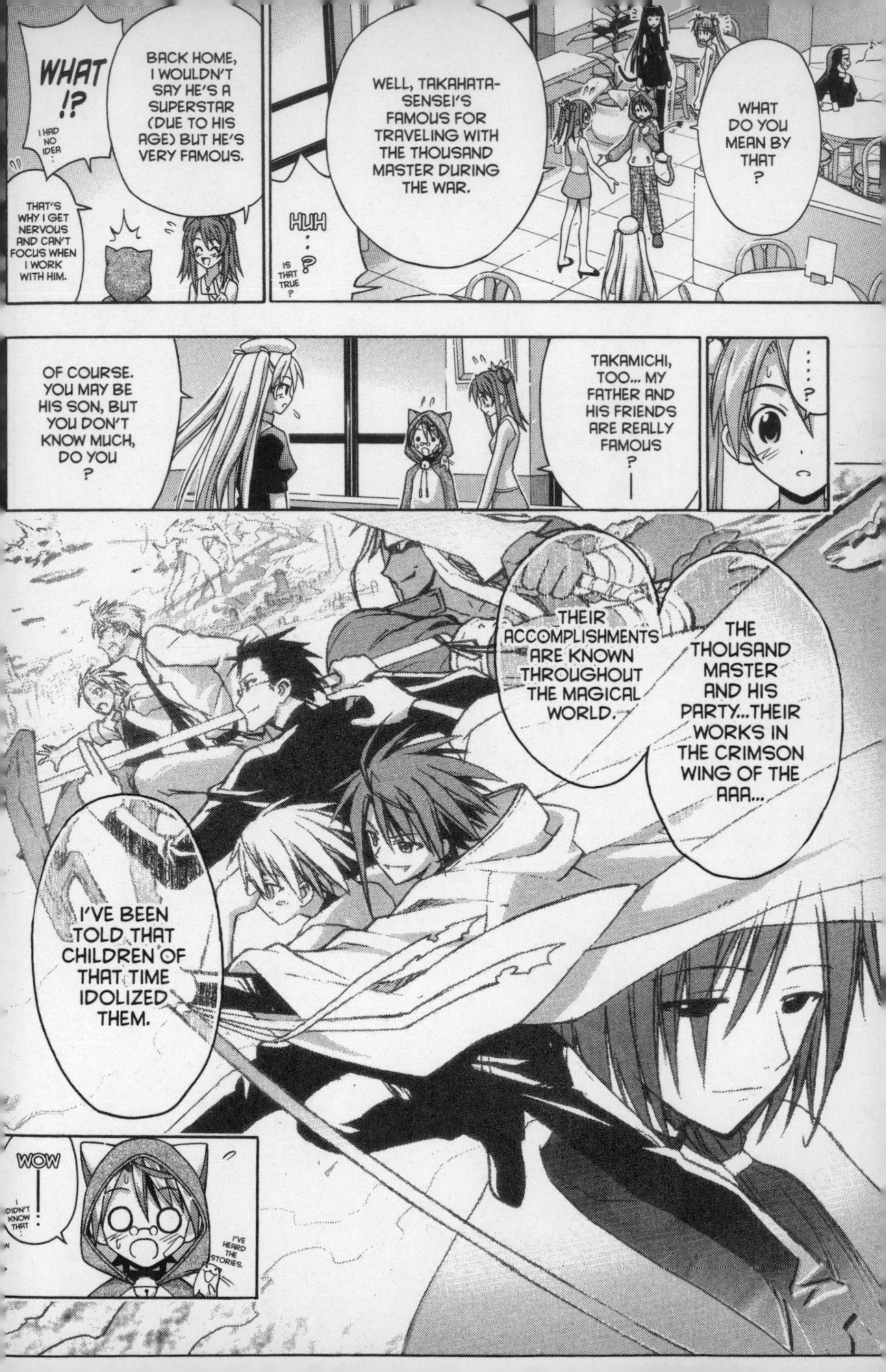
WHAT DO YOU MEAN BY THAT?
WELL, TAKAHATA-SENSEI'S FAMOUS FOR TRAVELING WITH THE THOUSAND MASTER DURING THE WAR.
HUH...?
IS THAT TRUE?
BACK HOME, I WOULDN'T SAY HE'S A SUPERSTAR (DUE TO HIS AGE) BUT HE'S VERY FAMOUS.
WHAT!?
I HAD NO IDEA
THAT'S WHY I GET NERVOUS AND CAN'T FOCUS WHEN I WORK WITH HIM.
...?
TAKAMICHI, TOO... MY FATHER AND HIS FRIENDS ARE REALLY FAMOUS?
OF COURSE. YOU MAY BE HIS SON, BUT YOU DON'T KNOW MUCH, DO YOU?
THE THOUSAND MASTER AND HIS PARTY...THEIR WORKS IN THE CRIMSON WING OF THE AAA...
THEIR ACCOMPLISHMENTS ARE KNOWN THROUGHOUT THE MAGICAL WORLD.
I'VE BEEN TOLD THAT CHILDREN OF THAT TIME IDOLIZED THEM.
WOW!
I DIDN'T KNOW THAT
I'VE HEARD THE STORIES.

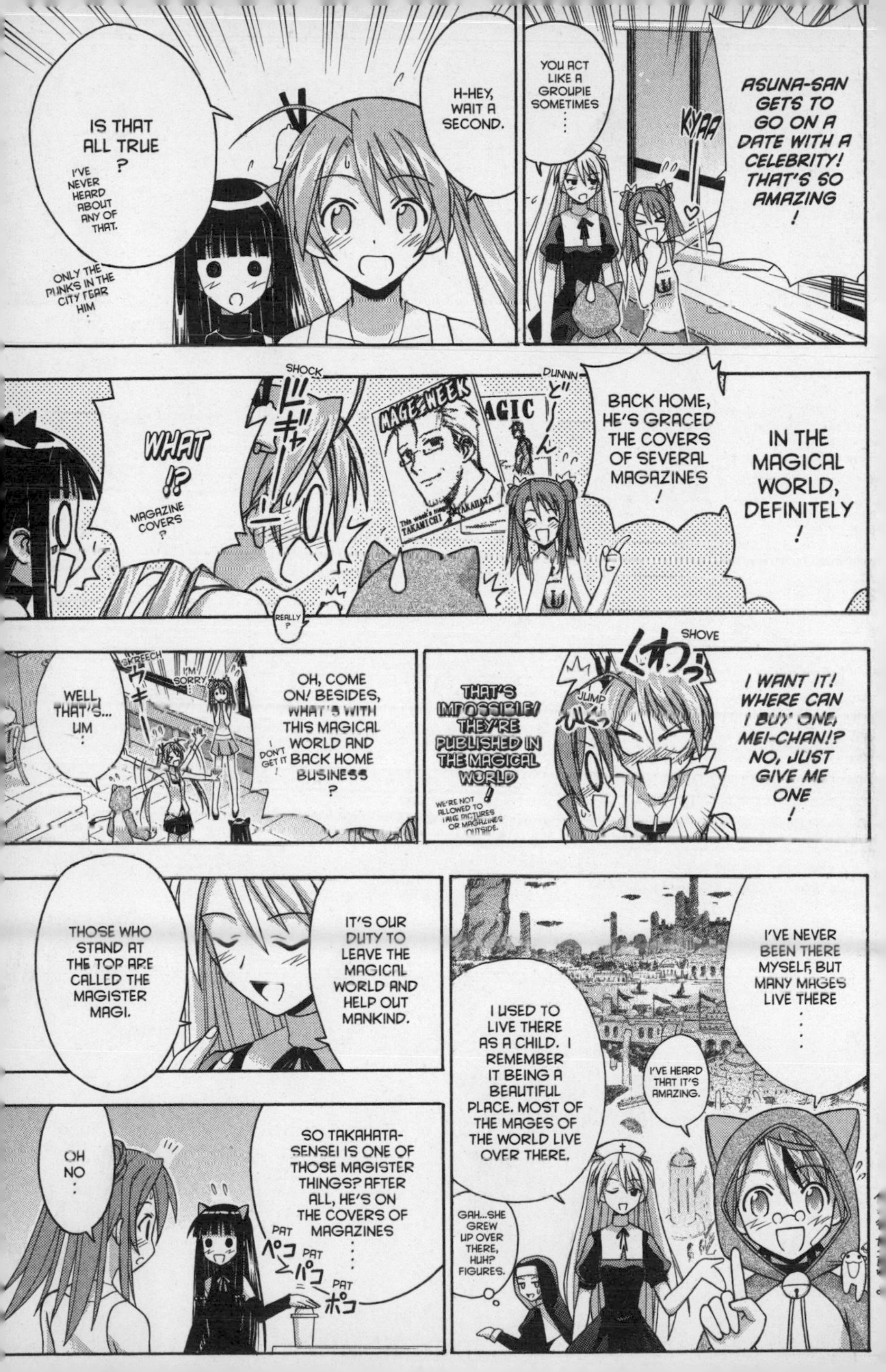
ASUNA-SAN GETS TO GO ON A DATE WITH A CELEBRITY! THAT'S SO AMAZING!
KYAA
YOU ACT LIKE A GROUPIE SOMETIMES...
H-HEY, WAIT A SECOND.
IS THAT ALL TRUE?
I'VE NEVER HEARD ABOUT ANY OF THAT.
ONLY THE PUNKS IN THE CITY FEAR HIM.
IN THE MAGICAL WORLD, DEFINITELY!
BACK HOME, HE'S GRACED THE COVERS OF SEVERAL MAGAZINES!
DUNNN
MAGE WEEK
This week's mage: TAKAMICHI TAKAHATA
AGIC
SHOCK
WHAT!?
MAGAZINE COVERS?
REALLY?
I WANT IT! WHERE CAN I BUY ONE, MEI-CHAN!? NO, JUST GIVE ME ONE!
SHOVE
JUMP
THAT'S IMPOSSIBLE! THEY'RE PUBLISHED IN THE MAGICAL WORLD!
WE'RE NOT ALLOWED TO TAKE PICTURES OR MAGAZINES OUTSIDE.
OH, COME ON! BESIDES, WHAT'S WITH THIS MAGICAL WORLD AND BACK HOME BUSINESS?
I DON'T GET IT!
I'M SORRY
SKREECH
WELL, THAT'S... UM...
I'VE NEVER BEEN THERE MYSELF, BUT MANY MAGES LIVE THERE...
I'VE HEARD THAT IT'S AMAZING.
I USED TO LIVE THERE AS A CHILD. I REMEMBER IT BEING A BEAUTIFUL PLACE. MOST OF THE MAGES OF THE WORLD LIVE OVER THERE.
GAH...SHE GREW UP OVER THERE, HUH? FIGURES.
IT'S OUR DUTY TO LEAVE THE MAGICAL WORLD AND HELP OUT MANKIND.
THOSE WHO STAND AT THE TOP ARE CALLED THE MAGISTER MAGI.
SO TAKAHATA-SENSEI IS ONE OF THOSE MAGISTER THINGS? AFTER ALL, HE'S ON THE COVERS OF MAGAZINES...
PAT PAT PAT
OH NO...

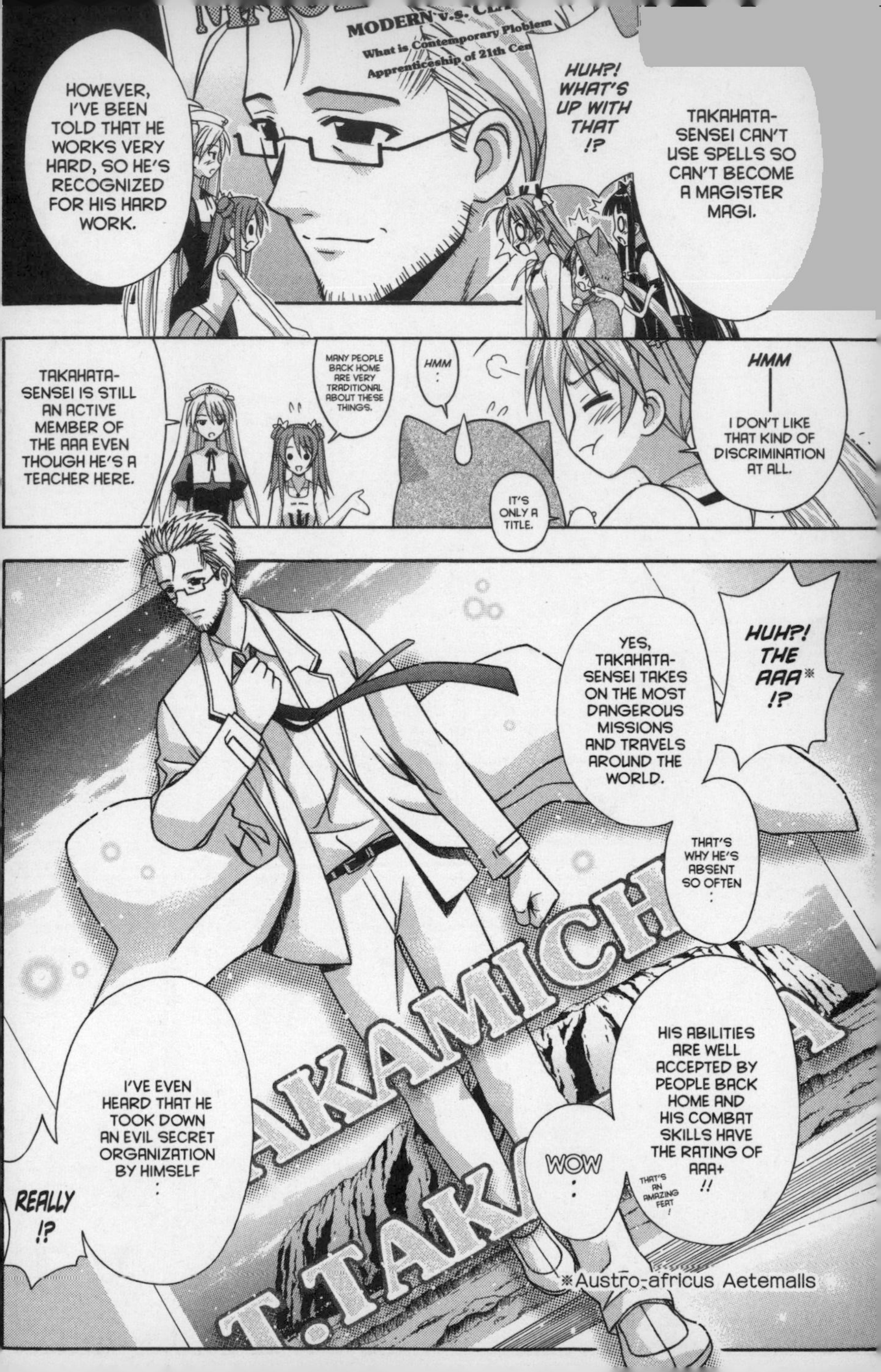
MODERN v.s.
What is Contemporary Ploblem
TAKAHATA-SENSEI CAN'T USE SPELLS SO CAN'T BECOME A MAGISTER MAGI.
HUH?! WHAT'S UP WITH THAT !?
HOWEVER, I'VE BEEN TOLD THAT HE WORKS VERY HARD, SO HE'S RECOGNIZED FOR HIS HARD WORK.
HMM — I DON'T LIKE THAT KIND OF DISCRIMINATION AT ALL.
IT'S ONLY A TITLE.
HMM :
MANY PEOPLE BACK HOME ARE VERY TRADITIONAL ABOUT THESE THINGS.
TAKAHATA-SENSEI IS STILL AN ACTIVE MEMBER OF THE AAA EVEN THOUGH HE'S A TEACHER HERE.
HUH?! THE AAA※ !?
YES, TAKAHATA-SENSEI TAKES ON THE MOST DANGEROUS MISSIONS AND TRAVELS AROUND THE WORLD.
THAT'S WHY HE'S ABSENT SO OFTEN :
HIS ABILITIES ARE WELL ACCEPTED BY PEOPLE BACK HOME AND HIS COMBAT SKILLS HAVE THE RATING OF AAA+ !!
THAT'S AN AMAZING FEAT!
WOW :
I'VE EVEN HEARD THAT HE TOOK DOWN AN EVIL SECRET ORGANIZATION BY HIMSELF :
REALLY !?
※Austro-africus Aetemalls

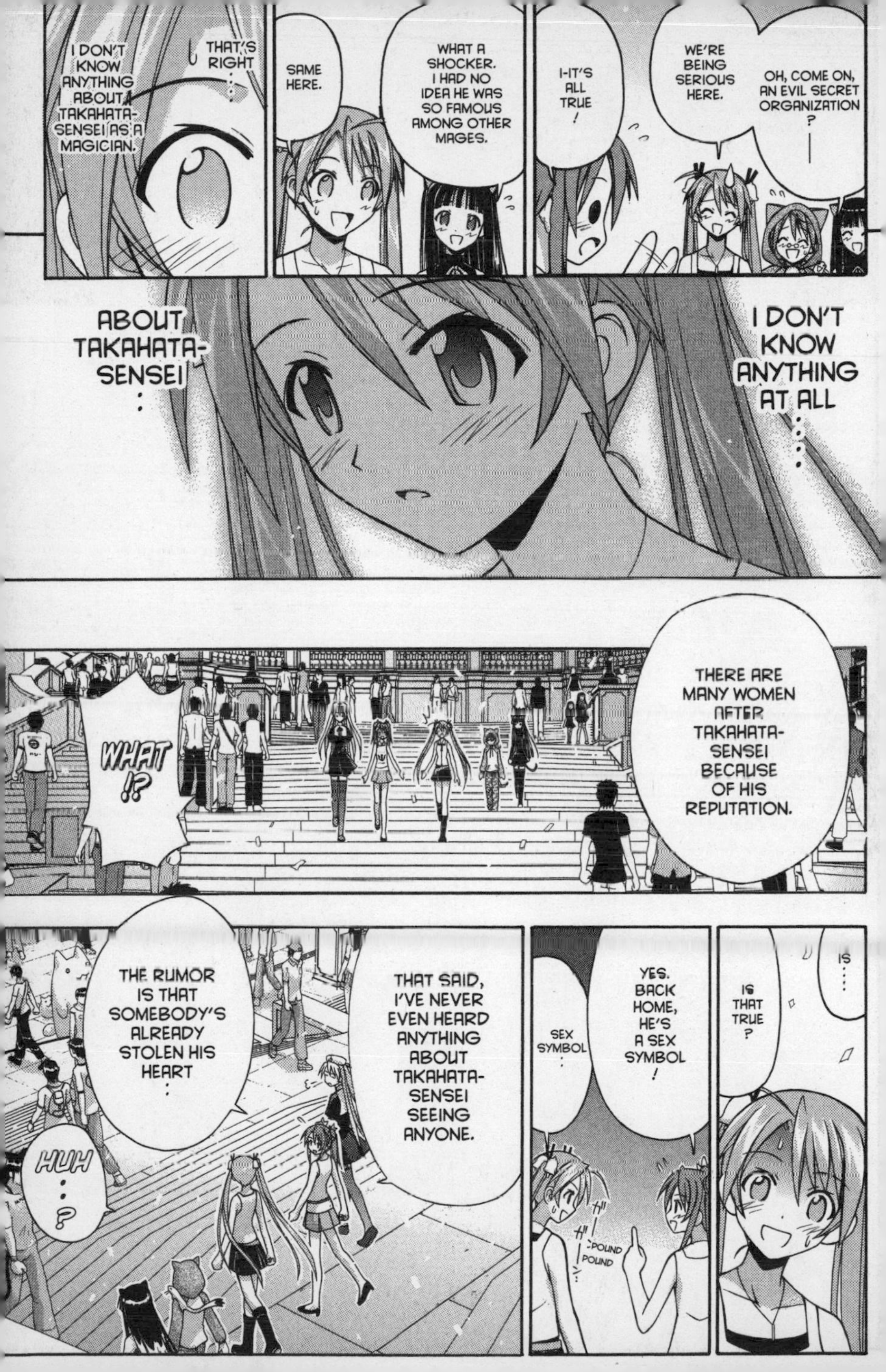
OH, COME ON, AN EVIL SECRET ORGANIZATION?
WE'RE BEING SERIOUS HERE.
I-IT'S ALL TRUE!
WHAT A SHOCKER. I HAD NO IDEA HE WAS SO FAMOUS AMONG OTHER MAGES.
SAME HERE.
THAT'S RIGHT...
I DON'T KNOW ANYTHING ABOUT TAKAHATA-SENSEI AS A MAGICIAN.
I DON'T KNOW ANYTHING AT ALL...
ABOUT TAKAHATA-SENSEI:
THERE ARE MANY WOMEN AFTER TAKAHATA-SENSEI BECAUSE OF HIS REPUTATION.
WHAT!?
IS....
IS THAT TRUE?
YES. BACK HOME, HE'S A SEX SYMBOL!
SEX SYMBOL:
POUND
POUND
THAT SAID, I'VE NEVER EVEN HEARD ANYTHING ABOUT TAKAHATA-SENSEI SEEING ANYONE.
THE RUMOR IS THAT SOMEBODY'S ALREADY STOLEN HIS HEART:
HUH...?

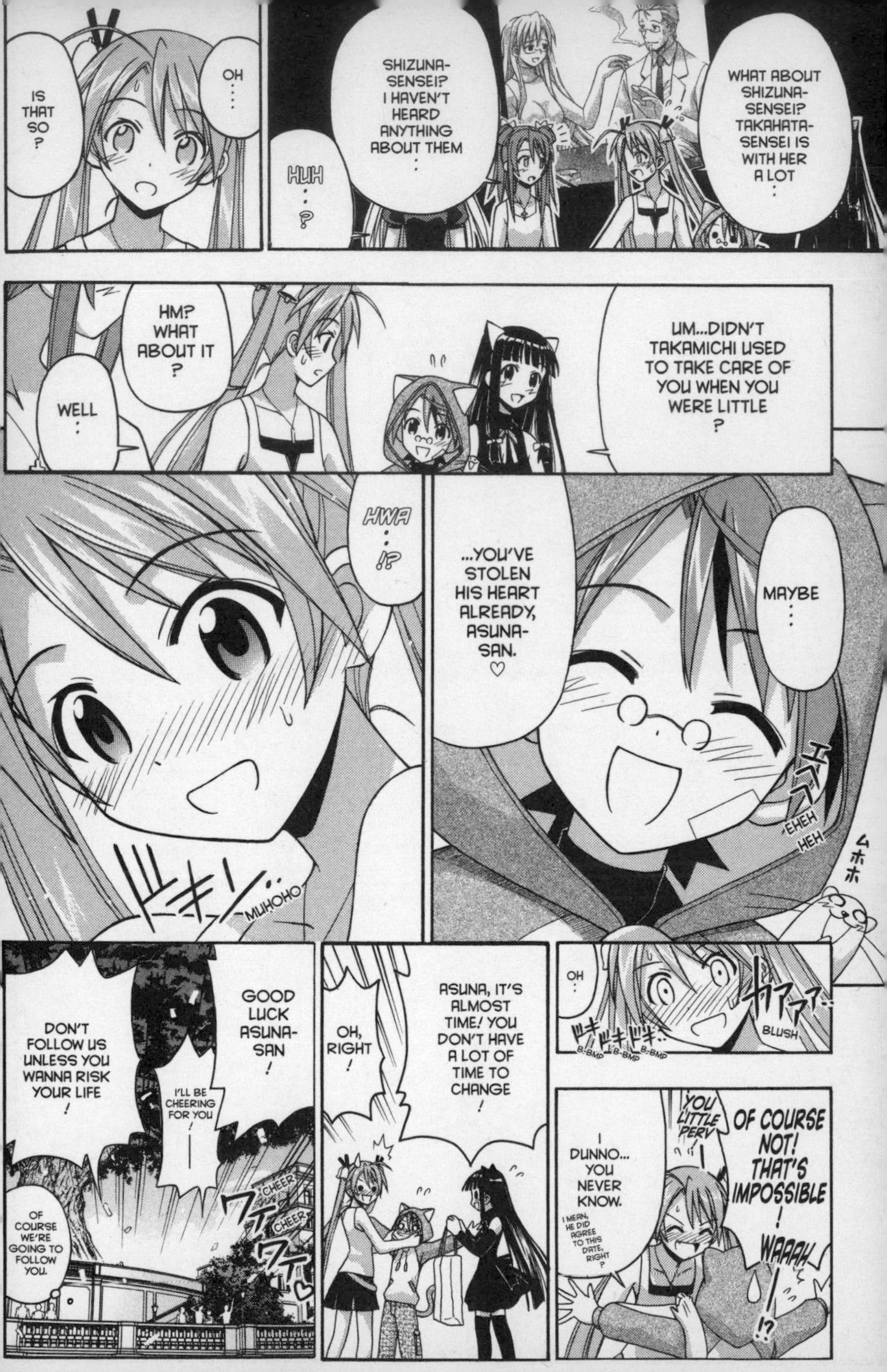
WHAT ABOUT SHIZUNA-SENSEI? TAKAHATA-SENSEI IS WITH HER A LOT...
SHIZUNA-SENSEI? I HAVEN'T HEARD ANYTHING ABOUT THEM...
HUH...?
OH....
IS THAT SO?
UM...DIDN'T TAKAMICHI USED TO TAKE CARE OF YOU WHEN YOU WERE LITTLE?
HM? WHAT ABOUT IT?
WELL...
MAYBE...
...YOU'VE STOLEN HIS HEART ALREADY, ASUNA-SAN. ♡
EHEH HEH
ムホホ
HWA...!?
MUHOHO
OH...
BLUSH
B-BMP B-BMP B-BMP
OF COURSE NOT! THAT'S IMPOSSIBLE!
YOU LITTLE PERV!
I DUNNO... YOU NEVER KNOW.
I MEAN, HE DID AGREE TO THIS DATE, RIGHT?
WAAAH!!?
ASUNA, IT'S ALMOST TIME! YOU DON'T HAVE A LOT OF TIME TO CHANGE!
OH, RIGHT!
GOOD LUCK ASUNA-SAN!
DON'T FOLLOW US UNLESS YOU WANNA RISK YOUR LIFE!
I'LL BE CHEERING FOR YOU!
CHEER CHEER
OF COURSE WE'RE GOING TO FOLLOW YOU.

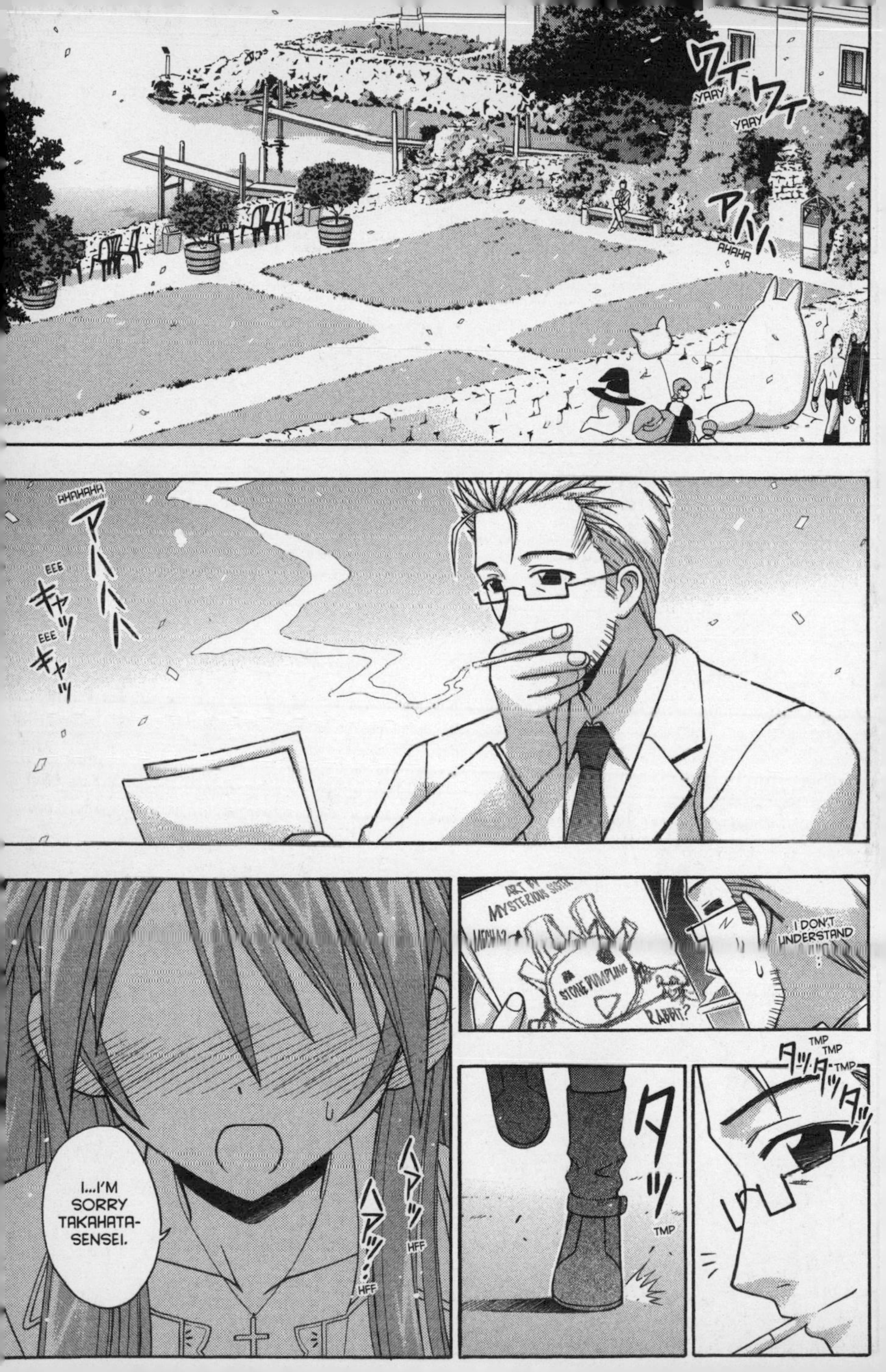
ワイワイ
YAAY YAAY
アハハ
AHAHA
アハハハ
AHAHAHA
キャッ
EEE
キャッ
EEE
ART BY MYSTERIOUS SISTER
STONE DUMPLING
RABBIT?
I DON'T UNDERSTAND...
タッタッタッ
TMP TMP TMP
タッ
TMP
I...I'M SORRY TAKAHATA-SENSEI.
ハァッ
HFF
ハァッ
HFF

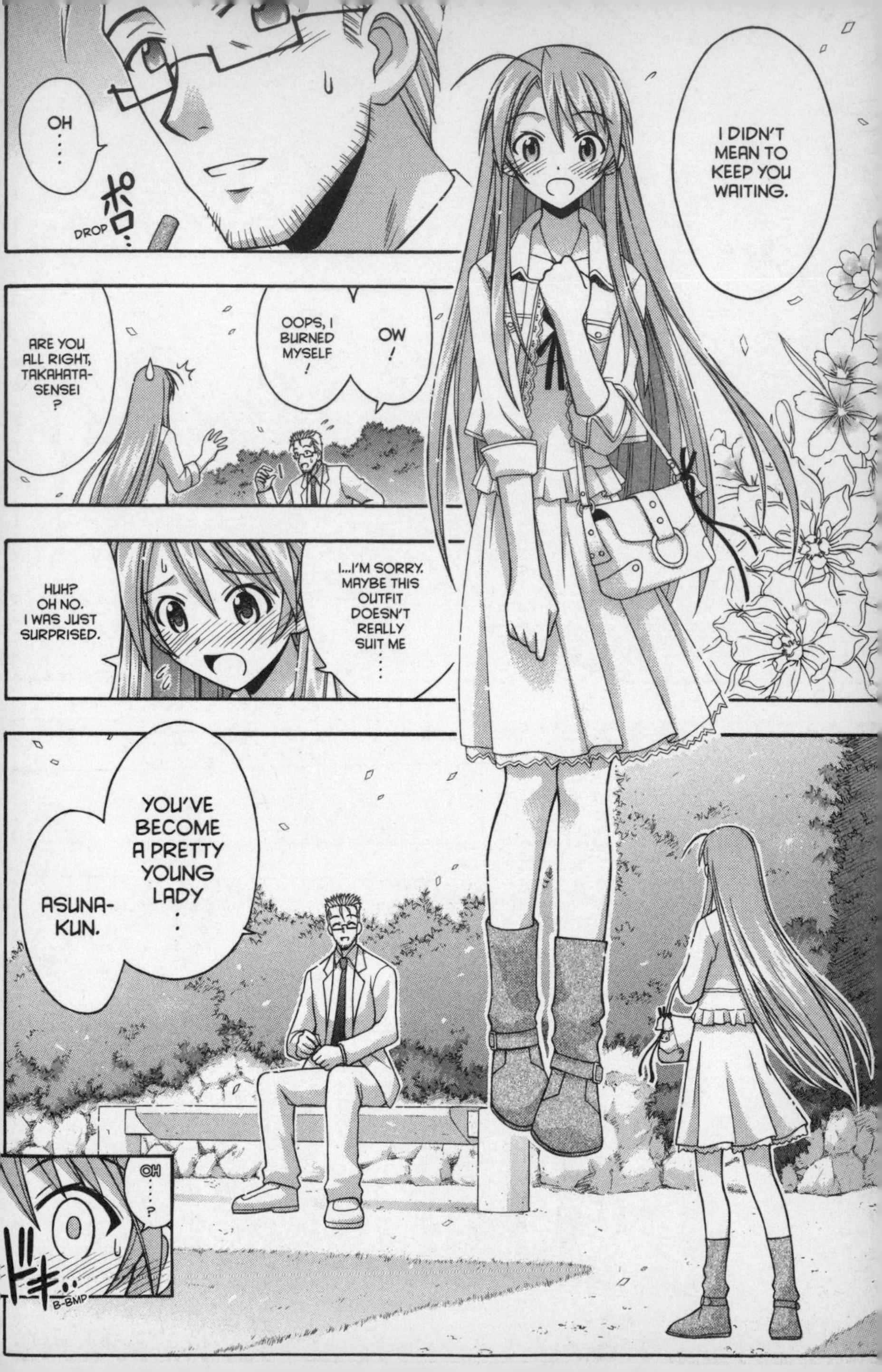
I DIDN'T MEAN TO KEEP YOU WAITING.
OH.....
ポロ
DROP
OOPS, I BURNED MYSELF!
OW!
ARE YOU ALL RIGHT, TAKAHATA-SENSEI?
I...I'M SORRY. MAYBE THIS OUTFIT DOESN'T REALLY SUIT ME...
HUH? OH NO. I WAS JUST SURPRISED.
YOU'VE BECOME A PRETTY YOUNG LADY..
ASUNA-KUN.
OH....?
ドキ
B-BMP

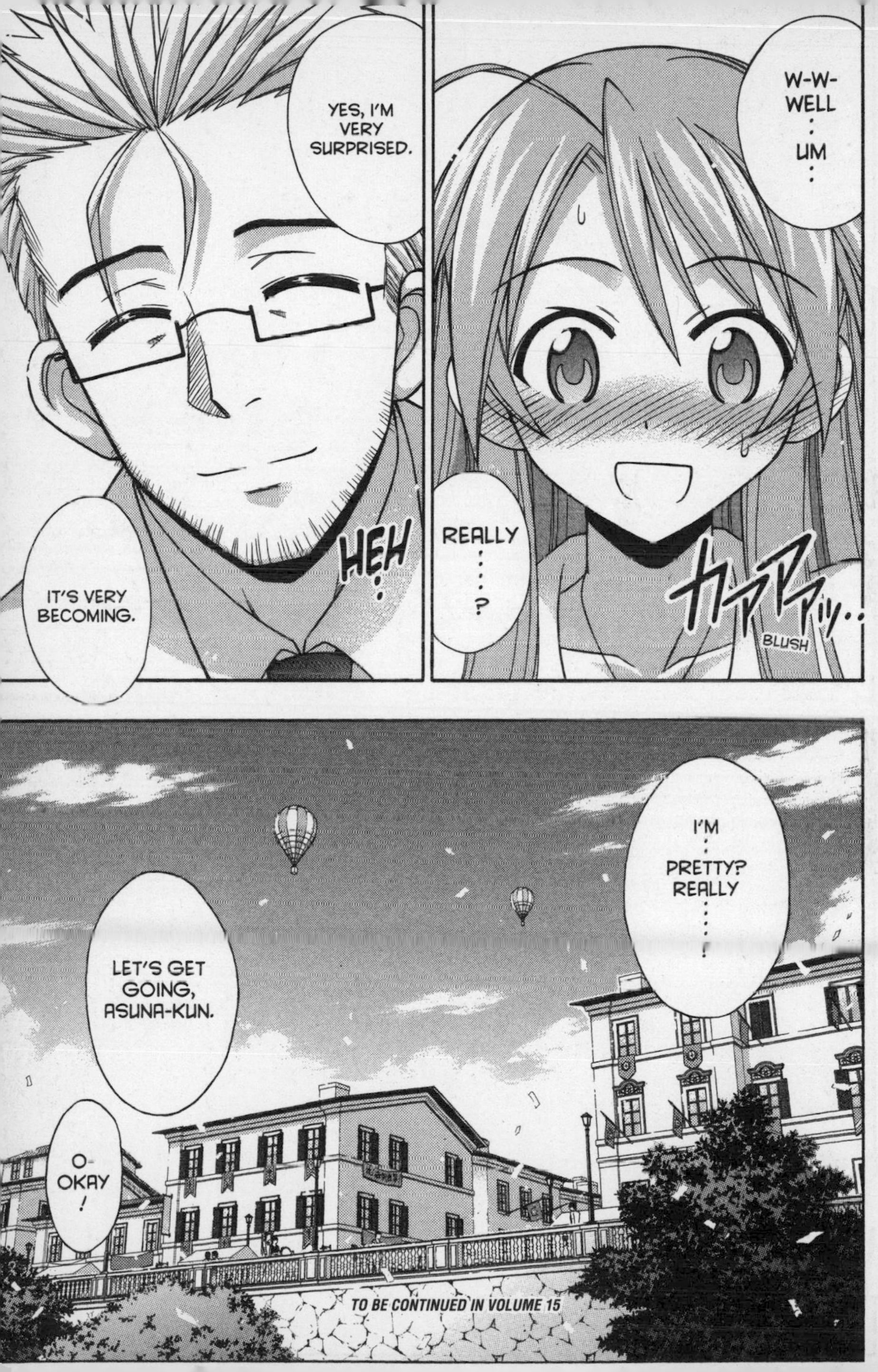
W-W-WELL... UM...
REALLY...?
カァァァッ..
BLUSH
YES, I'M VERY SURPRISED.
HEH
IT'S VERY BECOMING.
I'M... PRETTY? REALLY...
LET'S GET GOING, ASUNA-KUN.
O-OKAY!
TO BE CONTINUED IN VOLUME 15

-STAFF-

Ken Akamatsu
Takashi Takemoto
Kenichi Nakamura
Masaki Ohyama
Keiichi Yamashita
Tadashi Maki
Tohru Mitsuhashi

Thanks to
Ran Ayanaga

LIBRARY EXPLORATION CLUB

EXPEDITION EVENT

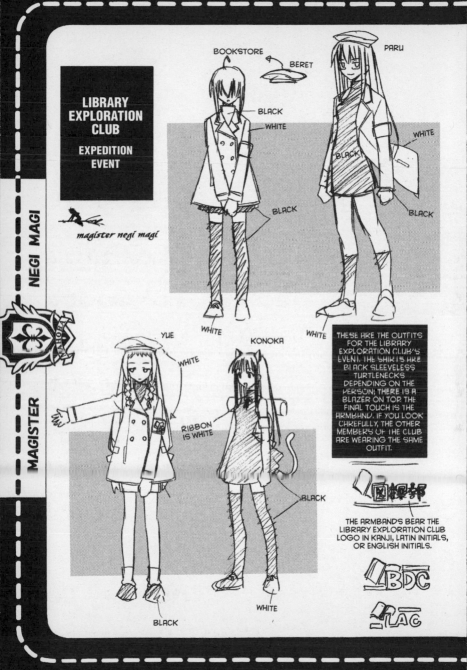

magister negi magi

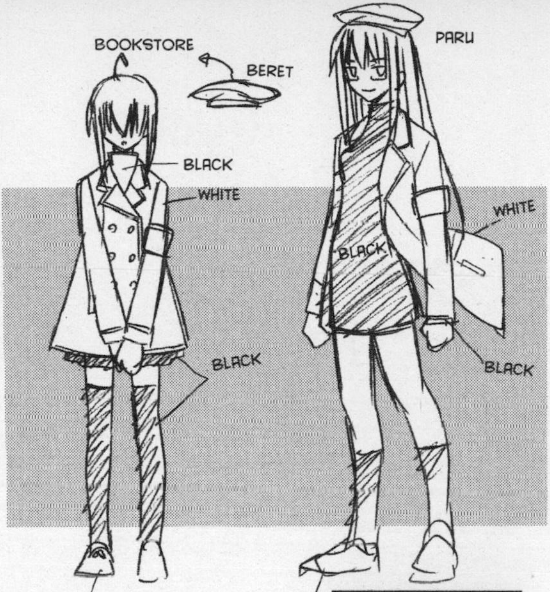
BOOKSTORE
BERET
PARU
BLACK
WHITE
WHITE
BLACK
BLACK
BLACK
WHITE
WHITE

THESE ARE THE OUTFITS FOR THE LIBRARY EXPLORATION CLUB'S EVENT. THE SHIRTS ARE BLACK SLEEVELESS TURTLENECKS DEPENDING ON THE PERSON; THERE IS A BLAZER ON TOP THE FINAL TOUCH IS THE ARMBAND. IF YOU LOOK CAREFULLY, THE OTHER MEMBERS OF THE CLUB ARE WEARING THE SAME OUTFIT.

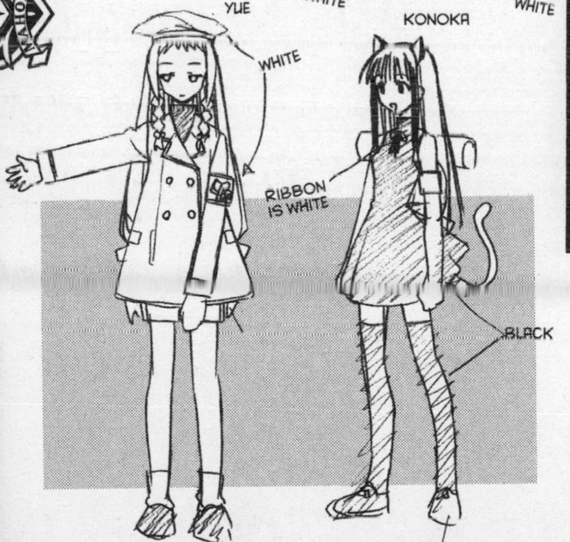
YUE
KONOKA
WHITE
RIBBON IS WHITE
BLACK
WHITE
BLACK

図探部

THE ARMBANDS BEAR THE LIBRARY EXPLORATION CLUB LOGO IN KANJI, LATIN INITIALS, OR ENGLISH INITIALS.

BDC

LAC

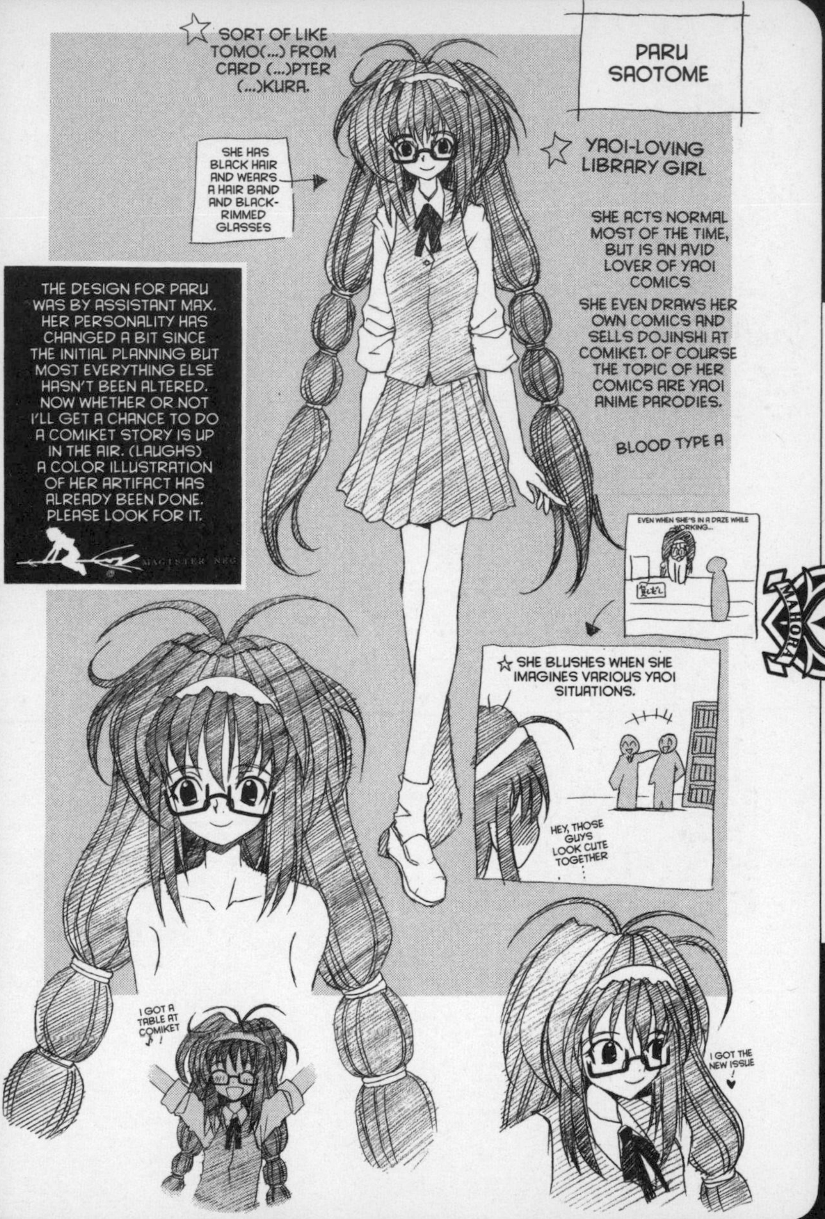
PARU SAOTOME
SORT OF LIKE TOMO(...) FROM CARD (...)PTER (...)KURA.
YAOI-LOVING LIBRARY GIRL
SHE HAS BLACK HAIR AND WEARS A HAIR BAND AND BLACK-RIMMED GLASSES
SHE ACTS NORMAL MOST OF THE TIME, BUT IS AN AVID LOVER OF YAOI COMICS
SHE EVEN DRAWS HER OWN COMICS AND SELLS DOJINSHI AT COMIKET. OF COURSE THE TOPIC OF HER COMICS ARE YAOI ANIME PARODIES.
BLOOD TYPE A
THE DESIGN FOR PARU WAS BY ASSISTANT MAX. HER PERSONALITY HAS CHANGED A BIT SINCE THE INITIAL PLANNING BUT MOST EVERYTHING ELSE HASN'T BEEN ALTERED. NOW WHETHER OR NOT I'LL GET A CHANCE TO DO A COMIKET STORY IS UP IN THE AIR. (LAUGHS) A COLOR ILLUSTRATION OF HER ARTIFACT HAS ALREADY BEEN DONE. PLEASE LOOK FOR IT.
MAGISTER NEGI
EVEN WHEN SHE'S IN A DAZE WHILE WORKING...
SHE BLUSHES WHEN SHE IMAGINES VARIOUS YAOI SITUATIONS.
HEY, THOSE GUYS LOOK CUTE TOGETHER
I GOT A TABLE AT COMIKET
I GOT THE NEW ISSUE

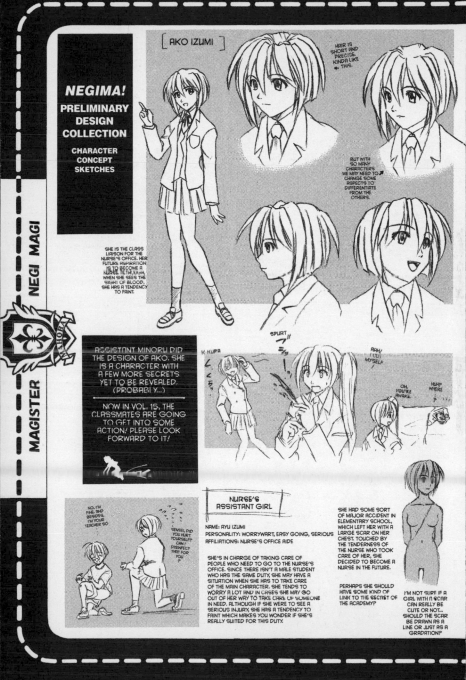

NEGIMA!
PRELIMINARY
DESIGN
COLLECTION

CHARACTER
CONCEPT
SKETCHES

[AKO IZUMI]

HAIR IS SHORT AND PRECISE, KINDA LIKE ← THIS.

BUT WITH SO MANY CHARACTERS WE MAY NEED TO CHANGE SOME ASPECTS TO DIFFERENTIATE FROM THE OTHERS.

SHE IS THE CLASS LIAISON FOR THE NURSE'S OFFICE. HER FUTURE ASPIRATION IS TO BECOME A NURSE. IN THE FUTURE, WHEN SHE SEES THE SIGHT OF BLOOD, SHE HAS A TENDENCY TO FAINT.

ASSISTANT MINORU DID THE DESIGN OF AKO. SHE IS A CHARACTER WITH A FEW MORE SECRETS YET TO BE REVEALED. (PROBABLY...)

NOW IN VOL. 15, THE CLASSMATES ARE GOING TO GET INTO SOME ACTION! PLEASE LOOK FORWARD TO IT!

SPURT
K KURA
AAH! YOU MYSELF
OH, YOU'RE AWAKE.
HUH? WHERE

NO, I'M FINE. AND BESIDES, I'M YOUR TEACHER SO

SENSEI DID YOU HURT YOURSELF? CAN I DISINFECT THAT FOR YOU?

NURSE'S
ASSISTANT GIRL

NAME: RYU IZUMI
PERSONALITY: WORRYWART, EASY GOING, SERIOUS
AFFILIATIONS: NURSE'S OFFICE AIDE

SHE'S IN CHARGE OF TAKING CARE OF PEOPLE WHO NEED TO GO TO THE NURSE'S OFFICE. SINCE THERE ISN'T A MALE STUDENT WHO HAS THE SAME DUTY, SHE MAY HAVE A SITUATION WHEN SHE HAS TO TAKE CARE OF THE MAIN CHARACTER. SHE TENDS TO WORRY A LOT AND IN CASES SHE MAY GO OUT OF HER WAY TO TAKE CARE OF SOMEONE IN NEED. ALTHOUGH IF SHE WERE TO SEE A SERIOUS INJURY, SHE HAS A TENDENCY TO FAINT WHICH MAKES YOU WONDER IF SHE'S REALLY SUITED FOR THIS DUTY.

SHE HAD SOME SORT OF MAJOR ACCIDENT IN ELEMENTARY SCHOOL, WHICH LEFT HER WITH A LARGE SCAR ON HER CHEST. TOUCHED BY THE TENDERNESS OF THE NURSE WHO TOOK CARE OF HER, SHE DECIDED TO BECOME A NURSE IN THE FUTURE.

PERHAPS SHE SHOULD HAVE SOME KIND OF LINK TO THE SECRET OF THE ACADEMY?

I'M NOT SURE IF A GIRL WITH A SCAR CAN REALLY BE CUTE OR NOT... SHOULD THE SCAR BE DRAWN AS A LINE OR JUST AS A GRADATION?

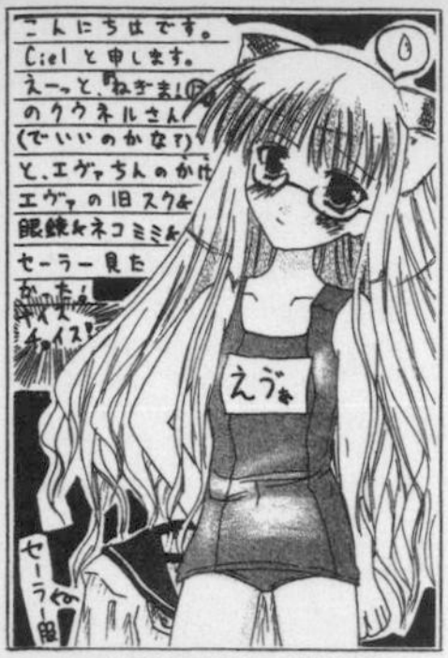
こんにちはです。
えヴぁ

▲ THANKS FOR THE CAT-EARED ASUNA.

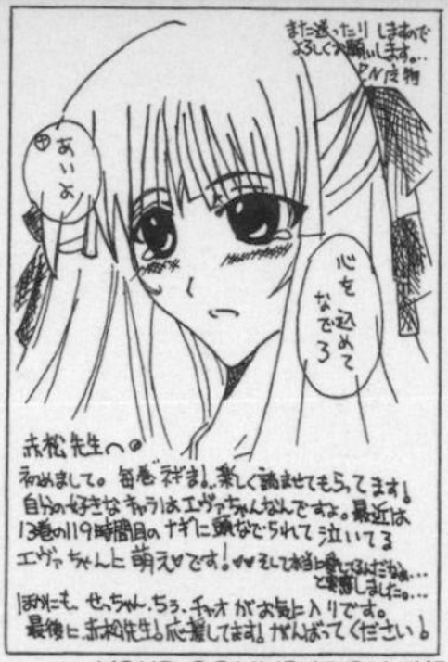
赤松先生へ

▲ YOUR COMMENT ON THE CHARACTERS MAKES US HAPPY.

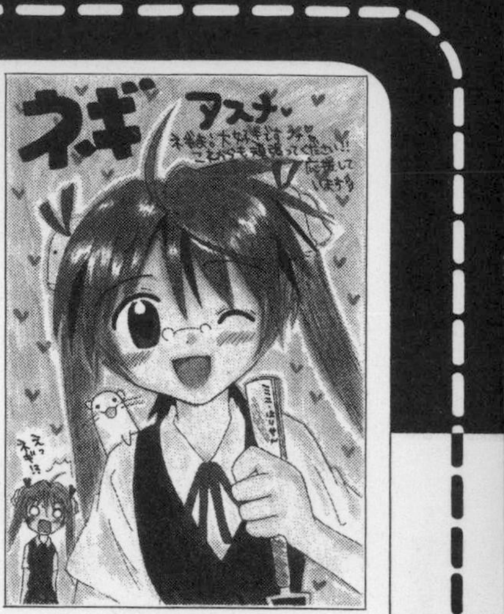
ネギ
アスナ

A CUTE NEGI-SENSEI? (LAUGHS) ▶

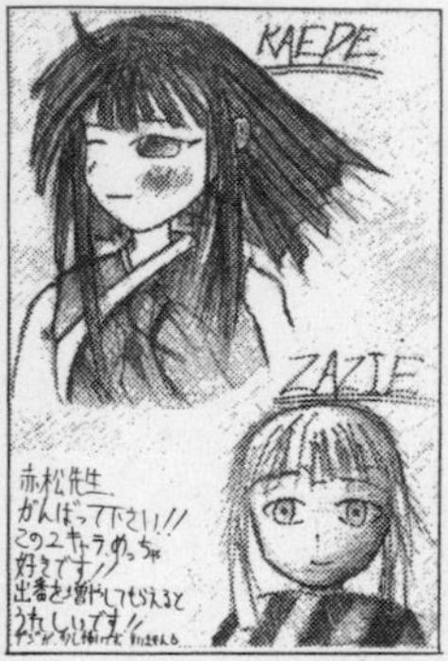
KAEDE
ZAZIE
赤松先生、
がんばって下さい!!

▲ WE LIKE HOW CUTE ZAZIE LOOKS IN THIS PICTURE!

NEGIMA!
FAN ART CORNER

THANKS TO ALL OF YOU, FOR ALL THE FANTASTIC ILLUSTRATIONS YOU'VE BEEN SENDING IN! (^^) TRUTHFULLY, WE WISH WE COULD SHOW YOU EVERYTHING WE RECEIVED!

LOOKING AT THE RECENT SUBMISSIONS, THERE'S BEEN A RISE IN THE NUMBER OF KU:NEL ILLUSTRATIONS. (^O^) SO LET'S SEE WHAT WE HAVE TO PRESENT THIS TIME AROUND! ALSO, WHEN SENDING SUBMISSIONS IN, REMEMBER TO NOT MAKE THEM TOO BIG SO THAT THE ARTWORK WON'T SUFFER WHEN WE SHRINK THEM DOWN FOR THIS SECTION. ABOUT A SIZE OF A POST CARD WOULD BE THE BEST. YOU CAN SEND YOUR ILLUSTRATIONS TO THE EDITORIAL OFFICES OF "KODANSHA COMICS."

– ASS'T MAX

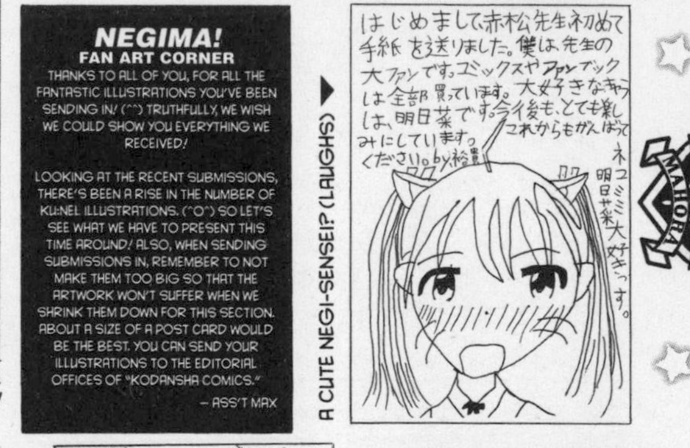
はじめまして赤松先生初めて手紙を送りました。僕は、先生の大ファンです。コミックスやファンブックは全部買っています。大好きなキャラは、明日菜です。今後も、とても楽しみにしています。
これからもがんばってください。
ネコミミ明日菜大好きっす。

A CUTE NEGI-SENSEI? (LAUGHS) ▶

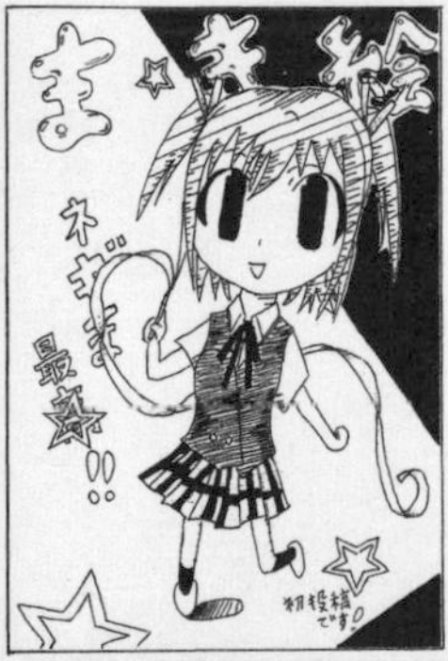

▲ ARE MAKIE PICTURES ON THE DECLINE LATELY?

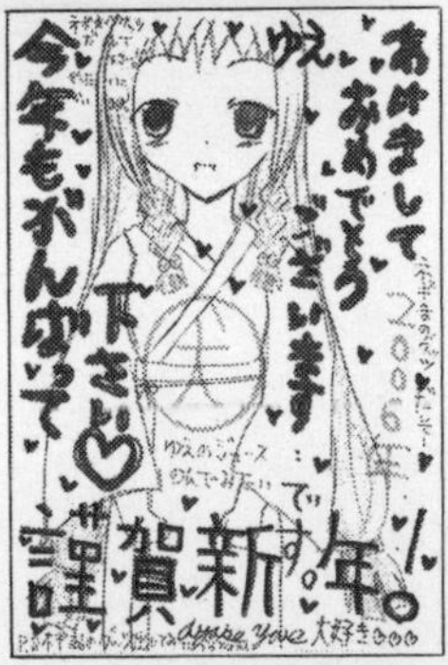
あけましておめでとうございます
今年もがんばって下さい
謹賀新年。

▲ THANK YOU FOR THIS NICE NEW YEAR'S GREETING! ☆

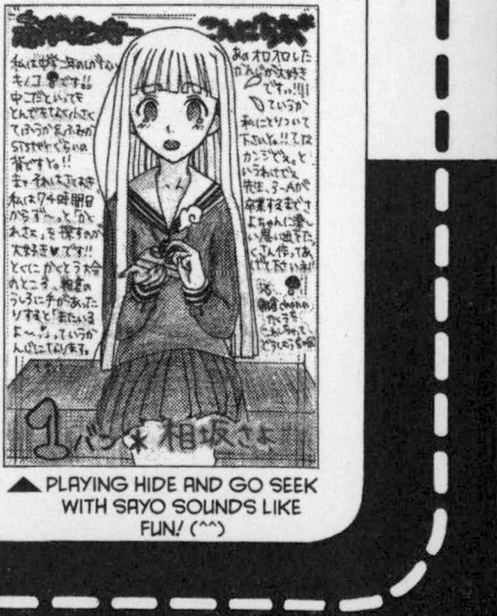
相坂さよ

▲ PLAYING HIDE AND GO SEEK WITH SAYO SOUNDS LIKE FUN! (^^)

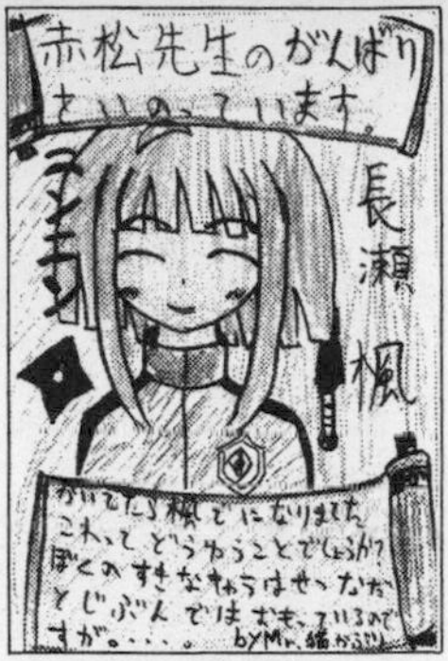
赤松先生のがんばりをいのっています。
長瀬楓

▲ NIN NIN ♪

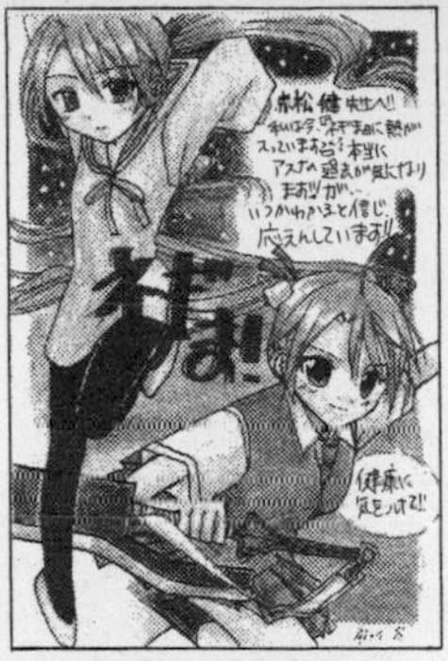

▲ HER PAST MAKES YOU WONDER, DOESN'T IT?

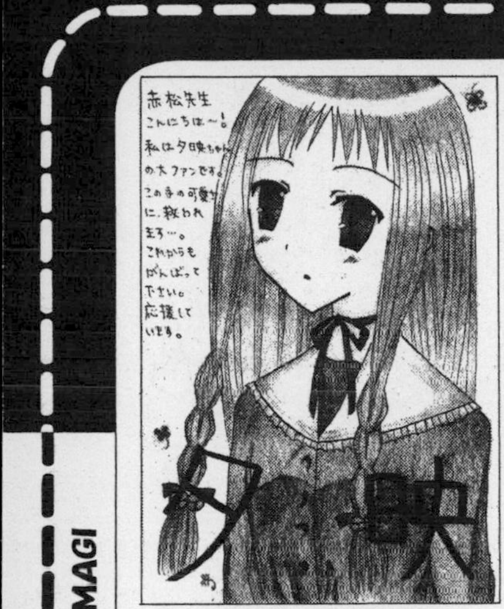
赤松先生
こんにちは～。
夕映

▲ THIS IS A VERY PRETTY PICTURE OF YUE! ☆

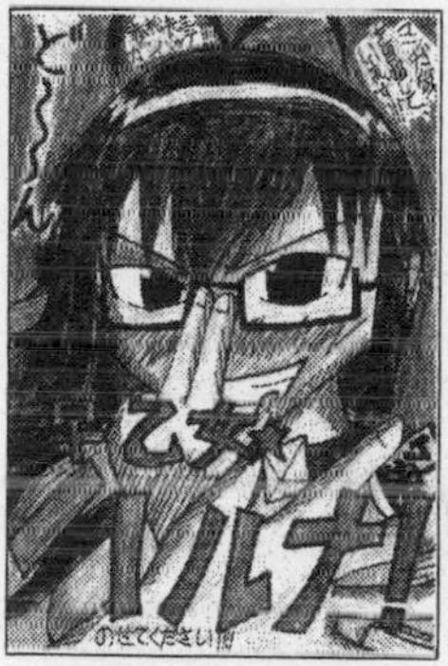

▲ WE LIKE THE INTENSITY OF HARUNA IN THIS PICTURE!

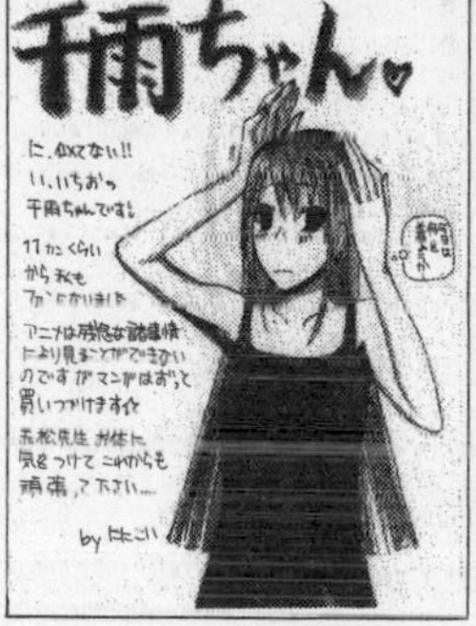
千雨ちゃん♡

▲ WE LIKE THIS UPDATED LOOK OF CHISAME HERE.

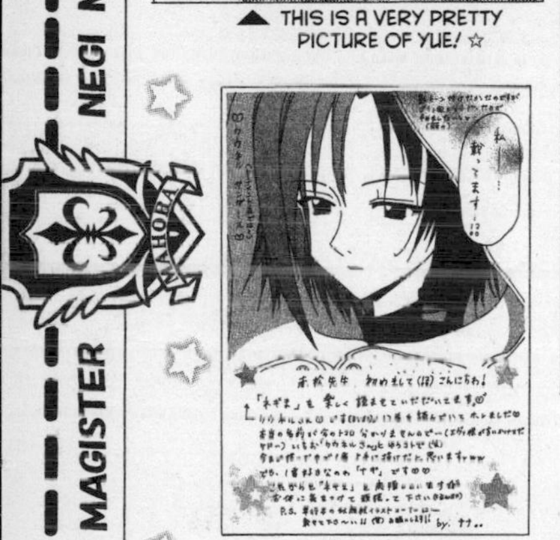

▲ KŪ:NEL IS SURE GETTING POPULAR THESE DAYS! (^^)

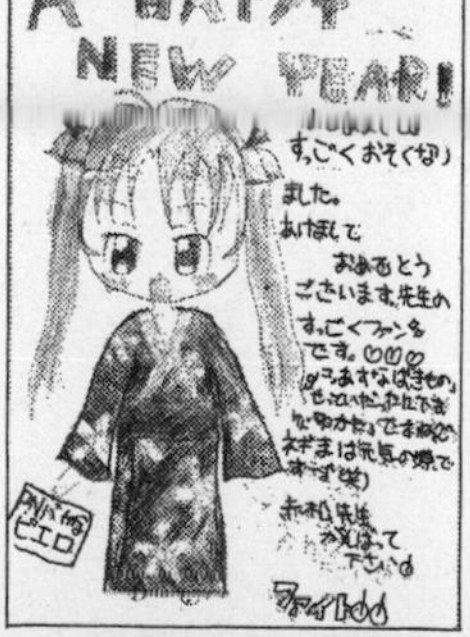
A HAPPY NEW YEAR!

▲ WE THINK THAT YUKATA LOOKS VERY CUTE! (^^)

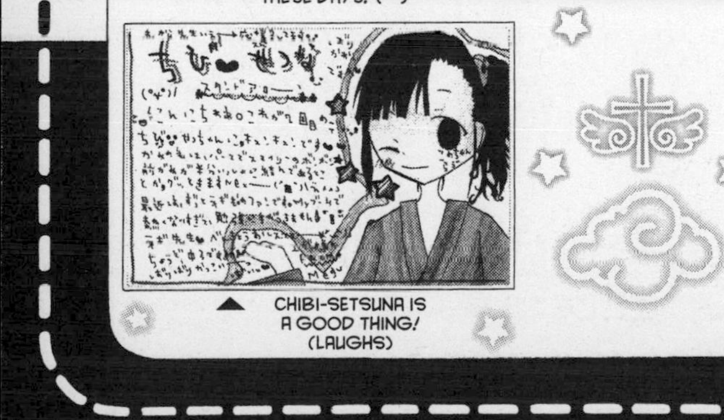

▲ CHIBI-SETSUNA IS A GOOD THING! (LAUGHS)

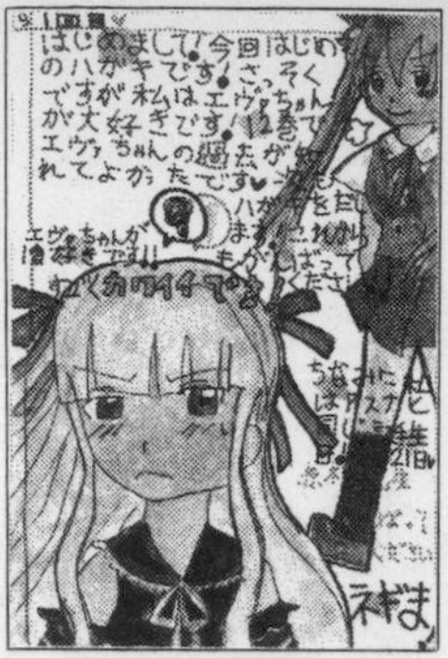
はじめまして! 今回はじめてのハガキです! さっそくですが私はエヴァちゃんが大好きです! 12巻でエヴァちゃんの過去が
ネギま

▲ IS EVA TROUBLED BY SOMETHING HERE? (^^)

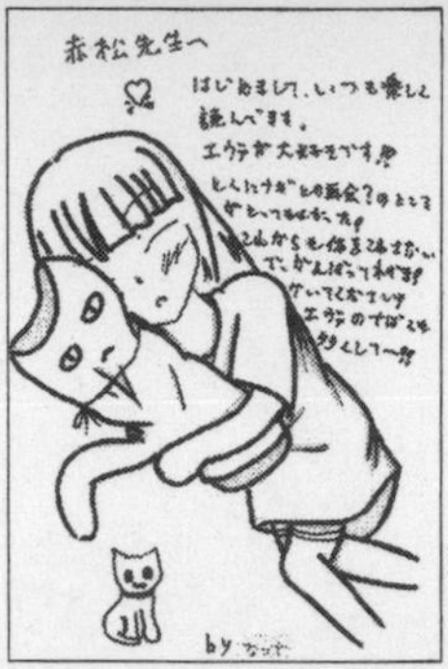
赤松先生へ
はじめまして、いつも楽しく読んでます。
エヴァが大好きです。

▲ EVA LOOKS VERY CUTE HERE ☆

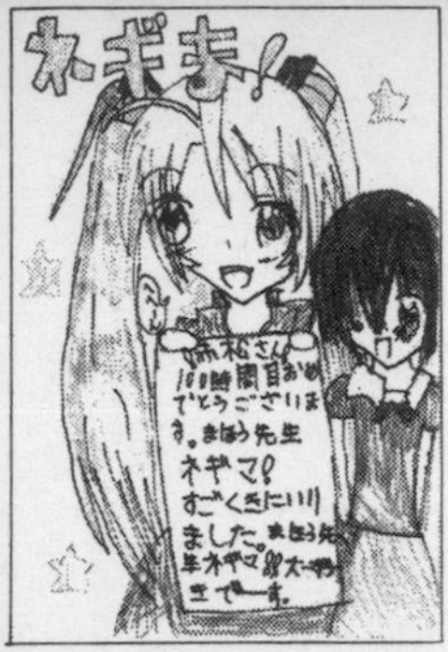
ネギま!
赤松さん 100時間目おめでとうございます。まほう先生ネギマ! すごくきに入りました。

▲ THANK YOU FOR ALL YOUR SUPPORT! (^^)

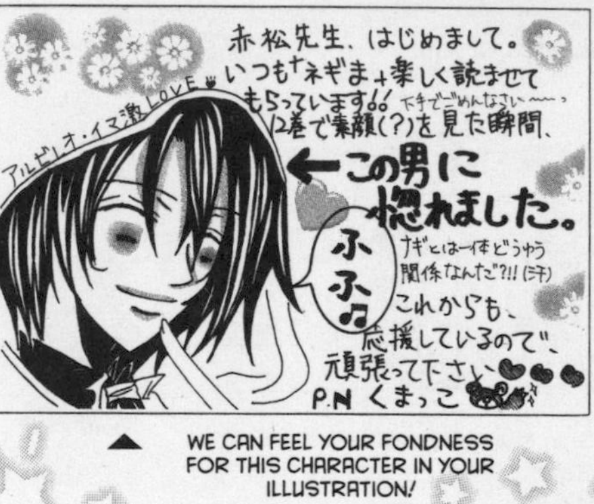
赤松先生、はじめまして。
いつも「ネギま」楽しく読ませてもらっています!!
下手でごめんなさい〜〜
アルビレオ・イマ激LOVE
12巻で素顔(?)を見た瞬間、
←この男に惚れました。
ふふ♪
ナギとは一体どういう関係なんだ?!!(汗)
これからも、応援しているので、頑張って下さい
P.N くまっこ

▲ WE CAN FEEL YOUR FONDNESS FOR THIS CHARACTER IN YOUR ILLUSTRATION!

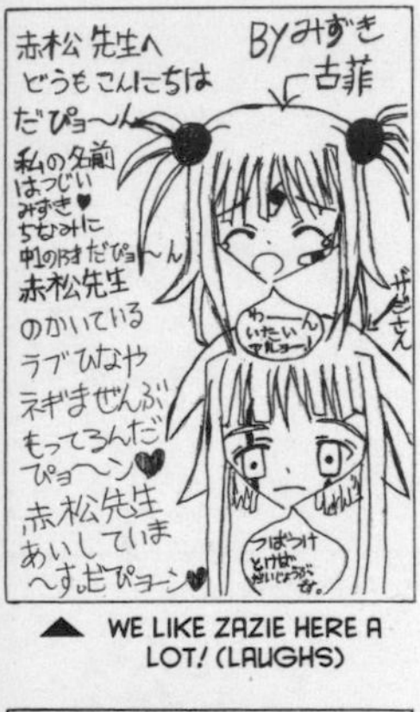
BYみずき
古菲
赤松先生へ
どうもこんにちは
だぴょ〜ん
私の名前
みずき
赤松先生
のかいている
ラブひなや
ネギまぜんぶ
もってるんだ
ぴょ〜ン
赤松先生
あいしていま
〜す!だぴょ〜ン

▲ WE LIKE ZAZIE HERE A LOT! (LAUGHS)

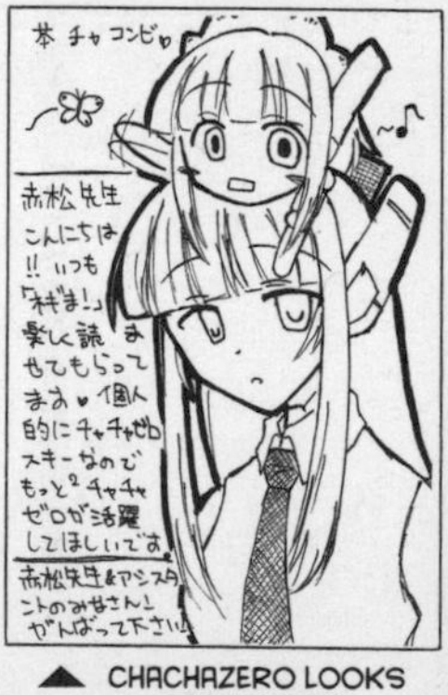
赤松先生
こんにちは!! いつも「ネギま!」楽しく読ませてもらってます♥ 個人的にチャチャゼロスキーなのでもっと²チャチャゼロが活躍してほしいです
赤松先生&アシスタントのみなさん! がんばって下さい

▲ CHACHAZERO LOOKS REALLY CUTE!

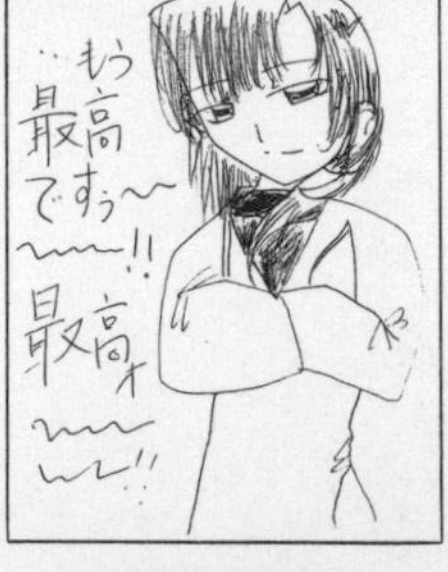
アルビレオ
…もう最高ですぅ〜
〜〜!!
最高ォ
〜〜!!

▲ WE CAN REALLY TELL HOW WONDERFUL YOU THINK HE IS. (^^)

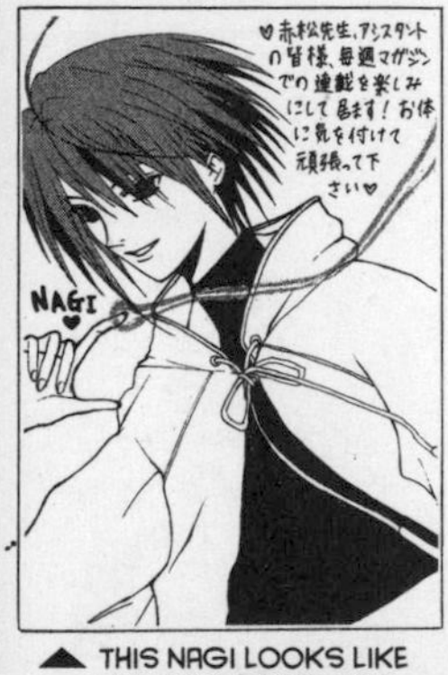
赤松先生、アシスタントの皆様、毎週マガジンでの連載を楽しみにして居ます! お体に気を付けて頑張って下さい♥
NAGI

▲ THIS NAGI LOOKS LIKE HE COULD STAR IN A SHOJO MANGA. ☆

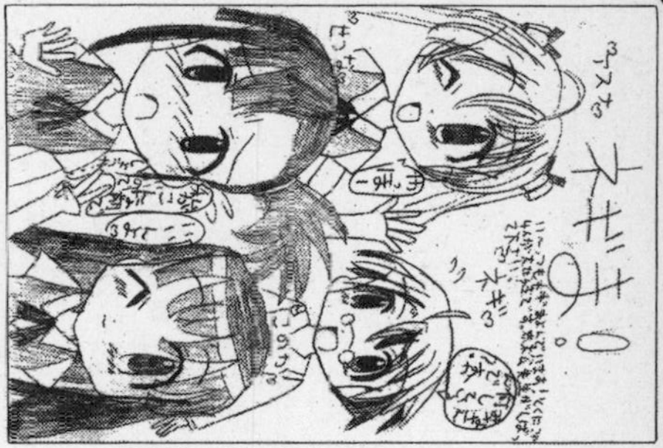
ネギま!

WE LOVE THE TROUBLED EXPRESSION ON SETSUNA.

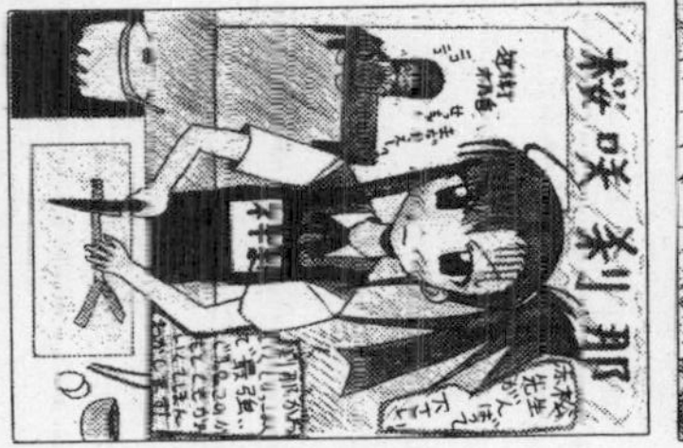
桜咲刹那

SEEING SETSUNA COOKING IS A GOOD THING.

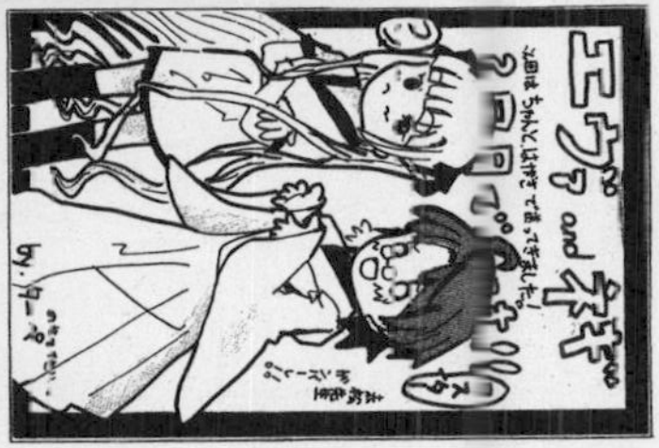
エヴァ and ネギ

WE LIKE THE RELAXED ART STYLE IN THIS PICTURE.

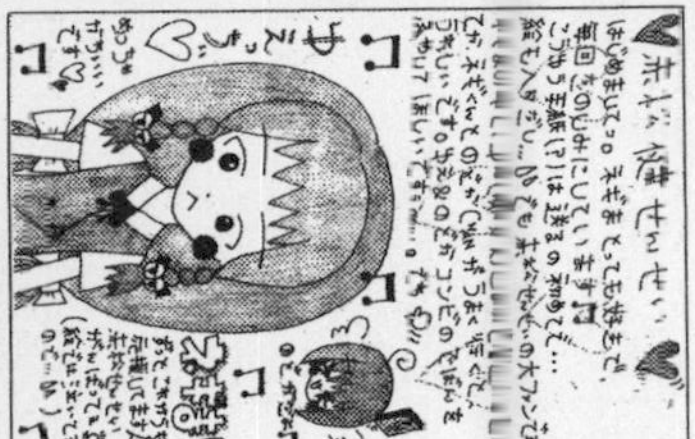
赤松健せんせい

KEEP UP YOUR SUPPORT OF YUECCHI! (^^)

THANK YOUR FOR YOUR SUPPORT!

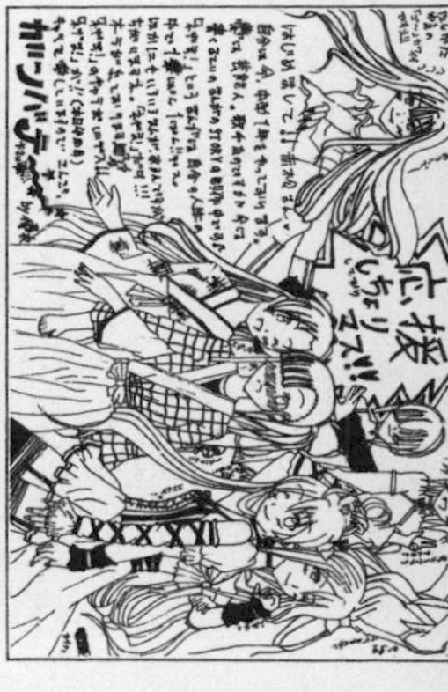
応援しちょリマス!!

THE TAIL ON SAKURAKO IS REALLY CUTE! (LAUGHS)

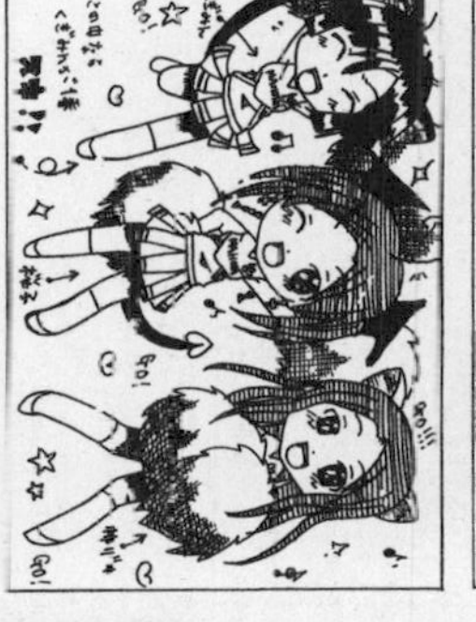

I HOPE MISORA MAKES MORE APPEARANCES FOR YOU.

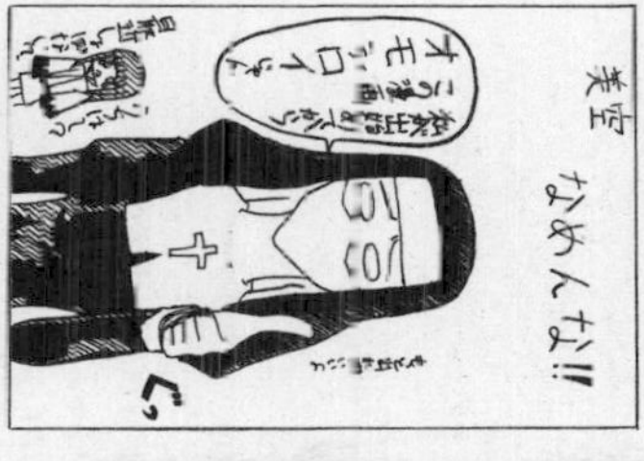
美空
なめんな!!
オモシロイじゃん
ぐっ

NOW DID HARUNA MAKE A CONTRACT OR NOT? (LAUGHS)

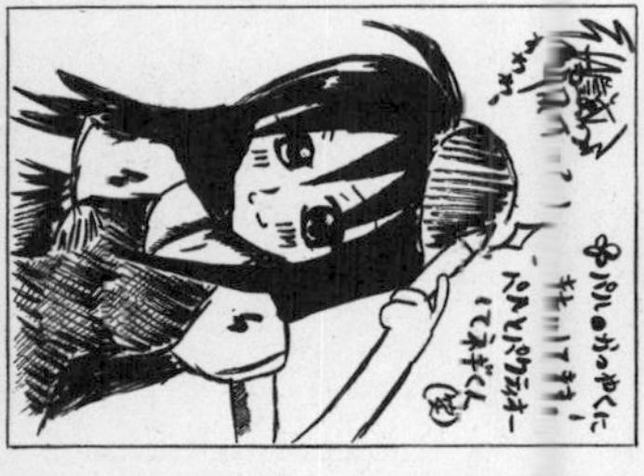

3-D BACKGROUNDS EXPLANATION CORNER

YES, ONCE AGAIN IT'S THE 3-D BACKGROUND EXPLANATIONS YOU'VE COME TO LOVE AND EXPECT! AND IN THIS VOLUME, THE NUMBER OF 3-D BACKGROUNDS HAS REALLY INCREASED! LET'S TAKE A LOOK AT SOME OF THEM.

~ PARKS SECTION ~

• JAPANESE GARDEN
SCENE NAME: J-GARDEN
POLYGON COUNT: 97,204

THIS IS THE JAPANESE-STYLE GARDEN USED FOR THE TEA CEREMONY CLUB'S *NODATE*. MAHORA ACADEMY SURE HAS A LOT OF NICE PLACES, DOESN'T IT? (LAUGHS)

BY THE WAY, THE ONLY NEW THING WE CREATED FOR THIS SCENE WAS THE BRIDGE AND THE TEA ROOM AND THE REST WE ADAPTED FROM ALREADY EXISTING 3-D ITEMS.

I GUESS BEING ABLE TO REUSE ITEMS IS ANOTHER BENEFIT OF WORKING WITH 3-D BACKGROUNDS.

UNUSUALLY, EVEN THE TREES WERE CREATED AS 3-D ITEMS.

• BRIDGE AND TEA HOUSE

• TEA ROOM
SCENE NAME: TEA ROOM
POLYGON COUNT: 8,459

THE EXTERIOR WAS HAND-DRAWN BUT THE INTERIOR IS MADE UP COMPLETELY OF 3-D ITEMS. THIS TEA ROOM IS DIFFERENT FROM THE ONE THE TEA CEREMONY CLUB NORMALLY USES.

BY THE WAY, IF YOU RECOGNIZED THIS ROOM FROM BEFORE, YOU ARE REALLY SHARP! THIS WAS ADAPTED FROM THE "TEMPORARY DRESSING ROOM" FROM VOL. 12. IT MIGHT BE FUN TO SEE IF YOU CAN SPOT ALL THE CHANGES WE MADE. (LAUGHS)

• FOUNTAIN PARK
SCENE NAME: FOUNTAIN PARK
POLYGON COUNT: 29,927

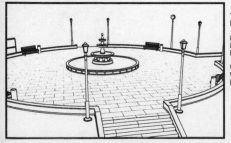

THIS IS THE PARK WITH THE FOUNTAIN WHERE AKO FAINTED.

IT'S LOCATED ATOP A HILL AND SAID TO BE A BEAUTIFUL PLACE TO WATCH THE NIGHTSCAPE.

THE TREES IN THIS PARK WERE HAND-DRAWN SO WITHOUT THEM, IT LOOKS KIND OF LONELY. (^^;)

THIS IS THE CLOCK IN THE PARK. ON A SIDE NOTE, THE HANDS OF THE CLOCK CAN BE MOVED FREELY.

~ AMUSEMENT SECTION ~

• MAHORA GREAT FERRIS WHEEL

SCENE NAME: FERRIS WHEEL
POLYGON COUNT: 281,162

THIS IS THE GREAT FERRIS WHEEL THAT STANDS 90 M TALL. IT'S AMAZING TO THINK THAT THIS STRUCTURE WAS BUILT JUST FOR THE MAHORA FESTIVAL! (LAUGHS)

BY THE WAY, THE "MAHORA FESTIVAL" ON THE WHEEL ROTATES SO IF YOU LOOK AT THE COMIC CAREFULLY, YOU'LL SEE IT IN DIFFERENT POSITIONS. (LAUGHS)

MAHORA
FESTIVAL

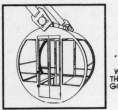

• GONDOLA

WE EVEN CREATED THE INTERIORS OF THE GONDOLA AS WELL.

• CONCERT STAGE

SCENE NAME: CONCERT STAGE
POLYGON COUNT: 3,007,607

麻帆良 ROCK FESTIVAL '03

THIS STAGE FIRST MADE AN APPEARANCE IN VOL. 8. WE'D PLANNED TO USE IT FOR THE FESTIVAL WHEN WE CREATED IT, BUT WE'RE HAPPY TO FINALLY BE ABLE TO USE IT IN THIS VOLUME. (LAUGHS)

SO, IN ORDER TO MAKE TO MORE LIKE A CONCERT STAGE, WE ADDED A FEW MORE ELEMENTS. THE HARDEST TO CREATE WAS THIS DRUM SET. YOU CAN'T REALLY SEE IT VERY WELL IN THE COMIC, BUT WE SPENT A LOT OF TIME CREATING IT. (^^;)

• EVENT STAGE

SCENE NAME: SMALL STAGE
POLYGON COUNT: [illegible]

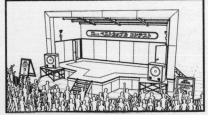

THIS IS THE STAGE THAT WAS USED FOR THE BEST COUPLE CONTEST. EVEN HERE, THE POLY-MEN ARE OUT IN FULL FORCE. (LAUGHS)

• CONCERT DRESSING ROOM

SCENE NAME: DRESSING ROOM
POLYGON COUNT: 8,962

THIS IS THE DRESSING ROOM WHERE AKO WAS CHANGING. WE HAD A HARD TIME GETTING HER REFLECTION IN THE MIRROR TO LOOK RIGHT. (^_^;)

• EXPEDITION DEPARTURE HALL
SCENE NAME: CHAPEL
POLYGON COUNT: 554,812

THIS IS WHERE THE PEOPLE GATHERED TO LEAVE ON THE EXPEDITION TOUR OF THE LIBRARY. IN A PREVIOUS VOLUME, IT WAS USED FOR THE COSPLAY CONTEST. THE ROOMS ON THE SECOND LEVEL WERE NEWLY CREATED FOR THIS VOLUME.

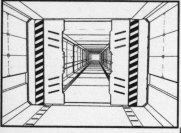

• GREAT NORTHERN CLIFF
SCENE NAME: BOOKWALL
POLYGON COUNT: 389,202

WHY WOULD SOMETHING LIKE THIS EVEN BE IN HERE? (LAUGHS)

• WORLD TREE MODEL REST AREA
SCENE NAME: LIBRARY REST AREA
POLYGON COUNT: 371,676

IT WAS HARD TO TELL IN THE ACTUAL STORY, BUT THIS ROOM CONTAINS A MINIATURE VERSION OF THE WORLD TREE. THE TREE WAS HAND-DRAWN IN THIS CASE AND MERGED WITH THE 3-D IMAGE.

• PASSAGEWAY WITH FIREPROOF DOORS
SCENE NAME: PASSAGE
POLYGON COUNT: 27,094

THIS IS AN AWFULLY MODERN-LOOKING PASSAGEWAY FOR THE LIBRARY. THIS PLACE SURE HAS A LOT OF MYSTERIES ABOUT IT. (LAUGHS)

• BALCONY
SCENE NAME: LIBRARY BALCONY
POLYGON COUNT: 260,397

IT'S REASSURING TO SEE THAT EVEN A STRANGE LIBRARY SUCH AS THIS CAN HAVE A NORMAL-LOOKING AND FABULOUS BALCONY ONCE YOU GET OUTSIDE. (LAUGHS)

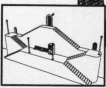

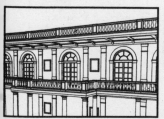

• WATERFALL OBSERVATION DECK
SCENE NAME: LIBRARY FALL
POLYGON COUNT: 266,714

YET ANOTHER LOCATION THAT'S HARD TO EXPLAIN. (LAUGHS) ON A SIDE NOTE, EVEN THE BLURRED EFFECTS OF THE MIST WERE DONE IN 3-D.

~ CITYSCAPE SECTION ~

• STONE BRIDGE WITH GATE

SCENE NAME: STONE BRIDGE

POLYGON COUNT: 1,333,776

THIS IS ONE OF THE GREAT STONE BRIDGES THAT SPANS OVER ONE OF THE RIVERS IN MAHORA CITY. IT DEFINITELY HAS AN AIR OF IMPORTANCE ABOUT IT, DOESN'T IT?

IT SEEMS THAT THIS IS A VERY POPULAR PLACE ON A NORMAL DAY.

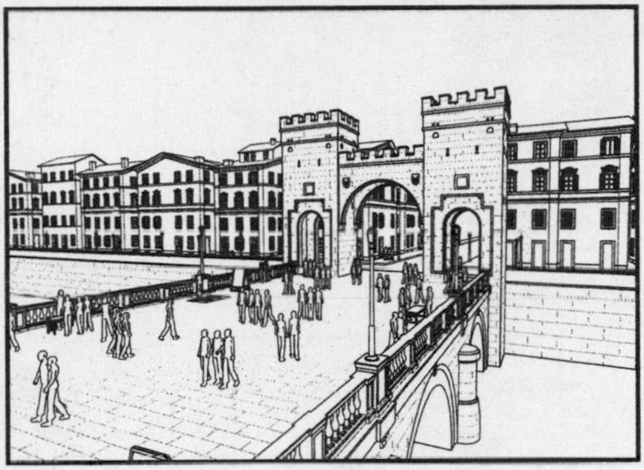

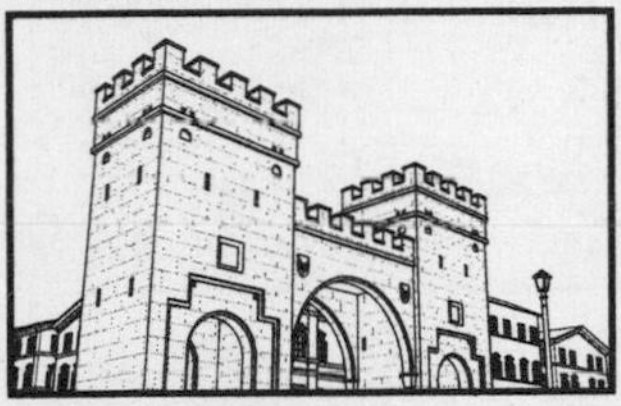

• GATE TOWER

HOW KOTARO AND THE OTHERS GOT UP THERE IS A MYSTERY. (LAUGHS)

• MAHORA'S CAFÉ

SCENE NAME: MAHORA'S CAFÉ

POLYGON COUNT: 8,962

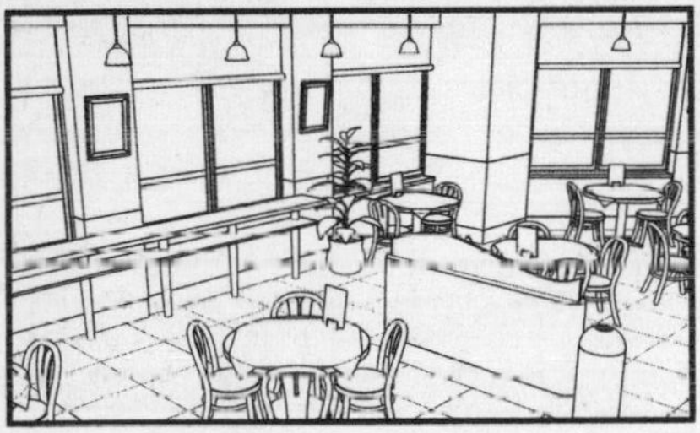

THIS IS THE PLACE WHERE ASUNA AND THE OTHERS WERE MAKING THE BATTLE PLANS (?) FOR HER DATE. THE PLACE LOOKS VERY FASHIONABLE WITH ITS COUNTERS ALONG THE WINDOWS.

WE HAVE TO ADMIT HERE THAT THE CAFE DOESN'T HAVE ANYTHING CREATED ON THE OTHER SIDE OF THE WINDOWS. (^^;)

• LIBRARY OUTDOOR CAFÉ

SCENE NAME: BRIDGE CAFÉ

POLYGON COUNT: 8,962

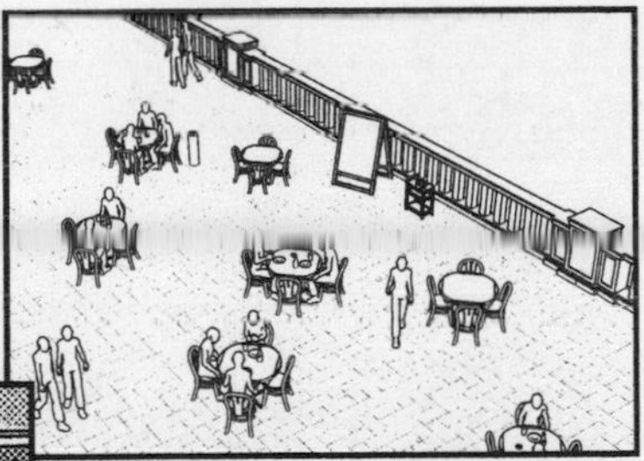

THIS IS THE CAFÉ THAT'S BEEN SET UP ON THE BRIDGE TO LIBRARY ISLAND. LOOKING AT THE LOGO ON TOP OF THE SIGN, YOU CAN SEE THAT IT'S AFFILIATED WITH THE EVER-POPULAR STARBOOKS CAFÉ. THEIR NAME BEING WHAT IT IS, SETTING UP RIGHT OUTSIDE THE LIBRARY IS PROBABLY A PERFECT PLACEMENT. (LAUGHS)

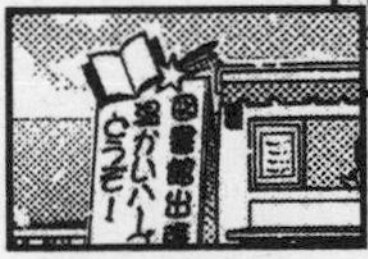

SEE? RIGHT HERE! (LAUGHS)

- BONUS -

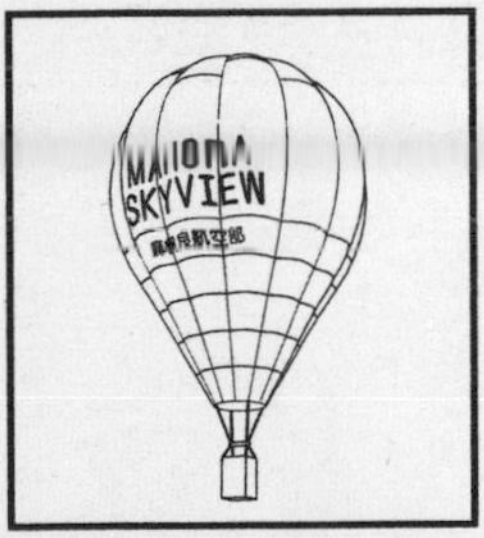
SKYVIEW

• HOT AIR BALLOONS OF THE MAHORA FLYING CLUB

YOU SEE THESE FLYING ALL OVER THE PLACE. IT MIGHT BE FUN TO SEE HOW MANY YOU CAN SPOT! (LAUGHS)

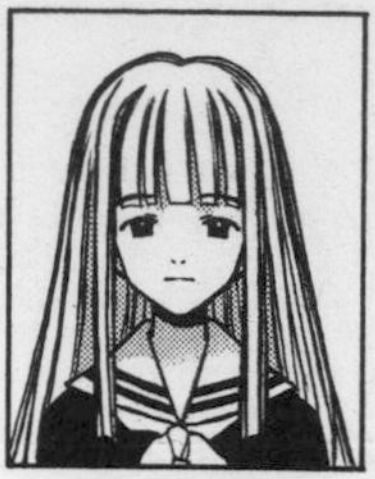

1. SAYO AISAKA

1940~
DON'T CHANGE HER SEATING

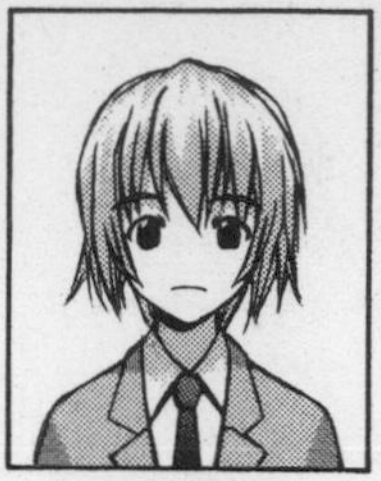

5. AKO IZUMI
NURSE'S OFFICE AIDE
SOCCER TEAM
(NON-SCHOOL ACTIVITY)

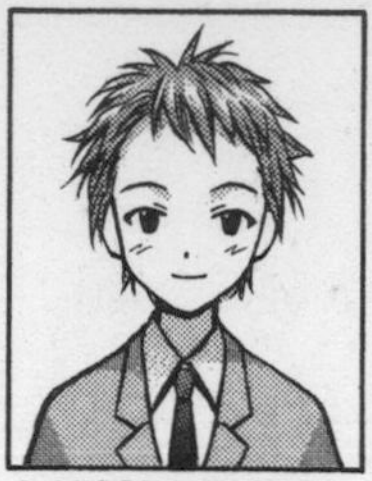

9. MISORA KASUGA
TRACK & FIELD

GRANDDAUGHTER OF SCHOOL DEAN

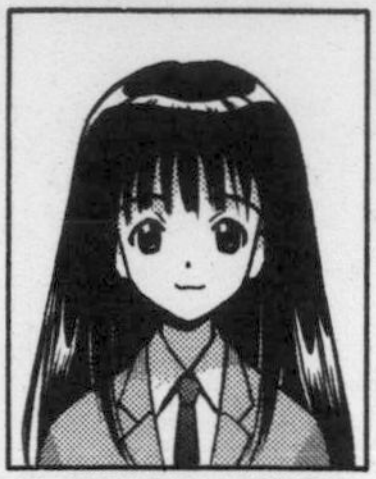

13. KONOKA KONOE
SECRETARY
FORTUNE-TELLING CLUB
LIBRARY EXPLORATION CLUB

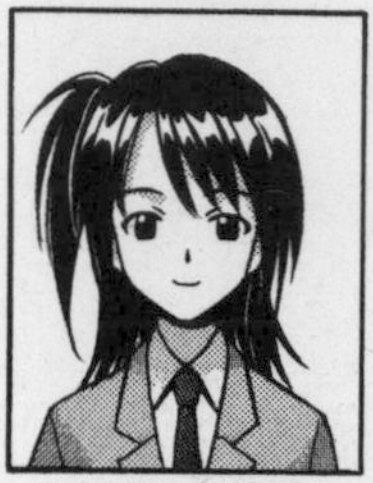

2. YUNA AKASHI
BASKETBALL TEAM

PROFESSOR AKASHI'S DAUGHTER

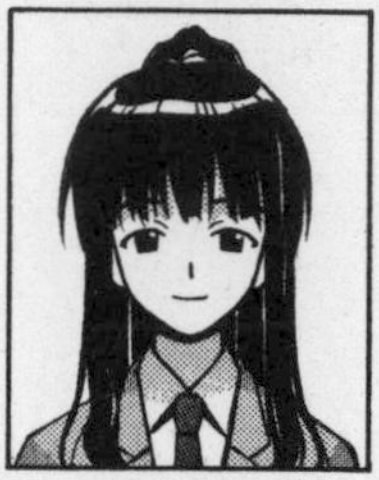

6. AKIRA OKOCHI
SWIM TEAM

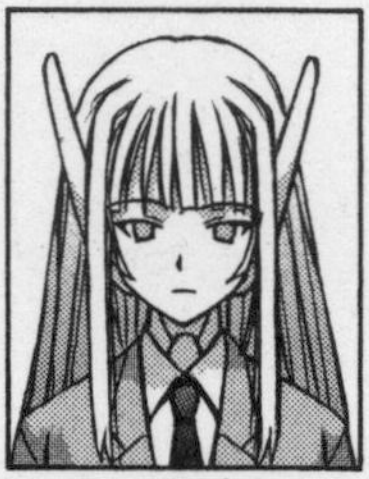

10. CHACHAMARU KARAKURI
TEA CEREMONY CLUB
GO CLUB

CALL ENGINEERING (ext. A08-7796) IN CASE OF EMERGENCY

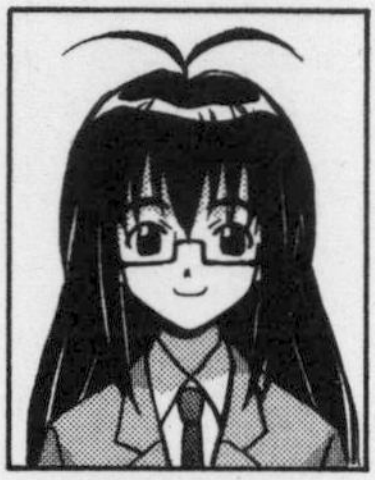

14. HARUNA SAOTOME
MANGA CLUB
LIBRARY EXPLORATION CLUB

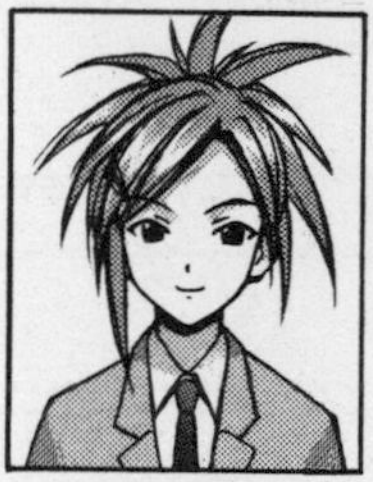

3. KAZUMI ASAKURA
SCHOOL NEWSPAPER

MAHORA NEWS (ext. B09-3780)

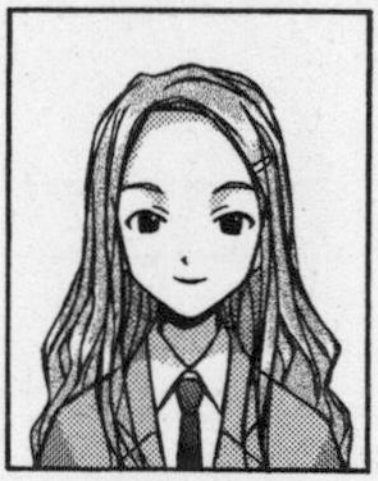

7. MISA KAKIZAKI
CHEERLEADER
CHORUS

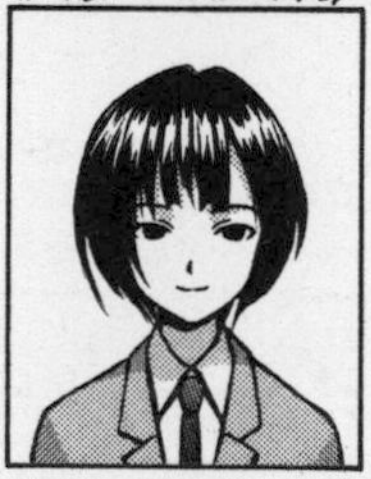

11. MADOKA KUGIMIYA
CHEERLEADER

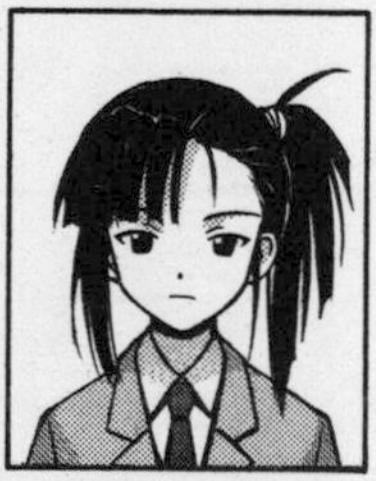

15 SETSUNA SAKURAZAKI
KENDO CLUB

KYOTO SHINMEI STYLE

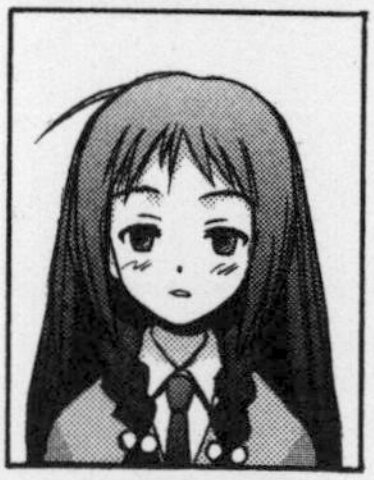

4. YUE AYASE
KIDS' LIT CLUB
PHILOSOPHY CLUB
LIBRARY EXPLORATION CLUB

A GOOD PERSON JUST AS I THOUGHT.

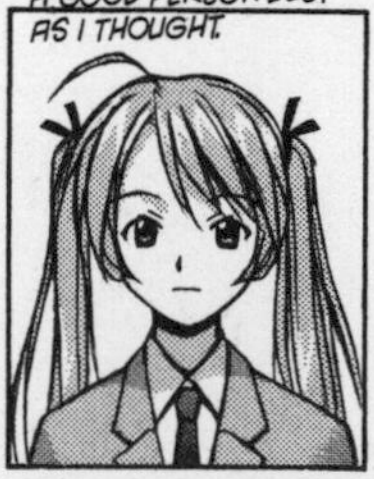

8. ASUNA KAGURAZAKA
ART CLUB

HAS A TERRIBLE KICK

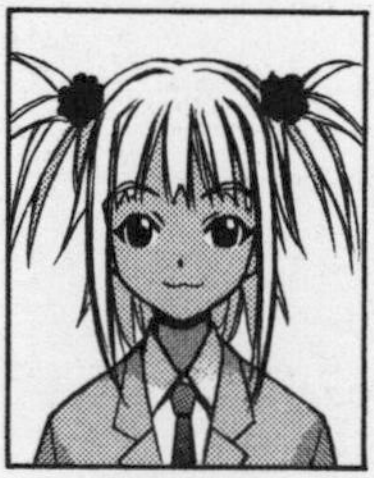

12. KŪ FEI
CHINESE MARTIAL ARTS CLUB

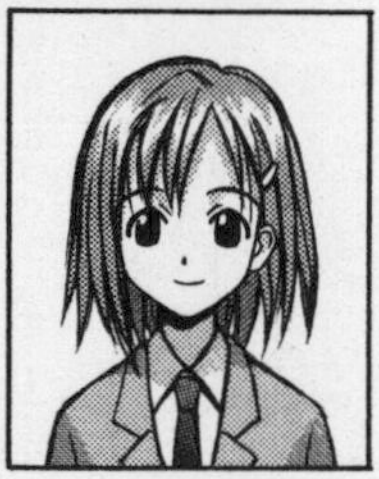

16. MAKIE SASAKI
GYMNASTICS

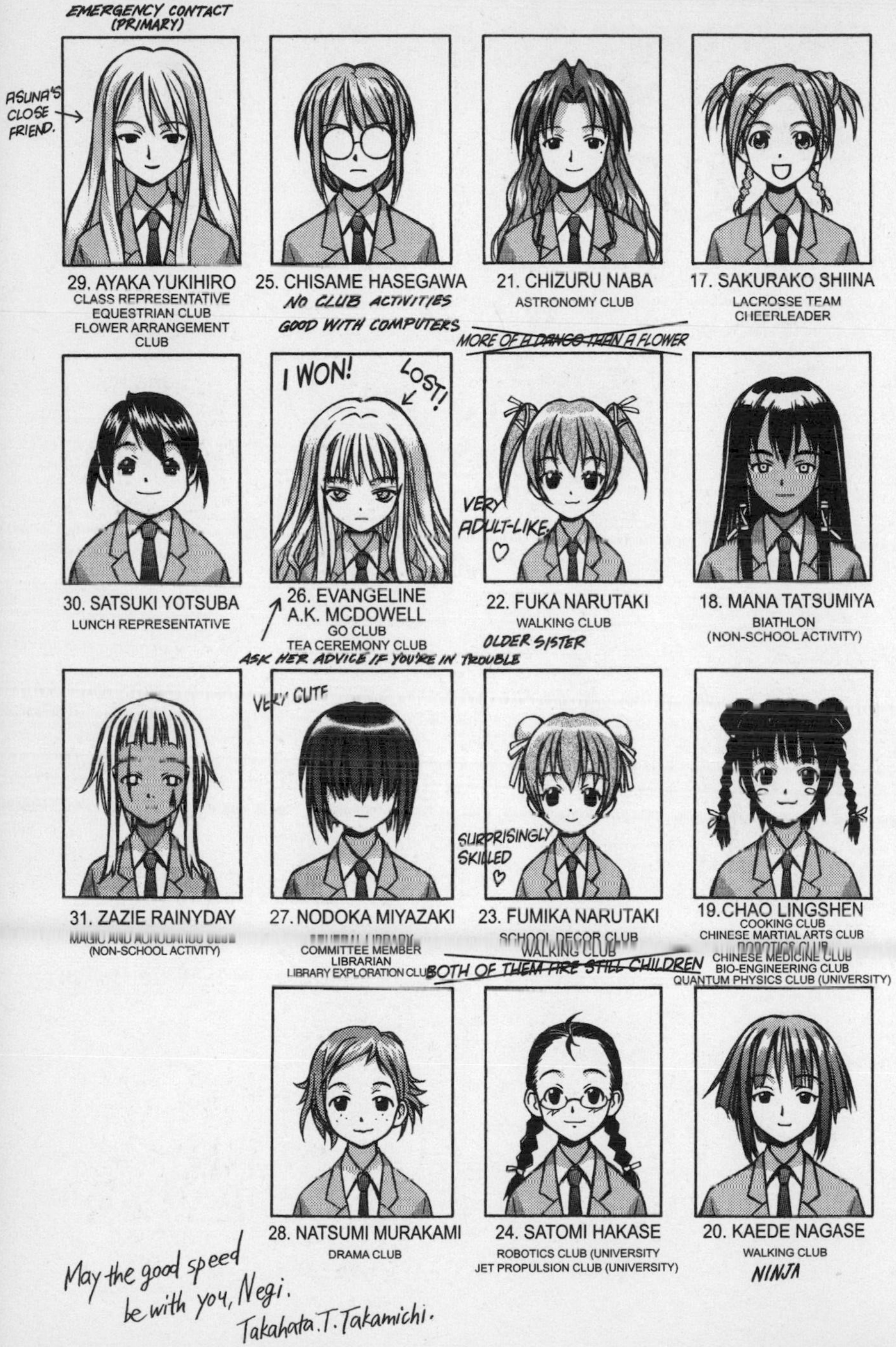

17. SAKURAKO SHIINA
LACROSSE TEAM
CHEERLEADER
MORE OF A DANGO THAN A FLOWER
21. CHIZURU NABA
ASTRONOMY CLUB
25. CHISAME HASEGAWA
NO CLUB ACTIVITIES
GOOD WITH COMPUTERS
EMERGENCY CONTACT (PRIMARY)
ASUNA'S CLOSE FRIEND.
29. AYAKA YUKIHIRO
CLASS REPRESENTATIVE
EQUESTRIAN CLUB
FLOWER ARRANGEMENT CLUB
18. MANA TATSUMIYA
BIATHLON
(NON-SCHOOL ACTIVITY)
VERY ADULT-LIKE ♡
22. FUKA NARUTAKI
WALKING CLUB
OLDER SISTER
I WON!
LOST!
26. EVANGELINE A.K. MCDOWELL
GO CLUB
TEA CEREMONY CLUB
ASK HER ADVICE IF YOU'RE IN TROUBLE
30. SATSUKI YOTSUBA
LUNCH REPRESENTATIVE
19. CHAO LINGSHEN
COOKING CLUB
CHINESE MARTIAL ARTS CLUB
CHINESE MEDICINE CLUB
BIO-ENGINEERING CLUB
QUANTUM PHYSICS CLUB (UNIVERSITY)
SURPRISINGLY SKILLED ♡
23. FUMIKA NARUTAKI
SCHOOL DECOR CLUB
WALKING CLUB
BOTH OF THEM ARE STILL CHILDREN
VERY CUTE
27. NODOKA MIYAZAKI
COMMITTEE MEMBER
LIBRARIAN
LIBRARY EXPLORATION CLUB
31. ZAZIE RAINYDAY
(NON-SCHOOL ACTIVITY)
20. KAEDE NAGASE
WALKING CLUB
NINJA
24. SATOMI HAKASE
ROBOTICS CLUB (UNIVERSITY
JET PROPULSION CLUB (UNIVERSITY)
28. NATSUMI MURAKAMI
DRAMA CLUB
May the good speed be with you, Negi.
Takahata.T.Takamichi.

魔法先生 ネギま! MAGISTER NEGI MAGI

赤松 健 SHONEN MAGAZINE COMICS
KEN AKAMATSU

14

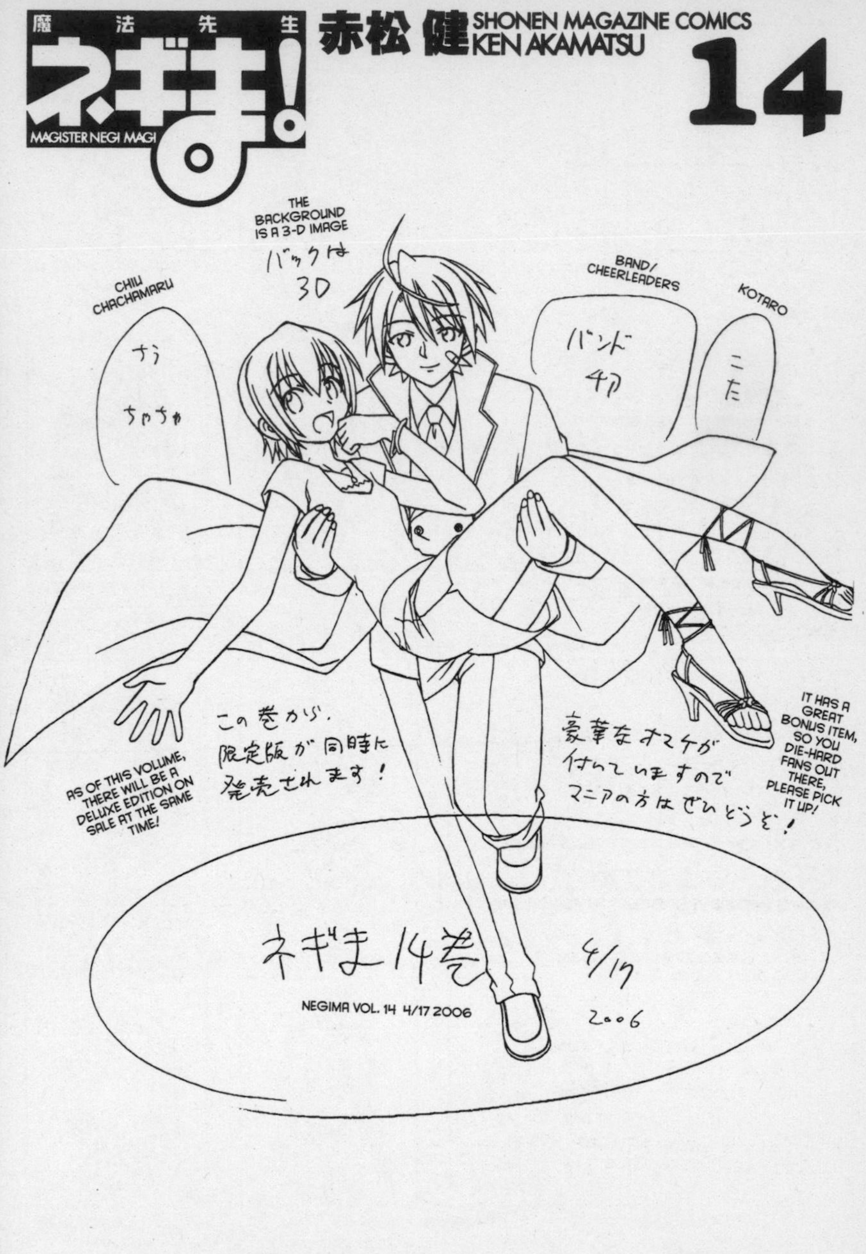
THE BACKGROUND IS A 3-D IMAGE
バックは 3D
CHIU CHACHAMARU
ちう ちゃちゃ
BAND/ CHEERLEADERS
バンド チア
KOTARO
こた
この巻から、限定版が同時に発売されます！
AS OF THIS VOLUME, THERE WILL BE A DELUXE EDITION ON SALE AT THE SAME TIME!
豪華なオマケが付いていますので マニアの方はぜひどうぞ！
IT HAS A GREAT BONUS ITEM, SO YOU DIE-HARD FANS OUT THERE, PLEASE PICK IT UP!
ネギま14巻 4/17 2006
NEGIMA VOL. 14 4/17 2006

キャラ解説
CHARACTER PROFILE

⑭早乙女ハルナ
⑭ HARUNA SAOTOME

アニメ版では一足早く
IN THE ANIME VERSION SHE GOT
アーティファクトが出ていま
HER ARTIFACT VERY EARLY ON,
したが、マンガ版でも
BUT WHETHER OR NOT ITS POWERS
同じ能力なのかどうかは
WILL BE THE SAME IN THE MANGA VERSION
ヒミツです。
OR NOT IS A SECRET!

…っていうか、仮契約した
...IF ANYTHING, DID SHE EVEN MAKE A
のかな？(^^;) ゆえの後で。
PROBATIONARY CONTRACT? (^^;) AFTER YUE THAT IS...

CVは石毛佐和さん。
HER VOICE ACTOR IS SAWA ISHIGE. I THINK
ふざけつつも色っぽい感じが
THE SEXY TONE OF HER VOICE EVEN WHEN SHE'S
ピッタリで、お気に入りです。
KIDDING AROUND IS A PERFECT FIT FOR HARUNA
歌もうまいんですよ〜♡
SHE'S REALLY GOOD AT SINGING TOO!
AND I'M REALLY FOND OF IT. ♡

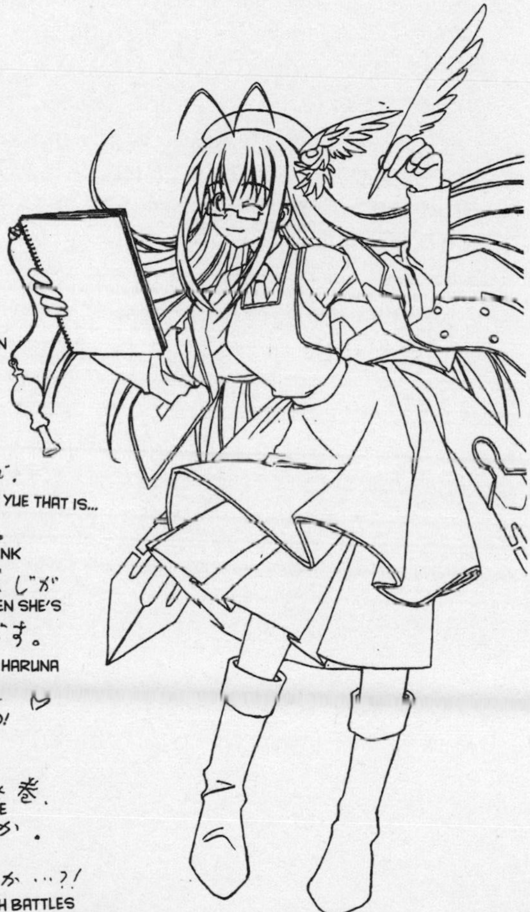

さて、全編ラブコメの14巻、
NOW, VOLUME 14 WAS ENTIRELY A LOVE
いかがでしたでしょうか。
COMEDY. I HOPE YOU ENJOYED IT.

次はバトルかラブコメか…?!
WILL THE NEXT VOLUME BE FILLED WITH BATTLES
OR MORE LOVE COMEDY...!?

赤松
AKAMATSU

About the Creator

Negima! is only Ken Akamatsu's third manga, although he started working in the field in 1994 with *AI Ga Tomaranai* (released in the United States with the title *A.I. Love You*). Like all of Akamatsu's work to date, it was published in Kodansha's *Shonen Magazine*. *AI Ga Tomaranai* ran for five years before concluding in 1999. In 1998, however, Akamatsu began the work that would make him one of the most popular manga artists in Japan: *Love Hina*. *Love Hina* ran for four years, and before its conclusion in 2002, it would cause Akamatsu to be granted the prestigious Manga of the Year Award from Kodansha, as well as go on to become one of the bestselling manga in the United States.

Translation Notes

Japanese is a tricky language for most westerners, and translation is often more art than science. For your edification and reading pleasure, here are notes on some of the places where we could have gone in a different direction in our translation of the work, or where a Japanese cultural reference is used.

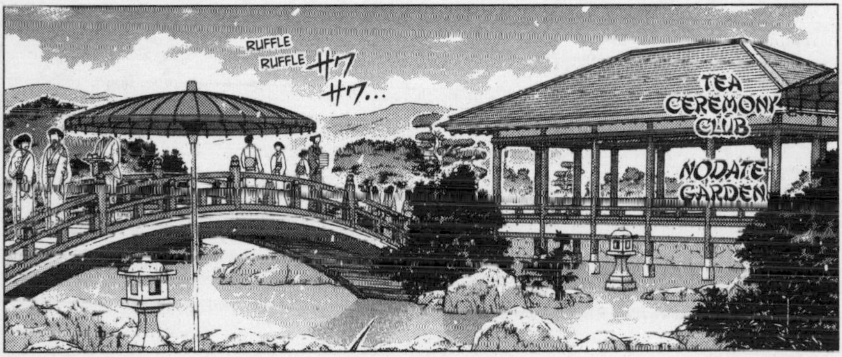
RUFFLE
RUFFLE
TEA CEREMONY CLUB
NODATE GARDEN

Nodate, page 7

Nodate is a traditional Japanese tea ceremony. It is held outdoors, usually in the autumn or spring, when the ambience and scenery can be enjoyed along with the traditional tea service.

On page 13, panel 2, note that Negi is drinking his tea as one should during a tea ceremony: with the thumb of his right hand resting on top of the tea cup, and the fingers and thumb of his left hand resting on the side of the cup and pointing away.

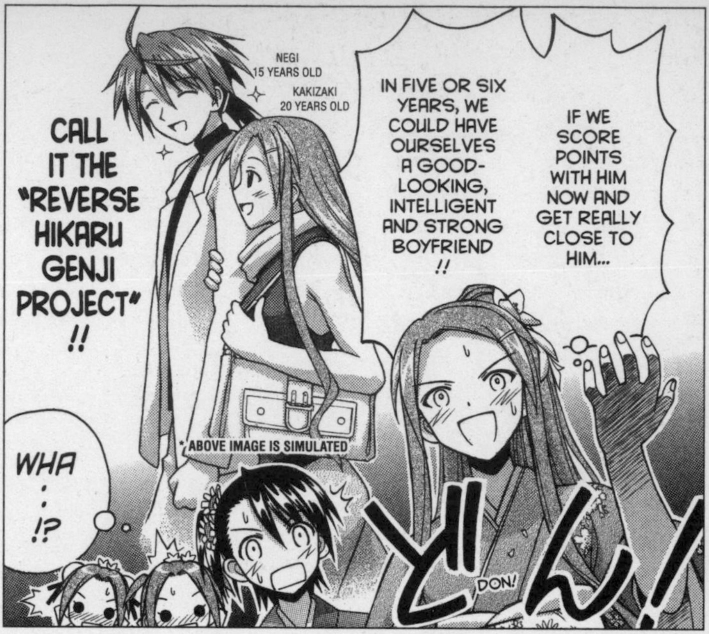
IF WE SCORE POINTS WITH HIM NOW AND GET REALLY CLOSE TO HIM...
IN FIVE OR SIX YEARS, WE COULD HAVE OURSELVES A GOOD-LOOKING, INTELLIGENT AND STRONG BOYFRIEND !!
NEGI 15 YEARS OLD
KAKIZAKI 20 YEARS OLD
CALL IT THE "REVERSE HIKARU GENJI PROJECT" !!
*ABOVE IMAGE IS SIMULATED
どん!
DON!
WHA : !?

Reverse Hikaru Genji Project, page 14

Kakizaki's plan is inspired by a famous episode in the classic Japanese novel *The Tale of Genji* by Murasaki Shikibu. In the book, Genji takes in a young girl named Wakamurasaki so that he can raise her to become his ideal woman.

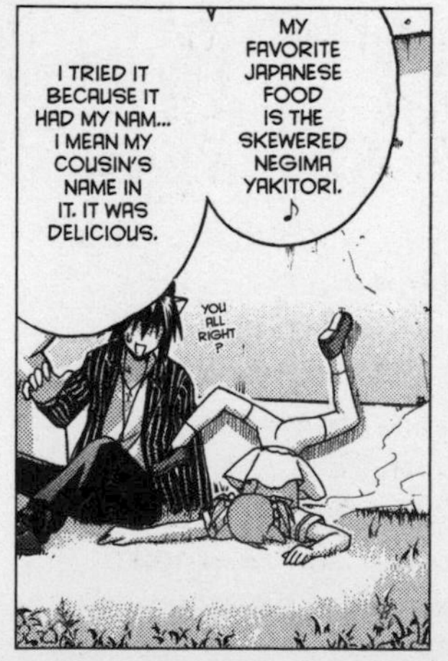
MY FAVORITE JAPANESE FOOD IS THE SKEWERED NEGIMA YAKITORI. ♪
I TRIED IT BECAUSE IT HAD MY NAM... I MEAN MY COUSIN'S NAME IN IT. IT WAS DELICIOUS.
YOU ALL RIGHT ?

Negima, page 91

When, in her failed attempt to confess her love, Ako asks Negi whether he likes dried squid, Negi replies that he likes the *yakitori* skewer called *negima*. *Negima* literally means "*negi* (green onion) in between." So the dish consists of pieces of chicken alternating on a skewer with pieces of green onion.

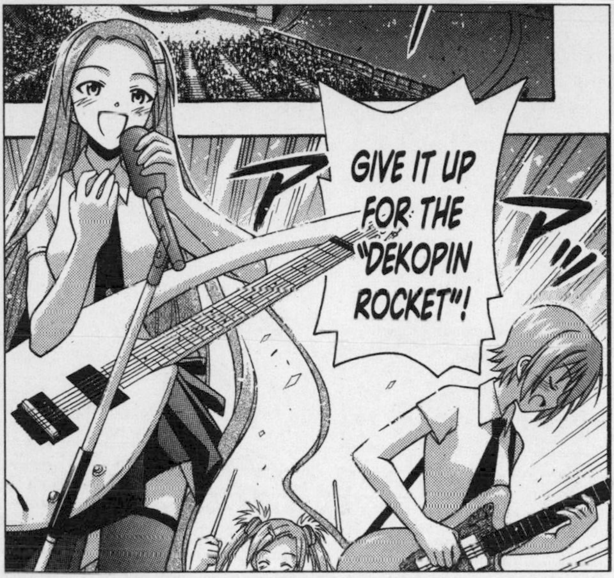
GIVE IT UP FOR THE "DEKOPIN ROCKET"!

Dekopin, page 103

The four girls in Classroom 3-A have named their band Dekopin Rocket. *Dekopin* is slang for the act of flicking one's finger at the forehead of another. *Deko* is short for *odeko*, meaning "forehead," and *pin* is onomatopoeia for the sound of the finger impacting on the head. You can see an example of this in vol. 2, page 32, panel 1.

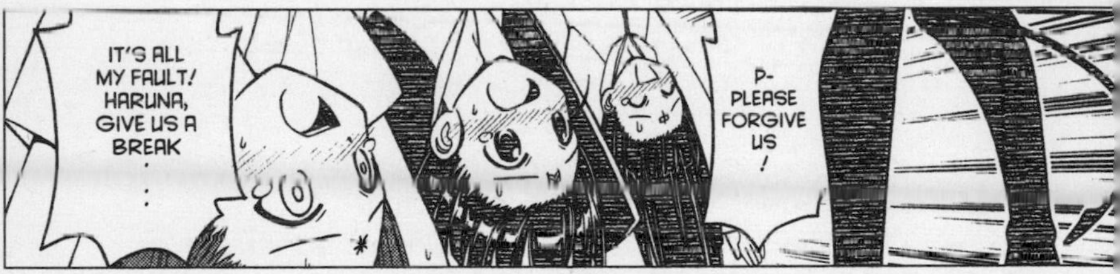
P-PLEASE FORGIVE US!
IT'S ALL MY FAULT! HARUNA, GIVE US A BREAK...

Kinnikuman homage, page 109

In Haruna's manga page, there are kanji characters for *niku* (meat) on Nodoka, *chu* (middle, or the first character in the kanji for China) on Konoka, and *kome* (rice, or the first character in the kanji characters for the United States) on Yue. This is an homage to the manga *Kinnukuman* (known as *Ultimate Muscle* in the U.S.) by Yudetamgo. The main character, Kinnikuman, has the kanji character *niku* on his forehead, the character Ramenman from China has the character *chu* on his forehead, and Terryman (an homage himself to American wrestler Terry Funk) from the U.S. has the character *kome* on his forehead. It's a throwaway gag, but people who know will recognize it.

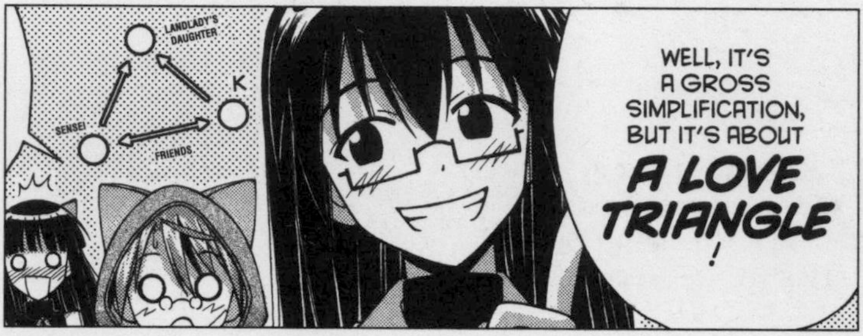
WELL, IT'S A GROSS SIMPLIFICATION, BUT IT'S ABOUT A LOVE TRIANGLE!
LANDLADY'S DAUGHTER
K
SENSEI
FRIENDS

Love triangle, pages 131-132

Soseki Natsume's novel *Kokoro* is featured. The quote on panel 6, "Anyone who has no spiritual aspirations is an idiot," is a key line that causes K severe psychological damage, driving him to slit his carotid artery with a knife.

One of the other books that Haruna shows Negi is Dostoyevsky's *The Idiot*. In this book, the love triangle is between Myshkin and his friend Rogozhin for the love of the beautiful Nastasya. This tale ends tragically: one person dies, one is sent to Siberia, and the other becomes an idiot over the loss of his love.

MY HEAVENLY HOCKEY CLUB

BY AI MORINAGA

WHERE THE BOYS ARE!

MY HEAVENLY HOCKEY CLUB
1 AI MORINAGA

Hana Suzuki loves only two things in life: eating and sleeping. So when handsome classmate Izumi Oda asks Hana—his major crush—to join the school hockey club, convincing her proves to be a difficult task. True, the Grand Hockey Club is full of boys—and all the boys are super-cute—but, given a choice, Hana prefers a sizzling steak to a hot date. Then Izumi mentions the field trips to fancy resorts. Now Hana can't wait for the first away game, with its promise of delicious food and luxurious linens. Of course there's the getting up early, working hard, and playing well with others. How will Hana survive?

Special extras in each volume! Read them all!

RATING AGES T 13+

VISIT WWW.DELREYMANGA.COM TO:

- Read sample pages
- View release date calendars for upcoming volumes
- Sign up for Del Rey's free manga e-newsletter
- Find out the latest about new Del Rey Manga series

DEL REY MANGA デルレイ

The Otaku's Choice™

Le Chevalier d'Eon

STORY BY TOU UBUKATA
MANGA BY KIRIKO YUMEJI

DARKNESS FALLS ON PARIS

A mysterious cult is sacrificing beautiful young women to a demonic force that threatens the entire country. Only one man can save Paris from chaos and terror, the king's top secret agent: The Chevalier d'Eon.

- Available on DVD from ADV Films.

Le Chevalier d'Eon I
TOU UBUKATA
KIRIKO YUMEJI

Special extras in each volume! Read them all!

VISIT WWW.DELREYMANGA.COM TO:
- Read sample pages
- View release date calendars for upcoming volumes
- Sign up for Del Rey's free manga e-newsletter
- Find out the latest about new Del Rey Manga series

RATING OT AGES 16+

DEL REY MANGA デルレイ
The Otaku's Choice™

TOMARE!

[STOP!]

You're going the wrong way!

Manga is a completely different type of reading experience.

To start at the *beginning*, go to the *end*!

That's right! Authentic manga is read the traditional Japanese way—from right to left. Exactly the *opposite* of how American books are read. It's easy to follow: Just go to the other end of the book, and read each page—and each panel—from right side to left side, starting at the top right. Now you're experiencing manga as it was meant to be.